英语听力教程：2

LISTEN TO 2

英 语 中 级 听 力

（教师用书）

北京外国语大学

何其莘　金利民

王　敏　夏玉和　编

外语教学与研究出版社

FOREIGN LANGUAGE TEACHING AND RESEARCH PRESS

北京　BEIJING

图书在版编目(CIP)数据

英语中级听力教师用书／何其莘等编．— 北京：外语教学与研究出版社，1993.8（2010.5 重印）
ISBN 978－7－5600－0670－3

Ⅰ．英… Ⅱ．何… Ⅲ．英语—听说教学—高等学校—教学参考资料 Ⅳ．H319.9

中国版本图书馆 CIP 数据核字（2007）第 022912 号

悠游网—外语学习 一网打尽
www.2u4u.com.cn
阅读、视听、测试、交流、共享

封底刮刮卡，获积分！在线阅读、学习、交流、换礼包！

出 版 人：于春迟
责任编辑：赵瑞超
封面设计：诸中英　王秋水
出版发行：外语教学与研究出版社
社　　址：北京市西三环北路 19 号（100089）
网　　址：http://www.fltrp.com
印　　刷：北京京科印刷有限公司
开　　本：850×1168　1/32
印　　张：22.75
版　　次：1993 年 8 月第 1 版　2010 年 6 月第 33 次印刷
书　　号：ISBN 978－7－5600－0670－3
定　　价：35.90 元
＊　　＊　　＊
购书咨询：(010)88819929　　电子邮箱：club@fltrp.com
如有印刷、装订质量问题，请与出版社联系
联系电话：(010)61207896　　电子邮箱：zhijian@fltrp.com
制售盗版必究 举报查实奖励
版权保护办公室举报电话：(010)88817519
物料号：106700101

前　　言

　　听力是英语教学中五项基本技能之一，也是中国学生的一个难点。突破这个难关不仅有助于其他单项技能的训练，同时也为培养学生的英语交际能力奠定一个良好的基础。在国家教育部颁布的《高等学校英语专业英语教学大纲》中，对于大学一至四年级学生在听力方面应该达到的标准都作出了详细的规定。*Listen to This* 就是按照这个大纲的要求，根据中国英语教学的特点而编写的一套听力教程。

　　整套教程共分为三册。第一册适合大学一年级学生和英语初学者使用；第二册的对象是大学二年级学生和有中等英语水平的自学者；第三册可供大学三四年级学生和有较高英语水平的自学者使用。每册均含《学生用书》（Student's Book）和《教师用书》（Teacher's Book），功用不同，相辅相成。《学生用书》以录音材料中的生词表、文化背景注释和配套的练习为主。《教师用书》则包含录音的书面材料、练习答案和相关文化背景知识的补充读物。

　　和国内现有的听力教程相比，*Listen to This* 有以下几个特点：

　　1. 教程的第三册适合英语专业高年级学生使用，以达到大纲中第六级和第八级对听力的要求。

　　2. 内容全面，听力材料均选自国外的有声资料。

　　3. 录音以标准的美音或英音为主，声音清晰。

　　4. 练习形式活泼。练习的设计参考了美国 TOEFL 考试和英国 Cambridge Certificate 考试的形式，并增加了是非题、填空题、听写、讲座摘记和根据笔记回答问题等多种形式。

　　5. 《教师用书》中的补充读物均摘自英美报刊和书籍，不仅能够为教师备课提供必要的历史文化背景，也可以作为学生的课外阅读材料，以扩大学生的知识面。

以上特点不仅使该教程适合课堂教学，同时也为英语专业学生和社会各层次的英语爱好者提供了自学的良好模式。

Listen to This 2 适用于大学二年级学生和有一定基础的英语自学者。录音材料选自英美的有声资料。全书共有 36 课，每课由三个部分组成。形式活泼多样，涉及了日常生活和社交活动的各个方面，不仅有助于提高学生的听力技能，也有益于提高学生的英语交际能力。全书的课文按录音材料的难易程度编排，循序渐进，既注意与第一册衔接又为学生继续使用第三册打下了基础。

《学生用书》包括生词表、文化背景注释和配套练习三个部分。在使用时应要求学生事先熟悉生词表中所列的词汇，并阅读文化背景注释。由于第二册中增加了根据上下文作出推测、记笔记和整理讲座提纲等几项训练，因此，在第 1、7、13、19、25 和 31 课的第三部分分别加上了对这些练习的示范说明。在做这部分练习前应要求学生熟悉这些训练的目的和要求。

《教师用书》包括录音的书面材料、练习答案和补充阅读材料三个部分。为了便于教师上课时使用，配有答案的练习排印在每部分的书面材料之后。第二册的补充阅读材料均以课文中所涉及的英美风俗和文化特色为主题。教师可以在教学中选择部分内容向学生作一些介绍，以扩大学生的知识面。

在编写过程中我们得到了徐国良、魏兰、赵秀英、王念华、刘俊凤、李铁、王德杰、杨建初等同志的帮助，我们在此谨表诚挚的谢意。同时，我们也愿借此机会对外语教学与研究出版社和北京外语音像出版社所给予的支持表示感谢。

编者

CONTENTS

4

Lesson 1

Section One:

Tapescript:

Task 1: This Is Your Life!

'This is Your Life' is one of the most popular programmes on British and American television. Every week a famous person is invited to a television studio, without knowing that he or she will be the subject of the programme. The compère meets the person outside the studio and says 'This is your life!'. The person then meets friends and relatives from his or her past and present. Studio 4 is where the programme is recorded. The programme begins at eight o'clock. It's 6.45 now and the director is checking the preparations with his new production assistant (PA). The subject of tonight's show will be an actor, Jason Douglas. The compère, as usual, will be Terry Donovan.

Director: Let's just check the arrangements. We're bringing Jason Douglas here in a studio car — he thinks he's coming to a discussion programme! The driver has been told to arrive at exactly 7.55. Now, the programme begins at eight o'clock. At that time Jason will be walking to the studio. Terry Donovan will start his introduction at 8.01, and Jason will arrive at 8.02. Terry will meet him at the studio entrance ... Camera 4 will be there. Then he'll take him to that seat. It'll be on Camera 3.

1

Jason will be sitting there during the whole programme. For most of the show Terry will be standing in the middle, and he'll be on Camera 2. The guests will come through that door, talk to Terry and Jason ... and then sit over there.

Director: Now, is that all clear?

PA: Yes...there's just one thing.

Director: Well, what is it?

PA: Who's going to look after the guests during the show?

Director: Pauline is.

PA: And where will they be waiting during the show?

Director: In Room 401, as usual. Pauline will be waiting with them, and she'll be watching the show on the monitor. She'll tell them two minutes before they enter.

PA: I think that's everything.

Terry: Good evening and welcome to 'This is Your Life'. This is Terry Donovan speaking. We're waiting for the subject of tonight's programme. He's one of the world's leading actors, and he thinks he's coming here to take part in a discussion programme ... I can hear him now ... yes, here he is! Jason Douglas ... This is your life!

Jason: Oh, no ... I don't believe it! Not me ...

Terry: Yes, you! Now come over here and sit down. Jason, you were born at number 28 Balaclava Street in East Ham, London on July 2nd, 1947. You were one of six children, and your father was a taxi driver. Of course, your name was then Graham Smith.

Terry: Now, do you know this voice? 'I remember Jason when he was two. He used to scream and shout all day.'

Jason: Susan!

Terry: Yes ... all the way from Sydney, Australia ... She flew here specially for this programme. It's your sister, Susan Fraser!

Jason: Susan ... Why didn't you tell me ... oh, this is wonderful!

Terry: Yes, you haven't seen each other for 13 years ... take a seat next to him, Susan. You started school at the age of five, in 1952, and in 1958 you moved to Lane End Secondary School.

Terry: Do you remember this voice? 'Smith! Stop looking out of the window!'

Jason: Oh, no! It's Mr Hooper!

Terry: Your English teacher, Mr Stanley Hooper. Was Jason a good student, Mr Hooper?

Mr Hooper: Eh? No, he was the worst in the class ... but he was a brilliant actor, even in those days. He could imitate all the teachers.

Terry: Thank you, Mr Hooper. You can speak to Jason, later. Well, you went to the London School of Drama in 1966, and left in 1969. In 1973 you went to Hollywood.

Terry: Do you know this voice? 'Hi Jason ... Can you ride a horse yet?'

Jason: Maria!

Terry: Maria Montrose ... who's come from Hollywood to be with you tonight.

Maria: Hello, Jason ... it's great to be here. Hello, Terry. Jason and I were in a movie together in 1974. Jason had to learn to ride a horse ... Well, Jason doesn't like horses very much.

Jason: Like them! I'm terrified of them!

3

Maria: Anyway, he practised for two weeks. Then he went to the director ... it was Charles Orson ... and said, 'What do you want me to do?' Charles said, 'I want you to fall off the horse'. Jason was furious. He said, 'What? Fall off! I've been practising for two weeks ... I could fall off the first day .. without any practice!'

Task 2: What Are Your Ambitions?

Interviewer: Good morning, sir. I'm from radio station QRX, and I wonder if you'd mind answering a few questions for our survey today.

David: Uh ... sure, why not?

Interviewer: What's your name?

David: Uh, my name is David George.

Interviewer: David, what do you do for a living?

David: I'm a professional baseball player.

Interviewer: Really?

David: Mm – hmm.

Interviewer: That's terrific. What do you do for fun?

David: Well, I like to read the classics – you know, Dickens, Shakespeare, ... uh ... books like that.

Interviewer: Fabulous. And what's the most exciting thing that's happened to you recently?

David: Just call me Dad. My wife and I ... uh ... had our first baby.

Interviewer: Oh, (Yeah. A little girl.) that's wonderful.

David: Mm – hmm.

Interviewer: Who do you admire most in this world?

David : Well , I admire my wife . . . uh . . . . she ' s terrific . She ' s

4

going to be a great mother, great mother.

Interviewer: Terrific. What do you want to be doing five years from now?

David: Well, ...uh ... five years from now I'd like to be a father of five. I'd like to have lots of kids around the house.

Interviewer: That's fabulous.

David: Yeah.

Interviewer: Thanks very much for talking to us, David.

David: Well, thank you.

Interviewer: Good morning. I'm from radio station QRX, and I wondered if you'd mind answering a few questions today for our survey.

Suzanne: Not at all.

Interviewer: What's your name?

Suzanne: Suzanne Brown.

Interviewer: Suzanne, what do you do for a living?

Suzanne: I'm a lawyer.

Interviewer: A lawyer? And what do you do for fun?

Suzanne: I like to run.

Interviewer: Uh – huh. Running, like – –

Suzanne: Jogging.

Interviewer: Jogging. And what's the most exciting thing that's happened to you recently?

Suzanne: I got to run in the Boston Marathon.

Interviewer: Congratulations. And who do you admire most in the world?

Suzanne: Oh, well, I'd have to say Martin Luther King, Jr.

Interviewer: Mmm, yes. And what do you want to be doing five years from today?

Suzanne: Well, dare I say win the Boston Marathon?

Interviewer: Wonderful. Thanks a lot for talking to us today, Suzanne.

Suzanne: You're welcome.

Interviewer: Good morning, sir. I'm from radio station QRX, and I wonder if you could answer a few questions for our survey this morning.

Adolfo: Oh, yes, yes.

Interviewer: What's your name?

Adolfo: My name is Adolfo Vasquez.

Interviewer: Adolfo, what do you do for a living?

Adolfo: I'm a dancer.

Interviewer: A dancer. And what do you do for fun?

Adolfo: I watch ... uh ... musical movies.

Interviewer: Musical movies. And what's the most exciting thing that's happened to you recently?

Adolfo: Oh, about six years ago I moved to United States, (Uh - huh.) and that's quite exciting for me.

Interviewer: Yes, that is very exciting. What do you – who do you admire most in the world?

Adolfo: I admire a lot ... um ... Sophia Loren, the movie actress.

Interviewer: I understand completely. (Mm - hmm.) What do you want to be doing five years from now?

Adolfo: I like very much what I'm doing right now, so I really would like to keep doing it.

Interviewer: Very good. (Mm - hmm.) Thanks for speaking to us today, Adolfo.

Adolfo: Okay. You're welcome.

Interviewer: Good morning, Miss. I'm from radio station QRX,

6

and I wonder if you could answer a few questions for our survey.

Linda: Sure.

Interviewer: What's your name?

Linda: Linda Montgomery.

Interviewer: Linda, what do you do for a living?

Linda: Uh, well, right now I'm going to beauty school.

Interviewer: Beauty school?

Linda: Yeah.

Interviewer: Uh‑huh. And what do you do for fun?

Linda: Oh, why for fun, I hang out with my friends – you know, go for pizza, stuff like that.

Interviewer: I understand. What's the most exciting thing that's happened to you recently?

Linda: Oh, this was so great! (Yeah?) Four of my friends and I, we went to a Bruce Springsteen concert. We actually – we got tickets.

Interviewer: Wonderful.

Linda: It was the best.

Interviewer: Who do you admire most in the world?

Linda: Who do I admi – I guess (Mm‑hmm.) my dad, (Uh‑huh.) probably my dad. Yeah.

Interviewer: And what do you want to be doing five years from now?

Linda: I would love it if I could have my own beauty salon.

Interviewer: Uh‑huh.

Linda: That would be great.

Interviewer: Thanks very much for talking to us today.

Linda: Okay.

Key to Exercises:

Task 1: This Is Your Life!

A. Choose the best answer (a, b or c) to complete each of the following statements.

1. "This Is Your Life" is _____.

    a. the most popular programme on British and American television

    b. one of the most popular programmes on British and American radio

  * c. one of the most popular programmes on British and American television

2. "This Is Your Life" is a _____ programme.

  * a. weekly

    b. monthly

    c. daily

3. The programme is recorded in _____.

  * a. studio 4

    b. studio 3

    c. studio 2

4. The programme begins at _____.

    a. 6.45

    b. 7.55

  * c. 8.00

5. The subject of tonight's show will be _____.

    a. Terry Donovan

  * b. Jason Douglas

    c. Pauline

6. Camera _____ will be at the studio entrance.

  * a. four

b. three

c. two

B. True or False Questions. Write a T in front of a statement if it is true according to the recording and write an F if it is false.

1. (T) The person invited to "This Is Your Life" does not know that he or she will be the subject of the programme.

2. (F) The subject can meet only friends and relatives from his or her past at the studio.

3. (F) Terry Donovan is the compère only for tonight's show.

4. (F) Jason Douglas will arrive at the studio at eight sharp.

5. (F) Jason will be sitting in the middle for most of the show.

6. (T) Usually the guests wait in Room 401 and Pauline tells them when they should enter.

C. Identification. Match each name in Column I with a description in Column II to identify the person.

Column I	Column II
(1) Jason Douglas	(a) Jason's English teacher
(2) Terry Donovan	(b) the subject of tonight's programme
(3) Pauline	(c) an actress who worked with Jason in 1974
(4) Susan Fraser	(d) the compère
(5) Stanley Hooper	(e) a director
(6) Maria Montrose	(f) the person who waits with the guests in Room 401
(7) Charles Orson	(g) Jason's sister

Answer: (1) – (b) (2) – (d) (3) – (f) (4) – (g)
(5) – (a) (6) – (c) (7) – (e)

D. Complete the following résumé for Jason Douglas.

Name: Jason Douglas
Former name: (Graham Smith)
Profession: (actor)
Date of birth: (July 2, 1947)
1952: (started school)
1958: (moved to Lane End Secondary School)
1966: (went to the London School of Drama)
1969: (left the London School of Drama)
1973: (went to Hollywood)
1974: (were in a movie with Maria Montrose)

Task 2: What Are Your Ambitions?
A. Give brief answers to the following questions.
1. Where is the interviewer from ?
   Answer: Radio Station QRX.
2. Why does he ask these questions?
   Answer: For a survey.
3. How many people have been interviewed?
   Answer: Four.
4. How many questions does each interviewee answer?
   Answer: Six.
5. What are the questions ?
   Answer: (1) What's your name?
           (2) What do you do for a living?
           (3) What do you do for fun?

(4) What's the most exciting thing that's happened to you recently?

(5) Who do you admire most in this world?

(6) What do you want to be doing five years from now?

B. Fill in the following chart with answers that each interviewee gives to the questions.

	Interviewee 1	Interviewee 2	Interviewee 3	Interviewee 4
Question 1	David George	Suzanne Brown	Adolfo Vasquez	Linda Montgomery
Question 2	professional baseball player	lawyer	dancer	student at school
Question 3	read classics – Dickens, Shakespeare	running – jogging	watch musical movies	hang out with friends- go for pizza
Question 4	had his first baby	got to run in the Boston Marathon	moved to the US	went to a Bruce Springsteen concert
Question 5	his wife	Martin Luther King, Jr.	Sophia Loren	her dad
Question 6	be a father of five in five years	win the Boston Marathon	do what he's doing right now	has her own beauty salon

Section Two:

In Your Own Words

Announcer: And now, at 10.50 it's time for In Your Own Words, in which we interview people with unusual stories to tell. Here to introduce the programme is Patricia Newell. Good morning, Patricia.

Patricia: Good morning, and good morning everyone. With me in the studio now is this morning's guest, Trevor Cartridge. Good morning, Trevor.

Trevor: Good morning, Patricia.

Patricia: Trevor, you have one of the most unusual stories I've ever heard. Yet, nowadays, you seem to lead a very ordinary life.

Trevor: Yes, Patricia. I'm a dentist. I live and work in London.

Patricia: But at one time you used to have a different job?

Trevor: Yes, I was a soldier.

Patricia: A soldier?

Trevor: That's right.

Patricia: And how long ago was that?

Trevor: Oh, about two thousand years ago.

Patricia: That's right. Trevor Cartridge believes that he was a soldier in the army of Julius Caesar. He remembers coming to Britain with the Roman army two thousand years ago. Trevor, tell us your remarkable story ... in your own words!

Trevor: Well, funnily enough, it all began because I wanted to give up smoking.

Patricia: Give up smoking!

Trevor: Mm, I used to smoke too much and I tried to give up several times, but I always started smoking again a few days later. In

12

the end I went to a hypnotist. He hypnotised me, and I stopped smoking at once. I was delighted, as you can imagine.

Patricia: Yes?

Trevor: That made me very interested in hypnotism, and I talked to the hypnotist about it. He told me that some people could remember their past lives when they were hypnotised, and he asked if I wanted to try. I didn't believe it at first, but in the end I agreed. He hypnotised me, and sure enough, I remembered. I was a Roman soldier in Caesar's army.

Patricia: You didn't believe it at first?

Trevor: I didn't believe it before we tried the experiment. Now I'm absolutely convinced it's true.

Patricia: What do you remember?

Trevor: Oh, all kinds of things, but the most interesting thing I remember is the night we landed in Britain.

Patricia: You remember that?

Trevor: Oh yes. It was a terrible, stormy night. There were a hundred or more of us in the boat. We were all shut in, because the weather was so bad and most people were sick, because it was very stuffy. There was a terrible smell of petrol, I remember. Lots of men thought we should go back to France. It wasn't called 'France' then, of course.

Patricia: And there was a smell of petrol?

Trevor: Yes, it was terrible. The weather got worse and worse. We thought we were going to die. In the end the boat was pushed up onto the sands, and we all climbed out. I remember jumping into the water and struggling to the beach. The water was up to my shoulders and it was a freezing night. A lot of men were killed by the cold or drowned in the storm, but I

13

managed to get ashore.

Patricia: You did?

Trevor: Yes. There were about ten survivors from our boat, but even then our troubles weren't over. We found a farmhouse, but it was deserted. When the people read the newspapers, and knew that we were coming, they were terrified. They took all their animals and all their food, and ran away into the hills. Of course, there were no proper roads in those days. Well, we went into the house and tried to light a fire, but we couldn't even do that. We always kept our matches in our trousers pockets, so naturally they were all soaked. We couldn't find anything to eat, except one tin of cat food. We were so hungry, we broke it open with our knives, and ate it. We found a tap, but the water was frozen. In the end we drank rainwater from the tin. We sat very close together and tried to keep warm. We could hear wolves but we didn't have any weapons, because our guns were full of seawater. By the morning, the storm was over. We went on to the beach and found what was left of the boat. We managed to find some food, and we hoped there was some wine too, but when we opened the box, all the bottles were broken.

Patricia: So what happened?

Trevor: We waited. Finally another boat came and took us away, and we joined the other soldiers. I remember going into the camp, and getting a hot meal, and clean clothes. Oh! It was wonderful. We were given our pay, too. I remember the date on the coins, 50 BC. It was an exciting time.

Patricia: And did you stay in Britain?

Trevor: Oh yes, I was here for five years, from 50 BC to 55 BC. I

14

enjoyed my stay in Britain very much.

Patricia: And then you went back to Rome?

Trevor: I can't remember anything after that.

Patricia: Well, Trevor Cartridge, thank you for telling us your
story, in your own words.

Key to Exercises:

A. Choose the best answer (a, b or c) for each of the following
questions.

　1. When does the programme "In Your Own Words" start?
　* a. 10.50.
　　b. 10.15.
　　c. 9.50.
　2. What is the programme about?
　　a. Patricia will tell stories about some unusual people.
　* b. Some people are invited to tell their unusual stories.
　　c. Anyone can be invited to talk about themselves in their
　　　own words.
　3. What does Trevor Cartridge do?
　* a. He is a dentist.
　　b. He is a soldier.
　　c. He is an announcer.
　4. Where does he work and live?
　　a. In Paris.
　　b. In Rome.
　* c. In London.
　5. What is Trevor's story mainly about?
　　a. How he gave up smoking.
　　b. How he became interested in hypnotism.

* c. His experience as a soldier in the army of Julius Caesar.

6. Where did Trevor live two thousand years ago according to his story?

    a. In Britain.

* b. In France.

    c. In Italy.

B. True or False Questions. Write a T in front of a statement if it is true according to the recording and write an F if it is false.

1. (F) When Trevor decided to stop smoking, he gave it up at once.

2. (T) Trevor became interested in hypnotism because a hypnotist helped him give up smoking.

3. (F) The hypnotist told Trevor that hypnotism could also help him remember his past life and, of course, Trevor believed him immediately.

4. (F) After being hypnotised, Trevor could only remember the night he landed in Britain as a soldier of the Roman army.

C. Fill in the following chart with information about the journey the Roman army made according to Trevor.

Designation: D Company

Number of men: (one hundred or more)

Journey from (France) to (Britain)

Means of transport: (boat)

Weather conditions: (stormy)

Food: (cat food)

Drink: (rain water)

Condition of weapons after landing: (useless)

16

Fighting: (none)

Equipment lost or damaged: (boat lost, guns full of water, supplies of wine lost)

Soldiers killed or wounded: (about ten survivors, all others drowned or killed by cold)

D. Point out what is not true in Trevor's story.

Answer: The following did not exist in Roman times:

petrol, newspaper, matches, trousers,

tinned food, taps, guns, wine bottles.

50 BC could not appear on a coin.

50 – 55 BC is counting backwards.

E. Fill in the blanks according to what you hear on the tape.

1. It was a (terrible), (stormy) night. There were a hundred (or more of us) in the boat. We were all (shut in), because the weather was (so bad) and most people were (sick), because it was very (stuffy).

2. We thought we were going to die. In the end the boat was (pushed up onto the sands), and we all (climbed out). I remember (jumping into the) water, and (struggling to the) beach. The water was (up to my shoulder) and it was a (freezing) night.

3. Finally another boat (came and took us away), and we (joined) the other soldiers. I remember (going into the camp), and getting (a hot meal), and (clean clothes). It was wonderful. We were (given our pay), too.

Section Three:

Study Skills: How to Predict?

When you listen to a person speaking your own language, in many situations you can be one step ahead of the speaker. You can very often predict what that person is going to say next — perhaps not always the exact words, but at least the main ideas. Have you ever found yourself finishing other people's sentences for them? This is often something we do without even thinking about it.

The more you can predict, the easier it becomes to understand — in a foreign language too. In fact, you will probably be surprised at how much you can predict in English. Train yourself to predict as much as possible. Do this consciously.

There are many things which can help you to predict while you are listening, for example:

1. how much you know about: the topic

   the situation

   the country in which the language is spoken

2. intonation, for example: When presenting a list, rising intonation signals that more items will follow and a falling intonation signals the end of the list: 'I'd like to buy some eggs, cheese, tomatoes and a cake.'

3. signals such as: 'I'm afraid that ...' (signals something negative will follow) 'There's one point I'd like to make...' (signals an opinion will follow)

The phrases in group 3 are called semantic markers. They serve as signals for the meaning and structure of the lecture or text. They tell us how the ideas are organized. There are many other semantic markers in English, which are classified here accord-

18

ing to their function.

1. The markers used for listing, such as:

firstly	thirdly
in the first place	my next point is
secondly	last/finally

2. Markers that show us the cause and effect relationship between one idea and another:

so	because
therefore	since
thus (we see)	

3. Markers which indicate that the speaker or writer is going to illustrate his ideas by giving examples:

for instance	let's take ...
for example	an example/instance of this was...

4. Markers that introduce an idea which runs against what has been said, or is going to be said:

but	and yet
nevertheless	although
on the other hand	

5. Markers which indicate that the speaker or writer is about to sum up his message, or part of it:

to summarize	it amounts to this
in other words	if I can just sum up
what I have been saying is this	

6. Semantic markers used to express a time relationship:

then	previously
next	while
after that	when

7. Markers used to indicate the relative importance of something:

19

it is worth noting

I would like to direct your attention to

8. Markers used to rephrase what has already been said, or to introduce a definition:

in other words   to put it another way

let me put it this way   that is to say

9. Markers that express a condition:

if   assuming that

unless

These are only a few examples of semantic markers. Train yourself to listen for these key words and phrases.

Tapescript:

Task 1: Learning to Predict

1. Bob, do you think you could possibly turn off that radio? I'm (pause) trying to write a letter.

2. A: I don't want a double room. I want a single room.

   B: I'm sorry, sir, but I'm afraid 43 (pause) is the only single room available at the moment.

3. A: Just look what I've got.

   B: Let me see. Fifty pounds! (pause) Where on earth did you get it?

4. A: Oh bother the Sex Discrimination Act. Surely they can't force me to take on a married woman.

   B: They can't force you to, Mr Clark, but (pause) you mustn't discriminate against someone just because they're married.

5. A: I'm glad I'm not a princess. It must be a dreadful life.

   B: Dreadful? (pause) I wouldn't mind being a prince.

6. I'm a reasonably hard-working person. But (pause) I'm not a

workaholic.

7. A: Had your brother been nervous about it himself?

   B: Well, he didn't say, but possibly (pause) he had been.

Key to Exercises:

Task 1: Learning to Predict

Listen to the following sentences. When you hear "pause", stop your recorder and guess what the speaker is going to say next. Discuss your answer with your classmates and then let the speaker finish his or her sentence.

1. Answer: trying to write a letter

   Reason: The speaker's question suggests he needs a quiet surrounding to do something.

2. Hint: the first speaker is a guest complaining about the conditions of Room 43 which is a single room. The second speaker is a hotel clerk who suggests that the guest move to a double room.

   Answer: is the only single room available at the moment

   Reason: The phrase "I'm afraid" often suggests a negative or unsatisfying answer.

3. Answer: Where on earth did you get it?

   Reason: The second speaker's surprised tone shows that the money is out of her expectation and she must be curious about how it is gained.

4. Answer: You mustn't discriminate against someone just because they are married.

   Reason: The word "but" suggests an opposite meaning.

5. Answer: I wouldn't mind being a prince.

   Reason: The man's questioning tone shows he doesn't agree

21

with the woman.

6. Answer: I'm not a workaholic.

   Reason: The word "but" suggests an opposite meaning.

7. Answer: he had been.

   Reason: "But" and "possibly" both give some hint.

Task 2: Dictation

The Knowledge

Becoming a London taxi driver isn't easy. In order to obtain a licence to drive a taxi in London, candidates have to pass a detailed examination. They have to learn not only the streets, landmarks and hotels, but also the quickest way to get there. This is called 'The Knowledge' by London cab drivers and it can take years of study and practice to get 'The Knowledge'. Candidates are examined not only on the quickest routes but also on the quickest routes at different times of the day. People who want to pass the examination spend much of their free time driving or even cycling around London, studying maps and learning the huge street directory by heart.

The Underground

Travelling on the London underground (the 'tube') presents few difficulties for visitors because of the clear colour – coded maps. It's always useful to have plenty of spare change with you because there are often long queues at the larger stations. If you have enough change you can buy your ticket from a machine. You will find signs which list the stations in alphabetical order, with the correct fares, near the machines. There are automatic barriers which are operated by the tickets. You should keep the ticket, because it's checked at the destination.

22

Lesson 2

Section One:

Tapescript:

Task 1: Film Editing

Interviewer: Is film editing a complicated job?

Film Editor: Oh yes, a lot of people probably don't know how complicated a job it can be. It's far more than just sticking pieces of film together.

Interviewer: How long does it take to edit a film?

Film Editor: Well, it depends. You can probably expect to edit a ten-minute film in about a week. A 35-minute documentary, like the one I'm editing at present, takes a minimum of four to five weeks to edit.

Interviewer: Can you explain to me how film editing works?

Film Editor: There are different steps. 'Synching up', for example.

Interviewer: What do you mean by synching up?

Film Editor: It means matching sound and pictures and that is usually done by my assistant. The film and the sound tape have numbers stamped along the edge which have to be matched. The details of the film and the sound are also recorded in a log book, so it's quick and easy to find a particular take and its soundtrack. This operation is called logging and is again done

23

by my assistant.

Interviewer: So what do you usually do yourself?

Film Editor: A lot of things, of course. First, I have to view all the material to make a first selection of the best takes. There's a lot of film to look through because to make a sequence work the way you want, you need a lot of shots to choose from.

Interviewer: Does that mean that you have to discard sequences?

Film Editor: Oh yes. On average for every foot of edited film, you need twelve times as much unedited film and therefore you have to compromise and, of course, discard some of it.

Interviewer: What do you do after selecting the material?

Film Editor: First of all, I prepare an initial version of the film, a 'rough cut' as it is called. That means that I actually cut the film into pieces and stick them together again in the new order.

Interviewer: And after this 'rough cut' what happens?

Film Editor: Well, after the 'rough cut' comes the 'fine cut' when the film takes its final form. The producer and the director come in for a viewing. Some small changes may then be necessary, but when the 'fine cut' has been approved by everyone, this is the final version of the film.

Interviewer: At this point is the film ready for distribution?

Film Editor: Oh no. After the final version of the film has been approved, there is the dubbing, there are voices, music, background noises and sometimes special effects to be put together for the soundtrack. And after the dubbing, the edited film is sent to the 'neg' cutters.

Interviewer: What do the 'neg' cutters do?

Film Editor: They cut the original negatives on the films, so that these match the edited film exactly. And after all that comes the best part – I can sit down quietly with my feet up and enjoy watching the film!

Task 2: A Vision of the Future

Man: Hi.

Woman: Hi.

Man: What'd you do last night?

Woman: I watched TV. There was a really good movie called *Soylent Green*.

Man: *Soylent Green*?

Woman: Yeah. Charlton Heston was in it.

Man: What's it about?

Woman: Oh, it's about life in New York in the year 2022.

Man: I wonder if New York will still be here in 2022.

Woman: In this movie, in 2022...

Man: Yeah?

Woman: ...New York has forty million people.

Man: Ouch!

Woman: And twenty million of them are unemployed.

Man: How many people live in New York now? About seven or eight million?

Woman: Yeah, I think that's right.

Man: Mm – hmm. You know, if it's hard enough to find an apartment now in New York City, what's it going to be like in 2022?

Woman: Well, in this movie most people have no apartment. So thousands sleep on the steps of buildings. (Uh – huh.) People who do have a place to live have to crawl over sleeping people to get inside. And there are shortages of everything. The soil is so polluted that nothing will grow. (Ooo.) And the air is so polluted they never see the sun. It's really awful.

Man: I think I'm going to avoid going to New York City in the year 2022.

Woman: And there was this scene where the star, Charlton Heston, goes into a house where some very rich people live.

Man: Uh - huh.

Woman: He can't believe it, because they have running water and they have soap.

Man: Really?

Woman: And then he goes into the kitchen and they have tomatoes and lettuce and beef. He almost cries because he's never seen real food in his life, you know, especially the beef. It was amazing for him.

Man: Well, if most people have no real food, what do they eat?

Woman: They eat something called *soylent*.

Man: Soylent?

Woman: Yeah. There's soylent red and soylent yellow and soylent green. The first two are made out of soybeans. But the soylent green is made out of ocean plants. (Ugh.) The people eat it like crackers. That's all they have to eat.

Man: That sounds disgusting.

Woman: Well, you know, it really isn't that far from reality.

Man: No?

Woman: Yeah. Because, you know the greenhouse effect that's beginning now and heating up the earth...

Man: Oh, yeah, I've heard about that.

Woman: ... because we're putting the pollutants in the atmosphere, you know?

Man: Mm – hmm.

Woman: I mean, in this movie New York has ninety degree weather all year long. And it could really happen. Uh ... like now, we ... we have fuel shortages. And in the movie there's so little electricity that people have to ride bicycles to make it.

Man: You know something? I don't think that movie is a true prediction of the future.

Woman: I don't know. It scares me. I think it might be.

Man: Really?

Woman: Well, yeah.

Key to Exercises:

Task 1: Film Editing

A. True or False Questions. Write a T in front of a statement if it is true according to the recording and write an F if it is false.

1. (T) According to the film editor, many people think that film editing is simply sticking pieces of film together.

2. (F) According to the film editor, it takes an average of four to five weeks for him to edit a film.

T) "Synching up" and "logging" are often done by the editor's assistant.

4. (F) After the "fine cut" is made the film editor can enjoy watching the film.

B. Fill in the following blanks to give a clear picture of what needs to be done before a film is ready for distribution.

1. The assistant:

a. ("Synching up") which means (matching sound and

27

pictures according to the numbers stamped along the edge of the film and sound tape.)

b. ("Logging") which means (recording the detail of the film and the sound in a log book.)

2. The film editor:

a. (Make a first selection of the best takes.)

b. (Prepare a "rough cut") – – (an initial version of the film.)

c. (Prepare the "fine cut") – – (the final form of the film.)

3. Others:

a. (Approve the fine cut.)

b. ("Dubbing") which means (voices, music, background noises and sometimes special effects are put together.)

c. (The "neg" cutters cut the original negatives on the film, so that these match the edited film exactly.)

Task 2: A Vision of the Future

A. Choose the best answer (a, b or c) for each of the following questions.

1. What did the woman do last night?

* a. She watched TV.

b. She went to a movie.

c. She went to New York.

2. Who is Charlton Heston?

a. The man in the dialogue.

* b. An actor performing in Soylent Green.

c. A person in the story of Soylent Green.

3. What is the film about?

* a. Life in New York in 2022.

28

b. Life in New York in 2020.

c. Life in New York in 2002.

4. How many people does New York have in the movie?

    a. Eight million.

    b. Fourteen million.

* c. Forty million.

5. Which of the following mentioned in the film is not a result of pollution?

    a. The soil produces nothing.

    b. New York has ninety degree weather all year long.

* c. People ride bicycles instead of driving cars.

6. Which of the following is made out of ocean plants?

    a. Soylent red.

    b. Soylent yellow.

* c. Soylent green.

B. True or False Questions. Write a T in front of a statement if it is true according to the recording and write an F if it is false.

1. (T) In the movie only rich people can have real food.

2. (F) Most people eat crackers.

3. (T) Greenhouse effect is a result of pollution.

4. (F) The woman believes that the film is a true prediction of the future, though the man disagrees with her.

C. Fill in the following blanks to give a clear picture of the problems New York faces in the movie.

1. Over population: New York has (forty million) people.

2. Housing shortage: Most people (have no apartment). Thousands(sleep on the steps of the building). People who do have

29

a place to live have to (crawl over sleeping people to get inside).

3. The soil is so polluted that (nothing will grow). The air is so polluted that (they never see the sun).

4. Most people have no real food. They eat something called (soylent): (soylent red), (soylent yellow), and (soylent-green). The first (two) are made out of (soybeans). The (soylent green) is made out of (ocean plants).

5. New York has (ninety degree) weather all year long.

6. Fuel shortages: There is so little (electricity) that people have to (ride bicycles to make it).

Section Two:

Tapescript:

Task 1: American Indians

The native Americans, the people we call 'Indians', had been in America for many thousands of years before Christopher Columbus arrived in 1492. Columbus thought he had arrived in India, so he called the native people 'Indians'.

The Indians were kind to the early settlers. They were not afraid of them and they wanted to help them. They showed the settlers the new world around them; they taught them about the local crops like sweet potatoes, corn and peanuts; they introduced the Europeans to chocolate and to the turkey; and the Europeans did business with the Indians.

But soon the settlers wanted bigger farms and more land for themselves and their families. More and more immigrants were coming from Europe and all these people needed land. So the Europeans started to take the land from the Indians. The Indians had to move back into the centre of the continent because the settlers were taking all their land.

The Indians couldn't understand this. They had a very different idea of land from the Europeans. For the Indians, the land, the earth, was their mother. Everything came from their mother, the land, and everything went back to it. The land was for everyone and it was impossible for one man to own it. How could the White Man divide the earth into parts? How could he put fences round it, buy it and sell it?

Naturally, when the White Man started taking all the Indians' land, the Indians started fighting back. They wanted to keep their land, they wanted to stop the White Man taking it all for himself. But the White Man was stronger and cleverer. Slowly he pushed the Indians into those parts of the continent that he didn't want—the parts where it was too cold or too dry or too mountainous to live comfortably.

By 1875 the Indians had lost the fight: they were living in special places called 'reservations'. But even here the White Man took land from them—perhaps he wanted the wood, or perhaps the land had important minerals in it, or he even wanted to make national parks there. So even on their reservations the Indians were not safe from the White Man.

There are many Hollywood films about the fight between the Indians and the White Man. Usually in these films the Indians are bad and the White Man is good and brave. But was it really like that? What do you think? Do you think the Indians were right or wrong to fight the White Man?

Task 2: New Australians

31

Interviewer: Today, there are more than 15 million people living in Australia. Only 160,000 of these are Aborigines, so where have the rest come from? Well, until 1850 most of the settlers came from Britain and Ireland and, as we know, many of these were convicts. Then in 1851 something happened which changed everything. Gold was discovered in south-eastern Australia. During the next ten years, nearly 700,000 people went to Australia to find gold and become rich. Many of them were Chinese. China is quite near to Australia. Since then many different groups of immigrants have gone to Australia for many different reasons. Today I'm going to talk to Mario whose family came from Italy and to Helena from Greece. Mario, when did the first Italians arrive in Australia?

Mario: The first Italians went there, like the Chinese, in the gold-rushes, hoping to find gold and become rich. But many also went there for political reasons. During the 1850s and 1860s different states in Italy were fighting for independence and some Italians were forced to leave their homelands because they were in danger of being put in prison for political reasons.

Interviewer: I believe there are a lot of Italians in the sugar industry.

Mario: Yes, that's right. In 1891 the first group of 300 Italians went to work in the sugar-cane fields of northern Australia. They worked very hard and many saved enough money to buy their own land. In this way they came to dominate the sugar industry on many parts of the Queensland coast.

Interviewer: But not all Italians work in the sugar industry, do they?

Mario: No. A lot of them are in the fishing industry. Italy has a long coastline, as you know, and Italians have always been good fishermen. At the end of the nineteenth century some of these went to western Australia to make a new life for themselves. Again, many of them, including my grandfather, were successful.

Interviewer: And what about the Greeks, Helena?

Helena: Well, the Greeks are the fourth largest national group in Australia, after the British, the Irish and the Italians. Most Greeks arrived after the Second World War but in the 1890s there were already about 500 Greeks living in Australia.

Interviewer: So when did the first Greeks arrive?

Helena: Probably in 1830, they went to work in vineyards in southeastern Australia. The Greeks have been making wine for centuries so their experience was very valuable.

Interviewer: But didn't some of them go into the coalmines?

Helena: Yes, they weren't all able to enjoy the pleasant outdoor life of the vineyards. Some of them went to work in the coalmines in Sydney. Others started cafes and bars and restaurants. By 1890 there were Greek cafes and restaurants all over Sydney and out in the countryside (or the bush, as the Australians call it) as well.

Interviewer: And then, as you said, many Greeks arrived after the Second World War, didn't they?

Helena: Yes, yes, that's right. Conditions in Greece were very bad: there was very little work and many people were very poor. Australia needed more workers and so offered to pay the boat fare. People who already had members of their family in Australia took advantage of this offer and, well, went to find a better life there.

33

Interviewer: Well, thank you, Mario and Helena. Next week we will be talking to Juan from Spain and Margaret from Scotland.

Key to Exercises:

Task 1: American Indians

A. Answer the following questions briefly.

1. When did Christopher Columbus arrive in what he believed to be "India"?

   Answer: 1492.

2. Why did he call the native Americans "Indians"?

   Answer: He thought that he had arrived in India.

3. How did the Indians treat the early settlers?

   Answer: They were kind to them and wanted to help.

4. Why did the Europeans start to take the land from the Indians?

   Answer: (1) They wanted bigger farms and more land for themselves;

   (2) More immigrants came from Europe.

5. How did the Indians think of the land?

   Answer: It was their mother. Everything came from and went back to their mother. And it was for everybody.

6. How did the Indians react when the white began to take their land?

   Answer: They started fighting back.

7. What was the result?

   Answer: By 1875 the Indians had lost the fight and had to live in "reservations".

8. How are the Indians and the White Man portrayed in Holly-

wood films?

Answer: The Indians are bad and the White Man is good and
brave in Hollywood films.

B. Choose the best answer (a, b or c) for each of the following
questions.

1. Which of the following word describes the relationship
between the Indians and the early settlers?

* a. Friendly.

b. Estranged.

c. Hostile.

2. Which of the following is not mentioned in the text?

a. Peanuts.

b. Corn.

* c. Potatoes.

3. Which of the following does not describe the land the Indians
were left with?

a. Too cold.

* b. Too hot.

c. Too dry.

4. Which of the following does not explain why the White Man
took land from the "reservations"?

a. It had important minerals in it.

b. He wanted to make national parks there.

* c. He needed more land for new immigrants.

Task 2: New Australians

A. Identification:

1. Match a name in Column I with a place in Column II to find

where the person is from.

Column I	Column II
(1) Margaret	a. Greece
(2) Mario	b. Italy
(3) Helena	c. Spain
(4) Juan	d. Scotland

Answer: (1) – (d) (2) – (b) (3) – (a) (4) – (c)

2. Write in Column II the number connected with each event mentioned in Column I.

Column I	Column II
(1) The population of Australia	(a) (more than 15 million)
(2) The number of Aborigines	(b) (160,000)
(3) Gold was discovered	(c) (the year 1851)
(4) People went to Australia from 1851 to 1861	(d) (700,000)

B. True or False Questions. Write a T in front of a statement if it is true according to the recording and write an F if it is false.

1. (F) Most of the settlers in Australia came from Britain until 1850.

2. (T) Many of the immigrants to Australia from 1851 to 1861 were from China, because China is near to Australia.

3. (F) The Italians dominate the sugar industry of Australia.

4. (F) The Greeks are the fourth largest national group in Australia, after the British, the Scottish and the Italians.

5. (T) The Greeks went to work in vineyards or coalmines or started cafes and bars and restaurants.

36

6. (T) Many Greeks went to Australia after WWII because the conditions in Greece were bad, whereas Australia offered to pay the boat fare to Australia.

C. Fill in the blanks with events connected with the following time expressions.

1. Italians
   a. the 1850s and 1860s: (Different states in Italy were fighting for independence and some Italians went to Australia for political reasons. Some others went there for gold.)
   b. 1891: (The first group of three hundred Italians went to work in the sugar – cane fields of northern Australia.)
   c. the end of the nineteenth century: (Some good Italian fishermen went to western Australia.)

2. Greeks
   a. 1830: (The first Greeks went to work in vineyards in south – eastern Australia.)
   b. the 1890s: (There were about five hundred Greeks in Australia.)
   c. 1890: (There were Greek cafes and restaurants all over Sydney and out in the countryside.)
   d. after WWII: (Many Greeks arrived in Australia.)

Section Three:
Tapescript:
Task 1: Learning to Predict
1. A: It doesn't sound much like dancing to me.
   B: It is; it's great.
   A: More like some competition in the Olympic Games.

C: Yeah. It's (pause) good exercise. Keeps you fit.

2. A: But you can't just start dancing in the street like that.

   B: Why not? We take the portable cassette recorder and when we find a nice street, we (pause) turn the music up really loud and start dancing.

3. A: We have competitions to see who can do it the fastest without falling over. Malc's the winner so far.

   B: Yeah, I'm the best. I teach the others but (pause) they can't do it like me yet.

4. A: You're reading a new book, John?

   B: Yes. Actually, (pause) it's a very old book.

5. A: Now, can you deliver all this to my house?

   B: Certainly. Just (pause) write your address and I'll get the boy to bring them round.

6. A: Good. I've made a nice curry. I hope you do like curry?

   B: Yes, I love curry, I used to work in India, as a matter of fact.

   A: Really? How interesting. You must (pause) tell us all about it over dinner.

Key to Exercises:

Task 1: Learning to Predict

Listen to the following sentences. When you hear "pause", stop your recorder and guess what the speaker is going to say next. Discuss your answer with your classmates and then let the speaker finish his or her sentence.

1. Answer: It's good exercise. Keeps you fit.

   Reason: The word "yeah" suggests that the boy will say something in agreement with the woman's comment.

2. Answer: We turn the music up really loud and start dancing.

   Reason: The phrase "why not" suggests that the boys will simply dance in the street.

3. Answer: They can't do it like me yet.

   Reason: The word "but" suggests an opposite meaning.

4. Answer: It's a very old book.

   Reason: The word "actually" also suggests an opposite meaning.

5. Answer: Write down your address and I'll get the boy to bring them round.

   Reason: The conversation takes place in a store. If the store owner agrees to deliver the goods, the only thing he wants to know will be the address of the customer.

6. Answer: Tell us all about it over dinner.

   Reason: The woman sounds very much interested in the man's experience. So she will certainly ask the man to tell her something about it.

Task 2: Dictation

The Foolish Frog

Once upon a time a big, fat frog lived in a tiny shallow pond. He knew every plant and stone in it, and he could swim across it easily. He was the biggest creature in the pond, so he was very important. When he croaked, the water-snails listened politely. And the water-beetles always swam behind him. He was very happy there.

One day, while he was catching flies, a pretty dragon-fly passed by. 'You're a very fine frog,' she sang, 'but why don't you live in a bigger pond? Come to my pond. You'll find a lot of frogs there. You'll meet some fine fish, and you'll see the danger-ous ducks. And you must see our lovely water-lilies. Life in a large pond is wonderful!'

'Perhaps it is rather dull here,' thought the foolish frog. So he hopped after the dragon-fly.

But he didn't like the big, deep pond. It was full of strange plants. The water-snails were rude to him, and he was afraid of the ducks. The fish didn't like him, and he was the smallest frog there. He was lonely and unhappy.

He sat on a water-lily leaf and croaked sadly to himself, 'I don't like it here. I think I'll go home tomorrow.'

But a hungry heron flew down and swallowed him up for sup-per.

Supplementary Reading:
American Indians

North America was the home of the Indians long before Euro-peans came to the New World. Many centuries before the arrival of Columbus, Indians hunted, fished, and planted crops in the eastern forests. They brought the bison to earth with bows and arrows on the Great Plains. They fished for salmon in the rivers of British Columbia and gathered rye seeds in the Great Basin and acorns in California. They farmed the land in Arizona and southern Mexico. When Columbus arrived, Indians held all the territory within the great triangle formed by Panama, Alaska, and Labrador. They were masters of the North American continent.

However, after the European conquest of the New World, there was much suffering and much change in all of the Indian areas. Between 1500 and 1900 the Indian population of the area that

40

is now the United States declined from close to 1, 000, 000 to 300,000. And for those who remained, the agony was great. Many were forced to take land in new and strange places. They were introduced to new tools, implements, and techniques. They were forced to abandon their old ways of life.

Many of the tribes were resettled on reservations in the west. The land belonged to the United States Government but was reserved tax-free for the Indians. The federal government provided the tribes with rations, tools, and equipment. Boarding and day schools were set up. In many cases responsible agents were sent to administer the reservations.

But the change from a free life to the restricted life of the reservations brought the Indians near despair. They did not change easily.

In 1887 the General allotment Act (Dawes Act) was passed. Heads of Indian families were permitted to buy a quarter-section (160 acres) of land. It was expected that the Indians would jump at the chance to farm acres of their own. Many land purchases were made, but results were disappointing. Most of the Indians did not make happy farmers.

In 1934 the Indian Reorganization Act was passed. It ended the allotment system. It permitted the tribes to organize themselves politically so they could enjoy selfgovernment under the protection of the United States. The act provided money for scholarship loans, made provisions easier for Indians to enter the Civil Service, and allowed the tribes to engage in business.

In 1953 Congress passed a resolution calling for a policy of "termination" in Indian affairs. Termination meant freeing tribes from federal supervision and control. The Menomini of the old Wild Rice

Area were one of the tribes that were terminated. They were expected to move slowly but surely toward selfgovernment and self-support. A county in Wisconsin (Menominee) was carved out of their old reservation land. They took control of local mill operations. They worked hard. But the going was difficult.

In 1961, following meetings at the University of Chicago, a Declaration of Indian Purpose was published. It called for an end to the termination policy, and emphasized instead the government's responsibilities toward Indian peoples. It called for reviewing the conditions that produced Indian poverty. It asked that each Indian community and its problems be treated separately. It called for the expansion of health services, for better housing, for improvements in Indian education. The 1960's was a time of growing concern about poverty and minority rights in the United States. Reports on the plight of the American Indian continued to be made. One major report pointed out that the economic position of the Indians was worse than that of any other American minority group. Most Indian communities were barely getting by. Some of the nation's worst slums were to be found on Indian reservations. Unemployment was high. Indians had inadequate sanitary facilities and water supplies, substandard housing, and food deficiencies.

Meanwhile Indians were moving in greater numbers to the nation's cities. New York, Chicago, Detroit, Minneapolis, Houston, Denver, and Los Angeles could all boast growing Indian populations. Many Indians moved into poverty rows. It was hard for them to find jobs. It was hard—almost impossible—to compete with the white man in the white man's world. Many Indians returned to the reservation. But if the reservation had been broken up there was no place to go. The gap between Indian American and white American was growing wider. The government gave up the termination policy and sought to help the Indians through its various antipoverty programs. In 1968 President Lyndon B. Johnson, in his Message from the President of the United States, spelled out the Indians' plight.

Fifty thousand Indian families lived in unsanitary, dilapidated dwellings—many in huts, shanties, even abandoned automobiles.

The unemployment rate among Indians was nearly 40 percent, more than 10 times the national average.

Fifty percent of Indian school children, double the national average, were dropping out of school before completing high school.

Indian literacy rates were among the lowest in the nation, the rates of sickness and poverty among the highest.

Thousands of Indians who had migrated to the cities found themselves untrained for jobs and unprepared for urban life.

The average age of death of an American Indian was 44 years, for all other Americans it was 65.

President Johnson pleaded for the following goals:

A standard of living for the Indians equal to that of the country as a whole.

Freedom of choice: An opportunity to remain in their homelands, if they chose, without surrendering their dignity; an opportunity to move to the towns and cities of America, if they chose, equipped with the skills to live in equality and dignity.

Full participation in the life of modern America, with a full share of economic power and social justice.

As other American minority groups have become increasingly militant in their own behalf, so have the Indians. On November 9, 1969, a group of young Indians landed on Alcatraz Island in San

Francisco Bay. They had captured Alcatraz, the site of an abandoned federal prison. Poverty, ill health, and the depressing conditions on the reservations as well as their own failure in college had spurred these young Indians to act. Authorities forced them to leave Alcatraz, but they returned in greater numbers. They claimed Alcatraz as Indian territory and proposed to build on it an Indian cultural centre. Their action drew widespread publicity. It also drew sympathy and support from many Americans across the country.

So did the events at Wounded Knee. For many years the Oglala Sioux on the Pine Ridge Reservation in South Dakota had complained of their poverty, poor housing, inadequate water supply, and poor health care. They had complained about the corruption and inefficiency of the BIA (Bureau of Indian Affairs) and the failure on the reservation's economic programs. There were those who complained about the chairman of the tribal council, who was believed to be in league with the BIA. In December, 1972, therefore, a Civil Rights Organization was formed on the reservation. The wrongs of the past were to be made right. Members of AIM (American Indian Movement) were called in to help.

On February 27, 1973, a car caravan made up largely of Oglala raiders left Pine Ridge. At Wounded Knee the raiders piled out of their cars and quickly occupied the Roman Catholic Church. They raided the trading post and store and collected guns, ammunition, food, and supplies. They took eleven "hostages."

The national government responded quickly. Federal marshalls and FBI agents were called in to protect life and property. Representatives from the Department of Justice were sent in to negotiate with the Indians.

Lines for battle and for negotiation were drawn. The Indians

44

dug in and fought from bunkers. So did the government forces. For 70 days the "battle" raged. Sometimes nothing happened. Occasionally there were bursts of gunfire from both sides. Two Indians were killed, one agent was paralysed, and at least nine other persons were injured.

A disarmament pact was finally announced on May 6. All weapons were to leave Wounded Knee by May 9. The battle was over.

But Wounded Knee was a shambles. The trading post was destroyed, the museum vandalized, and individual homes ransacked. The bridge on the road to nearby Porcupine was destroyed. Dead cattle and dogs could be seen scattered over the landscape. The Catholic Church was pockmarked with bullet holes. There were those who vowed that they would never again live in the village.

Alcatraz and Wounded Knee are both perhaps symbols of our times. They show the deep frustrations of the long neglected and long oppressed American Indians. They may also contain the seeds for new beginnings and new hopes. For both have made the American people more aware of the Indians' problems.

Meanwhile the Indians have been working hard in their own interests. They are building new communities, establishing new industries, and erecting new schools. They are developing motels and other recreational schemes on the reservations. There is a growing Pan-Indian movement. Indians have become active in writing and publishing. Some tribes have benefited through settlement of their land or other claims against the government. They are using the funds for their own development. Perhaps a new day has already dawned for the American Indians.

Lesson 3

Section One:

Tapescript:

Task 1: I Don't See It That Way

Conversation One:

Clerk: Hello, sir. What can I do for you?

Customer: Hi. Uh ... I have this ... uh ... cassette player (Mm
　　－hmm.) here that I bought about six months ago. And it just
　　ruined four of my favourite cassettes.

Clerk: Oh dear, I'm sorry.

Customer: So I ... um ... wanted you to fix it. I'm sure it will be
　　no problem, right?

Clerk: Your sales slip, please?

Customer: Yeah, here it is. Uh.

Clerk: I'm sorry, sir. Your warranty's expired.

Customer: Well, it ... uh ... ran out ten days ago, but I'm sure
　　that you'll ... you'll ... fix the machine for free, because the
　　machine was obviously defective when I bought it. I...

Clerk: I'm sorry, sir. Your warranty has run out. There's nothing
　　I can do.

Customer: No. No, look. No. I didn't drop it off a building or
　　anything. I mean, what difference can ten days make? I mean
　　you ... you can—

Clerk: Sir, I'm sorry, we have the six-month rule for a reason. We

46

can't ...

Customer: Well, but you can bend the rule a little bit.

Clerk: ... make an exception for you. Then we'll have to make an exception for everybody. (Well, but look ...) You could say it's only a month, it's only two months.

Customer: I just lost twenty dollars worth of tapes.

Clerk: Sir, I'm sorry, it's too late.

Customer: It actually ate the tapes. I mean, they're destroyed. I mean—

Clerk: Well, sir, you knew (I...) when your warranty ran out. You should (Well ...) have brought it in before. It was (Well ... look ...) guaranteed for six months. I'm sorry, there's nothing I can do.

Customer: Paying for this is adding insult to injury. I mean, surely you're going to make good on this cassette player. It's ... it's ... it's a good cassette player, but it's just defective. I mean, I can't pay for this.

Clerk: Well, sir, I'm sorry, you should have brought it in earlier.

Customer: But surely you won't hold me to ten days on this.

Clerk: Sir, the rules are the rules. I'm sorry, but there's nothing I can do.

Conversation Two:

Norma: You know, Brian, it doesn't look like you've vacuumed the living room or cleaned the bathroom.

Brian: No, I haven't. Ugh. I had the worst day. I am so tired. Look, I promise I'll do it this weekend.

Norma: Listen, I know the feeling. I'm tired, too. But I came home and I did my share of the housework. I mean, that's the agreement, right?

Brian: All right. We agreed. I'll do it in a minute.

Norma: Come on. Don't be that way. You know, (What?) I shouldn't have to ask you to do anything. I mean, we both work, we both live in the house, we agreed that housework is ... is both of our responsibility. I don't like to have to keep reminding you about it. It makes me feel like an old nag or something.

Brian: Sometimes you are an old nag.

Norma: Oh, great!

Brian: No, it's just that I don't notice when things get dirty like you do. Look, all you have to do is tell me, and I'll do it.

Norma: No, I don't want to be put in that position. I mean, you can see dirt as well as I can. Otherwise— I mean, that puts all the responsibility on me.

Brian: It's just that cleanliness is not a high priority with me. There are other things I would much rather do. Besides, the living room floor does not look that dirty.

Norma: Brian.

Brian: Okay, a couple of crumbs.

Conversation Three:

Bob: Mr Weaver, I have been with this company now for five years. And I've always been very loyal to the company. And I feel that I've worked quite hard here. And I've never been promoted. It's getting to the point now in my life where, you know, I need more money. I would like to buy a car. I'd like to start a family, and maybe buy a house, all of which is impossible with the current salary you're paying me.

Mr Weaver: Bob, I know you've been with the company for a while, but raises here are based on merit, not on length of employment. Now, you do your job adequately, but you don't do it well enough to deserve a raise at this time. Now, I've told you before, to earn a raise you need to take more initiative and show more enthusiasm for the job. Uh, for instance, maybe find a way to make the office run more efficiently.

Bob: All right. Maybe I could show a little more enthusiasm. I still think that I work hard here. But a company does have at least an obligation to pay its employees enough to live on. And the salary I'm getting here isn't enough. I mean rents are rising, the price of food is going up, inflation is high, and I can barely cover my expenses.

Mr Weaver: Bob, again, I pay people what they're worth to the company, now, not what they think they need to live on comfortably. If you did that the company would go out of business.

Bob: Yes, but I have ... I have been here for five years and I have been very loyal. And it's absolutely necessary for me to have a raise or I cannot justify keeping this job any more.

Mr Weaver: Well, that's a decision you'll have to make for yourself, Bob.

Task 2: Marriage Customs

Here is an extract from a radio talk on marriage customs in different parts of the world by Professor Robin Stuart:

Despite the recent growth in the number of divorces, we in the West still tend to regard courtship and marriage through the eyes of a Hollywood producer. For us it's a romantic business. Boy meets girl, boy falls in love with girl, boy asks girl to marry him, girl accepts. Wedding, flowers, big celebration.

But in other parts of the world things work differently. In India, for instance, arranged marriage is still very common. An intermediary, usually a married lady, learns that a young man wishes to get married and she undertakes to find him a suitable bride. The young couple meet for the first time on the day of the wedding.

In Japan, too, arranged marriages still take place. But there things are organized in a different way. A girl wishes to find a husband, and the girl's mother, or an aunt perhaps, approaches the mother of a suitable young man and the young couple are introduced. They get a chance to have a look at one another and if one of them says 'Oh, no, I could never marry him or her', they call the whole thing off. But if they like one another, then the wedding goes ahead.

In parts of Africa, a man is allowed to have several wives. Now that sounds fine from the man's point of view, but in fact the man is taking on a great responsibility. When he takes a new wife and buys her a nice present, he has to buy all his other wives presents of equal value and, although we are obviously speaking of a male-dominated society, the wives often become very close and so, if there is a disagreement in the family, the husband has three or four wives to argue with instead of just one.

Now, most listeners, being used to the Western style of courtship and marriage, will assume that this is the best system and the one with the greatest chance of producing a happy marriage. But pause and reflect. Marriage must always be something of a gamble. Going out with somebody for six months is very different from being married to them for six years.

50

It is true that American women, brought up in the United States, who married Africans and went to live in Africa, have sometimes found it exceedingly difficult to assume the role of the wife of an African living in Africa. However, my observations have led me to believe that various forms of arranged marriage have just as much chance of bringing happiness to the husband and wife as our Western system of choosing marriage partners.

Key to Exercises:
Task 1: I Don't See It That Way
A. Conversation One:
1. Choose the best answer (a, b or c) to complete each of the following statements.
   (1) The customer comes to the shop _____.
       a. to repair his cassette player
     * b. to have his cassette player repaired
       c. to complain about his cassette player
   (2) The clerk refuses to repair the cassette player for free because _____.
     * a. the customer's warranty is expired
       b. the customer dropped it off a building and ruined it himself
       c. the customer bought the cassette player more than six months ago
2. Give brief answers to the following questions.
   (1) When did the customer buy the cassette player?
   Answer: About six months ago.
   (2) What's wrong with the cassette player now?
   Answer: It is defective and has ruined four of the

customer's favorite cassettes.

(3) How long is the cassette player guaranteed to free repairment?

Answer: Six months.

(4) When did the warranty run out?

Answer: Ten days ago.

3. Fill in the following blanks.

(1) Customer: Well, but you can (bend the rule) a little bit.

Clerk: . . . (make an exception for) you. Then we'll have to (make an exception for) everybody.

(2) Pay for this is (adding insult to injury). I mean, surely you're going to (make good on) this cassette player.

(3) Clerk: Well, sir, I'm sorry, you should have (brought it in) earlier.

Customer: But surely you won't (hold me to) ten days (on) this.

B. Conversation Two:

1. Choose the best answer (a, b or c) for each of the following questions.

(1) When does the dialogue take place?

  a. A weekday afternoon.

  * b. A weekday evening.

  c. A weekend evening.

(2) What is the agreement between husband and wife?

  * a. They two will share the housework.

  b. The wife should remind the husband about his housework.

    c. The husband should clean the living room when it looks
    dirty.

2. True or False Questions. Write a T in front of a statement if it is
true according to the recording and write an F if it is false.
   (1) (F) The man hasn't vacuumed the living room or cleaned
       the bedroom because he is tired.
   (2) (T) Though the woman is tired too, she has already done
       her share of the housework.
   (3) (T) The wife hopes that the husband will do the housework
       voluntarily, but the husband's eyes are not sensitive to
       dirt.
   (4) (T) The husband does not think that cleanliness is very im-
       portant.

C. Conversation Three:
1. Give brief answers to the following questions.
   (1) Is Bob married or single?
       Answer: Single.
   (2) How long has Bob worked for the company?
       Answer: Five years.
   (3) What's his attitude towards work?
       Answer: He has been loyal to the company and worked quite
               hard.
   (4) What's his purpose of speaking to Mr Weaver?
       Answer: Asking for a raise.
   (5) What's Mr Weaver's comment on Bob's work?
       Answer: Bob does his job adequately, but he doesn't do it
               well enough to deserve a raise.

(6) What does Mr Weaver suggest that Bob should do?

    Answer: Take more initiative and show more enthusiam for the job.

(7) What does Bob threaten to do if he can't get the raise?

    Answer: To quit his job.

(8) What's Mr Weaver's answer?

    Answer: That's a decision Bob will have to make for himself.

Task 2: Marriage Customs

A. Fill in the blanks to give a brief outline of the talk.

    Speaker: (Professor Robin Stuart)

    Topic: (Marriage customs in different parts of the world)

        In the West marriage is a (romantic business).

        In India (arranged marriage) is very common. The young couple meet for the first time (on the day of the wedding).

        In Japan (arranged marriages) still take place. But the young couple get a chance (to have a look at one another) and if one of them says 'Oh, no, I could never marry him or her', they (call the whole thing off). If they like one another, then (the wedding goes ahead).

        In parts of Africa polygamy is quite common. A man can have (several wives).

        Conclusion: Professor Stuart believes that various forms of arranged marriage have (just as much chance of bringing happiness to the husband and wife as the Western system of choosing marriage partners).

B. True or False Questions. Write a T in front of a statement if it is true according to the recording and write an F if it is false.

1. (T) In the West people believe that marriage should be based on romantic love.
2. (F) In Japan marriage is often arranged by an intermediary, usually the girl's aunt.
3. (T) According to the professor, though polygamy sounds fine from the man's point of view, the man in fact takes on a great responsibility and economic burden.

Section Two:

Tapescript:

Task 1: At the Dentist's

Dentist: There we are. Now, open wide. Now, this won't hurt a bit. You won't feel a thing.

Patient: Aaaagh!

Dentist: Come along, now. Open your mouth. I can't give you the injection with your mouth closed, can I?

Patient: I ... I ... I don't want an injection. I hate needles.

Dentist: But it won't hurt you, I promise. None of us likes injections but sometimes they're necessary.

Patient: It will hurt, I know.

Dentist: Not at all. Look, I often deal with little children and they never complain; they're always very brave. Now, open wide.

Patient: I don't want an injection.

Dentist: But how else can I take out your tooth? It would hurt even more without an injection, wouldn't it? And the reason we're taking it out is because it's hurting you, isn't it? Once you've had an injection and I've taken out the tooth you won't have

55

any more pain at all. So let's be brave. Open wide.

Patient: Aaaagh.

Dentist: But I haven't touched you yet. What are you shouting for?

Patient: You're going to touch me.

Dentist: Well, of course I am. I can't give you an injection without touching you. As soon as you've had the injection your gum will freeze and you won't feel a thing.

Patient: How do I know what you'll do while I'm asleep? You might rob me.

Dentist: Now, let's not be silly. You won't go to sleep. We don't do that nowadays. This will just freeze the area around the tooth so that you can't feel any pain while I'm pulling out the tooth. That's all. You won't go to sleep. You can watch everything I do in that mirror above you. Come along now.

Patient: I don't want to watch. I'll faint.

Dentist: Then don't look in the mirror. But there won't be a lot of blood. I promise you.

Patient: Blood! Blood! Why did you have to say that? I can't afford to lose any blood.

Dentist: Now let's not be silly. You can't take out a tooth without losing some blood.

Patient: Blood...!

Dentist: But it's a tiny amount . You'll make it up in a day.

Patient: A night.

Dentist: All right, in a night, then. But as I said it's only a small amount of blood ...

Patient: Blood! Blood!

Dentist: ... and it isn't going to kill you.

Patient: Kill! Kill!

Dentist: Oh, don't be silly; of course it won't. You can't die from having a tooth pulled out.

Patient: Die! Die!

Dentist: I shall get cross in a minute.

Patient: Cross! Cross!

Dentist: Now look, I've had just about enough of this. You come in here screaming in pain, saying that you've been in agony all night because you bit on a bone or something, and you ask me to do something to stop the pain but the minute I do try to do something you won't let me. Now, just what exactly am I expected to do? You're a grown man and I'm a very busy lady. I have a lot of patients waiting in the other room and you're taking up my time, which is very expensive. Now, pull yourself together and let's get on with it.

Patient: I can't. Couldn't you just give me some painkillers?

Dentist: Well, I could, but that isn't going to solve the problem. On the other hand, perhaps that's the best thing if you're so nervous about me doing the extraction today. Yes, perhaps that's best. You take some painkillers and let's make an appointment for next week when you're feeling less nervous. Now, which day would you like, Mr...? Sorry I didn't catch your name.

Patient: Dracula.

Task 2: Hiccups

Man : Rose (hic). Rose (hic). Rosemary. Can (hic) can you (hic) help me?

Rosemary: What's the matter? Oh, you've got the hiccups.

Man : I've had them for (hic) three hours (hic, hic).

Rosemary: Oh, there must be something we can do. Now, what are the different remedies for hiccups?

Man: I've tried everything (hic) I can think of.

Rosemary: Have you tried holding your breath?

Man: I've tried (hic) holding it (hic) but I hiccuped.

Rosemary: Well, you obviously haven't held it long enough.

Man : How can (hic) I hold it long enough when I (hic) hiccup in the middle?

Rosemary: Now what's the other thing I've heard? Now come along, something to do with a glass of water. That's right, you have to drink from the other side of a glass. Have you tried that?

Man : Well, how (hic) do you mean (hic) drink (hic) from the other side of a glass?

Rosemary: Well, you know how you drink normally...

Man: Yes (hic).

Rosemary: Then you drink from the opposite side.

Man: You mean (hic) you turn the glass round (hic)?

Rosemary: You bend over with your head towards the floor, then you put your lips to the far side of the glass and you try to drink it like that.

Man: Ah, (hic) you mean like this?

Rosemary: Oh no, you're getting it all over the carpet. Now what's the other thing? Key down the back of your neck.

Man: No (hic), that's for when your ... your nose's bleeding.

Rosemary: Oh, is it?(hic) What about a coin on your forehead (hic)?

Man: I've never (hic, hic) heard of that (hic).

Rosemary: Now what's that other thing for hiccups? A shock, a shock. I'll have to frighten you ... Erm ... let me burst a paper bag.

Man : (Hic) But (hic) I know you (hic) are going to frighten me so I (hic) won't be frightened, will I (hic)?

Rosemary: Now what else is there?(hic)Now, look, I know. I'll give you five pounds if you hiccup again, you give me five pounds if you can't.

Man: Yes, all right.

Rosemary: Did you understand what I said?

Man: Of course I did. You give me five pounds if I hiccup again.

Rosemary: Yes, but you stopped hiccuping, so that means you owe me five pounds.

Man: Oh, no (hic)!

Key to Exercises:

Task 1: At the Dentist's

A. Choose the best answer (a, b or c) for each of the following questions.

1. Why does the dentist ask the man to open his mouth wide?

    a. To give him a general check-up.

 * b. To give him an injection.

    c. To pull out one of his teeth.

2. Why doesn't the patient open his mouth?

 * a. He hates to have injections.

    b. His tooth aches.

    c. He hates the dentist.

3. Why does the dentist want to give the patient an injection?

    a. To let him sleep so that he won't be so noisy.

    b. To rob him while he is asleep.

 * c. To reduce the pain while the tooth is being pulled out.

4. What does the dentist finally give the man?

    a. An injection.

    b. A pull-out.

* c. Some painkillers.

B. True or False Questions. Write a T in front of a statement if it is true according to the recording and write an F if it is false.

1. (F) The patient has come to see the dentist because his tooth has been aching for a week.

2. (T) The injection will only freeze the area around the tooth rather than let the patient go to sleep.

3. (F) The patient doesn't want to watch in the mirror in front of him because he'll faint.

4. (F) According to the dentist, the patient will make up the blood that he will lose in a night.

5. (T) The dentist is angry with the patient because he is wasting her precious time.

6. (T) The patient will probably have his tooth pulled out next week.

Task 2: Hiccups

A. Give brief answers to the following questions.

1. Why does the man call Rosemary?

    Answer: He wants her to help him stop his hiccups.

2. How long has he been hiccupping?

    Answer: Three hours.

3. What has he tried to do?

    Answer: Everything he can think of.

4. What does Rosemary finally suggest?

60

Answer: She'll give the man five pounds if he hiccups again,
and he gives her five pounds if he can't.

5. What's the result?

Answer: The man has stopped hiccupping and owes Rosemary five pounds.

B. Identification. Match the suggestions Rosemary has made in Column I with the man's reaction in Column II.

Column I	Column II
(1) Hold the breath.	(a) Never heard of that.
(2) Drink from the oth-er side of a glass.	(b) Hiccupped in the middle.
(3) Key down the back of his neck.	(c) Won't be frightened when knowing it beforehand.
(4) Put a coin on the fore-head.	(d) Dropping water all over the carpet.
(5) Have to be frightened.	(e) That's for nose bleeding.

Answer: (1) – (b) (2) – (d) (3) – (e) (4) – (a) (5) – (c)

Section Three:

Tapescript:

Task 1: Learning to Predict

1. A: But the whole office complains that I smell of garlic for a
week after we've been to the French restaurant.

B: Well, how about (pause) the Chinese then?

2. A: Look, if you're determined to eat, why don't you go down
to the take-away and bring us back a nice packet of fish and
chips?

B: Fish and chips?

A: Well, it's better than nothing, isn't it? Go on. It's down the road and if you're quick, (pause) they'll still be hot when you get back.

3. A: Hurry up and you'll be in time for the next programme.

   B: Not if (pause) there's a queue.

4. A: Hi George. Where are you off to ?

   B: Home, do you want to come and listen to some jazz?

   A: Yes, that sounds (pause) a good idea.

5. A: But I don't think I'm going to take it.

   B: Why not? Not enough money?

   A: No, it's not that; the money's good. About 200 a week. It's just that we'll be working in a hotel playing for the tourists and they just want the same old tunes over and over to dance to and I get so bored. It's not like playing music, it's like being a machine.

   B: I wouldn't mind (pause) being a machine for that money.

6. But if all I wanted was money I could do an ordinary job. I play drums because (pause) I want to play drums.

Key to Exercises:

Task 1: Learning to Predict

Listen to the following sentences. When you hear "pause", stop your recorder and guess what the speaker is going to say next. Discuss your answer with your classmates and then let the speaker finish his or her sentence.

1. Answer: the Chinese then?

   Reason: "What about" suggests an alternative.

2. Answer: they'll still be hot when you get back.

   Reason: The woman's words suggest that the shop is very close

62

to their home.

3. Hint: The woman is asking the man to buy a pack of fish and chips from a nearby shop.

   Answer: there's a queue.

   Reason: The phrase "not if" suggests a condition that hinders the fulfilment of an action.

4. Answer: a good idea.

   Reason: The word "yes" shows an agreement.

5. Answer: being a machine for that money.

   Reason: "I wouldn't mind" suggests that the man will do what the woman doesn't want because of certain attractive conditions.

6. Answer: I want to play drums.

   Reason: The earlier sentence suggests that the man does not play drum for money. Consequently the explanation must be that he enjoys playing it.

Task 2: Dictation

Sleep

It's clear that everyone needs to sleep. Most people rarely think about how or why they sleep, however. We know that if we sleep well, we feel rested. If we don't sleep enough, we often feel tired and irritable. It seems there are two purposes of sleep: physical rest and emotional or psychological rest. We need to rest our bodies and our minds. Both are important in order for us to be healthy. Each night we alternate between two kinds of sleep: active sleep and passive sleep. The passive sleep gives our body the rest that's needed and prepares us for active sleep, in which dreaming occurs.

Throughout the night, people alternate between passive and active sleep. The brain rests, then it becomes active, then dreaming occurs. The cycle is repeated: the brain rests, then it becomes active, then dreaming occurs. This cycle is repeated several times throughout the night. During eight hours of sleep, people dream for a total of one and half hours on the average.

Supplementary Reading:

Marriage

When viewed within the entire range of past and present human societies, marriage can be described as a more or less durable union, sanctioned by society, between one or more men and one or more women. To obtain the sanction of society it is necessary that the relationship be formed and conducted in accordance with unwritten customs and taboos, as in primitive societies, or in accordance with established laws, as in more sophisticated societies. The sanction of society distinguishes marriage from other relationships between men and women and from pair bonding, a reasonably long-term relationship between male and female. All societies have rules or shared patterns of behaviour that regulate sexuality, birth, and child rearing. Marriage is the institution that encompasses these rules and patterns of behaviour.

According to one definition, which emphasizes relationship between the spouses, marriage is a socially legitimate sexual union. It is begun with a public announcement and usually with a public rite in a form recognized by the society. The union is undertaken with some idea of permanence and with a contract that defines the obligations between the spouses and of the spouses toward any children they may have.

Another definition emphasizes the importance of marriage as a means of providing social legitimacy for the children of the union. In this sense marriage is a relationship between a woman and one or more persons that provides that any child she bears under the rules of the relationship will receive the status and rights common to other members of the society. In this view, the importance of marriage is that it provides a way to distinguish between legitimate and illegitimate births. The assumption is that the child must have a "social father" to ensure proper social development and entrance into the social order. According to this definition, marriage is a "licensing of parenthood."

In nearly all societies the greatest emphasis is on having acceptable social fatherhood, which is quite different from physiological fatherhood. Social fatherhood can be assumed by a variety of individuals and by women as well as men. Not all societies have well-defined rules based on physiological fatherhood.

Forms of Marriage

An enormous variety of relationships between men and women, singly and in groups, meet the definition of marriage. Often the forms of marriage sanctioned by a society are related to the needs of that society. Marriage between two individuals, one male and one female, is known as monogamy. Marriage of three or more individuals is known as polygamy.

Polygyny is a form of polygamy in which one male is married to more than one female. Polyandry is a form of polygamy in which one female is married to more than one male. Still another form of polygamy is group marriage, in which two or more males are married to two or more females. In some societies a polyandrous marriage of two men with one woman may become a group marriage through the addition of a second woman. Not uncommonly in these marriages, the co-husbands are brothers and the added woman is the first wife's sister.

Monogamy. Throughout the world, probably in all societies at all times, some form of monogamy has been the prevalent form of marriage. This has been so because of economic necessity and also because, under normal conditions, the number of males and females in any society is relatively equal. Thus if a man is permitted to take a second wife, it may mean that some other man will not have any.

Although monogamy is the most prevalent form of marriage, studies have shown that it is not considered the ideal or preferred type. In a sample of 565 of the world's societies, 75% favoured polygyny, slightly less than 25% favoured monogamy, and less than 1% preferred polyandry. Nevertheless, most of the marriages in these societies are monogamous.

In many countries in which monogamy is the only socially sanctioned and legal form of marriage, "successive polygamy" is permitted by the device of divorce. In these countries two or three wives or husbands during a lifetime are not exceptional, although the society demands that they be taken one at a time, thus upholding the principle of monogamy.

Polygyny. In general, polygyny presupposes a considerable accumulation of wealth and is therefore rarely practised. A polygynous marriage requires more economic resources than a monogamous marriage because in most societies each wife and her children, unless they are sisters, have their own sleeping quarters and sometimes also their own cooking facilities.

Where polygyny exists, it is practised largely by the wealthy and the ruling classes, because only these can afford the luxury of having more than one wife. Generally it is the older men, who have lived long enough to acquire capital, who have more than one wife. Younger men have either one wife or none. In some societies where there is an extension of the marriageable ages for women, such as from 13 to 45 years, and a compression of marriageable ages for men, a larger pool of female partners is available, without an overall unbalanced sex ratio. This, too, leads to older men having several wives.

Polygyny can be traced principally to military and economic activities. In early warfare, such as that of the American Indians, a common practice was to kill the men and carry off the women for secondary wives. Extra wives were not only an outward sign of a man's wealth but also a means of increasing the wealth he already had. For example, among the Blackfoot Indians polygyny, which had been practised in a limited way by chiefs and other influential persons, was greatly expanded when the fur trade changed from beaver to buffalo. Buffalo skins were tanned almost exclusively by women. The enlarged market for buffalo skins led to a need for more female workers, which was met by the accumulation of more wives.

In a polygynous marriage sexual jealousy is minimized through clearly defining the marital rights and obligations of co-spouses. Usually a senior or first wife has authority over subsequent wives. By means of a rotation system, each wife is allotted an equal period of cohabitation with the husband. It is also common for co-wives (unless they are sisters) to have their own separate dwellings. These practices help minimize jealousy, whose public expression is discouraged by the society. Co-wives are not expected to be jealous of one another, and even if jealousy is present it is regarded as an individual response to a particular situation, one that the larger society does not encourage.

Polygyny has been practised within practically all societies, even though the overall numbers involved have been small. Where it lacked legal sanction, it frequently existed in a more or less illegal form of concubinage, as among the Chinese up to the beginning of the 20th century. In many cases polygyny has received the explicit sanction of religion, as in Islam and Mormonism. But the practice has tended to die out, owing in large part to the diffusion of western European culture and particularly to the spread of Christianity. The ethical views of Christianity have opposed any form of marriage other than monogamy.

Polyandry. The union of one woman with several men is a rare form of marriage found in Tibet, among certain other Himalayan societies, and to some extent in American Indian and Eskimo cultures. Polyandry, however, has never been widespread.

Polyandry generally does not mean that one woman has the privilege of having more than one husband, but rather that several men combine and share one wife. It seems to exist only under certain economic and social conditions. For example, the scarcity of women and the difficulty that one man confronts in trying to support a family in the barren regions of Tibet led to the development of polyandry there.

The most frequent form of polyandry is the fraternal or Tibetan form, in which a group of brothers have a common wife, the oldest brother being the head of the household and the social father of all the children. Among the Nayar of southern India, however, a nonfraternal form of polyandry exists. Polyandry, in contrast to polygyny, has developed among members of the lower social strata. This

68

was the case in Tibet, where because they were poor, two or more brothers would share one wife. Thus they were able to establish a single conjugal group and maintain it in the interests of the wife's children. This type of polyandry tended to keep family lands and property intact, allowing them to be passed on to the next generation.

Other Kinds of Marriage. Regardless of the forms of marriage sanctioned by society, the chief function is to provide social legitimacy for the adults and their children. The human infant in contrast with the infants of other species, requires long and continual care. Human culture is acquired, not inherited. Human infants cannot survive and become functioning socialized adults unless socialized adults care for them. Social arrangements are therefore necessary to ensure that the infants will survive and learn the culture. Sometimes other forms of marriage are developed to accomplish these goals.

Among the Dahomey, a West African people the type of marriage is determined by the particular arrangements of economic exchange. In one type of marriage, for example, a woman can marry one or more other women. This occurs when the woman (who already may be married to a man) pays a bride-price (a payment to the bride's family for the bride's reproductive and productive services) and becomes a "female husband." She forms a domestic group of her own, and her "wives" become pregnant through relationships with designated males. She is not the biological but the sociological father and assumes control over the destiny of her wives and their offspring.

Among the Nuer in Sudan, a widow marries a close relative of her dead husband, but the children she bears continue to be "fathered" by the dead first husband.

69

In the past, among the Nayar of India a girl was ritually married at puberty. However, she did not remain with her "husband", and in fact never saw him again. She returned home, where she shared a household with her matrilineal kin: her mother, her mother's sisters, her own sibling and their children. Here she was permitted to take a series of lovers. Formal paternity of subsequent children was assigned to the man who paid delivery expenses for the child. However formal paternity did not mean assumption of guardianship or continued support for either mother or child. Guardianship and support were the responsibility of the matrilineal kinfolk.

Problems of Marriage. Both polygynous and monogamous unions have been criticized by those concerned with equal rights for women. Polygynous marriage has been condemned on the ground that it debases women. Monogamous marriage also has been condemned on the ground that it keeps the wife dependent on, and therefore unequal in status with, the husband.

Marriage is intimately connected to other aspects of society. The consequences for the men and women involved depend on a host of economic, ideological, and demographic factors. In no setting can marriage solve the larger social problems of economic exploitation and the institutional factors of sexism.

Each marital form presents a different structural problem to the marital partners. In monogamous unions, particularly in Western society, the dominant relationship is the married couple. The marriage is expected to fulfil virtually all the social and psychic needs of the partners.

By contrast, in a polygynous society marriage is not viewed as an independent tie between two individuals. Polygynous marriages

70

are seen in relation to group interests that take precedence over individual interest. Polygyny is enmeshed in a larger kinship unit in which the marital tie is not expected to be the dominant one. Husband and wife have little opportunity for intimacy. They do not expect to receive love, companionship, sexual satisfaction, economic sustenance, or domestic support from one individual, as in a monogamous marriage.

Lesson 4

Section One:

Tapescript:

Task 1: Weather Forecast

Announcer: And now over to Marsha Davenport for today's weather forecast. Marsha?

Weather reporter: Thanks, Peter. Well, as you can see from the weather map, there's varied weather activity across the United States and Canada today. Let's start with the west coast, where it's raining from British Columbia down to northern California. The high in Seattle will be 50 degrees. Southern California will be in better shape today—they'll have sunny skies and warmer temperatures. We're looking for a high of 78 degrees in San Diego. The midwest will be having clear but windy weather. Oklahoma City will see a high of 65 and sunny skies, with very strong winds. Down in Houston we're looking for cloudy skies and a high of 69. Over to the east in Miami we expect the thermometer to reach 64 degrees, but it'll be cloudy and quite windy. Up in the northeast, it looks like winter just won't let go! New York City will be having another day of heavy rains, high winds, and cold temperatures, with a high of only 35 degrees expected. Further north in Montreal it's even colder—28 degrees, with snow flurries expected today. Over in Toronto it's sunny but a cold 30 degrees.

And that's this morning's weather forecast. We'll have a complete weather update today at noon.

Task 2: The 5 O'Clock News

News anchor: Good evening. I'm Charles McKay, and this is the 5 o'clock evening news. The top story this hour: The town of Delta has been declared a health hazard. The entire town of Delta was closed down by government authorities yesterday, after testing confirmed that the town had been poisoned by the dumping of toxic chemicals in town dumps. Suspicions were first aroused three weeks ago, when 200 people telephoned the hospital complaining of headaches, stomachaches, faintness, and dizziness. An investigation revealed that toxic wastes had leaked into the ground and contaminated the water supply. People were being poisoned by their drinking water and by the fruits and vegetables they were eating from their gardens. In fact, any contact they had with soil or water was dangerous. Government authorities have ordered all residents to leave the area until the chemical company responsible for the toxic waste can determine whether the town can be cleaned up and made safe again.

And now here's Sarah Cooper with tonight's Consumer Report. Sarah?

Consumer reporter: Thank you Charles, and good evening. There was some good news for beer drinkers today: A recent study of 17,000 Canadians shows that people who drink beer moderately are healthier than people who drink other alcoholic beverages, such as wine or liquor. Researchers say they don't yet know exactly why this is so. They found, however, that moderate

73

beer drinkers reported less illness and appeared to have a lower risk of death from heart disease. Good health seemed to be connected to the amount of beer consumed and the regularity of drinking. People who drank beer one or more times a day reported the least amount of illness. Heavy drinkers, however— people who drank 35 or more pints of beer a week—reported more illness.

The war against cigarette smoking is heating up again. Legislation was introduced today that would make it illegal to advertise cigarettes, cigars, or any other tobacco product in any form of media. That means ads would be banned from newspapers, magazines, television, radio, and billboards. The legislation would also prevent tobacco manufacturers from sponsoring sporting events and from giving away free samples. This is the strongest anti-smoking legislation that has been introduced to date. Cigarette manufacturers insist that the legislation would be useless. In fact, they claim that in parts of the country where advertising has already been prohibited, cigarette smoking has actually increased.

That concludes the Consumer Report for tonight. Let's go over now to Jerry Ryan and find out what's happening in the world of sports. Jerry?

Sports announcer: Thanks, Sarah, and good evening sports fans. It was an exciting day in world soccer. Mexico defeated France 7 to 6, in a close game that offered spectators plenty of excitement. The game between Canada and Argentina ended in a tie, 3 to 3. And in a game that's still in progress, Italy is leading Haiti 2 to 1, with 30 minutes left to go.

Tune in tonight at 11 for a complete sports update.

Key to Exercises:

Task 1: Weather Forecast

A. Choose the best answer (a, b or c) to complete each of the following statements.

1. The weather reporter for today is _____.
   * a. Marsha
   b. Peter
   c. Margaret

2. The weather report covers the weather activity of _____.
   a. the United States
   b. Canada
   * c. the United States and Canada

B. Fill in the following chart.

	Weather Description	Temperature
British Columbia down to northern California	raining	
Seattle		50 degrees
Southern California	sunny	warmer temperature
San Diego		78 degrees
Midwest	clear but windy	
Oklahoma City	sunny with strong winds	65 degrees
Houston	cloudy	69 degrees
Miami	cloudy, windy	64 degrees
New York City	heavy rains and high winds	35 degrees
Montreal	snow flurries	28 degrees
Toronto	sunny	30 degrees

Task 2: The 5 O'Clock News

A. Fill in the following chart.

Title	Name	Summary of the Report
News anchor	Charles Mckay	Delta has been declared a health hazard.
Consumer reporter	Sarah Cooper	a. Drinking beer moderately is good for health. b. The war against cigarette smoking is heating up.
Sports announcer	Jerry Ryan	Results of some soccer games.

B. Give brief answers to the following questions based on the news report.

1. What happened to Delta yesterday?

   Answer: It was closed down by government authorities.

2. Why did that happen?

   Answer: Testing confirmed that the town had been poisoned by the dumping of toxic chemicals in town dumps.

3. When were suspicions first aroused?

   Answer: Three weeks ago.

4. How many people telephoned the hospital?

   Answer: Two hundred.

5. What did they complain of?

   Answer: Headaches, stomachaches, faintness and dizziness.

6. What did the investigation reveal?

   Answer: Toxic wastes had leaked into the ground and contaminated the water supply.

7. What have government authorities ordered?

Answer: All the residents should leave the area, until the chemical company responsible for the toxic waste can determine whether the town can be cleaned up and made safe again.

C. True or False Questions. Write a T in front of a statement if it is true according to the recording and write an F if it is false (based on the consumer report).

1. (F) A recent study of 70,000 Canadians shows that drinking beer moderately is better than drinking no beer at all.

2. (T) Researchers haven't yet discovered why drinking beer moderately is good for health.

3. (T) According to the study, drinking a little beer every day is better than drinking a lot at one time.

4. (F) Legislation was introduced today to make it illegal to produce cigarettes, cigars, or any other tobacco products.

5. (F) The legislation would also prevent tobacco manufacturers to sponsor any kind of public events.

6. (T) Cigarette manufacturers insist that the legislation would be useless, and this had already been proved in parts of the country.

D. Fill in the following blanks (based on the sports report).

Teams Playing	Result
(1) Mexico – – (France)	(seven to six)
(2) (Canada) – – Argentina	(three to three)
(3) (Italy) – – Haiti	(two to one)
(with (30 minutes) left to go)	

Tapescript:

Task 1: What Do You Like for Entertainment?

Reporter: Well here I am at the Brooklyn Academy of Dramatic Arts. I'm asking students here about their favourite forms of artistic entertainment. Pop or classical concerts? Art galleries or the theatre? The ballet or the opera? The first person I'm going to talk to is Benny Gross. Benny comes from New York and he's 20 years old and he's studying the piano. Benny, hello and welcome to our programme.

Benny: Hi, thanks.

Reporter: So, first question Benny - have you ever been to an art gallery?

Benny: Yes, lots of times.

Reporter: And the ballet, have you ever been to the ballet?

Benny: Yes, a few times. It's all right, I quite like it.

Reporter: And what about classical concerts?

Benny: Yes, of course, many many times.

Reporter: Erm - next - have you ever been to an exhibition, Benny?

Benny: Oh, yes - I love going to photographic exhibitions.

Reporter: Do you? Now, next question - what about a ... folk concert?

Benny: No, never. I think folk music is awful.

Reporter: Ok. And the opera? Have you ever been to the opera?

Benny: Yes. Two or three times. It's a little difficult but I quite like it.

Reporter: And a pop concert?

Benny: No, never.

Reporter: Finally — have you ever been to the theatre?

Benny: Yes, once or twice, but I didn't like it much.

Reporter: Ok Benny. Now the next thing is — which do you like best from this list of eight forms of artistic entertainment?

Benny: Well I like going to classical concerts best because I'm a musician, and I love classical music.

Reporter: Ok and what next?

Benny: Erm let's see — next, art galleries I think. And then, exhibitions.

Reporter: OK — art galleries, then exhibitions. Then? The theatre?

Benny: No, I don't think so, I don't really like the theatre.

Reporter: The ballet? The opera? Well, which do you prefer of those two?

Benny: The opera.

Reporter: So of the theatre and the ballet, which do you prefer?

Benny: Erm, the ballet I think because there's the music. I can always enjoy the music if I don't always like the dancing.

Reporter: Right, well, thanks very much, Benny.

Benny: You're welcome.

Reporter: My next guest is Kimberley Martins. What are you studying here, Kimberley?

Kimberley: Modern dance. I want to be a professional dancer when I leave.

Reporter: OK, so here we go. First question — have you ever been to an art gallery?

Kimberley: Yes, lots of times.

Reporter: And have you ever been to the ballet? Oh, stupid question I think.

Kimberley: Yes, a bit. Of course I have. I go almost every night if I can.

Reporter: And what about classical concerts?

Kimberley: Yes – there are classical concerts here a lot – the other students perform here and I go to those when I can.

Reporter: What about exhibitions – have you ever been–?

Kimberley: Oh yes, lots of times – I like exhibitions – exhibitions about famous people – dancers, actors, you know –

Reporter: Mmm. And what about a folk concert? Have you ever been to one of them?

Kimberley: No, I don't like folk music very much.

Reporter: What about the opera?

Kimberley: No, never. I don't really like opera. It's a bit too heavy for me.

Reporter: A pop concert?

Kimberley: Yes. I saw Madonna once. She was fantastic – she's a really great dancer.

Reporter: And have you ever been to the theatre?

Kimberley: Yes, I have.

Reporter: Right. Thank you Kimberley. My next question is – which do you like best of all? And I think I know the answer.

Kimberley: Yes – ballet, of course. After that, exhibitions. And after that, art galleries.

Reporter: OK.

Kimberley: Erm, what's left? Can I see the list?

Reporter: Yes, of course.

Kimberley: Erm, let me see – oh, it's difficult – I suppose – what next? – er – classical concerts, pop concerts, the theatre. Well, I think pop concerts next, I like going to those.

Then I don't know . .Classical concerts or the theatre? Classical concerts I think. So that leaves the theatre after them. OK?

Reporter: Great. And many thanks for talking to us, Kimberley.

Kimberley: You're welcome.

Task 2: Are You a Heavy Smoker?

Salesgirl: Yes?

Mrs Bradley: Six packets of Rothmans and three of Silk Cut please.

Salesgirl: Six Rothmans ... and three Silk Cut. That's ... six fifty-fives—three pound thirty ... three Silk Cut—one forty-four ... That's four pound seventy-four altogether. Thank you. 26p. change ... and your stamps.

Interviewer: Excuse me, madam.

Mrs Bradley: Yes?

Interviewer: I wonder whether you'd help us. We're doing a survey on smokers' habits. Would you mind ... ?

Mrs Bradley: Well ... I'm in a bit of a hurry actually.

Interviewer: It'll only take a few minutes. We'd very much appreciate your help.

Mrs Bradley: Well all right. I ... I can spare that I suppose.

Interviewer: Thank you. You are a smoker of course?

Mrs Bradley: Yes I'm afraid I am. My husband is too. As you can see ... I've just bought the week's ration.

Interviewer: Would you describe yourself as being a heavy smoker?

Mrs Bradley: Heavy ... no. I wouldn't call three packets of twenty a week heavy smoking. That's not even ten a day. No ... a light smoker. My husband ... he's different...

Interviewer: Yes?

Mrs Bradley: I get in twice as many a week for him. He smokes twenty or more a day.

Interviewer: You wouldn't describe him as a chain-smoker?

Mrs Bradley: No ... he's not as bad as that.

Interviewer: Right ... Thank you Mrs...?

Mrs Bradley: Oh, Bradley. Doris Bradley.

Interviewer: ... Mrs Bradley. You and your husband smoke cigarettes I see. What about cigars ... a pipe ... Does your husband ...?

Mrs Bradley: Oh he's never smoked a pipe. He's the restless, nervy type. I always associate pipe-smoking with people of another kind ... the calm contented type ... As for cigars I suppose he never smokes more than one a year—after his Christmas dinner. Of course I only smoke cigarettes.

Interviewer: Right. Now let's keep to you Mrs Bradley. When and why—if that's not asking too much—did you begin to smoke? Can you remember?

Mrs Bradley: Yes ... I remember very well. I'm thirty-two now ... so I must have been ... er ... yes ... seventeen ... when I had my first cigarette. It was at a party and—you know—at that age you want to do everything your friends do. So when my boyfriend—not my husband—when he offered me a cigarette I accepted it. I remember feeling awfully grown-up about it. Then I started smoking ... let's see now ... just two or three a day ... and I gradually increased.

Interviewer: I see. That's very clear. Now ... Might I ask if you have ever tried to give up smoking?

Mrs Bradley: Yes—twice. The first time about six months before getting married. Oh that was because I was saving up and ...

yes ... I used to smoke more in those days. Sometimes thirty a day. So I decided to give it up—but only succeeded I'm afraid in cutting it down. I still smoked a little...

Interviewer: And the second time?

Mrs Bradley: Oh the second time I did manage to give up completely for a while. I was expecting ... and the doctor advised me not to smoke at all. I went for about .. seven or eight months ... without a single cigarette.

Interviewer: Then you took it up again.

Mrs Bradley: Yes ... a couple of weeks after the baby was born. It was all right then because the baby was being bottlefed anyway.

Interviewer: Good. That's interesting. So if you'd been breast-feeding you would have gone for longer without smoking?

Mrs Bradley: Definitely. It's what the doctors advise. Though not all mothers do as their doctors say...

Interviewer: Now Mrs Bradley. When do you smoke most?

Mrs Bradley: Erm... When I'm sitting watching TV or ... or reading a book ... but especially I'm with ... when I'm in company. Yes ... that's it ... when I'm with friends. I never smoke when I'm doing the housework ... never ... There's always too much to do.

Interviewer: Do you ever smoke at meal-times?

Mrs Bradley: I always have ... one cigarette after a meal. Never on an empty stomach. Which reminds me—I must be going. My husband will be waiting for his lunch. And Keith ... he's my son.

Interviewer: Just one more question and that'll be all.

Mrs Bradley: Well if you insist.

Interviewer: How would you describe the effect that smoking has on you?

Mrs Bradley: What do you mean?

Interviewer: Well ... Does smoking—for example—make you excitable ... keep you awake...?

Mrs Bradley: Oh no — quite the contrary. As I told you before I smoke most at times when I'm most relaxed. Though quite honestly I ... don't really know whether I smoke because I'm relaxed or ... er ... you know ... in order to relax. Now I really must be ... Please excuse me. I see you're ... you're carrying a tape-recorder. This won't be on the radio, will it?

Interviewer: No Mrs Bradley ... I'm afraid not. But we do thank you all the same.

Mrs Bradley: Right. Goodbye.

Interviewer: Goodbye Mrs Bradley.

Pause.

Salesgirl: How's it going then?

Interviewer: Fine. Give us a packet of Seniors, will you. I'm dying for a smoke.

Salesgirl: That's 60p.

Interviewer: What about you. Don't you smoke ...?

Key to Exercises:

Task 1: What Do You Like for Entertainment?

A. Fill in the following blanks.

Reporter: Deborah Tyler

Interviewee: Students of the (Brooklyn Acadamy of Dramatic Arts)

Major: Benny Gross—(piano)

84

Kimberley Martins—(modern dance)

B. Fill in the following chart about how often Benny and Kimberley go to the eight forms of artistic entertainment.

	Benny	Kimberley
(1) Art gallery	lots of times	lots of times
(2) Ballet	a few times	almost every night
(3) Classic concerts	many times	sometimes
(4) Exhibition	photographic ones	those about famous people
(5) Folk concert	never	never
(6) Opera	two or three times	never
(7) Pop concert	never	Madonna once
(8) Theatre	once or twice	yes

C. Re-arrange the forms of artistic entertainment that Benny and Kimberley like, beginning with the form that each one likes best.

Benny: (3)—(1)—(4)—(6)—(2)—(8)

Kimberley: (2)—(4)—(1)—(7)—(3)—(8)

Task 2: Are You a Heavy Smoker?

A. True or False Questions. Write a T in front of a statement if it is true according to the recording and write an F if it is false.

1. (T) The conversation probably takes place at the cigarettes counter in a large supermarket.

2. (F) Mrs Bradley has bought ten packets of cigarettes for herself.

3. (T) The interviewer asks Mrs Bradley questions for a survey on smokers' habits.

4. (T) Though Mrs Bradley is in a hurry, she finally agrees to answer the questions.

5. (F) Mrs Bradley says that she smokes because she wants to be relaxed.

6. (T) The interviewer himself is a smoker, too.

B. Choose the best answer (a, b or c) to complete each of the following statements.

1. A Silk Cut costs _____.
    a. one pound forty-four
    b. twenty-six pence
* c. thirty-eight pence

2. Mrs Bradley gives the salesgirl _____.
    a. four pounds
* b. five pounds
    c. six pounds

3. Mrs Bradley smokes _____ a week.
    a. three cigarettes
    b. twenty cigarettes
* c. sixty cigarettes

4. Mrs Bradley will describe her husband as _____.
    a. a chain smoker
* b. a heavy smoker
    c. a light smoker

5. Mr Bradley has never smoked _____.
* a. a pipe
    b. a cigar
    c. a cigarette

6. Mrs Bradley has _____.

a. no children
　　　b. a daughter
＊　c. a son

C. Fill in the following chart about Mrs Bradley's smoking experi-
　　ence.
　　Name: (Doris Bradley)
　　Sex: (female)
　　Age: (thirty-two)
　　Amount: (three packets of twenty a week)
　　First experience:
　　　　Time: (at the age of seventeen)
　　　　Place: (at a party)
　　　　Offered by: (boyfriend, not husband)
　　　　Feeling: (awfully grown-up)
　　Later: started smoking (2 or 3) a day and gradually (increased).
　　Experience of giving up smoking: twice
　　　　1. Time: (six months before getting married)
　　　　　Reason: (saving up)
　　　　　Result: (only cut it down from 30 a day, still smoked a
　　　　　　　　　little)
　　　　2. Time: (when expecting a baby)
　　　　　Reason: (according to doctor's advice)
　　　　　Result: (gave up completely for 7 or 8 months and took
　　　　　　　　　it up a couple of weeks after the baby was born,
　　　　　　　　　because the baby was being bottle-fed)
　　Time when she smokes most:
　　　　1. (watching TV)
　　　　2. (reading books)

3. (in company)
4. (with friends)

Time when she never smokes:
1. (doing the house work)
2. (on an empty stomach)

Section Three:

Tapescript:

Task 1: Learning to Predict

1. Interviewer: Why do the actors wear roller-skates?

   Designer: Well, they're all playing trains, you see.

   Interviewer: Trains?

   Designer: Yes, singing trains and they have to skate all round the audience at very high speeds. We've designed special lightweight costumes for them out of foam rubber, otherwise (pause) they'd be exhausted at the end of each performance.

2. I found it took me rather a long time to get into the book. I mean, I kept wondering when we were going to begin with the plot, when we were going to get the actual story. Apart from that I must say that (pause) I enjoyed it very much.

3. I found it very exciting and moving. I couldn't put it down and (pause) I stayed up very late to finish it.

4. Well, I do agree with Jane that the book took a long time to start. In fact, for me, it's only honest to say that (pause) the book never really got started at all.

5. I'm one of those impatient readers who want to get straight into a book from the beginning. Otherwise (pause) I tend to skip parts that don't really hold my interest.

6. A: I'm afraid I did quite a lot of skipping with Alan Bailey's novel. And with over five hundred pages it was a bit of a disappointment really.

   B: Yes, I must admit that (pause) it *was* rather long.

Key to Exercises:

Task 1: Learning to Predict

Listen to the following sentences. When you hear "pause", stop your recorder and guess what the speaker is going to say next. Discuss your answer with your classmates and then let the speaker finish his or her sentence.

1. Answer: (They'd be exhausted at the end of each performance.)

   Reason: ("Otherwise" suggests a result of the opposite condition.)

2. Answer: (I enjoyed it very much.)

   Reason: ("Apart from that I must say" often suggests an opposite statement to earlier comments.)

3. Answer: (I stayed up late to finish it.)

   Reason: ("And" suggests that the speaker would finish the book at one sit.)

4. Answer: (the book never really got started at all.)

   Reason: (After an opinion of agreement, the phrase "in fact" suggests a further comment; the expression "it's only honest to say" usually introduces a confession—something which is probably not as good as the one mentioned.)

5. Answer: (I tend to skip parts that don't really hold my interest.)

   Reason: ("Otherwise" suggests a result of the opposite

89

6. Answer: (it was rather long.)

 Reason: ("I must admit" suggests an agreement to the other person's opinion.)

Task 2: Dictation

Books Belong to the Past

Sir,

 I visited my old school yesterday. It hasn't changed in thirty years. The pupils were sitting in the same desks and reading the same books. When are schools going to move into the modern world? Books belong to the past. In our homes radio and television bring us knowledge of the world. We can see and hear the truth for ourselves. If we want entertainment most of us prefer a modern film to a classical novel. In the business world computers store information, so that we no longer need encyclopaedias and dictionaries. But in the schools teachers and pupils still use books. There should be a radio and television set in every classroom, and a library of tapes and records in every school. The children of today will rarely open a book when they leave school. The children of tomorrow won't need to read and write at all.

M. P. Miller

London

Supplementary Reading:

Smoking and Health

 For centuries the smoking of tobacco in cigarettes, cigars, and pipes has produced controversy over possible health hazards, but only since the 1950's has sufficient scientific evidence accumulated to

90

make possible a thorough evaluation of the health risk.

Scientific investigations of the relationship of smoking and health gained impetus after the beginning of the 20th century, when an increase in lung cancer was noted. As the use of tobacco increased, studies improved. Although some gaps in knowledge still exist, the information now available is sufficient to permit making sound judgements, based on the converging lines of evidence.

Investigators have directed their principal consideration to cigarette smoking, because the health consequences attributed to it far exceed those due to smoking cigars and pipes. The widespread popularity of cigarettes is comparatively recent in man's use of tobacco. The smoking pattern began to change at the beginning of the 20th century. Since then, cigarettes have steadily become more popular than cigars and pipes. In the United States, per capita cigarette consumption – calculated for all persons 15 years of age and older, regardless of whether they smoked – rose from 49 per year in 1900 to 3,888 in 1960. Per capita consumption of cigars, pipe tobacco, and chewing tobacco declined sharply in the same period. Data presented in 1966 indicated a sharp reduction in cigarette smoking in the United States for men under the age of 55 with the trend continuing to 1970. Further increase in cigarette consumption for women of all ages was reported in 1966 and no further increase was noted between 1966 and 1970. However, in 1970 overall per capita cigarette consumption rose.

By 1962 the Royal College of Physicians of London reported: "Cigarette smoking is a cause of lung cancer and bronchitis, and various other less common diseases. It delays healing of gastric and duodenal ulcers." Some scientists, however, expressed dissenting opinions.

The most widely publicized report in the United States was issued in 1964 by the Surgeon General's Advisory Committee on Smoking and Health. The principal judgement in the committee's 150,000-word report was: "Cigarette smoking is a health hazard of sufficient importance in the United States to warrant appropriate remedial action." The smokers of pipes and cigars were found to incur much less health risk. However, the incidence of cancer and heart disease among them was found to be greater than among nonsmokers.

Smoking and Health (1964), the original report to the Surgeon General, had its findings confirmed and its conclusions extended by a review (1967) with two supplements (1968, 1969) and a new report titled *The Health Consequences of Smoking* (1971). For instance, cigarette smoking is now regarded as the most important cause of non-neoplastic bronchopulmonary disease in the United States, whereas the earlier conclusion limited the causal relationship to chronic bronchitis alone. The decrease in life expectancy among young men who smoke two packs of cigarettes a day is now more precisely defined as an average reduction of eight years and an average reduction of four years for those who smoke less than half a pack per day. The relationship of pregnancy and smoking has also been further clarified, new evidence indicating that smoking increases chances of stillbirth, neonatal death, prematurity, and low birth weight.

Antismoking Movements

A medical indictment of the habitual use of tobacco was published in 1798 by Dr. Benjamin Rush, a signer of the Declaration of Independence. The importance of this report was not its scientific contribution but its action in sparking antismoking movements several decades later.

Such well-known persons as John Quincy Adams, Horace Greeley, John Brown, and P. T. Barnum supported the movements. Antismoking campaigns continued throughout the 19th century, but the expanding tobacco industry did not significantly impede the increasing popularity of tobacco smoking.

A Broad Campaign. In the 1950's accumulating scientific evidence linking cigarette smoking and lung cancer made a distinct impact on the smoking public. During this period many health agencies declared smoking to be a health hazard. US Surgeon General Leroy E. Burney said in 1957: "The weight of the evidence is increasingly pointing to one direction: that excessive smoking is one of the causative factors in lung cancer." The initial reports had the heaviest impact, so that total cigarette production dropped in 1953 and again in 1954. Subsequent reports appeared to have less effect on smoking habits, and by 1957 cigarette production had risen above the 1952 level.

After four voluntary health organizations urged president John F. Kennedy to establish a commission to study the widespread implications of the tobacco problem, the Surgeon General's Advisory Committee on Smoking and Health was appointed in 1962 to review and evaluate all available scientific data. When its report, *Smoking and Health*, was released in early 1964, cigarette consumption again declined temporarily. Pipe and cigar smoking increased. More than 350,000 copies of the report were distributed and sold. Numerous abstracts and pamphlets were prepared by the Public Health Service and other organizations in a massive educational campaign on the hazards of cigarette smoking.

At least 80 professional health organizations, research organizations, medical societies, and government health agencies in the United States and other countries have concluded that cigarette smoking is an important health hazard. These include the American Medical Association, the American Cancer Society, the American Heart Association, the American Public Health Association, the National Tuberculosis Association, the American College of Chest Physicians, and the World Health Organization. The unifomity of opinions is reflected in a statement by US Surgeon General Luther Terry: "I know of no organized medical or scientific body in the world which states that cigarette smoking is not a serious health hazard." A National Interagency Council on Smoking and Health, composed of 18 major health, educational, and youth leadership organizations, provides leadership and liaison for nationwide educational programs in the United States.

In 1966, as a result of legislation passed by the US Congress in 1965, the federal government instituted a requirement that each package, box, or container of cigarettes carry a label reading "Caution: cigarette smoking may be hazardous to your health." On Jan. 2, 1971, a US government ban on all cigarette advertising on radio and television became effective.

The Industry's Stand. The tobacco industry in 1954 established the Tobacco Industry Research Council, later redesignated the Council for Tobacco Research – U. S. A. In 10 years the council granted more than $ 7 million to scientists for research into the question of tobacco and health. In 1964, after *Smoking and Health* had been released, the council issued its own 71-page *Report of the Scientific Director*, in which Dr. Clarence Cook Little wrote:

"After 10 years, the fact remains that knowledge is insufficient either to provide adequate proof of any hypothesis or to define the

94

basic mechanisms of health and disease with which we are concerned. It is true now as it was in 1954 that continued research in all areas where knowledge is deficient offers the best hope for the future." The report said "the results [of studies] lend little to support the hypothesis that cigarette smoke can act as a direct contact carcinogen in the human lung."

The tobacco industry announced its own code of self-censorship on cigarette advertising in 1964. The code banned advertising directed at persons under 21 years of age and prohibited advertising suggesting that cigarette smoking is essential to social prominence, athletic prowess, business success, or sex appeal. It ended claims that a filter makes cigarettes less harmful. In addition, the industry provided many millions of dollars to further research on smoking and health.

Other Countries. Government and private groups in several countries other than the United States have taken steps to discourage cigarette smoking. In Britain, the government in 1965 banned cigarette advertising on television. Three years earlier, a report on the hazards of smoking issued by the Royal College of Physicians had caused a temporary drop in cigarette consumption, but a subsequent extensive education effort failed to influence smoking habits significantly.

In Italy, the government passed legislation in 1962 forbidding any form of advertisement for tobacco. In the two years preceding the ban, cigarette sales had increased 6% annually; in the year following the ban, the rate of increase declined to 1.5%. In Denmark, the Danish Cancer Society launched an extensive educational campaign against smoking in 1960.

Lesson 5

Tapescript:

Task 1: An Unpleasant Trip

Herbert Wilson and his wife went to the Isle of Wight for their summer holiday. But they were by no means pleased with their hotel. As soon as they returned home, Herbert decided to write to the Manager of Happytours.

Herbert: Can you spare a moment, dear? I want you to listen to this letter.

Margaret: Go ahead, then.

Herbert: Dear Sir, my wife and I arrived home last night after a holiday arranged by your firm, in Jersey. We stayed at the hotel described in your brochure as a comfortable, medium-sized hotel, with a magnificent view of the sea, offering courteous, old fashioned service and excellent food, served in a relaxed friendly atmosphere.

Margaret: Yes, that's what the brochure said.

Herbett: In fact the hotel is situated at least half a mile from the sea. Our room overlooked a car park...

Margaret: Through the gates of which motor vehicles were constantly arriving or departing.

Herbert: Yes, that's good. The food was strictly beefburgers and chips or fish and chips. Wine was available, but at exorbitant

96

prices, and as for the courteous, old fashioned service, the majority of the staff were foreign and virtually incapable of speaking or understanding the English language.

Margaret: Yes, that's quite true.

Herbert: In addition to this, we were most unhappy with the arrangements for our journey home. We were instructed to catch the 11.00 am ferry...

Margaret: Wasn't it 12.00?

Herbert: No, 11.00... but this was apparently delayed and we did not get away till 6 o'clock in the evening. Now that our holiday is over, it seems fairly pointless writing this letter, but I should like you to know that we were most disappointed with the hotel and travel arrangements and shall certainly not be booking any future holidays through Happytours. Yours faithfully, Herbert Wilson.

Margaret: Yes dear, that's a very good letter.

Task 2: At the Travel Agency

Miss Bush is talking to a travel agent in London.

Travel Agent: Good morning. Can I help you?

Miss Bush: Hello. Er, my name's Miss Bush and I'm intending to go to a conference in Sydney for three weeks.

Travel Agent: I see. Er, do you want the excursion fare or the full return fare.

Miss Bush: Now, can I get a stopover on an excursion fare?

Travel Agent: Yes, you're allowed only one stopover on the excursion fare.

Miss Bush: Oh, I see, only one.

Travel Agent: Yes. But of course, if you pay the full return fare then you can have unlimited stopovers.

Miss Bush: Oh that's much better. Yes. You see, the thing is that I've got two weeks' holiday after the conference and I've never been out that way before at all to Australia or the Far East, and I, I wanted to go, you know, shopping or seeing Hong Kong or India or somewhere round there.

Travel Agent: Yes. Uhum.

Miss Bush: Um, where exactly can I go?

Travel Agent: Well, lots of places. There's Singapore or um, Teheran, Kuwait, Athens, you've really got quite a lot of choice you know.

Miss Bush: Mm. Well, it sounds marvellous. Um, how much would that cost? How much is the full fare?

Travel Agent: The full fare? Well, that's really quite a lot. It's £1204.

Miss Bush: (laughs) Yes, a thousand two hundred and four. Well, it's once in a lifetime, you know, I've never been.

Travel Agent: Mm.

Miss Bush: The thing is, actually that, um, I'm absolutely terrified of flying. I've never done it before.

Travel Agent: Oh dear. Uhum

Miss Bush: And er, um, I'm hoping that I can persuade my two friends, who are also going to the conference, to stop over with me on the way back.

Travel Agent: Yes, that would be a good idea, yes.

Miss Bush: Mm, yes. By the way, one of them's in Cairo at the moment. Would it be possible for me to stop over there on my way to Sydney?

Travel Agent: Yes of course. There are plenty of flights to Cairo

98

and, and then plenty more onwards from Cairo to Sydney. And then you can stay, there, in Cairo, for as long as you like.

Miss Bush: Oh that's great? Now, the thing is, I think I'd better go and persuade Mr Adams that, you know, he'd like to stop with me in Cairo...

Travel Agent: I see.

Miss Bush: ... go and discuss it with him and then come back to you in a day or two, if that's all right.

Travel Agent: Yes. Certainly. Of course, madam.

Miss Bush: Oh, thank you very much. O.K. Goodbye.

Travel Agent: Thank you. Goodbye.

Key to Exercises:

Task 1: An Unpleasant Trip

A. Give brief answers to the following questions.

1. Where did Mr and Mrs Wilson go for their summer holiday?
   Answer: The Isle of Wight.

2. How did they feel about the tour?
   Answer: They were not pleased with their hotel.

3. What did Mr Wilson decide to do when they returned home?
   Answer: He decided to write to the Manager of Happytours.

4. What is Happytours?
   Answer: A travel agency.

5. What did Mr Wilson complain about in his letter?
   Answer: The hotel and travel arrangements.

6. What will the Wilsons do in the future?
   Answer: They will never book any future holidays through Happytours.

B. Fill in the blanks with the words used in the brochure and by Mr Wilson to describe the hotel and travel arrangement.

	Brochure	Mr Wilson
Hotel	comfortable, medium-sized, with a magnificent view of the sea	half a mile from the sea, with our room overlooking a car park
Service	courteous, old fashioned	The majority of the staff were foreigners and couldn't speak or understand English
Food	excellent	strictly beefburgers and chips or fish and chips, wine at exorbitant prices
Atmosphere	relaxed, friendly	
Journey home	11.00 am ferry	didn't get away till 6 pm

Task 2: At the Travel Agency

A. Choose the best answer (a, b or c) to complete each of the following statements.

1. Miss Bush comes to the travel agency to _____.

   * a. ask for some information

   b. buy a ticket

   c. talk to a friend

2. Miss Bush's main purpose of the trip is _____.

   a. sightseeing in Australia and the Far East

   b. visiting a friend in Cairo

   * c. attending a conference in Sydney

3. Miss Bush will probably buy _____.

   a. an excursion fare

   * b. a full return ticket

   c. a single ticket

4. The full fare costs _____.

   a. 1402 pounds

* b. 1204 pounds

   c. 2104 pounds

5. Miss Bush's trip will probably be _____.

   a. London – – Sydney – – Cairo

   b. London – – Kuwait – – Sydney

* c. London – – Cairo – – Sydney

6. Miss Bush will probably come to the travel agency again

_____.

* a. the day after tomorrow

   b. next week

   c. in two weeks

B. True or False Questions. Write a T in front a statement if it is true according to the recording and write an F if it is false.

1. (T) Miss Bush's conference in Sydney will last for three weeks.

2. (F) Miss Bush thinks that the full return fare is better than the excursion fare because she can have a stopover.

3. (T) Miss Bush wants to visit not only Australia but also the Far East this time.

4. (T) Though Miss Bush thinks that the full return ticket is quite expensive, she will accept that because it is once in a lifetime.

5. (F) Though Miss Bush is used to travelling by air, she's still frightened this time.

6. (T) A friend of Miss Bush's in Cairo is also going to attend the conference in Sydney.

C. Fill in the blanks with the two things that Miss Bush will do.

1. Persuade (her two friends), who are also going to the conference, (to stop over with her on the way back).

2. Persuade (Mr Adams to stop with her in Cairo).

Section Two:

Tapescript:

A Saturday Afternoon

Gillian felt slightly uneasy as the porter unlocked the gates and
waved her through. St Alfred's Hospital was not an ordinary mental
institution. It was the most exclusive institution of its type in the
country. You had to be not only mentally ill, but also extremely
wealthy to be accepted as a patient. She parked her car outside the
main entrance of the imposing eighteenth century building. She
paused on the steps to look at the superb ornamental gardens and
surrounding parkland. An old man in a white panama hat was watering the flowerbed beside the steps. He smiled at her.

Old man: Good afternoon, miss. A lovely day, isn't it?

Gillian: Yes, it certainly is.

Old man: Are you a new patient?

Gillian: Oh, not a patient. I'm just here to do some research.

Old man: Will you be staying long?

Gillian: I really don't know. I wonder if you could direct me to
Dr Carmichael's office?

Old man: Certainly, miss. Just go through the main door, turn
left, walk down to the end of the corridor, and it's the last
door on the right.

Gillian: Thank you very much indeed.

102

Dr Carmichael was waiting for her. He had been looking forward to meeting his new research assistant. He himself had always been interested in the special problems of long-stay patients. Dr Carmichael was very proud of his hospital and she was impressed by the relaxed and informal atmosphere. She spent the mornings interviewing patients, and the afternoons writing up the results of her research in the gardens. Some of the patients were withdrawn and depressed, some seemed almost normal. Only one or two had to be kept locked up. She found it hard to believe that all of them had been thought too dangerous to live in normal society. She often saw the old man in the panama hat. He spent most of his time working in the gardens, but he always stopped to speak to her. She found out that his name was Maurice Featherstone. He was a gentle and mild-mannered old fellow, with clear, blue, honest eyes, white hair and a pinkish complexion. He always looked pleased with life. She became particularly curious about him, but Dr Carmichael had never asked her to interview him, and she wondered why. One night, at dinner, she asked about Mr Featherstone.

Dr Carmichael: Ah, yes, Maurice. Nice old chap. He's been here longer than anybody.

Gillian: What's wrong with him?

Dr Carmichael: Nothing. His family put him here thirty-five years ago. They never come to visit him, but the bills are always paid on time.

Gillian: But what had he done?

Dr Carmichael: Oh, I'll show you his file. It seems that he burnt down his school when he was seventeen. His family tried to keep the incident quiet. Over the next few years there were a number of mysterious fires in his neighbourhood, but the family did noth-

103

ing until he tried to set fire to the family mansion. He was in here the next day. Maurice never protested.

Gillian: And that was thirty-five years ago?

Dr Carmichael: I'm afraid so. If I'd had my way, I'd have let him out years ago.

Gillian: But he can't still be dangerous!

Dr Carmichael: No. He's had plenty of opportunities. We even let him smoke. If he'd wanted to start a fire, he could have done it at any time.

Gillian was shocked by the story. She became determined to do something about it. She wrote letters to Maurice's family, but never received a reply. He had never been officially certified as insane, and legally, he could leave at any time. Dr Carmichael was easily persuaded to let her talk to Maurice.

Gillian: Maurice, have you ever thought about leaving this place?

Maurice: No, miss. I'm very happy here. This is my home. And anyway, I've got nowhere to go.

Gillian: But wouldn't you like to go into the village sometimes ... to walk around, to buy your own tobacco?

Maurice: I've never thought about it, miss. I suppose it would be nice. But I wouldn't want to stay away for long. I've spent twenty years working on this garden. I know every flower and tree. What would happen to them if I weren't here?

Gillian realized that it would be unkind to make him leave the hospital. However, she found out that the next Saturday was his birthday. She arranged with the staff to give him a party. They wanted it to be a surprise and Dr Carmichael agreed to let him go out for the afternoon. There was a flower show in the village. Maurice left at two o'clock. He seemed quite excited. They expected him to

104

return about four o'clock. The cook had made a birthday cake and the staff had decorated the lounge.

Gillian was standing in the window when she saw him. He was early. He was walking up the drive towards the house, whistling cheerfully. Behind him, above the trees, several thick black columns of smoke were beginning to rise slowly into the clear blue sky.

Key to Exercises:

A. Identification. Identify briefly the following characters in the story.

Name	Identification
Gillian	(Dr Carmichael's new research assistant)
Dr Carmichael	(the president of St Alfred's Hospital)
Maurice Featherstone	(the gardener of the hospital)

B. Choose the best answer (a, b or c) to complete each of the following statements.

1. St Alfred's Hospital is considered most exclusive because _____.

    a. it accepts all people with mental illness

    b. it only accepts people with serious mental illness

  * c. it only accepts extremely rich people with mental illness

2. Gillian parked her car _____.

    a. outside the hospital gates

  * b. outside the main entrance of the hospital building

    c. in the park of the hospital

3. Gillian came to the hospital to _____.

  * a. research on the problems of long-stay patients

105

b. solve the problems of Maurice Featherstone

c. be a doctor in the hospital

4. After Maurice entered the hospital, _____.

* a. he never went out

b. he only went to the village on weekends

c. he only went out to see flower shows

5. Maurice had been the gardener of the hospital for _____ years.

a. forty – five

b. thirty – five

* c. twenty

6. Maurice returned to the hospital for his birthday party _____.

* a. before 4 o'clock

b. at 4 o'clock

c. after 4 o'clock

C. True or False Questions. Write a T in front of a statement if it is true according to the recording and write an F if it is false.

1. (F) The first time Gillian met Maurice, he was watering the flowerbeds near the gates of the hospital.

2. (F) If you want to see Mr Carmichael in his office, you should go through the main door, turn right, walk down to the end of the corridor. It's the last but one door on the right.

3. (T) Dr Carmichael knew that Gillian was coming.

4. (F) Gillian interviewed the patients during the day and write up results in the evening.

5. (T) Dr Carmichael never asked Gillian to interview Maurice,

because Maurice was already a normal person in his mind.

6. (F) Maurice did not set fires in the hospital because he had never been given a chance.

7. (T) Gillian tried to persuade Maurice to leave the hospital, but Maurice was unwilling to do so.

8. (T) The end of the story suggests that it was Maurice who set the fire.

D. Fill in the blanks with information about Maurice.

Name: (Maurice Featherstone)

Sex: (male)

Age: (old)

Appearance: (clear, blue, honest eyes; white hair and a pinkish complexion)

Temperament: (gentle and mild-mannered)

Length of stay in the hospital: (thirty-five years)

Reasons for entering the hospital:

1. When he was seventeen, (he burnt down his school).

2. Over the next few years, (there were a number of mysterious fires in his neighbourhood).

3. Later (he tried to set fire to the family mansion).

Visits from family members: (No)

Bills: (paid on time)

E. Fill in the blanks.

1. Gillian felt (slightly uneasy) as the porter (unlocked the gates) and (waved her through).

2. Some of the patients were (withdrawn) and (depressed), some seemed almost (normal). Only one or two

had to be (kept locked up). She found it hard to believe that (all of them) had been thought (too dangerous to live in normal society).

3. She arranged (with the staff) to give him a party. They wanted it to be (a surprise) and Dr Carmicheal agreed to (let him go out for the afternoon). There was a (flower show) in the village. Maurice seemed (quite excited). The cook had made (a birthday cake) and the staff had (decorated the lounge).

Section Three:

Tapescript:

Task 1: Learning to Predict

1. The student, puzzled about a particular point, decides to ask a question. As so often happens when under pressure, he tends to concentrate most of his attention on the subject matter and he pays practically no attention to the language. Consequently, (pause) he fails to employ the correct question form.

2. However, even though the student does employ an appropriate question form, (pause) difficulties may still arise.

3. The basic difficulty may, in fact, be one of several different types. It may lie in the student's limited aural perception, in other words, (pause) the student may not have clearly heard what was said.

4. Learners of English have, for example, said to me such things as "See me here tomorrow" or "Explain this". Fortunately, as I deal with non-native speakers and as I understand their language problems, I interpret this as inadequacy in the language rather than rudeness. Other teachers, however, (pause) may feel angry at receiving such orders.

5. Today I'm going to consider, very briefly, a problem concerned with the competition for land use, that i... that is (pause) whether crops should be used to produce food or to... should be used to produce fuel.

6. A particularly interesting possibility for many developing countries has been the conversion of plant material to alcohol. Th ... this is interesting because in many developing countries there is a large agricultural sector, and at the same time (pause) a small industrial sector.

Key to Exercises:

Task 1: Learning to Predict

Listen to the following sentences. When you hear "pause" stop your recorder and guess what the speaker is going to say next. Discuss your answer with your classmates and then let the speaker finish his or her sentence.

1. Answer: (he fails to employ the correct question form.)
   Reason: ("Consequently" suggests a result of the facts mentioned earlier.)

2. Answer: (difficulties may still arise.)
   Reason: ("even when" suggests that in spite of the following facts, something else still exists.)

3. Answer: (the student may not have clearly heard what was said.)
   Reason: ("In other words" is often followed by an explanation in clearer and easier words.)

4. Answer: (may feel angry at receiving such orders.)
   Reason: ("However" suggests an opposite fact.)

5. Answer: (whether crops should be used to produce food or

109

should be used to produce fuel.)

Reason: ("That is" is also followed by an explanation.)

6. Answer: (a small industrial sector.)

Reason: ("At the same time" suggests the coexistence of two things. Here prediction is also based on common knowledge.

Task 2: Dictation

The School Holidays Are Too Long

Today the children of this country have at last returned to work. After two months' holiday pupils have started a new term. How many adults get such long holidays? Two to four weeks in the summer and public holidays—that's all the working man gets. As for the average woman, she's lucky to get a holiday at all. Children don't need such long holidays. In term-time they start work later and finish earlier than anyone else.

In the holidays most of them get bored, and some get into trouble. What a waste! If their overworked parents were given more free time instead, everyone would be happier.

This isn't just a national problem either—it's worldwide. Dates may be different from country to country, but the pattern's the same. Why should children do half as much work and get twice as much holiday as their parents?

Lesson 6

Section One:

Tapescript:

Task 1: In the Path of the Earthquake

Reporter: And now, Mrs Skinner, can you tell us your story? What happened at your farm when the earthquake passed?

Mrs Skinner: Oh, it was terrible. I'll never forget it to my dying day. I hope I never see anything like that again. It was terrible. (Um.) Well, we always get up, Jack and me, at about a quarter to five. He has to milk the cows early, you see, and while he's doing that I make his breakfast. I was in the kitchen when it came. Suddenly the whole house was moving. The coffee pot flew through the window and I was on my back on the kitchen floor. The noise was terrible. Well, I knew what I had to do. You have to get outside, you know, it's safer there. So I ran through the house and opened the front door. Then I stopped – I couldn't believe it – everything was different, everything had changed, nothing was in the right place any more. You know outside our house there is a path to the gate – there was I should say – well, the path wasn't there any more. In front of the front door was our rose-garden, not the path! And next to the rose-garden were the eucalyptus trees, and behind them the raspberry patch – just as before, but they had all moved, moved about five metres, five metres to the left, to the south that is. On each side of the garden path we had a line of beautiful old cypress trees.

111

Well these had now moved right down to the end of the house, to the left again that is. And the path had completely disappeared.

Reporter: But that's incredible, Mrs Skinner. Do you mean that everything in front of your house had moved—what? —five metres to the left, I mean to the south? The raspberry patch, the eucalyptus trees, the rose-garden, the two lines of cypress trees—all had moved?

Mrs Skinner: Yes, everything had moved into the place of the other!

Reporter: But your front path had completely disappeared?

Mrs Skinner: Yes, that's right. Oh it was terrible, terrible.

Reporter: And your husband Jack? Was he all right?

Mrs Skinner: Yes—but the cowshed had moved too—it had moved several metres. Jack was all right—I could see him running round after the cows—all the cows had escaped you see. They were running all over the place—it was impossible to catch them.

Reporter: So Jack, your husband, was all right.

Mrs Skinner: Well he was a bit shocked like me, but he was all right. Oh, I forgot to tell you about the granary—that had moved south too. Its normal place was behind the house and now it was near the cowshed. Can you believe it?

Reporter: Incredible, Mrs Skinner. And the house itself—what about your house?

Mrs Skinner: Well then we saw what had happened. Everything had moved one way—that is, to the south—except the house. The house—can you believe it? —had moved the other way— the house had moved north. So the house went one way and ev-

112

erything else—the garden, the trees, the granary—went the other way.

Reporter: Incredible, Mrs Skinner, absolutely incredible.

Task 2: A Funny Thing Happened to Me ...

A funny thing happened to me last Friday. I'd gone to London to do some shopping. I wanted to get some Christmas presents, and I needed to find some books for my course at college (you see, I'm a student). I caught an early train to London, so by early afternoon I'd bought everything that I wanted. Anyway, I'm not very fond of London, all the noise and traffic, and I'd made some arrangements for that evening. So, I took a taxi to Waterloo station. I can't really afford taxis, but I wanted to get the 3.30 train. Unfortunately the taxi got stuck in a traffic jam, and by the time I got to Waterloo, the train had just gone. I had to wait an hour for the next one. I bought an evening news paper, the 'Standard', and wandered over to the station buffet. At that time of day it's nearly empty, so I bought a coffee and a packet of biscuits ... chocolate biscuits. I'm very fond of chocolate biscuits. There were plenty of empty tables and I found one near the window. I sat down and began doing the crossword. I always enjoy doing crossword puzzles.

After a couple of minutes a man sat down opposite me. There was nothing special about him, except that he was very tall. In fact he looked like a typical city businessman ... you know, dark suit and briefcase. I didn't say anything and I carried on with my crossword. Suddenly he reached across the table, opened my packet of biscuits, took one, dipped it into his coffee and popped it into his mouth. I couldn't believe my eyes! I was too shocked to say anything. Anyway, I didn't want to make a fuss, so I decided to

113

ignore it. I always avoid trouble if I can. I just took a biscuit myself and went back to my crossword.

When the man took a second biscuit, I didn't look up and I didn't make a sound. I pretended to be very interested in the puzzle. After a couple of minutes, I casually put out my hand, took the last biscuit and glanced at the man. He was staring at me furiously. I nervously put the biscuit in my mouth, and decided to leave. I was ready to get up and go when the man suddenly pushed back his chair, stood up and hurried out of the buffet. I felt very relieved and decided to wait two or three minutes before going myself. I finished my coffee, folded my newspaper and stood up. And there, on the table, where my newspaper had been, was my packet of biscuits.

Key to Exercises:

Task 1: In the Path of the Earthquake

A. True or False Questions. Write a T in front of a statement if it is true according to the recording and write an F if it is false.

1. (F) On the day when the earthquake took place, Mr Skinner got up at about a quarter to five because he wanted to milk the cows earlier that day.

2. (T) When the earthquake came, Mrs Skinner was in the kitchen preparing breakfast.

3. (F) Mrs Skinner tried to run out of the kitchen and went into the rose-garden, because it was safer there.

4. (T) Jack Skinner was the husband's name.

5. (F) Mr Skinner was running after the cows, because he was frightened by the earthquake and didn't know what to do.

6. (F) Everything on the Skinners' farm moved five metres to

114

the south during the quake.

B. Map 1 is a layout of the Skinners' farm. Mark out the plants and buildings in the map. Then in map 2 draw a new plan of the Skinners' farm after the quake.

Map 1:

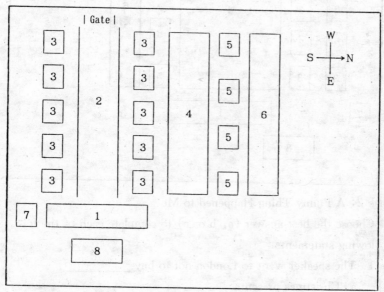

1. (farm house)
3. (cypress trees)
5. (eucalyptus trees)
7. (cow shed)

2. (garden path)
4. (rose garden)
6. (raspberry patch)
8. (granary)

Map 2:

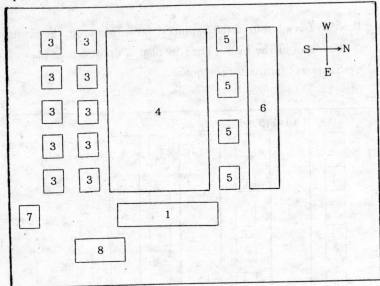

Task 2: A Funny Thing Happened to Me ...

A. Choose the best answer (a, b or c) to complete each of the following statements.

1. The speaker went to London not to buy _____ .

   a. Christmas presents

   b. books

* c. Christmas cards

2. The speaker wanted to catch the early afternoon train not
because _____ .

* a. it was the only train back

   b. he didn't like the noise of London

   c. he had made some arrangements for that evening

3. The train he wanted to catch was the _____ train.

   a. 3.13

116

* b. 3.30
 c. 3.33
4. While waiting for the train, he didn't buy _____.
   a. a newspaper
* b. a bar of chocolate
   c. a packet of chocolate biscuits
5. The packet contained _____ biscuits.
   a. two
   b. three
* c. four
6. The packet of biscuits they ate actually belonged to
* a. the man
   b. the speaker
   c. somebody else

B. Give brief answers to the following questions.
   1. When did the incident happen?
      Answer: Last Friday.
   2. What did the speaker do at college?
      Answer: He was a student.
   3. Where is Waterloo station?
      Answer: In London.
   4. How did the speaker go there?
      Answer: By taxi.
   5. Why didn't he catch the train?
      Answer: The taxi got stuck in a traffic jam and the train
              had left by the time he got to the station.
   6. How long did he have to wait for the next train?
      Answer: One hour.

7. Where did he wait?

   Answer: The station buffet.

8. What newspaper did he buy?

   Answer: An evening newspaper, the "Standard".

9. Where did he sit?

   Answer: At a table near the window.

10. What did he do?

    Answer: He did the crossword puzzle.

C. True or False Questions. Write a T in front of a statement if it is true according to the recording and write an F if it is false.

1. (F) The man sat opposite to the speaker because they were friends.

2. (F) The man looked like a typical businessman and there was nothing special about him.

3. (T) When the man took a biscuit from the packet near the speaker, the speaker was shocked because he thought it was his packet.

4. (T) Though the speaker was shocked, he didn't say anything but pretended to be interested in his puzzle.

5. (F) When the speaker took his first biscuit from the packet, he found the man looking at him furiously.

6. (T) The speaker's biscuits were actually under his news-paper.

D. Fill in the blanks.

1. Suddenly he (reached across) the table, (opened) my packet of biscuits, (took one), (dipped) it (into) his coffee and (popped it into) his mouth.

118

2. I was ready to (get up and go) when the man suddenly (pushed back) his chair, (stood up) and (hurried out of) the buffet.

Section Two:
Tapescript:
Consolidation: A Very Beautiful Story

Inspector: Morning, Sergeant. What have you got for me today?

Sergeant: We've got that tape from Gentleman Jim, sir. It was sent to us yesterday. They want to know if it's all right to send it to his wife.

Inspector: And is it?

Sergeant: I don't know sir. I'm sure there's a message hidden in the tape, but I don't know what it is. It's been examined by half the police force in London, and nothing was found. But there is something very peculiar about that tape.

Inspector: Well, what is it?

Sergeant: Well, sir, he talks about happy memories and things. And really, Inspector, I don't think Gentleman Jim really feels like that about anything. Mm, I don't think he means any of it. I'm sure there is something else on the tape, and it's hidden in what he says. But I can't find it.

Inspector: The tape is all right, is it? It wasn't tampered with when Gentleman Jim recorded the message?

Sergeant: The tape was carefully examined by three different experts, and they didn't find anything. Whatever it is, it's in the words.

Inspector: Well, I think I'd better listen to this tape, and see if I can find this mystery message.

119

Sergeant: Right you are sir, it's waiting for you.

Jim: Hello my dear wife. I want you to listen very carefully to this recording. Play it over and over again, and enjoy all the *beautiful* things I want to remind you about. Don't worry about me, just think about the *beautiful* things, and I'm sure you will be very happy, and you will find something very comforting in my words. Are you ready? I want to remind you of some really happy memories. Do you remember the day when we first met? You were *very beautiful*. There was a lot of sunshine that day, do you remember? There aren't many girls who are *very beautiful*, are there? But you were lovely. And our children. They're *very beautiful*. Two lovely girls, and a handsome boy, although they're all in prison now. I remember when our son was small, he had lovely blue eyes, and *very beautiful* gold curly hair. Do you remember the toys he used to play with? I remember his teddy bear, and also some *very beautiful* bricks, which he used to play with on the bedroom floor. Those were happy days. Do you remember, dear wife, the first dance we went to? You wore a blue dress and you looked *very beautiful* in the moonlight, and we danced until the morning, and then I took you home on my motorbike. Your mother was waiting for us, and she looked *very beautiful*. The next day I asked you to marry me. I don't think your mother was very pleased. She wanted us to buy the house next to her, do you remember? But we wanted a bigger house, with a *very beautiful* garden and we found one. I like our house very much. I remember coming home one day in the winter, and looking at our house. It looked *very beautiful* under the white snow, and I knew that you were waiting in the

120

kitchen with a cup of hot soup, and my dear friend Ginger. Poor Ginger. He has been in prison too. He says that you are *very beautiful*. The important thing in prison is to have happy memories. And I've got wonderful memories. Do you remember Ginger's cat? It was a *very beautiful* big black cat. Ginger liked it very much. He bought it fish to eat, and a *very beautiful* red ribbon, which he tied around its neck. I always liked Ginger's cat. I'm sorry I did not want to see you when you came. I wanted to send you this message instead. When I come home, I will buy you some expensive perfume, or a *very beautiful* rose. Play this recording many times, and think carefully about my words. Think about what came after all these beautiful things, and walk into the country, sit down beside the river, under a *very beautiful* tree, and think about me. Your loving Gentleman Jim.

Inspector: Mm, is that all?

Sergeant: Yes, that's all.

Inspector: You're quite right. There is something very peculiar about that message. Look, I've written some questions for you.

Inspector: Well, I think Gentleman Jim has hidden a message in the tape.

Sergeant: Yes sir, so do I. He keeps telling his wife to play the message over and over again.

Inspector: He tells her that she'll *find* something comforting. What do you think he means by that?

Sergeant: Well sir, perhaps there is money hidden somewhere, and this message tells his wife where to look?

121

Inspector: I wish he'd tell us where to look. Then perhaps we'd find the message.

Sergeant: I think he *has* told us, Inspector.

Inspector: What do you mean?

Sergeant: Well, did you notice that he keeps saying the same words over again?

Inspector: Yes, of course. He says everything is *very beautiful*.

Sergeant: Mm, that's right. And he tells his wife to think about these beautiful things. That must be a clue.

Inspector: Well, what does he say? His wife is beautiful, the girls are beautiful, his son is beautiful, the bricks were beautiful...

Sergeant: That's a very funny thing to say.

Inspector: Yes, it is. But wife, girls, son, bricks. It doesn't make any sense. 'Very beautiful bricks,' he said. It's nonsense!

Sergeant: Just a minute. do you remember what Gentleman Jim said at the end of the recording?

Inspector: What was that?

Sergeant: He said, 'Think about what *came after* all these beautiful things.' I think that's the answer, Inspector. Play it again, and every time he says 'very beautiful' write down the next word. I think we'll find Gentleman Jim's message.

Inspector: Right Sergeant. That's very clever of you. Well done!

Key to Exercises:

A. Listen to the first part of the policemen's discussion and give brief answers to the following questions.

   1. What are the two policemen discussing about?

     Answer: A tape from Gentleman Jim.

   2. .When was it sent to the police?

122

Answer: Yesterday.

3. Whom was it for?

Answer: Jim's wife.

4. What did the police suspect?

Answer: There was a message hidden in the tape.

5. Who had examined it?

Answer: Half the police force in London and three experts.

6. What was the result?

Answer: Nothing had been found yet.

7. What did Jim talk about?

Answer: Happy memories and things.

8. Where was the message suspected to be existing?

Answer: In his words.

B. Listen to Gentleman Jim's recording and write a T in front of a statement if it is true according to the recording and write an F if it is false.

1. (F) Gentleman Jim wants his wife to play the tape over and over again because he sincerely hopes his wife can enjoy all the beautiful things of the past.

2. (T) Jim and his wife first met on a sunny day.

3. (F) Jim has two sons and a daughter who are now all in prison.

4. (F) As a small boy, Jim's son used to play with teddy bear and bricks on the bed.

5. (T) Jim wanted to marry his wife after their first dance.

6. (T) Jim didn't buy the house next to his wife's mother because it was too small.

7. (F) Jim's friend Ginger had a very beautiful cat with a black

ribbon tied around its neck.

8. (T) Jim sounds a very romantic person, but in fact he doesn't feel about things like that.

C. Discuss with your classmates what message is hidden in Gentleman Jim's recording.

D. Listen to the second part of the policemen's discussion and list all the things they feel unusual about Gentleman Jim's recording.

1. (Jim keeps telling his wife to play the message over and over again.)

2. (Jim tells his wife that she'll find something comforting.)

3. (Jim keeps saying "very beautiful" over and over again.)

4. (The speech doesn't sound natural.)

E. Listen to Gentleman Jim's recording again and work out the message.

Answer: (There are two gold bricks in the garden under the big red rose tree.)

Section Three:

Tapescript:

Task 1: Learning to Predict

1. When it has been decided what's to be read — a chapter of a book, for example — then it's helpful to get an overview of the contents before starting to read. This can be done by reading the introduction, usually the opening paragraph, and the conclusion, usually the final paragraph. In addition, (pause) a glance at the

headings of sections or subsections will show the order in which the items are introduced.

2. Finally, the students should ask themselves a specific question connected with the main part of their reading. They should then endeavour to answer it by making appropriate notes as they read. This will help them to focus on the reading as well as (pause) providing a summary which can be re-read later.

3. When the student is writing a dissertation or doing a piece of research then he will need to consult a specialized bibliography. This is a book which lists all the published materials on a particular subject, and in some cases gives a brief summary of each item. Very recent research, however, (pause) may not appear in a bibliography.

4. There's the type of error which leads to misunderstanding or, even worse, to a total breakdown in communication. The causes of such misunderstandings and breakdowns are numerous, and I'll therefore be able to (pause) do no more than try to cover the most important ones here.

5. Very often those students who come from a language background which is Indo-European, mis-use English words which have a similar form to those in their native language. Spanish speakers, for example, expect the English word "actually" to mean the same as the Spanish word "actualmente". Unfortunately, (pause) it doesn't.

6. Finally, we come to the third type of error. This is the least damaging of the three, though (pause) it's still important.

Key to Exercises:

Task 1: Learning to Predict

125

Listen to the following sentences. When you hear "pause", stop your recorder and guess what the speaker is going to say next. Discuss your answer with your classmates and then let the speaker finish his or her sentence.

1. Answer: (a glance at the headings of sections or sub-sections will show the order in which the items are introduced.)

    Reason: ("In addition" is followed by a supplementary idea. Prediction here is also based on common knowledge.)

2. Answer: (providing a summary which can be re-read later.)

    Reason: ("As well as" is often followed by an idea of the same importance as the one before "as well as".)

3. Answer: (may not appear in a bibliography.)

    Reason: ("However" suggests an opposite idea.)

4. Answer: (no more than try to cover the most important ones here.)

    Reason: ("Therefore" suggests a result.)

5. Answer: (it doesn't.)

    Reason: ("Unfortunately" suggests that something opposite to one's expectation will happen.)

6. Answer: (it's still important.)

    Reason: ("Though" suggests that in spite of the fact that follows, something still happens.)

Task 2: Dictation

Sign Language

Deaf people, people who can't hear, are still able to communicate quite well with a special language. It's called sign language. The speaker of sign language uses hand gestures in order to communicate. Basic sign language has been used for a long, long time, but

126

sign language wasn't really developed until about 250 years ago. In the middle of the 1700s a Frenchman named Epée developed sign language. Epée was able to speak and hear, but he worked during most of his life as a teacher of deaf people in France. Epée developed a large number of vocabulary words for sign language. Epée taught these words to his deaf students. Epée's system used mostly picture image signs. We call them picture image signs because the signs create a picture. For example, the sign for sleep is to put both hands together, and then to place the hands flat against the right side of your face, and then to lower your head slightly to the right. This action was meant to show the position of sleep. So we call it a picture image sign.

Section Four:
Enjoy Your English:
Tapescript:

Try to Remember

Try to remember the kind of September
When life was slow and also mellow
Try to remember the kind of September
When grass was green and grain was yellow
Try to remember the kind of September
When you were a tender and callow fellow
Try to remember and if you remember
Then follow follow

Try to remember when life was so tender
That no one wept except the willow

Try to remember the kind of September
When love was an ember about to billow
Try to remember and if you remember
Then follow follow

Deep in December it's nice to remember
Although you know the snow will follow
Deep in December it's nice to remember
The fire of September that made us mellow
Deep in December our heart should remember
And follow follow follow

Lesson 7

Section One:
Tapescript:

Task 1: Learning a Foreign Language

Professor Ernest Watson was answering questions on a radio phone-in programme on the subject of learning a foreign language.

Listener: Hello, Professor, can you hear me?

Prof W: Yes, we can hear you fine.

Listener: My name is Humphries, Albert Humphries, and I live in Balham, in London.

Prof W: Yes, good evening Mr Humphries. What is your question?

Mr H: I've been studying Spanish for some years. I go to Spain on holiday sometimes. I've learnt quite a lot of grammar and vocabulary. But I find it very difficult to speak, and when I went to Spain this summer, I couldn't understand the Spanish people at all. I got really disheartened.

Prof W: Yes, it is a problem. How long have you been studying Spanish?

Mr H: About four years.

Prof W: Yes, how exactly? Going to an evening class, using tapes...?

Mr H : I've been going to an evening class and I've watched quite a lot of the BBC television programmes.

Prof W: Oh, yes. They're very good. Did you buy the BBC book?

129

Mr H : No, we use a different book in the class. But I watched the programmes.

Prof W: Yes, I see ... Mr Humphries, I always think that learning a language is rather like learning to drive. Now, you couldn't learn to drive a car by sitting in a classroom or watching television. I think what you need is a lot of practice in using the language.

Mr H : That's all very well if you live in the country where they speak the language but I don't.

Prof W: Yes, I understand the problem. Though even if you live in the country where the language is spoken, you have to reach a certain standard before you are able to have conversations with the natives. I was thinking perhaps you might arrange with another student or students to have regular conversation practice.

Mr H: But the other students make the same mistakes as I do.

Prof W: I...I...I think you're confusing learning with practising. Remember what I said about driving a car. Learning to speak means being able to put together the right groups of words and to say them in a reasonably accurate way.

Mr H: And what about learning to understand real Spanish?

Prof W: Well, again, you need practice in hearing the Spanish language spoken by Spanish speakers. There are Spanish speakers in London. Get one of them to read some extracts from a Spanish newspaper onto a cassette. Have you got a cassette recorder?

Mr H: Yes.

Prof W: Then you want to listen and listen and listen to the recordings until you almost know them by heart, just as if you were learning to drive, you'd practise parking the car, over and over

130

again, till you could do it perfectly. Learning to speak a language is a very hard business. You don't need a huge vocabulary. You need a small vocabulary that you can use really efficiently, and to be able to do that you need lots and lots of practice.

Task 2: In the Library

Woman: Good morning.

Librarian: Morning, can I help you?

Woman: Yes, I'd like to join the library. We're new to the district you see.

Librarian: Certainly. Well all we need is some sort of identification with your name and address on it.

Woman: Oh dear. We just moved, you see, and everything has my old address.

Librarian: A driving licence, perhaps?

Woman: No, I don't drive.

Librarian: Your husband's would do.

Woman: Yes, but his licence will still have the old address on it.

Librarian: Perhaps you have a letter addressed to you at your new house?

Woman: No, I'm afraid not. We've only been there a few days you see and no one's written to us yet.

Librarian: What about your bank book?

Woman: That's just the same. Oh dear, and I did want to get some books out this weekend. We're going on holiday to relax after the move, you see, and I wanted to take something with me to read.

Librarian: Well, I'm sorry, but we can't possibly issue tickets

131

without some form of identification. What about your passport?

Woman: What? Oh yes, how silly of me. I've just got a new one and it does have our new address. I've just been to book our tickets so I have it on me. Just a minute. Here you are.

Librarian: Thank you. Well, that's all right. Now if you'd like to go and choose your books your tickets will be ready for you when you come back to the desk to have them stamped out.

Woman: Oh, thank you. Er, how many books am I allowed to take out?

Librarian: You can take four books out at a time and you also get two tickets to take out magazines or periodicals. Newspapers, I'm afraid can't be taken out; they have to be read here.

Woman: Oh that's fine. We have our own daily newspaper delivered to the house. Oh, do you have a record library? Some libraries do, I know.

Librarian: Yes, we do. You have to pay a deposit of £ 5 in case you damage them. But that entitles you to take out two records at a time. We also have everything available on cassette if you prefer it. Cassettes seem to be much more popular than records lately.

Woman: Oh yes, as a matter of fact, I would prefer cassettes but I won't take any out today. I'll leave it until we come back from our holidays. Could you show me where your history and biography sections are, please?

Librarian: Yes, just over there to your right. If there's any particular book you want you can look it up in the catalogue, which you'll find just round the corner.

Woman: Thank you. Oh, and how long am I allowed to keep the

books for?

Librarian: For three weeks. After that you must telephone to renew the books if you wish to keep them longer. Otherwise we charge 20p a day fine for each book.

Woman: Oh dear. We're going away for six weeks. Can I renew them now?

Librarian: I'm afraid not. You must do that at the end of three weeks. Someone else might want them you see. And in that case we have to ask you to return them.

Woman: You mean, if someone wants them after my three weeks are up I have to bring them back?

Librarian: Yes, but just telephone and we'll see what we can do.

Woman: But I'm going to Tahiti. It would cost a fortune.

librarian: Well. . .

Woman: Oh, never mind. I'll leave it until we get back. It's not worth all the bother. I'll get some paperbacks in the airport. Well, thank you. I'm sorry I've been such a nuisance. Good morning.

Librarian: Not at all. Good morning.

Key to Exercises:

Task 1: Learning a Foreign Language

A. Choose the best answer (a, b or c) to complete each of the following statements.

   1. Professor Ernest Watson was answering questions on _____ on the subject of learning a foreign language.

      a. the phone

   * b. the radio

      c. T. V.

2. Mr Humphries wanted to know _____.

   a. how to study Spanish grammar

   b. how to enlarge his Spanish vocabulary

* c. how to improve his speaking and listening in Spanish

3. Professor Watson compared learning a language to

   _____.

* a. learning to drive

   b. driving a car

   c. watching T. V.

4. Professor Watson's advice was to _____.

* a. practice more in using the language

   b. go to live in the country where the language is spoken

   c. watch more T. V. programmes

B. True or False Questions. Write a T in front of a statement if it is true according to the recording and write an F if it is false.

  1. (F) Mr Humphries often went to Spain on holiday to practice his Spanish.

  2. (T) When Mr Humphries went to Spain this summer, he got disheartened because he still couldn't understand the Spanish people.

  3. (T) According to Professor Watson, Mr Humphries could improve his oral Spanish by practising with another student.

  4. (F) According to Professor Watson, Mr Humphries could improve his listening in Spanish by speaking to Spanish speakers in London.

C. Give brief answers to the following questions.

  1. What is the listener's name?

134

Answer: Albert Humphries.

2. Where does he live?

Answer: Balham, London.

3. How long has he been studying Spanish?

Answer: Four years.

4. How has he been learning Spanish?

Answer: He has been going to an evening class and has watched quite a lot of the BBC television programmes.

5. Why hasn't he bought the BBC book?

Answer: They use a different book in the class.

6. Why doesn't Mr Humphries want to practice oral Spanish with another student?

Answer: They make the same mistakes as he does.

7. What does learning to speak mean, according to the professor?

Answer: It means being able to put together the right groups of words and to say them in a reasonably accurate way.

Task 2: In the Library

A. Choose the best answer (a, b or c) to complete each of the following statements.

1. One needs to _____ to join this library.

   a. write down one's name and address

  * b. show some kind of identification with one's name and address on it

   c. give one's address

2. The woman wants to borrow some books because _____.

a. she wants to read them and relax

* b. she wants to take them away on holiday this weekend

c. she enjoys reading and can't live without books

3. The woman is finally able to join the library by showing

_____ .

a. her driving licence

b. her bank book

* c. her passport

4. The woman can take out _____ books out at a time.

* a. four

b. two

c. six

5. The woman can also borrow _____ records by paying
_____ pounds as a deposit.

a. five; 2

b. four; 2

* c. two; 5

6. The woman can keep the books for _____ weeks.

* a. three

b. four

c. six

B. True or False Questions. Write a T in front of a statement if it is
true according to the recording and write an F if it is false.

1. (T) The woman wants to join the library now because she
has just moved to the district.

2. (T) The library can never issue tickets without some sort of
identification.

3. (F) The woman has just got her passport. That's why she

has it on her.

4. (T) The librarian suggests that the woman go and choose her books while her tickets are being prepared.

5. (F) Apart from books, the woman can also take away magazines, periodicals or newspapers.

6. (T) The woman probably wants to borrow some books on history and biography this time.

C. Give brief answers to the following questions.

1. Where is the catalogue?

Answer: Round the corner.

2. What is the punishment for failing to return the books on time?

Answer: A 20p a day fine for each book.

3. Where will the woman go on holiday?

Answer: Tahiti.

4. Does the woman finally borrow any books?

Answer: No.

D. Fill in the blanks.

1. You have to pay a deposit of (5 pounds) in case (you damage them). But that (entitles you) to take out (2 records at a time). We also have (everything availabale) on cassette if you prefer it. Cassettes seem to (be much more popular than) records lately.

2. After that you must (telephone to renew the books) if you wish to keep them longer.

3. Oh, never mind. I'll leave it until (we get back). It's not (worth all the bother). I'll get (some paperbacks in the air-

port). Well, thank you. I'm sorry (I've been such a nuisance).

Section Two:

Tapescript:

Task 1: United World Colleges

Receptionist: United World Colleges. Can I help you?

Julian: Yes, I'd like some information about the colleges, please.

Receptionist: Hold the line. I'll put you through to the International Secretary.

Creighton: Good morning. Robert Creighton speaking.

Julian: Good morning. My name's Julian Harris and I have a friend in Spain who's interested in applying for a place at one of the colleges. There are one or two questions which she'd like me to ask you.

Creighton: Go ahead.

Julian: Thanks. The first one is: What language is used for normal lessons?

Creighton: Well, the main language of instruction in all the colleges is English. But at Pacific College in Canada some subjects are taught in French, and at the College of the Adriatic some may be taught in Italian.

Julian: Right. Her next question is about fees. Is it expensive to go to one of the colleges?

Creighton: Students' parents don't have to be rich, if that's what you mean. There are scholarships for all colleges, but we do ask parents to help by paying what they can afford.

Julian: Good, she'll be glad to hear that. Now she wants to know something about getting into a college. Does she have to get high

138

marks in her examinations?

Creighton: Ah, yes, well she will have to do well, but academic ability is not the only thing that's important. We also look at personal qualities.

Julian: What sort of things do you mean?

Creighton: Maturity, the ability to get on well with people from different countries, that sort of thing.

Julian: Of course. I understand what you mean. Her last question is about her other interests. Can she do painting and modern dancing, for example?

Creighton: Yes, probably. It depends on the staff at the college she enters. Each college has its own special activities, such as theatre studies or environmental work, in which students can take part.

Julian: Good. I think that's all. Thank you very much for your help.

Creighton: You're welcome. I hope your friend sends in an application.

Julian: I'm sure she will. Thanks again. Goodbye.

Creighton: Goodbye.

Task 2: I Remember ...

Grace: It's so great seeing you guys again.

Curtis: Yeah.

Martin: I agree.

Grace: I can't believe it's been twenty years since we were all in college together.

Martin: You know something, I remember it as if it were yesterday.

Curtis: I do ... (Yeah.) I was just going to say, as if it were yes-

139

terday.

Martin: Incredible.

Grace: Martin, what do you remember most about our college days?

Martin: Oh, I remember most?

Grace: Uh – huh.

Martin: Curtis's hair ... down to his waist.

Curtis: Now, I remember how Grace looked. (Wha...) She always had a flower painted on her face, remember that?

Martin: Oh, yes. I remember that.

Grace: Now wait, wait. Let's not forget about Martin and his air-conditioned blue jeans. I never saw anybody with more holes in their jeans than Martin.

Martin: They're a classic. You know, I still have those blue jeans. (Oh.)

Grace: Still have them? I don't believe it.

Curtis: Oh. Incredible. I don't either.

Martin: And I still wear them, too.

Curtis: You know, I was just thinking the other day – it's funny – about that worst ... worst thing that happened in college.

Martin: The worst thing?

Grace: What was that?

Curtis: Yeah. The time we were driving home from college for a spring break, remember? (Oooh.) (Ooh. Yeah. Oooh.) It was a holiday, and every gas station was closed. And that darn gas gauge was on empty.

Martin: And (We were desperate.) we stopped at that gas station and tried to get some gas out of that pump.

Grace: And the neighbours saw us and called the police. We almost got arrested. (Oooh.) Gosh, I was scared stiff.

Martin: You were scared stiff? I was petrified. And - but, you know, it was a lot different from the time we actually did get arrested.

Curtis: Umm.

Grace: Yeah. you know, that's my best memory. That peace demonstration. (Yeah.) You know, somehow getting arrested for something you believe in isn't . . . isn't scary at all.

Curtis: No, it isn't at all.

Martin: You're right.

Curtis: But it did help that there were five hundred other students getting arrested along with us.

Martin: That was a great day, though.

Grace: Hey, hey, you all remember our last day of college?

Martin: What, you mean graduation?

Curtis: Graduation, what's to remember? None of you went to graduation. I didn't go.

Martin: Do you regret that, that. . . that after all these years you skipped out on the ceremony?

Grace: Not me. Hey, I've changed my mind about a lot of things in twenty years, but I don't think we missed anything that day.

Curtis: No, nothing at all. And that picnic that the three of us had by the stream, remember? (That was great.) (Oooh.) Drinking wine, playing guitar, singing. Oh, that was worth more to me than any graduation ceremony.

Martin: That was (Mm - hmm.) the best graduation ceremony there could have been.

Curtis: Mm - hmm.

141

Key to Exercises:

Task 1: United World Colleges

A. Give brief answers to the following questions.

1. Where does the dialogue take place?

   Answer: On the phone.

2. What does Julian want to know?

   Answer: Some information about the college.

3. What's the name of the International Secretary?

   Answer: Robert Creighton.

4. Who wants to apply to one of the colleges?

   Answer: Julian's friend in Spain.

5. What is the main language used for normal lessons?

   Answer: English.

6. Is it expensive to go to one of the colleges?

   Answer: No. There are scholarships for all colleges, but parents will have to pay too.

7. Does a student have to get high marks in her examinations?

   Answer: Yes. But academic ability is not the only thing important. Personal qualities will also be considered.

8. What does personal qualities refer to?

   Answer: Maturity, the ability to get on well with people from different countries.

B. Fill in the blanks.

1. Hold (the line). I'll (put you through to) the International Secretary.

2. But at (Pacific College) in Canada some subjects are taught in (French), and at the College of the Adriatic some (may be taught in Italian).

3. Julian: Her last question is about her other interests. Can she do (painting and modern dancing), for example?

   Creighton: Yes, (probably). It depends on (the staff at the college) she enters. Each college has its own (special activities), such as (theatre studies) or (environmental work), in which students can (take part).

Task 2: I Remember ...

A. Choose the best answer (a, b or c) for each of the following questions.

1. What's the possible relationship between the speakers?
   a. Friends.
   * b. Former classmates and friends.
   c. Colleagues.

2. When were they in college?
   * a. Twenty years ago.
   b. Twenty – five years ago.
   c. Thirty years ago.

3. What does Martin remember most about the college days?
   * a. Curtis's hair down to his waist.
   b. How Grace looked.
   c. The air – conditioned blue jeans.

4. What is Grace's best memory?
   a. The time they were driving home from college for a spring break.
   * b. The peace demonstration.
   c. The graduation day.

5. Who of the three went to the graduation ceremony?
   a. Martin.

     b. Curtis.

*   c. None of them.

6. How did Grace spend her graduation day?

*   a. She went for a picnic with Martin and Curtis.

     b. She attended the graduation ceremony.

     c. She drank wine in a bar.

B. True or False Questions. Write a T in front of a statement if it is true according to the recording and write an F if it is false.

1. (T) The time they were in college were probably the sixties.

2. (T) In college Grace used to paint a flower on her face.

3. (T) They called Martin's blue jeans air-conditioned because they had a lot of holes.

4. (F) Martin no longer has his air-conditioned blue jeans.

5. (F) When they were driving home for a spring break once, they got arrested for stealing gas.

6. (T) They got arrested when they took part in a peace demonstration. But they were not frightened because five hundred other students got arrested with them.

7. (T) Grace has never regretted for not having attended the graduation ceremony.

8. (T) The three of them spent the last day of college together by the stream, drinking wine, playing guitar and singing.

Section Three:

Study Skills: Note-taking 1

    As students you may often attend lectures delivered in English. You will want to write down as many of the details as possible as you listen so that you can remember them later. However, taking

144

notes on a lecture can be difficult. How can you write everything down quickly, especially when the words are long? You may still be writing one sentence while the lecturer is five sentences further along. By the time you have finished writing and can listen again you are lost! You no longer understand what the lecturer is talking about. Or, like many students, you may decide that it is more important just to listen, and so you stop taking notes. But then at the end of the lecture you have already forgotten many important details. This textbook will introduce some techniques which you can begin to use now to make sure that your listening and note-taking keep pace with the speaker's ideas.

Rephrasing Sentences for Note-Taking

Taking good notes requires you to be able to do two things very quickly: First, you must recognize main topics; second, you must be able to write down as many details and supporting examples as you can hear and understand. In other words, your hand must work as quickly as your ear.

Most students do not have special training in transcribing or copying speech. You don't need a course in secretarial skills or shorthand in order to do a good job taking notes. But you do need to practise a few simple techniques to help you to be thorough in your note-taking. You should use abbreviations. We will study that technique later in this book. You should also learn how to write only the most important words from each sentence, and ignore the rest.

When you send a telegram to somebody, you must pay by the word; and for many people, money is limited. That is why we send very short telegrams which include only the most important words. For example, compare these two messages:

1. "I will be arriving tomorrow, Monday, April 15, on TWA flight

number 222, at JFK airport."

2. "Arrive 15th TWA 222 JFK"

Which message would be more expensive?

When you take notes, you have a similar problem. In this case it is not money, but time, that is limited. Therefore, it is a good idea to practise listening for only the most important sentences in a section of speech, and only the most important words in those sentences.

Tapescript:

Task 1: Learning to Rephrase

1. Most of the subjects of the enquiry think that nearly every word in English has just one meaning.

2. While it's true, of course, that many words in English do have only one meaning, it can easily be shown that the majority have more than one.

3. The third important misconception on the part of the students is their idea that a word can be used correctly as soon as its meaning is known.

4. English has a larger vocabulary than any other language. The reason for this, of course, is that it has been influenced by several other languages. It has, in fact, borrowed words from many sources. It is, therefore, particularly rich in synonyms.

5. Perhaps more important is a grammatical matter, namely that some words which mean the same can only be used when certain other words are present.

6. Unfortunately, when many students pick up a book to read they tend to have no particular purpose in mind other than simply to read the book.

146

7. The result is that students frequently don't have an overall view of what they're reading; also, they tend to forget fairly soon what they've been reading.

8. One reason for poor comprehension from reading may be that students fail to make notes or to ask themselves questions about the text.

9. If the reading material was broken down every twenty-five pages by short tests, reminding him what he had read, he could go on without fatigue or loss of efficiency for periods of up to six hours.

10. If he can increase his reading speed without loss of comprehension, then he'll have become a more efficient reader.

Key to Exercises:

Task 1: Learning to Rephrase

Listen to the following sentences. Write the words you think are most important in the space given.

1. (most subjects: 1 English word, 1 meaning)
2. (most English words: more than 1 meaning)
3. (3rd misconception: word used correctly with meaning known)
4. (larger vocabulary: influenced by other languages; rich in synonyms)
5. (grammatical matter: words of same meaning used with certain other words)
6. (many students: no purpose than read)
7. (students: no overall view, forget soon)
8. (poor comprehension because no notes, no questions)
9. (25 pages a test: no fatigue or loss of efficiency up to 6 hours)
10. (increase speed, no loss of comprehension: more efficient

147

reader)

Credit Cards

Many businesses, such as department stores, restaurants, hotels and airline companies, use a credit system for selling their products and services. In a credit system, the seller agrees to sell something to the buyer without immediately receiving cash. The buyer receives the goods or services immediately and promises to pay for them later. This "buy – now – pay – later" credit system is quite old. People have been buying things on credit for centuries. But nowadays people use credit cards. There are two types of credit cards. One type is issued directly by a store to a customer. Many large department stores issue credit cards to their customers. The store credit card can be used to make purchases only at a particular store. The other kind of credit card is issued by a credit company. Credit cards from credit companies can be used to buy things almost anywhere. If you have a major credit card, you can buy airplane tickets, stay at hotels, and eat at restaurants with it. Most large credit companies are connected to large banks. So if you want a credit card from a credit company, you generally have to make an application at a bank. After an applicant receives a credit card, he or she can make purchases, using the card.

Supplementary Reading:

Credit Card

A credit card is a means of identification by which the owner may obtain consumer credit for the purchase of goods or services rather than pay cash. At the time of sale he presents his card to the seller, who records the purchaser's name and account number along with the price of the purchase. Records are sent to a central billing office that calculates the total price of purchases made by the card owner during the business month and sends him a bill. The purchaser returns his personal check, covering all or part of the total, to the central office, which allocates the money to the establishments entitled to it.

The credit card, an American innovation, first gained national popularity in 1938 when oil companies selling gasoline to consumers set up a national pool to honour each other's cards. Rapid growth, however, was not possible until the mid – 50's, when the development of electronic computers permitted fast, accurate billing and accounting. Department stores, airlines, banks, hotels, and other enterprises then entered the field and now offer credit to over 140 million card owners.

Charges and Interest. Service charges or interest rates levied against card owners vary with the types of retail establishments involved. For businesses where individual purchases are small (for example, among oil companies selling gasoline to consumers) and total charges are generally paid within one month, card owners usually pay no service charges, and no interest is charged on unpaid balances until after six months.

For department stores, individual purchases are often very large, and installment payments are common. Such stores need their funds for investment in inventories and cannot afford to allow card users to incur a large interest-free debt. Accordingly, their credit generally carries an interest charge on all purchases that are not paid for within one month. The rate is high, commonly 18 % per year.

In another type of credit system, the credit card is issued by banks or credit companies and can be used at a large number of licensed agencies, including hotels, retail establishments, and restaurants. Because the agency issuing the card has no direct role in the retail sale, it must take its profit by charging either the card owner or the retail establishment. Both techniques are employed: some agencies levy an annual service charge against the owner as well as charging interest on unpaid balances; others charge the retail establishments a percentage of their total billing.

Advantages and Disadvantages. Credit cards offer advantages to both parties in a sale. With only one monthly billing, credit card owners are better able to synchronize their receipts and expenditures. Companies that are too small to undertake the expense and risk of instituting their own credit system can affiliate with a national card system and offer credit.

One disadvantage of the system is that the extension of this type of credit is beyond the control of the Federal Reserve System. Another disadvantage is that the informality of the use of credit cards makes theft and fraud quite simple. Card owners are generally liable for all claims submitted on lost or stolen cards until the central office is notified of the loss.

Lesson 8

Section One:

Tapescript:

Task 1: Twins

Interviewer: We continue with the World of Investigation. Laura, an identical twin, has agreed to contribute to our investigations. I must apologize for the fact that Laura's twin cannot be here tonight. And I'd like to tell you, Laura, how sorry we are. You and your sister are very close, aren't you?

Laura: Of course we are.

Interviewer: Interesting! You said 'of course'. Don't you think there are quite a few sisters who aren't close?

Laura: Sarah and I aren't just sisters. We're identical twins.

Interviewer: I take your point. How identical are you, in fact?

Laura: Both blonde, with brown eyes. Same height, same weight, same size. Even shoes.

Interviewer: As you're the same size, have you always dressed alike?

Laura: Oh yes. I'm told it started when we were babies. Mum made a feature of her twins. And then we got into the habit of buying two of everything.

Interviewer: And you've never minded having a double identity? I mean. . . another person exactly like you?

Laura: Sarah isn't exactly like me. We may look identical, but. . . I

151

remember our boyfriends couldn't tell us apart.

Interviewer: Didn't that cause problems?

Laura: For them, perhaps. Not for us. We couldn't stop laughing.

Interviewer: I think you said you and Sarah weren't exactly alike? Just what did you mean by that?

Laura: Sarah has a well-fed happy husband and four healthy children. When she was washing up, I was learning to type. When she was knitting, I was writing articles for the school newspaper. When she was having her second child, I was in Panama, doing my first job for United Information Services. See what I mean?

Interviewer: And haven't you got a healthy husband and happy children?

Laura: You must be joking. There's never been the time...or the inclination.

Interviewer: Laura, you've made some very interesting points. I gather that you don't feel that behaviour is purely genetic... that there might be some element of environment or choice or even perhaps...

Laura: Shall I conclude? Sarah and I are identical twins... in appearance, that is ... but it's a fact that life has presented us with different opportunities, so we've led very different lives.

Task 2: Genetic Make-up

Alan and Barbara have just read an article about twins and coincidences. They are discussing the article over lunch. Listen to their discussion.

Alan : That idea about our genetic make-up is rather frightening, isn't it?

152

Barbara: Do you mean the idea that because of our genetic make-up we are bound to act in a particular way?

Alan : Yes. If it's true, then it suggests that criminals are born and not made.

Barbara: Not necessarily. It would only mean that somebody was born with the potential to become a criminal.

Alan: How do you mean?

Barbara: Well, if somebody was born with a particular set of genes that made him a potential criminal, it would be necessary for him to be brought up in a particular way if he was actually going to become a criminal.

Alan : He'd have to grow up in a family of criminals, you mean?

Barbara: Yes, in the sort of family that regarded crime as a way of life and saw the police as the enemy.

Alan: They say it takes a thief to catch a thief.

Barbara: What do you mean by that?

Alan : Well, I suppose I mean that similar qualities are necessary to become a successful criminal or a first-class policeman.

Barbara: That's a bit hard on the policeman, isn't it?

Alan : I don't think so. In time of war men who might easily be in jail win medals for gallantry.

Barbara: That's because they're the sort of men who aren't satisfied with a normal everyday job.

Alan : Yes, they're men who get bored with ordinary life and want action. They're usually pretty strong characters, too.

Key to Exercises:

Task 1: Twins

A. Choose the best answer (a, b or c) to complete each of the following questions.

1. Where does the conversation most probably take place?
   * a. On the radio.
   b. On the phone.
   c. In the laboratory.

2. When does the conversation take place?
   a. In the morning.
   b. In the afternoon.
   * c. In the evening.

3. What's the name of the programme?
   a. The World of Investigations.
   * b. The World of Investigation.
   c. The Word of Investigation.

4. What's the relationship between Laura and Sarah?
   a. They are sisters.
   b. They are twins.
   * c. They are identical twins.

5. In what ways are Laura and Sarah identical?
   * a. In appearance.
   b. In personality.
   c. In life style.

6. Which of the following statements is correct?
   a. The twin's mother often mixes them up.
   * b. The twin's boyfriends often mixes them up.
   c. The twin used to have problems in finding boyfriends.

B. Fill in the blanks with information about the twins.

Name: Laura and Sarah

Sex: (female)

154

Similarities: 1. (blonde)

               2. (brown eyes)

               3. (same height)

               4. (same weight)

               5. (same size)

               6. (same shoes)

Differences: 1. Laura is single, but Sarah has a (well-fed happy) husband and (four healthy) children.

               2. When Laura was learning to type, Sarah was (washing up).

               3. When Laura was writing articles for the (school newspaper), Sarah was (knitting).

               4. When Laura was in (Panama), doing her first job for (United Information Services), Sarah was (having her second child).

C. True or False Questions. Write a T in front of a statement if it is true according to the recording and write an F if it is false.

1. (T) Laura is still single not only because she is busy, but also because she does not want to get married.

2. (F) Laura and Sarah have different life styles because of the genes.

Task 2: Genetic Make-up

A. Give brief answers to the following questions.

1. Who are the speakers?

   Answer: Alan and Barbara.

2. When does the conversation take place?

   Answer: At lunch time.

3. What are they discussing about?

   Answer: An article about twins and coincidences.

4. Why does Alan think that the idea of genetic make-up is frightening?

   Answer: Because it suggests criminals are born and not made.

5. What does Barbara think the idea of genetic make-up means?

   Answer: Somebody was born with the potential to become a criminal.

6. What kind of families can bring up criminals according to Barbara?

   Answer: The ones that regard crime as a way of life and see the police as enemy.

7. What does it mean by saying "it takes a thief to catch a thief"?

   Answer: Similar qualities are necessary to become a successful criminal or a first-class policeman.

8. According to Alan, what kind of people win medals for gallantry?

   Answer: Men who might easily be in jail.

B. Fill in the blanks.

1. Do you mean the idea that because of our genetic make-up we are (bound to act in a particular way).

2. If somebody was born with (a particular set of genes) that made him a (potential criminal), it would be necessary for him to be (brought up in a particular way) if he was actually going to become a criminal.

3. They're men who (get bored with) ordinary life and (want

156

action). They're usually (pretty strong characters), too.

Section Two:

Tapescript:

Task 1: Can I Take a Message?

Secretary: Mr. Turner's office.

Caller 1: Hello. I'd like to speak to Mr. Turner, please.

Secretary: I'm sorry, he's in a meeting right now. May I take a message?

Caller 1: Uh, yes. This is Mary Roberts from the First National Bank. (Mm – hmm.) Would you ask him to call me at 772 – 1852?

Secretary: Okay. That's 772 – 18 – ?

Caller 1: 52.

Secretary: Okay.

Caller 1: He can reach me at this number until, say, twelve thirty, or between two and five this afternoon.

Secretary: That's fine, Ms. Roberts. I'll tell him. I'll give him your message.

Caller 1: Thank you very much. Goodbye.

Secretary: Goodbye...Mr. Turner's office.

Caller 2: Yes. Hello. Is Mr. Turner in, please.

Secretary: No, I'm sorry, he's in a meeting right now. May I take a message??

Caller 2: This is Mr. Brown calling. I have a lunch appointment with Mr. Turner for tomorrow noon that I have to cancel. I'm going to be out of town for a while. Would you offer my apologies to Mr. Turner and have him call me, please, to reschedule? My number here is 743 – 9821.

Secretary: Okay, Mr. Brown. I'll make sure he gets the message.

Caller 2: Thank you so much.

Secretary: You're welcome.

Caller 2: Bye-bye, now.

Secretary: Bye-bye ... Mr. Turner's office.

Caller 3: Hello, Jane. Is my husband in?

Secretary: Oh, no, Mrs. Turner. I'm sorry. He's in a meeting until noon.

Caller 3: Oh.

Secretary: Oh, excuse me just a minute. I have another call. Can you hold for a second?

Caller 3: Yes, sure.

Secretary: Mr. Turner's office. Will you hold please? Hello, Mrs. Turner. Uh...Would you like your husband to call you back?

Caller 3: No. That's not necessary. But would you just tell him, please, that I won't be home until eight o'clock? I'll be working late.

Secretary: Oh, sure. I'll tell him.

Caller 3: Thanks a lot. Bye-bye.

Secretary: Bye-bye. Thank you for holding. Uh...Can I help you?

Caller 4: Yeah. Hi. This is Wendy at Travel Agents International. Umm...I've got Mr. Turner booked on a flight for Puerto Rico next Tuesday. Can you take down the information?

Secretary: Sure.

Caller 4: Okay. It's Pan Am Flight two twenty-six, which leaves Tuesday the twelfth at eight a.m.

Secretary: Okay. That's Pan Am Flight two twenty-six, leaving Tuesday the twelfth at eight a.m.

Caller 4: Right. Umm...I'll send the ticket over later this afternoon, if that's okay.

Secretary: Oh, sure. That'd be fine.

Caller 4: Okay. Thanks lot. Bye.

Secretary: Bye-bye...Mr. Turner's office.

Caller 5: Hello. Uh...My name is Juan Salvador. I'm calling from Puerto Rico, and I want to speak to Mr. Turner.

Secretary: I'm sorry, sir, Mr. Turner is in a meeting. May I take a message?

Caller 5: I...think it would be better if I...uh...call him later. Uh...Will you please tell me when he's going to be free?

Secretary: He'll be free in about an hour.

Caller 5: Oh, thanks. Uh...Why don't you leave him a message saying that I called him and I will call him back? It's in regard to our meeting on next Wednesday.

Secretary: Okay. Uh... Could you give me your name again, please?

Caller 5: Yes, of course. Juan Salvador.

Secretary: Could you spell that, please?

Caller 5: Yes. S − a − l − v − a...

Secretary: Uh...Excuse me, sir. I'm having trouble hearing you. Could you repeat it, please?

Caller 5: Yes, of course. S − a − l − v − a − d − o − r.

Secretary: Thank you very much, Mr. Salvador. I'll give Mr. Turner the message.

Caller 5: Oh, thank you very much. Bye-bye.

Secretary: Bye-bye.

Task 2: Night Flight

'This is Captain Cook speaking. Our estimated time of arrival in Brisbane will be one a. m., so we've got a long flight ahead of us. I hope you enjoy it. Our hostesses will be serving dinner shortly. Thank you.'

It was Christmas Eve 1959, and the beginning of another routine flight. The hostesses started preparing the food trays. A few of the passengers were trying to get some sleep, but most of them were reading. There was nothing to see from the windows except the vast blackness of the Australian desert below. There was nothing unusual about the flight, except perhaps that the plane was nearly full. A lot of the passengers were travelling home to spend Christmas with their families. The hostesses started serving dinner.

It was a smooth and quiet flight. The hostesses had finished collecting the trays, and they were in the galley putting things away when the first buzzers sounded. One of the hostesses went along the aisle to check. When she came back she looked surprised. 'It's amazing,' she said. 'Even on a smooth flight like this two people have been sick.'

Twenty minutes later nearly half the passengers were ill – dramatically ill. Several were moaning and groaning, some were doubled up in pain, and two were unconscious. Fortunately there was a doctor on board, and he was helping the hostesses. He came to the galley and said, 'I'd better speak to the captain. This is a severe case of food poisoning. I think we'd better land as soon as possible.' 'What caused it?' asked one of the hostesses. 'Well,' replied the doctor, 'I had the beef for dinner, and I'm fine. The passengers who chose the fish are ill.' The hostess led him to the flight deck. She tried to open the door. 'I think it's jammed,' she said. The doctor helped her to push it open. The captain was lying behind the door. He was unconscious. The co-pilot was slumped

160

across the controls, and the radio operator was trying to revive him.

The doctor quickly examined the two pilots. 'They just collapsed,' said the radio operator. 'I don't feel too good myself.' 'Can you land the plane?' said the doctor. 'Me? No, I'm not a pilot. We've got to revive them!' he replied. 'The plane's on automatic pilot. We're OK for a couple of hours.' 'I don't know,' said the doctor. 'They could be out for a long time.' 'I'd better contact ground control,' said the radio operator. The doctor turned to the hostess. 'Perhaps you should make an announcement, try to find out if there's a pilot on board.' 'We can't do that!' she said, 'It'll cause a general panic.' 'Well, how the hell are we going to get this thing down?' said the doctor.

Suddenly the hostess remembered something. 'One of the passengers...I overheard him saying that he'd been a pilot in the war. I'll get him.' She found the man and asked him to come to the galley. 'Didn't you say you used to be a pilot?' she asked. 'Yes ... why? The pilot's all right, isn't he?' She led him to the flight deck. They explained the situation to him. 'You mean, you want me to fly the plane?' he said. 'You must be joking. I was a pilot, but I flew single-engined fighter planes, and that was fifteen years ago. This thing's got four engines!'

'Isn't there anybody else?' he asked. 'I'm afraid not,' said the hostess. The man sat down at the controls. His hands were shaking slightly. The radio operator connected him to Air Traffic Control. They told him to keep flying on automatic pilot towards Brisbane, and to wait for further instructions from an experienced pilot. An hour later the lights of Brisbane appeared on the horizon. He could see the lights of the runway shining brightly beyond the city. Air Traffic Control told him to keep circling until the fuel gauge registered almost empty. This gave him a chance to get used to handling the controls. In the cabin the hostesses and the doctor were busy attending to the sick. Several people were unconscious. The plane circled for over half an hour. The passengers had begun to realize that something was wrong. 'What's going on? Why don't we land?' shouted a middle-aged man. 'My wife's ill. We've got to get her to hospital!' A woman began sobbing quietly. At last the plane started its descent. Suddenly there was a bump which shook the plane. 'We're all going to die!' screamed a man. Even the hostesses looked worried as panic began to spread through the plane. 'It's all right!' someone said. 'The pilot's just lowered the wheels, that's all.' As the plane approached the runway they could see fire trucks and ambulances speeding along beside the runway with their lights flashing. There was a tremendous thump as the wheels hit the tarmac, bounced twice, raced along the runway and screeched to a halt. The first airport truck was there in seconds. 'That was nearly a perfect landing. Well done!' shouted the control tower. 'Thanks,' said the man. 'Any chance of a job?'

Key to Exercises:

Task 1: Can I Take a Message?

A. Choose the best answer (a, b or c) to complete each of the following statements.

    1. The conversations take place _____.

    * a. on the phone

      b. at Mr. Turner's office

      c. at Mr. Turner's home

    2. The first speaker is _____.

      a. Mrs Turner

162

b. Mary, the secretary

* c. Jane, the secretary

B. Fill in the following blanks.
1. Message 1:
   Caller's name: (Mary Roberts)
   Caller's number: (772 – 1852)
   Message: (Call back at that number till 12.30 or between 2
             and 5 this afternoon.)
2. Message 2:
   Caller's name: (Mr Brown)
   Caller's number: (743 – 9821)
   Message: (Cancel the lunch appointment for tomorrow noon,
             because he is out of town for a while. Please call
             and reschedule.)
3. Message 3:
   Caller's name: (Mrs Turner)
   Message: (She won't be home until 8 o'clock. She's work-
             ing late.)
4. Message 4:
   Caller's name: (Wendy)
   Message: (Ticket for Puerto Rico is booked. That's Pan Am
             Flight 226, leaving Tuesday the 12th at 8 am.
             Ticket will be sent over later this afternoon.)
5. Message 5:
   Caller's name: (Juan Salvade)
   Message: (He'll call back about the meeting next
             Wednesday.)

163

C. Fill in the following blanks.

1. I'm sorry, he's in a meeting right now. (May I take a message)?

2. I'm going to be (out of town) for a while. Would you (offer my apologies) to Mr Turner and (have him call me), please?

3. Oh, excuse me (just a minute). I have another call. (Can you hold for a second)?

4. Thank you for (holding). Can I help you?

Task 2: Night Flight

A. True or False Questions. Write a T in front of a statement if it is true according to the recording and write an F if it is false.

1. (F) The flight was conducted on Christmas Eve, 1969.

2. (T) The plane would reach its destination Brisbane at one Christmas morning.

3. (T) During the flight nearly half of the passengers got ill because of the fish they had eaten.

4. (F) The two pilots and the radio operator also got poisoned and fainted. That made the case extremely dangerous.

5. (T) Though the hostess did not announce the danger to the passengers, they still came to realize that something was wrong.

6. (F) The plane finally landed in Brisbane with the help of a passenger who was a pilot himself.

B. Choose the best answer (a, b or c) to complete each of the following statements.

1. While the hostesses started preparing the food trays, most of the passengers were _____.

164

a. sleeping

* b. reading

c. talking

2. The plane was usually _____.

* a. not full

b. nearly full

c. full

3. Two passengers got sick when _____.

a. the hostesses were collecting the trays

b. the hostesses were having dinner

* c. the hostesses were in the galley putting things away

4. According to the radio operator , the only way out was

_____.

a. for him to land the plane

* b. to revive the two pilots

c. to wait for help

5. Though the two pilots collapsed , the plane was still flying be-cause _____.

* a. it was on automatic pilot

b. the radio operator could fly the plane

c. a passenger knew how to fly a plane

6. The passenger at first refused to fly the plane because

_____.

a. he was boasting when he said he had been a pilot

b. he was too old to fly a plane

* c. he had never flown four-engined planes

7. The Air Traffic Control told the performing pilot to circle above Brisbane because _____.

a. they hadn't prepared well

165

*　b. they wanted him to use up most of the fuel

　　　c. there was no empty runway

　8. As the plane approached the runway, _____.

　　　a. the airport was on fire

　　　b. ambulances were ready for rescue

　　*　c. fire trucks and ambulances were ready for rescue

C. Fill in the blanks.

　1. Nearly half of the passengers were ill – (dramatically) ill. Several were (moaning and groaning), some were (doubled up) in pain, and two were (unconscious).

　2. The man sat down (at the controls). His hands were (shaking slightly).

　3. An hour later the lights of Brisbane appeared (on the horizon). He could see (the lights of the runway) shining brightly (beyond the city).

　4. There was a tremendous (thump) as the wheels (hit the tarmac), bounced twice, (raced along) the runway and screeched (to a halt).

D. Answer the following questions.

　1. What did one of the hostesses discover when the first buzzers sounded?

　　Answer: She discovered that two passengers had been sick.

　2. Why couldn't the hostess open the door to the flight deck?

　　Answer: Because the captain was lying behind the door unconscious.

　3. Why did the hostess refuse to make an announcement?

　　Answer: Because she was afraid that would cause a general

166

panic.

4. When did the passengers begin to realize that something was wrong?

Answer: When the plane had circled over Brisbane Airport for over half an hour.

Section Three:

Tapescript:

Task 1: Learning to Rephrase

1. Thousands of people die of heart attacks every year; heart disease is becoming so widespread that we can almost talk of an epidemic.

2. That is, people with heart disease often show one or more of these traits.

3. The answer is, a person's personality determines that he or she will be likely to develop this illness.

4. They set themselves unrealistic goals and force themselves to meet impossible deadlines.

5. Eventually their responses to life become less creative, more automatic, and all of their activities are performed under stress.

6. In the past, men have tended to show Type A behaviour more than women have, but with an increasing number of women entering the labour force, this also may change.

7. Stress seems to be caused by our highly technical, highly rushed modern way of life.

8. Now it is not uncommon for a sixty or fifty or even a forty-year-old to suffer a heart attack.

9. Too preoccupied with his own schedule, he has little capacity to concentrate on what other people are saying — unless, of

course, they are talking about work.

10. When he returns to work, he finds that the leisure time of the night before has helped him find a creative solution to his work problems.

Key to Exercises:

Task 1: Learning to Rephrase

Listen to the following sentences. Write the words you think are most important in the space given.

1. (thousands die/year; heart disease - - epidemic)
2. (people with heart disease: 1 or more traits)
3. (personality determines this illness)
4. (set unrealistic goals, meet impossible deadlines)
5. (responses less creative, activities performed under stress)
6. (past: more Type A men; now: more women work, this change)
7. (stress: caused by highly technical, rushed modern life)
8. (60 or 50 or 40, heart attack, common)
9. (too preoccupied with own schedule, can't concentrate, unless about work)
10. (work again, leisure time - - a creative solution to work problems)

Task 2: Dictation

The Boy Who Cried Wolf

Once upon a time there was a very naughty shepherd-boy. He often fell asleep while he was watching his sheep. And he told lies. The villagers shook their heads and said, 'That boy will come to a bad end.'

168

One day, when he was feeling very bored, the boy decided to play a practical joke on the villagers. He ran down the hill. 'Wolf, wolf!' he cried. 'Help, come quickly. Wolf!' All the villagers seized their spears and ran to help him. But there was no wolf. 'He heard you,' the naughty boy lied, 'and ran away.' When everyone had gone, he started to laugh.

Three weeks later, when he was feeling very bored indeed, he decided to play the same trick again. 'Wolf, wolf!' he shouted. 'Help, come quickly. Wolf!' Most of the villagers hurried to help him. This time the boy laughed at them. 'Ha, ha. There wasn't a wolf,' he said. 'What a good joke!' The villagers were very angry. 'Lies are not jokes,' they said.

Two days later the boy woke up suddenly. He had fallen asleep in the afternoon sun. What was that big dark animal coming towards his flock? Suddenly it seized a lamb. 'Wolf!' screamed the boy. 'Wolf. Help, come quickly. Wolf!' But none of the villagers came to help him. He screamed again. The wolf heard him and licked its lips. 'I like lamb,' it thought, 'but shepherd-boy tastes much nicer.'

When the shepherd-boy didn't come home that night, some of the villagers went to look for him. They found a few bones.

Supplementary Reading:

Multiple Birth

In humans most pregnancies result in the birth of one child. Twins, the most common multiple birth, occur in one out of 80 to 100 pregnancies. Triplets occur once in 10, 000 pregnancies and quadruplets about once in 600, 000. Higher multiple births occur with much lower frequencies. An approximation of higher multiple births, known as Hellin's law, is that the frequency of triplets is approximately the square of the twinning rate, that for quadruplets is the cube of the twinning rate, and so on. There have been a few cases of the birth of six or more infants, but in very few of these cases have all of the infants survived.

Types of Multiple Births. There are two types of twins. Some are so similar that they are called identical twins, while others are no more similar than ordinary siblings and are called nonidentical, or fraternal, twins.

Identical twins originate from a single egg fertilized by a single sperm. One-egg, or monozygotic, twins are the result of the division of a single fertilized egg, or zygote, into two independent embryonic structures that are genetically identical, barring somatic mutation. Monozygotic twins and higher multiple births resulting from a single fertilized egg (zygote) are the only source of human beings with identical genotypes, or genetic make-up. In these cases mitosis, or cell division, provides the cells of each twin (or triplet, and so on) with descendants of the same chromosomes originally carried by the single fertilized egg, or zygote. Monozygotic twins (MZ) are always of the same sex.

Nonidentical, or fraternal, twins come from two eggs, each fertilized by a separate sperm. Two-egg, or dizygotic, twins have different genetic make-ups. Dizygotic twins of the same sex occur about as often as do those of unlike sex.

Using a statistical method first proposed by the French physician-statistician Adolphe Bertillon in 1874 and later by the German physician Wilhelm Weinberg in 1901, one can predict how many twins in a population are monozygotic and how many are dizygotic. The calculation is based on the fact that Dizygotic twins (DZ) have

170

an equal probability of being of like sex or of unlike sex. If n is the number of twins of unlike sex (which must be dizygotic) in a randomly selected population (P) of twins, then the same number – n – of like sex twins must be also DZ, and the remainder of twins in the population (P – 2n) are monozygotic. Since the number of monozygotic twins is represented by the difference between all twins and the dizygotic twins, Weinberg's method is known as the differential method.

Monozygotic twins can be of any of four types. In one type, the fertilized egg, or zygote, may divide at the first cleavage, producing two independent embryonic structures. In other cases the separation into two structures may occur at a later stage of division. In some cases the single zygote may develop two inner cell masses, each of which develops into an embryo. Lastly, in some cases the division may be late or incomplete and result in conjoined, or Siamese, twins. The developing zygote is surrounded by membranes, an inner (*amnion*) and an outer (*chorion*). Monozygotic twins may develop in four ways: (1) with separate amnions, chorions, and placentas; (2) with separate amnions and chorions but a fused placenta; (3) with separate amnions but sharing a chorion and placenta; or (4) sharing a single amnion, chorion, and placenta. In dizygotic twins, each twin has completely separate membranes, although when implantation is close together the two placentas may fuse.

Triplets, quadruplets, and other higher multiple births may all arise from different zygotes when three or more eggs are each fertilized by separate sperm, from the same zygote when a single fertilized egg divides, or from a combination of monozygotic and dizygotic multiplication. For example, triplets may arise in three ways: monozygotic triplets are derived from a single fertilized egg and are

171

all identical; dizygotic triplets from two eggs, one of which divides to form two genetically identical embryos; and trizygotic triplets from three eggs.

Factors Affecting Frequency of Multiple Births. Several factors, including race, maternal age, and number of previous births, affect the frequency of multiple births. The frequency of twin births, generally about 1% – 1.5% of all births, shows considerable racial variation. For example, Japan has a low rate of twin births, about 0.7%, while Negroes have the highest rates, about 2.5% for African Negroes generally and as high as 4% for the Yorubas of Nigeria. Since monozygotic and dizygotic twins are biologically different, it is important to distinguish variation in rates between MZ and DZ twins. Twinning rates of monozygotic twins are not appreciably different from race to race. The racial difference in twinning rate is mostly due to differences in rates for dizygotic twins. In general, Negroids have the highest twinning rate, Caucasoids intermediate rates, and Mongoloids the lowest rates.

In the United States, whites have about ten twin births per 1,000 pregnancies, about 30% of them monozygotic. Nonwhites (mostly blacks) have about 13.5 twin births per 1,000 pregnancies.

Maternal age also affects the frequency of dizygotic twinning. The tendency of women to bear dizygotic twins increases from age 15 to 39 and drops after 40. The monozygotic twinning rate is fairly stable throughout the women's childbearing years. At all maternal ages, twinning rates increase steadily with birth order.

An incidence of dizygotic twinning that is higher than would be expected is observed in some families. Evidence suggests that a true increase in the dizygotic twinning rate occurs only in the female relatives of women who have had twins. This supports the hypothesis that the inheritance of a tendency to have dizygotic twins is a sex – linked genetic factor. Studies of interracial crosses show no paternal effect on the frequency of dizygotic twins.

Socioeconomic and nutritional factors may also affect the dizygotic twinning rate. In the United States and many European countries, dizygotic twinning rates have shown an unexplained decline since the 1950's.

Effect of Fertility Drugs. In the 1960's the introduction of pituitary hormones and other hormones for the treatment of some types of sterility led to striking cases of multiple births. Most of the multiple births resulting from treatment with fertility drugs were polyzygous – that is, resulting from the fertilization of more than one egg. Inexperience with the hormonal treatment, particularly with the dose levels needed, produced polyovulation, but by the 1970's increased experience resulted in fewer multiple births as a result of fertility drug use.

Twin Studies. In 1876 the English statistician Francis Galton proposed the twin method as a means of distinguishing between the roles of environment and heredity in the determination of human variation. The concordance-discordance method (concordant when both twins possess or both are free of a trait, discordant when only one of the pair has a trait) compares the degree of similarity of monozygotic twins—that is, twins with identical genetic make-up— to that of like sex, dizygotic twins – twins with different genetic make-ups. It also compares the degree of similarity of monozygotic twins that have been reared together to those that have been reared apart to determine the role of environment when genetic make-up is identical. These studies depend on precise knowledge of whether the twins are monozygotic or dizygotic. Such determinations are made on the basis of placenta examination and the study of the twins' external characteristics, blood types, and other criteria.

Lesson 9

Section One:

Tapescript:

Willing to Train

Catherine has just left school and she wants to find a job. She and her mother have come to speak to the Careers Advisory Officer.

Listen to their conversation.

Officer: Oh, come in, take a seat. I'm the Careers Officer. You're Cathy, aren't you?

Mother: That's right. This is Catherine Hunt, and I'm her mother.

Officer: How do you do, Mrs Hunt. Hello, Catherine.

Cathy: Hello. Pleased to meet you.

Officer: And you'd like some advice about choosing a career?

Mother: Yes, she would. Wouldn't you, Catherine?

Cathy: Yes, Please.

Officer: Well, just let me ask a few questions to begin with. How old are you, Catherine?

Mother: She's nineteen. Well, she's almost nineteen. She'll be nineteen next month.

Officer: And what qualifications have you got?

Mother: Well, qualifications from school of course. Very good results she got. And she's got certificates for ballet and for playing the piano.

175

Officer: Is that what you're interested in, Catherine, dancing and music?

Cathy: Well...

Mother: Ever since she was a little girl she's been very keen on her music and dancing. She ought to be a music teacher or something. She's quite willing to train for a few more years to get the right job, aren't you, Catherine?

Cathy: Well, if it's a good idea.

Mother: There you are, you see. She's good girl really. A bit lazy and disorganized sometimes, but she's very bright. I'm sure the Careers Officer will have lots of jobs for you.

Officer: Well, I'm afraid it's not as easy as that. There are many young people these days who can't find the job they want.

Mother: I told you so, Catherine. I told you you shouldn't wear that dress. You have to look smart to get a job these days.

Officer: I think she looks very nice. Mrs Hunt, will you come into the other office for a moment and look at some of the information we have there. I'm sure you'd like to see how we can help young people.

Mother: Yes, I'd love to. Mind you, I think Catherine would be a very nice teacher. She could work with young children. She'd like that. Or she could be a vet. She's always looking after sick animals.

Officer: I'm afraid there's a lot of competition. You need very good results to be a vet. This way, Mrs Hunt. Just wait a minute, Catherine.

*　　　*　　　*　　　*　　　*

Officer: There are just one or two more things, Catherine.

Cathy: Do call me Cathy.

176

Officer: OK, Cathy. Are you really interested in being a vet?

Cathy: Not really. Anyway, I'm not bright enough. I'm reasonably intelligent, but I'm not brilliant. I'm afraid my mother is a bit over-optimistic.

Officer: Yes, I guessed that. She's a bit overpowering, isn't she, your mum?

Cathy: A bit. But she's very kind.

Officer: I'm sure she is. So, you're interested in ballet and music, are you?

Cathy: Not really. My mother sent me to lessons when I was six, so I'm quite good, I suppose. But I don't want to do that for the rest of my life, especially music. It's so lonely.

Officer: What do you enjoy doing?

Cathy: Well, I like playing tennis, and swimming. Oh, I went to France with the school choir last year. I really enjoyed that. And I like talking to people. But I suppose you mean real interests — things that would help me to get a job?

Officer: No. I'm more interested in what you really want to do. You like talking to people, do you?

Cathy: Oh yes, I really enjoy meeting new people.

Officer: Do you think you would enjoy teaching?

Cathy: No, no, I don't really. I was never very interested in school work, and I'd like to do something different. Anyway, there's a teacher training college very near us. It would be just like going to school again.

Officer: So you don't want to go on training?

Cathy: Oh, I wouldn't mind at all, not for something useful. I wondered about being a hairdresser — you meet lots of people, and you learn to do something properly — but I don't know. It doesn't seem very worthwhile.

Officer: What about nursing?

Cathy: Nursing? In a hospital? Oh, I couldn't do that, I'm not good enough.

Officer: Yes, you are. You've got good qualifications in English and Maths. But it is very hard work.

Cathy: Oh, I don't mind that.

Officer: And it's not very pleasant sometimes.

Cathy: That doesn't worry me either. Mum's right. I do look after sick animals. I looked after our dog when it was run over by a car. My mother was sick, but I didn't mind. I was too worried about the dog. Do you really think I could be a nurse?

Officer: I think you could be a very good nurse. You'd have to leave home, of course.

Cathy: I rather think I should enjoy that.

Officer: Well, don't decide all at once. Here's some information about one or two other things which might suit you. Have a look through it before you make up your mind.

Key to Exercises:

A. True or False Questions. Write a T in front of a statement if it is true according to the recording and write an F if it is false.

1. (T) Catherine comes to the Careers Advisory Officer to see what job suits her most..

2. (T) Catherine's mother is overpowering.

3. (F) Catherine's mother knows her daughter well.

4. (T) The job that Catherine will probably choose is nursing.

B. Fill in the blanks with information about Catherine based on her own statement.

178

Name: Catherine (Hunt)

Age: (almost nineteen)

Qualifications: 1. (qualifications from school, very good
results)

2. (certificates for ballet and for playing the piano)

Interests: 1. (tennis)

2. (swimming)

3. (travelling)

4. (talking to people)

Intelligence: (reasonably intelligent)

C. Give brief answers to the following questions.

1. What does Catherine's mother believe that Cathy is interested in?

Answer: Dancing and music.

2. What does Cathy's mother think about her?

Answer: A good girl. A bit lazy and disorganized sometimes, but very bright.

3. What jobs does Cathy's mother think that she should do?

Answer: Be a teacher or a vet.

4. Why does her mother think so?

Answer: Because she believes that Cathy likes working with
young children and looking after sick animals.

5. Why does the officer ask Mrs Hunt to go to the other office?

Answer: She wants to talk to Cathy, not her mother.

6. Does Cathy want to do the work her mother has suggested?
Why or why not?

Answer: No. She is not bright enough to be a vet and wants

to find something different from school work.

7. Is Cathy willing to train?

Answer: Yes, if it is for something useful.

8. What job does the officer suggest? Why?

Answer: Nursing, because she has good qualifications in English and Maths.

9. How does the officer describe the job of nursing?

Answer: Very hard work, not very pleasant sometimes.

10. How does Cathy think about the officer's suggestion?

Answer: At first she is afraid she is not good enough. Later she thinks she should enjoy that.

D. Complete the following sentences.

1. Ever since she was (a little girl) she's been (very keen on) her music and dancing. She ought to be (a music teacher or something). She's quite willing (to train for) a few more years to get (the right job).

2. My mother sent me (to lessons) when I was (six), so I'm quite good, (I suppose). But I don't want to do that (for the rest of) my life, especially (music). It's so (lonely).

3. I went to (France) with (the school choir) last year. I really enjoyed that. And I like (talking to people). But I suppose you mean (real interests) − − things that would help me to get a job.

4. I wondered about (being a hairdresser) − − you meet lots of (people), and you learn to (do something properly) − − but I don't know. It doesn't seem (very worthwhile).

5. I (do look after) sick animals. I (looked after) our dog when it was (run over by a car). My mother was sick, but I

didn't (mind). I was (too worried) about the dog.

Section Two:

Tapescript:

Task 1: How Do Others Think of My Job?

Speaker 1. When I was at university, I was — I was horrified by what had happened to a lot of my friends by the time they reached the end of the course. Having spent their university careers being all the things one is at university — clever, artistic, very noisy — at the end of their time they all seemed to take entry exams for the ... the Civil Service, and there were some of them who went .. huh ... went as low as to go into the Tax Office huh. How grey, how grey, I thought. But now huh. well, look at me!

Speaker 2. The circular letters I get drive me absolutely mad, from American Express, etc. They're sent to my work address and they're all addressed to *Mr* S Andrews! Obviously they found the name on some published list and assumed that anybody who wasn't a secretary must of course be a man. It's stupid really, because the Company does put Mr or Ms in front of the names on its departmental lists, but perhaps because they naturally assume it's a man, they're just blind to the women's names amongst the heads of departments.

Speaker 3. I work in London at er ... a large hospital as a nursing officer. It's erm ... it's what a lot of people call a male nurse, which I think is the most ridiculous term I've ever come across. It...sort of implies that a nurse ought to be female and that by being male I'm different, but er ... the idea still carries on. The other thing is that people always say 'I suppose

181

you really wanted to be a doctor', just because I'm a man.
They can't imagine that I really wanted to be a nurse and that
er ... erm... it wasn't just that I failed to be a doctor. And
... what they don't realize is the work's completely different,
you know as a ... a male nurse you've much more contact with
the er ... patients and, you know, a long term responsibility
for their ... their welfare huh. There's no way I'd want to be
a doctor. Well, except for the money of course.

Speaker 4. Whenever I say I'm a bank manager, half the time people tend to laugh. I've never understood why. I suppose bank
managers do have a rather stuffy bourgeois image, but I can't
see why it's funny.

Speaker 5. I'm a sales representative, what used to be called a travelling salesman, and for some reason there's lots of dirty jokes
about travelling salesmen. Can't think why. Well, I suppose
it's because they tend to travel a lot, you know, a night here,
a night there. Well, people get the idea they're not particularly
dependable, sort of fly by nights I suppose, you know, wife in
every port. But it aint true, I promise you.

Speaker 6. I'm an apprentice hairdresser. I enjoy the work very
much. I'm learning a lot, not just about hair, but how to get
along with people. I'm gaining confidence 'cos I never had that
at school. I left as soon as I could. I hated it. I remember
teachers used to look down on jobs like hairdressing. They were
ever so stuck up. They thought that only girls who were a bit
dim went in for hairdressing, but I'm not dim at all. If I work
hard in the salon and get all my certificates, if I save hard, in a
few years I could start my own business, and I'd be earning
five times as much as those old bags at school!

Task 2: Job Stereotypes

Interviewer: Well, we heard some people just now who seem to feel that other people have a wrong idea about the work they do. Do you think this sort of thing is very widespread?

Sociologist: Oh absolutely. Most jobs or professions seem to have an image or a stereotype attached to them, often much to the irritation of the job-holders. But there is a serious point to all this, too, that maybe young people actually choose their careers under the influence of these false images. And certainly, there is evidence that they may even avoid certain careers because they have a negative image. Well, on a large scale, as you can imagine, this could cause problems for whole sectors of the economy.

Interviewer: Er, you say there's evidence?

Sociologist: Oh most definitely. There was a survey recently into children's attitudes to different professions.

Interviewer: How was that done, though? Because, after all, children don't know much about the world of work before they get into it.

Sociologist: Well, exactly. What the investigators wanted to get at was their impressions and their prejudices. They used a very simple technique. They gave the children twelve pairs of statements. In each pair one statement was positive, the other was its opposite.

Interviewer: For example?

Sociologist: Well, for example, 'Such and such a person is likely to be boring or interesting company.'

Interviewer: I see. What professions did they ask about?

Sociologist: (laugh) Do you want the whole list?

Interviewer: Well, why not?

Sociologist: OK. Here goes. They looked at: physicists, lawyers, economists, accountants, sales representatives, estate agents, biologists, and three types of engineer — mechanical engineers, electrical and civil. The children were asked to say which of the statements was 'most true' about each profession.

Interviewer: And the results?

Sociologist: Well, they were rather striking concerning one profession in particular, the poor old engineer. Of all the jobs mentioned, he came out really much worse than you might expect. The vast majority of children (90% in the case of the mechanical engineer), thought that engineering was a 'dirty job'. They also thought the job was of 'low status' and 'subordinate'; that is, the engineer is more likely to take orders than to give them. Oh, and insecure too. The only other person they thought more likely to actually lose his job was the sales representative. But, I must say there were good points too. Engineering was seen to be 'interesting, well paid' work.

Interviewer: Hmm, not such a rosy picture, really.

Sociologist: No... but it got better when the children were asked about how they imagined the engineer as a person. The majority of the children chose positive comments, except that they thought the engineer was likely to be badly rather than well dressed. (laugh)

Interviewer: Well, what about the other professions, then? Erm... what came out favourite, for example?

Sociologist: Oh the lawyer without a doubt. He collected by far the greatest number of positive opinions. The sales representative and then the estate agent were right at the bottom.

184

Interviewer: Oh, so the engineers weren't right down there?

Sociologist: Oh no! The children's ratings put them just above the poor old sales representative all bunched together. Probably the children don't have that much of an idea of their real work. I think they ... (laughs) ... they went by the titles, really, since civil engineer came out top, perhaps the suggestion of the name?

Interviewer: Oh, I see. You mean that he was a. . .a more civilized sort of chap than the others?

Sociologist: (laughs) Yes, right. Reasonable sounding, isn't it?

Interviewer: Yes. Quite sensible, I suppose. And I imagine the mechanical engineer came out bottom?

Sociologist: Absolutely right. In fact 90% of the children associated him with dirty work, as against 76% for the electrical engineer and 68% for the civil engineer.

Interviewer: And the other professions?

Sociologist: Well, after the lawyer came the accountant; then the scientists, the physicist first. The economist came just above the engineers. Funnily enough, he was the only one that the majority of children felt would be gloomy rather than cheerful.

Interviewer: A real sign of the times, that.

Sociologist: Yes. But I still think the most serious implication of the results of the survey was the children's apparent ignorance of the importance of the engineer's role in society.

Interviewer: Hmm.

Sociologist: After all, in most other European countries to be an engineer is to be somebody. And I imagine that this means that many bright children, who might really enjoy the profession and do well in it, probably never consider it, which is a great pity for the country as a whole. We do need good engineers after all.

Key to Exercises:

Task 1: How Do Others Think of My Job?

A. Fill in the following chart.

	Sex	Job	Stertotype of the Job
Speaker 1	male	work in Civil Service or Tax Office	grey
Speaker 2	female	manager of a department	It's a man's job.
Speaker 3	male	nursing officer in a hospital	He should be a doctor, for nursing is a woman's job.
Speaker 4	male	bank manager	stuffy, bourgeois, funny
Speaker 5	male	sales representative	not dependable, wife in every port
Speaker 6	female	apprentice hairdresser	for dim girls

B. Give brief answers to the following questions.

1. What does Speaker 1 think of university students?

   Answer: Clever, artistic, very noisy.

2. How are letters to Speaker 2 addressed?

   Answer: To Mr S. Andrews.

3. Why does she think it's stupid?

   Answer: The Company does put Mr or Ms in front of the names on its departmental list.

4. What job does Speaker 3 want to do? Why?

    Answer: Nursing. Being a male nurse, he has more contact with the patients and a long term responsibility for their welfare.

5. Why are there dirty jokes about travelling salesmen?

    Answer: They travel and have wife at every port.

6. Are the jokes true according to Speaker 5?

    Answer: No.

7. Why does Speaker 6 enjoy her work?

    Answer: She is learning a lot about hair and how to get along with people and is gaining confidence.

8. What will happen if she works hard and saves hard?

    Answer: She will be able to start her own business and earn five times as much as the teachers.

Task 2: Job Stereotypes

A. True or False Questions. Write a T in front of a statement if it is true according to the recording and write an F if it is false.

1. (T) One of the speakers is a sociologist.

2. (F) People have wrong images or stereotypes about all professions or jobs.

3. (T) Job stereotypes may produce a serious problem. People can be doing a job that has a positive image but does not suit them at all.

4. (F) The survey was about what kind of jobs children want to do.

5. (T) The children were given twelve pairs of statements, one is positive, the other is its opposite.

6. (F) The professions they looked at were physicists, lawyers,

accountants, sales representatives, travel agents and three types of engineer.

B. Choose the best answer (a, b or c) to complete each of the following statements.

1. The result of the survey is most striking concerning one pro - fession, _____.

   * a. the engineer
   b. the civil engineer
   c. the estate agent

2. According to the result , the person most likely to lose his job was the _____.

   a. estate agent
   * b. sales representative
   c. engineer

3. The children thought the engineer was likely to be _____.

   * a. badly dressed
   b. well dressed
   c. a bad person

4. The profession that had the greatest number of positive opin - ions was the _____.

   * a. lawyer
   b. physicist
   c. economist

5. About _____ of the children associated electrical engineer with dirty work.

   a. 90 %
   * b. 76 %

c. 68%

6. The majority of the children thought the economist was
   _____.

    a. funny

    b. cheerful

* c. gloomy

7. The most serious implication of the results of the survey was
   that _____.

    a. children often have prejudices against certain professions

* b. children are ignorant of the importance of the engineer's
   role in society

    c. children may never consider certain professions that they
   can do well in

8. In _____ to be an engineer is to be somebody.

    a. all European countries

* b. most European countries

    c. some European countries

C. Re-list the professions in the survey, beginning with the one that
the children took as the most favourite.

Answer: (1) (lawyer)   (2) (accountant)

       (3) (physicist)   (4) (biologist)

       (5) (economist)   (6) (civil engineer)

       (7) (electrical engineer) (8) (mechanical engineer)

       (9) (sales representative) (10) (estate agent)

D. Fill in the blanks.

1. The vast majority of children thought that engineering was a
   ("dirty job"). They also thought the job was of ("low

status") and ("subordinate"); that is, the engineer is more likely to (take orders) than to (give orders).

2. There were good points, too. Engineering was seen to be ("interesting, well paid") work.

Section Three:

Tapescript:

Task 1: Learning to Rephrase

1. Bartering is the process by which trade takes place through the exchange of goods.

2. Whereas in the past, seashells and spices had no specific value, this new money idea had a stated value.

3. However, due to recent economic developments, the world is once again conducting trade by bartering goods for goods.

4. We refer to the more valuable currency as hard currency while we term the less valuable money, soft currency.

5. In fact, hard currency is usually demanded by the seller, particularly if the seller is from a nation having hard currency.

6. Inflation refers to an abnormally rapid increase in prices.

7. As a result of the scarcity of hard currency in some nations and the recent high world-wide inflation, it's obvious that the conventional method of payment in hard currency must be supplemented by other types of payment such as bartering.

8. Not only is the following illustration a good example of bartering, it also reveals, to a small degree, consumer preferences in beverages in the USSR and the United States.

9. It seems that Pepsi-Cola was the first company to introduce cola into the USSR, much to the disappointment of Coca-Cola.

10. Of course, bartering presents some great problems that are not

190

always easy to overcome.

Key to Exercises:

Task 1: Learning to Rephrase

Listen to the following sentences. Write the words you think are most important in the space given.

1. (barter = trading goods for goods)
2. (past: seashells spices − − no value
         money − − stated value)
3. (because economic developments, trade done in barter)
4. (more valuable currency − − hard c.
   less valuable − − soft c.)
5. (seller demand hard c., esp, from nation with hard c.)
6. (inflation = abnormally rapid price increase)
7. (due to scarcity of hard c. in some nations & world-wide inflation, payments in hard c. be supplemented by other types, e.
   g. bartering)
8. (the following: example of bartering, consumer preferences in
   beverages in USSR & USA)
9. (Pepsi − Cola: 1st introduction of cola to USSR, Coca − Cola
   unhappy)
10. (Bartering presents serious difficult problems)

Task 2: Dictation

How to Make Wine

This is how wine is made in our winery. After the grapes are picked in late summer, they are pressed so that all the juice runs out. Then the juice is separated from the skins and pips and it is put into large containers and left to ferment. Later, it is put into smaller

191

containers. Then it is left for about a year when it is put into bottles. If it is a good wine, the bottles are kept for several years but the cheaper wines are sold immediately.

Alan Simpson

The mystery of the man found wandering in the city centre has now been solved. The man, whose name is now known to be Alan Simpson, is a medical student. Mr Simpson was taking part in an experiment conducted by the university department of psychology, when he walked away, unnoticed by the staff supervising the experiment. He has now regained his memory, and has left hospital. Several people, including his sister, April Simpson, telephoned the police to identify Mr Simpson after seeing his picture in the press.

Supplementary Reading:
Barter

Barter is the exchange of goods or services without the use of money. The earliest trade, before the invention of money, took the form of barter. Among nonliterate peoples in many parts of the world, barter is still widely practised; however, the use of money in the form of national currencies has everywhere tended to replace ancient barter customs.

Early Trading. Barter was the earliest basis for the development of markets, where the concept of "fair value" or "equivalent value" emerged even without a standardized medium of exchange. Such concepts as "value" and "price" generally developed in the process of bargaining or haggling, away of arriving at a fair price by consensus. A man wishing to acquire potatoes must find someone who has potatoes to dispose of and wishes to acquire something the would-be buyer has available. Then the two men must bargain to decide how many potatoes will be exchanged for the other commodity.

Anthropologists have found more examples of barter between tribes and communities than within such groups. This is most likely explained by the fact that internal exchanges often represent social and ceremonial gift-giving, whereas intergroup barter is a means of meeting economic needs. Tribal peoples, like nation-states, are seldom economically self-sufficient and must find ways of complementing what they themselves are able to produce.

Silent Trade. The most striking type of barter is the so-called "silent trade," in which no direct contact occurs between the parties to the exchange. One group leaves trade items at a designated place. Members of the second group come later and if they find the items desirable, leave goods of their own in place of those they take. Such barter has occurred between groups that have hostile relations or no relations at all with each other, and between people of mutually unintelligible languages.

Examples of silent trade were reported by ancient and medieval historians such as Herodotus and Ibn Battuta. Modern anthropologists have observed silent trade among tribes of California Indians, Pygmies and Bantus in the Congo, natives of New Guinea, and others. These examples show how the need to trade overrides what might appear to be insurmountable difficulties.

Trading Chains. Intertribal trade frequently involves the development of trade partnerships, some of which form chains passing through many groups and across hundreds of miles. Examples of this sort of barter have been found among Australian tribes in modern times: stone axes from southern sources are known to have been distributed in this manner to northern tribes. Such trading chains probably also explain why such items as barracuda jaws from the Gulf of Mexico and mica from the Rocky Mountains are found among the archaeological remains of the prehistoric Hopewell peoples of Ohio.

Even in industrialized societies, some bartering still goes on. In the United States, for example, "swapping" through the medium of newspaper columns is barter in pure form.

Lesson 10

Section One:

Tapescript:

Task 1: News Summary 1

Here's the news at 11:30.

Thousands of people have marched through the centre of Corby in Northamptonshire to protest against plans to close the steel works, the town's major employer. The marchers demonstrated outside the local British Steel Corporation's headquarters where union leaders are talking about closure plans with the management.

Hospital waiting lists in the south west of England have gone up by a quarter in the last five years. While the number of doctors, nurses and other staff have increased, the demand on the service has grown even faster.

The EEC is to give another £13 million to Britain's poorer areas. The aid from the regional development fund includes £13.5 million for Northern Ireland and £10 million for industrial improvement and road works in the north of England.

In a report on rabies controls, Kent County Council has said that 17 dogs, 5 cats, 2 rabbits and 2 hamsters have been landed illegally at Channel ports in the first nine months of this year. This was seven more than in the same period last year.

A derailed coal train at Thirsk in North Yorkshire has disrupted rail services between Newcastle and the south of England.

Task 2: News Summary 2

It's time for the news at 3.30 here on Radio I.

A girl aged 16 armed with a shotgun held up a class of children at a secondary school in Surrey this morning. Police said that soon after school began at Blair Hill Secondary School, Newton, the girl, armed with a double-barrelled shotgun belonging to her brother, went into one of the classrooms and threatened a teacher and about thirty pupils. A shot was fired into the ceiling as she was being overpowered by police officers.

Surgeons at Cambridge have successfully transplanted a pancreas — the organ that produces insulin — in two patients suffering from diabetes. One patient, a 23-year-old electronics worker also had a liver transplant. The other patient, a 55-year-old housewife, had a kidney transplanted at the same time. Both patients are doing well.

A stately home owner who allowed a pop concert to be staged in his grounds was fined yesterday for letting a rock band play overtime. The Honourable Frederick Sidgwick-Johnson admitted allowing the rock group Led Zepplin to play on after midnight during a concert at his home near Stevenage two months ago. Stevenage magistrates fined him £125 with £25 costs.

Three people have so far been killed in the storms sweeping across the north of England and southern Scotland. A woman was killed in Carlisle when a chimney on a house collapsed and two men were killed when their car crashed into a fallen tree on a country road near Melrose. More high winds and rain are forecast for tonight.

Key to Exercises:

Task 1: News Summary 1

A. True or False Questions. Write a T in front of a statement if it is true according to the recording and write an F if it is false.

1. (F) The purpose of demonstration was to protest against the town's major employer.

2. (F) The demand on hospital service has increased by a quarter in the last year in the south of England.

3. (T) The aid from EEC is to help develop Britain's poorer area.

4. (F) Kent County Council has been doing very well in rabies controls.

5. (T) The last news item is about the damage a derailed coal train has done.

B. Fill in the blanks.

1. The marchers demonstrated outside (the local British Steel Corporation's headquarters) where union leaders are talking about (closure plans) with the management.

2. While the number of (doctors, nurses and other staff) have increased, the demand on the service has (grown even faster).

3. The EEC is to give (another 31 million pounds) to Britain's (poorer areas). The aid from the (regional development fund) includes (13.5 million pounds) for Northern Ireland and (10 million pounds) for (industrial improvement) and (road works) in the north of England.

4. Kent County Council has said that (17) dogs, (5) cats, (2) rabbits and (2) hamsters have been (landed illegally) at

Channel port in (the first nine months) this year. This was (seven more) than in the same period last year.

5. A (derailed coal train) at Thirsk in North Yorkshire has (disrupted rail services) between Newcastle and (the south of England).

Task 2: News Summary 2

A. Choose the best answer (a, b or c) for each of the following statements.

1. _____ armed with a shotgun held up _____ at a secondary school this morning.
   a. Sixteen girls; a class of children
   * b. A girl of 16; a class of children
   c. A girl of 16; sixteen children

2. Surgeons at Cambridge have successfully completed transplantations in _____ patients who suffer from _____.
   a. two; liver cancer
   b. three; diabetes
   * c. two; diabetes

3. The stately home owner was fined because _____.
   * a. he let a rock band play overtime in his grounds.
   b. he let a rock band play in his grounds.
   c. he played rock music overtime.

4. Three people have been killed in the storms in _____.
   a. the north of England.
   b. southern Scotland.
   * c. the north of England and southern Scotland.

B. Answer the following questions briefly.

198

1. What kind of shotgun was used in news item one?

   Answer: A double-barrelled.

2. To whom did the shotgun belong?

   Answer: The girl's brother.

3. When was a shot fired?

   Answer: When the girl was being overpowered by police officers.

4. To which direction was the shot fired?

   Answer: Into the ceiling.

5. Who were the two patients mentioned in news item two?

   Answer: A 23-year-old electronics worker and a 55-year-old housewife.

6. How are the patients now?

   Answer: They are doing well.

7. When was the concert held?

   Answer: Two months ago.

8. How much was the home owner fined?

   Answer: 125 pounds with 25 pounds costs.

9. How were the three people in news item four killed in the storms?

   Answer: A woman was killed when a chimney on a house collapsed and two men were killed when their car crashed into a fallen tree.

10. What are forecast for tonight?

    Answer: More high winds and rain.

Section Two:

Tapescript:

Task 1: British Newspapers

Professor Richard Hill is talking about British newspapers.

It seems to me that many British newspapers aren't really newspapers at all. They contain news, it is true, but much of this news only appears in print because it is guaranteed to shock, surprise or cause a chuckle.

What should we expect to find in a real newspaper? Interesting political articles? Accurate reports of what has been happening in distant corners of the world? The latest news from the stock exchange? Full coverage of great sporting events? In-depth interviews with leading personalities?

It is a sad fact that in Britain the real newspapers, the ones that report the facts, sell in thousands, while the popular papers that set out to shock or amuse have a circulation of several million. One's inescapable conclusion is that the vast majority of British readers do not really want a proper newspaper at all. They just want a few pages of entertainment.

I buy the same newspaper every day. In this paper political matters, both British and foreign, are covered in full. The editorial column may support government policy on one issue and oppose it on another. There is a full page of book reviews and another devoted to the latest happenings in the theatre, the cinema and the world of art. Stock exchange prices are quoted daily. So are the exchange rates of the world's major currencies. The sports correspondents are among the best in the country, while the standard of the readers' letters is absolutely first class. If an intelligent person were to find a copy of this paper 50 years from now, he or she would still find it entertaining, interesting and instructive.

So my favourite newspaper is obviously very different from those popular papers that have a circulation of several million. But that does not mean that it is 'better' or that they are 'worse'. We are not comparing like with like. A publisher printing a newspaper with a circulation of several million is running a highly successful commercial operation. The people who buy his product are obviously satisfied customers and in a free society everybody should have the right to buy whatever kind of newspaper he pleases.

Task 2: Eccentricity

Dave: Dr Jones, how exactly would you define eccentricity?

Dr Jones: Well, we all have our own particular habits which others find irritating or amusing, but an eccentric is someone who behaves in a totally different manner from those in the society in which he lives.

Dave: When you talk about eccentricity, are you referring mainly to matters of appearance?

Dr Jones: Not specifically, no. There are many other ways in which eccentricity is displayed. For instance, some individuals like to leave their mark on this earth with bizarre buildings. Others have the craziest desires which influence their whole way of life.

Dave: Can you give me an example?

Dr Jones: Certainly. One that immediately springs to mind was a Victorian surgeon by the name of Buckland. Being a great animal lover he used to share his house openly with the strangest creatures, including snakes, bears, rats, monkeys and eagles.

Dave: That must've been quite dangerous at times.

Dr Jones: It was, particularly for visitors who weren't used to having 'pets' – for want of a better word – in the house. They used to get bitten and even attacked. And the good doctor was so interested in animals that he couldn't resist the temptation to

201

sample them as food. So guests who came to dinner had to be prepared for a most unusual menu, mice on toast, roast giraffe. Once he even tried to make soup from elephant's trunk. Strangely, though, his visitors seemed to go back for more.

Dave: They must've had very strong stomachs, that's all I can say. Dr Jones, what particular kind of eccentric are you most interested in from a psychologist's point of view?

Dr Jones: I think they're all fascinating, of course, but on the whole I'd say it's the hermit that I find the most intriguing, the type who cuts himself off from the world.

Dave: Does one of these stand out in your mind at all?

Dr Jones: Yes, I suppose this century has produced one of the most famous ones: the American billionaire, Howard Hughes.

Dave: But he wasn't a recluse all his life, was he?

Dr Jones: That's correct. In fact, he was just the opposite in his younger days. He was a rich young man who loved the Hollywood society of his day. But he began to disappear for long periods when he grew tired of high living. Finally, nobody was allowed to touch his food and he would wrap his hand in a tissue before picking anything up. He didn't even allow a barber to go near him too often and his hair and beard grew down to his waist.

Dave: Did he live completely alone?

Dr Jones: No, that was the strangest thing. He always stayed in luxury hotels with a group of servants to take care of him. He used to spend his days locked up in a penthouse suite watching adventure films over and over again and often eating nothing but ice cream and chocolate bars.

Dave: It sounds a very sad story.

Dr Jones: It does. But, as you said earlier, life wouldn't be the same without characters like him, would it?

Key to Exercises:

Task 1: British Newspapers

A. True or False Questions. Write a T in front of a statement if it is true according to the recording and write an F if it is false.

1. (F) Professor Hill does not think that many British newspapers are real newspapers because they don't contain news at all.

2. (T) The real newspapers are more serious than the popular papers but the latter have a larger circulation.

3. (T) Professor Hill thinks highly of the newspapers he buys every day.

4. (F) Professor Hill thinks that his favourite newspaper is much better than the popular papers and that others should read this paper, too.

B. Choose the best answer(a, b or c) to complete each of the following statements.

1. In Britain the popular papers are to do the following except _____ people.

   a. to shock

* b. to instruct

   c. to amuse

2. Facts show that the vast majority of British readers want _____.

* a. no proper papers at all

   b. a proper paper

c. more than a few papers of entertainment

3. If an intelligent person finds a copy of Professor Hill's favourite paper 50 years from now, he will still find it

_____.

　　a. entertaining and amusing

＊ b. interesting and instructive

　　c. shocking and surprising

C. Fill in the blanks with information about Professor Hill's favourite paper.

News: (1) Political matters are (covered in full).

　　　　(2) The editorial column may (support government policy) on one issue and (oppose it) on another.

Book Reviews: (a whole page for it)

Art: (a whole page for the latest happenings in the theatre, the cinema and the world of art)

Economics: (1) (Stock Exchange prices are quoted daily.)

　　　　　　(2) (Exchange rates of the world's major currencies are reported daily.)

Sports: (The correspondents are among the best.)

Readers' Letters: (The standard is first-class.)

Task 2: Eccentricity

A. Answer the following questions.

1. What is an eccentric, according to Dr Jones?

　Answer: A person who behaves in a totally different manner from those in the society he lives in.

2. Does eccentricity mainly refer to matters of appearance?

　Answer: Not specifically.

204

3. Why is the Victorian surgeon an eccentric?

   Answer: He used to share his house openly with the strangest
   animals and sample them as food.

4. What particular kind of eccentric is Dr Jones most interested
   in?

   Answer: The hermit.

B. True or False Questions. Write a T in front of a statement if it is
true according to the recording and write an F if it is false.

   1. (F) Only an eccentric has particular habits which others find
      irritating or amusing.

   2. (F) The Victorian surgeon lived at Buckland.

   3. (T) Visitors to the Victorian surgeon's house used to get bit-
      ten or even attacked by the animals that he kept there.
      However, the guests still liked to go back.

   4. (T) A hermit is a person who cuts himself off from the
      world.

   5. (T) Howard Hughes was not a hermit all his life.

   6. (T) Howard Hughes became a recluse because he was tired of
      high living.

   7. (F) Ever since Howard Hughs became a recluse, he cut him-
      self off completely from the world.

   8. (F) Howard Hughs used to spend his days watching adven-
      ture films without eating anything.

C. Fill in the blanks.

   1. Nobody was allowed to (touch his food) and he would
      (wrap) his hand (in a tissue) before (picking) anything
      (up). He didn't even allow (a barber) to go near him (too

205

often) and his hair and beard (grew down to his waist).

Section Three:
Tapescript:
Task 1: Learning to Rephrase
1. In the United States we are using more and more oil every day, and the future supply is very limited.
2. It is estimated that at the current rate of use, oil may not be a major source of energy after only 25 more years.
3. We have a lot of coal under the ground, but there are many problems with mining it, transporting it, and developing a way to burn it without polluting the air.
4. Production of new nuclear power plants has slowed down because of public concern over the safety of nuclear energy.
5. The government once thought that we would be getting 20 percent of our electricity from nuclear energy by the 1970's, but nuclear energy still produced only about 12 percent of our power as of 1979.
6. There is no need to purchase fuel to operate a solar heating system because sunshine is free to everyone.
7. Because solar systems depend on sunshine, they can't always provide 100% of your heat.
8. Solar heating can be used in most areas of the United States, but it is most practical in areas where there is a lot of winter sunshine, where heat is necessary, and where fuel is expensive.
9. A hot-liquid system operates in basically the same way except the hot-liquid system contains water instead of air; and the storage unit is a large hot water tank instead of a container of hot rocks.

10. Then energy from the sun may provide the answer to our need for a new, cheap, clean source of energy.

Key to Exercises:

Task 1: Learning to Rephrase

Listen to the following sentences. Write the words you think are most important in the space given below.

1. (US: use more oil/day, future supply − limited)
2. (current rate of use, oil not a major source of energy in 25 years)
3. (a lot of coal, but problem: mining, transporting & burning with pollution)
4. (production of new nuclear power plants, slow down, public concern over safty)
5. (government expected 20% electricity from nuclear energy 1970s, but only 12% 1979)
6. (no fuel for solar heating system, sunshine free)
7. (solar system can't provide 100% heat due to sunshine)
8. (solar heating possible in most US, better in areas: lot of winter sunshine, heat necessary, fuel expensive)
9. (hot-liquid system: basically same but contains water not air, a large hot water tank, not a container of hot rocks)
10. (energy from sun: answer to our need for new, cheap, clean source of energy)

Task 2: Dictation

Voice Analysis

If we want to measure voice features very accurately, we can use a voice analyser. A voice analyser can show four characteristics of a speaker's voice. No two speakers' voices are alike. To get a voice sample, you have to speak into the voice analyser. The voice analyser is connected to a computer. From just a few sentences of normal speech, the computer can show four types of information about your voice. It will show nasalization, loudness, frequency and length of articulation. The first element, nasalization, refers to how much air normally goes through your nose when you talk. The second feature of voice difference is loudness. Loudness is measured in decibels. The number of decibels in speaking is determined by the force of air that comes from the lungs. The third feature of voice variation is frequency. By frequency we mean the highness or lowness of sounds. The frequency of sound waves is measured in cycles per second. Each sound of a language will produce a different frequency. The final point of voice analysis concerns the length of articulation for each sound. This time length is measured in small fractions of a second. From all four of these voice features — length of articulation, frequency, loudness and nasalization — the voice analyser can give an exact picture of a person's voice.

Lesson 11

Tapescript:

Task 1: A Way of Life

Doctor: Well Mr Thomson. The first and important thing I have to tell you is that ... mm ... there is really nothing seriously wrong with you ... physically that is. My ... er ... my very thorough re-examination and the ... the analyst's report show that basically you are very fit. Yes ... very fit ...

Mr Thomson: So ... Why is it doctor that I'm always so nervy ... tense ... ready to jump on anybody—my wife, children, colleagues?

Doctor: I think ... erm ... I think your condition has a lot to do with er—What shall we call it? —Way of life? Habits?

Mr Thomson: Way of life? Habits?

Doctor: Yes ... now tell me Mr Thomson ... You smoke, don't you?

Mr Thomson: Yes ... I'm afraid ... I'm afraid I do doctor.

Doctor: And ... er ... rather heavily I imagine.

Mr Thomson: Well ... yes. I smoke—what ... about forty ... fifty a day I suppose.

Doctor: You should do your best to stop you know.

Mr Thomson: Yes ... I see ... But er ... Well ... it won't be the first time. I've tried to give up smoking several times but it's ... it's no good.

209

Doctor: You see...fifty a day is overdoing it ... you must admit. You must cut it down ... at least that. Oh yes. I know that when you're feeling tense you ... you probably feel that a cigarette relaxes you. But in the long run ... I do advise you to make ... to make a real effort.

Mr Thomson: Of course. But ... well ... it's easy to say give it up or cut it down ... but ... oh you know ...

Doctor: Well in my opinion you have no choice. Either you make a real effort or... or there's no real chance of your feeling better. You see ... well obviously I could prescribe some kind of tranquillizer ... but would that help? I'd prefer – and I'm quite sure you'll agree—I'd prefer to see you really back to normal ... not just seemingly so. And that's my reason for asking you several more questions about ... about your other habits.

Mr Thomson: Right.

Doctor: Your eating habits for example. What do you eat normally ... during a normal day?

Mr Thomson: Yes ... well ... I'm a good eater. Yes I'd say I'm a good eater. Now let's see ... Up at eight in the morning and my wife has a good breakfast ready.

Doctor: A good breakfast?

Mr Thomson: The usual. A cereal followed by bacon and eggs with fried bread and perhaps a tomato or two. Then toast and marmalade ... all washed down with a couple of cups of tea. I er ... yes ... I really enjoy my breakfast.

Doctor: Er ... yes ... I can see you do. But I'd advise you to eat rather less. We'll come to that later. Go on.

Mr Thomson: Then lunch ... no, first brunch. A cup of coffee and a bun at eleven. Lunch has to be quick because there's so much to do in the office about that time. So I have a pint and a sandwich in the pub. All very hurried.

Doctor: Try to be in less of a hurry.

Mr Thomson: But I make up for it in the evening. I get home at about seven. Dinner's round about eight. Er ... yes ... My wife's an excellent cook ... excellent. It's usually some meat dish...and we like spaghetti as a first course. Spaghetti, a meat dish, cheese, a sweet. But er ... but then ... at the end of the day shall we say ... then ... well then I begin to feel on edge again. Most evenings after dinner we read or watch TV ... but I ... I get this terrible feeling of tension.

Doctor: Well ... I'm sorry to have to say this because you obviously enjoy your food ... but ... er ... I really do recommend that you ... that you eat less and—secondly—that you eat *more healthily*. Instead of having that enormous breakfast for example ... er ... well ... try to be content with a fruit juice and some cereal.

Mr Thomson: I see ... but er ...

Doctor: Elevenses ... right ... well that's all right. But lunch should be more leisurely. Remember your health is at stake not your job. As for dinner ... er ... I'd advise you to eat a soup perhaps ... with a salad ... a salad followed by some fruit.

Mr Thomson: But my wife's cooking ...

Doctor: ... is superb. Granted. And she probably enjoys preparing delicious meals for you. If you like ... well ... er ... I'll have a word with your wife...

Mr Thomson: No ... that won't be necessary ... erm ... thanks just the same doctor. But no ...

211

Doctor: And on that subject Mr Thomson ... erm ... er ... Just one other thing... er ... I'm sure this won't embarrass you. You say you feel tense in the evenings after dinner. Might I ask, please forgive this question, but it's necessary, might I ask about your relationship—your sexual relationship that is—with your wife?

Mr Thomson: Well ... erm ... er ... you see ... er ...

Task 2: Do It Yourself

Do It Yourself magazine organizes a competition every summer to find the 'Handyman of the Year'. The winner this year is Mr Roy Miller, a Sheffield postman. A journalist and a photographer have come to his house. The journalist is interviewing Mr Miller for an article in the magazine.

Journalist: Well, I'm very impressed by all the work you've done on your house, Mr Miller. How long have you been working on it?

Mr Miller: I first became interested in do-it-yourself several years ago. You see, my son Paul is disabled. He's in a wheel-chair and I just had to make alterations to the house. I couldn't afford to pay workmen to do it. I had to learn to do it myself.

Journalist: Have you had any experience of this kind of work? Did you have any practical skills?

Mr Miller: No. I got a few books from the library but they didn't help very much. Then I decided to go to evening classes so that I could learn basic carpentry and electrics.

Journalist: What sort of changes did you make to the house?

Mr Miller: First of all, practical things to help Paul. You never really realize the problems handicapped people have until it affects your own family. Most government buildings, for example, have steps up to the door. They don't plan buildings so that disabled people can get in and out. We used to live in a flat, and of course, it was totally unsuitable. Just imagine the problems a disabled person would have in your house. We needed a large house with wide corridors so that Paul could get from one room to another. We didn't have much money and we had to buy this one. It's over ninety years old and it was in a very bad state of repair.

Journalist: Where did you begin?

Mr Miller: The electrics. I completely rewired the house so that Paul could reach all the switches. I had to lower the light switches and raise the power – points. I went on to do the whole house so that Paul could reach things and go where he wanted.

Journalist: What else did you do?

Mr Miller: By the time I'd altered everything for Paul, do-it-yourself had become a hobby. I really enjoyed doing things with my hands. Look, I even installed smoke-alarms.

Journalist: What was the purpose of that?

Mr Miller: I was very worried about fire. You see, Paul can't move very quickly. I fitted them so that we would have plenty of warning if there were a fire. I put in a complete burglar-alarm system. It took weeks. The front door opens auto-matically, and I'm going to put a device on Paul's wheelchair so that he'll be able to open and close it when he wants.

Journalist: What are you working on now?

Mr Miller: I've just finished the kitchen. I've designed it so that he can reach everything. Now I'm building an extension so that Paul will have a large room on the ground floor where he

213

can work.

Journalist: There's a £10,000 prize. How are you going to spend it?

Mr Miller: I am hoping to start my own business so that I can convert ordinary houses for disabled people. I think I've become an expert on the subject.

Key to Exercises:

Task 1: A Way of Life

A. Choose the best answer (a, b or c) to complete each of the following statements.

1. This conversation takes place _____.
   * a. at a doctor's surgery
   b. at an Indian restaurant
   c. between a chef and Mr Thomson

2. The doctor suggests that Mr Thomson should _____.
   a. stop smoking and eat more
   * b. stop smoking and eat less
   c. stop smoking and have good meals every day instead

3. Mr Thomson has come to see the doctor because he always feels _____.
   a. hungry
   * b. nervous
   c. unhappy with his work at office

4. It seems, according to the doctor's questions, Mr Thomson's condition has a lot to do with _____.
   a. Mr Thomson's way of life
   b. Mr Thomson's diet and everyday habits
   * c. both a and b

214

5. Actually, Mr Thomson's tension is caused by _____.
   a. his daily habits
 * b. his relationship with his wife
   c. his work

B. Complete the following sentences with what you hear on the tape.
   1. I'm always nervy, (tense), ready to (jump on) anybody.
   2. It's easy to say give it up or (cut it down).
   3. Either you (make a real effort) or there's (no real chance) of your feeling (better).
   4. I'd prefer to see you really (back to normal).
   5. Try to be in (less of a hurry).
   6. But then . . . (at the end of the day), I begin to feel (on edge) again.
   7. Remember your health is (at stake) not your (job).
   8. I'll (have a word with) your wife.

C. True or False Questions. Write a T in front of a statement if it is true according to the recording and write an F if it is false.
   1. (T) Mr Thomson is basically very fit.
   2. (F) Mr Thomson smokes at most thirty cigarettes a day.
   3. (F) The doctor does not think that Mr Thomson has to give up smoking.
   4. (F) Mrs Thomson isn't a good cook at all.
   5. (T) Mr Thomson always has a lot to eat for breakfast and dinner.
   6. (F) Mr Thomson never has a feeling of tension after dinner in the evening.

215

7. (T) The doctor suggests that Mr Thomson should have a fruit juice and some cereal for breakfast.

8. (T) The doctor's last question is embarrassing and personal.

Task 2: Do It Yourself

A. Choose the best answer (a, b or c) for each of the following questions.

1. Who is being interviewed?

    a. Paul.

* b. Mr Miller.

    c. A journalist.

2. What prize did Mr Miller win?

* a. "Handyman of the Year".

    b. "Most Popular Star".

    c. "Best Master of the Kitchen".

3. What has Mr Miller done to his house?

    a. He painted it.

    b. He renovated it.

* c. He altered it.

4. Why did Mr Miller do something to the house?

    a. For fun.

* b. For his disabled son.

    c. For the prize he won.

5. What does Mr Miller say he will do with the money he has won?

    a. To buy a new house.

* b. To start his own business.

    c. To become an expert.

6. How much is the prize?

216

* a. 10,000 pounds.
  b. 1,000 pounds.
  c. 100,000 pounds.

B. Give brief answers to the following questions.

1. How often does *Do It Yourself* magazine organize a competition?

   Answer: Every summer.

2. What does Mr Roy Miller do?

   Answer: He is a postman.

3. Where did Mr Miller learn do – it – yourself skills?

   Answer: At evening schools.

4. Why did Mr Miller make alternation to his house by himself?

   Answer: He could not afford to pay workmen.

C. True or False Questions. Write a T in front of a statement if it is true according to the recording and write an F if it is false.

1. (F) Though Paul is disabled, he managed to move in the house.

2. (T) Mr Miller enjoys doing things with his own hands.

3. (F) The front door to his home does not open antomatically.

4. (F) Mr Miller bought his house simply because the flat he used to live in was too expensive.

5. (F) Government buildings often have special paths for those handicapped.

6. (F) Paul could reach all the switches because they were originally installed at the right height for him.

7. (T) Do-it-yourself has become one of Mr Miller's hobbies.

8. (F) Mr Miller had known a lot about carpentry and electrics

217

before he was engaged in do-it-yourself.

Section Two:

Tapescript:

My First Job

The first job I ever had was as a waitress. I did it the summer before I started at university, when I was eighteen. I was working in a very nice hotel in a small town in Scotland where there are a lot of tourists in the summer so they were taking on extra staff. I arrived there in the evening and met some of the other girls who were working at the hotel — we all lived in a little house opposite the hotel. Anyway, they were all really friendly and we had dinner together and then sat around chatting and drinking coffee—I didn't get to bed until after one o'clock in the morning. I had to be at work in the dining room at seven ... seven thirty in the morning to start serving breakfast. Well, I didn't wake up'til seven fifteen! So I threw my clothes on, rushed over to the hotel. I must have looked a real mess because the head waiter just looked at me and told me to go to the bathroom to tidy myself up—I was so embarrassed!

The first thing I learned was that there were these two heavy swing doors into the kitchen from the restaurant — one for going into the kitchen and one for going out, so that the waiters coming in didn't bump into the ones going out. Anyway, that morning I was so frightened of the head waiter that I didn't listen properly to what he was saying, so when one of the waiters asked me to give him a hand and take two plates of eggs and bacon and an orange juice out to the restaurant, I went straight towards the wrong door and collided with another waiter coming in! You can't imagine the mess— eggs, bacon and orange juice all over the floor, the door, the waiter

218

and me. The other waiter thought it was quite funny, but the head waiter was furious and made me clear everything up straight away in case someone slipped and fell.

After serving breakfast, at about ten o'clock, we had our own breakfast. I was starving by then, and just wanted to sit down and eat quietly. But some of the waiters started making fun of my English accent — they were all Scottish. I think they were just trying to cheer me up and have a joke, but I was so upset and hungry that I just rushed off to the bathroom in tears! I thought everybody hated me! By the time I came back, they'd cleared up all the breakfast things, and I hadn't had a chance to eat anything!

Well, straight away we started getting the dining room ready for lunch — cleaning the silver, setting the tables, hoovering the floor. The room had a beautiful view over a river with the mountains behind, but of course, as soon as I stopped work to have a look out of the window, the head waiter spotted me and told me off again.

I didn't make too bad a job of serving lunch — one of the waiters looked after me and showed me how to do things. One of the customers ordered some expensive white wine, and I gave him a bottle from the cupboard, not from the fridge, so it wasn't cold enough. But fortunately the other waiters hid the bottle I'd opened wrongly and I gave him another bottle from the fridge so the head waiter didn't find out. I would have been quite happy, but I had another problem which was that I'd got up in such a hurry I just put on the shoes I'd been wearing the night before. Well, these shoes looked quite smart but they had really high heels, and after a few hours on my feet I was in agony and there was nothing I could do about it, there was certainly no time to go and change them. I can tell you I never wore those shoes to work again!

Anyway, after lunch we had our own lunch—I managed to get something to eat this time, and we were free in the afternoon. I went for a walk with one of the other girls and we got a bit lost so I didn't have time for any rest before we went back to work at six. By the time we finished serving dinner at about ten thirty I was completely exhausted. I'd never worked so hard in my life, I think. Of course, I stayed up chatting with the other girls that night too, and most of the other nights I was there. I fell into bed at night and out of it at seven the next morning, but I loved the job after a while, believe it or not, and I even went back to work there the next year! I never got on very well with the head waiter, though.

Key to Exercises:

A. Choose the best answer (a, b or c) to complete each of the following statements.

1. The story took place in _____.
   * a. Scotland
   b. England
   c. Ireland

2. The girl worked as a waitress _____.
   a. while she was a university student
   b. after she left university
   * c. before she started at university

3. The girl was _____.
   a. Scottish
   * b. English
   c. Welsh

4. The girl had to go to work at _____ every morning.

220

* a. 7.30
  b. 7.15
  c. 10.00
5. She got up at _____ the first time she started working.
   a. 7.30
 * b. 7.15
   c. 10.00
6. She picked up her first job at the age of _____.
 * a. 18
   b. 20
   c. 8

B. Answer the following questions briefly.
   1. Why were the hotels in that small Scottish town taking on extra staff?
      Answer: Because there were a lot of tourists that summer.
   2. What were the two heavy swing doors for?
      Answer: One is for coming into the kitchen and the other is for going out so that the waiters coming in would not bump into the ones going out.
   3. Why was the head waiter furious at her?
      Answer: Because she went to the wrong door and collided with a waiter. All the things she was carrying – – two plates of bacon and eggs and an orange juice fell onto the floor.
   4. Why was she late the first day she started working?
      Answer: Because the night before she had stayed up late chatting with other girls who worked in the hotel.

221

C. True or False Questions. Write a T in front of a statement if it is true according to the recording and write an F if it is false.

1. (F) She had a big breakfast that morning.

2. (T) She couldn't bear being laughed at so she burst into tears.

3. (T) Together with others, she started getting the dining room ready for lunch, having little time to enjoy the beautiful scenery outside the window.

4. (F) She started doing everything all by herself.

5. (F) The head waiter found out she had opened a bottle of wine wrongly.

6. (F) Her shoes looked smart and were very comfortable.

7. (T) In the afternoon she didn't take much rest even though she was free.

8. (F) She hated her job and never did it again.

9. (F) Actually she got on quite well with the head waiter.

10. (T) She worked very hard and was exhausted that day.

Section Three:

Tapescript:

Task 1: Learning to Rephrase

1. The Landsats are two butterfly-shaped spacecraft that were sent into orbit around the earth in 1972 and 1975.

2. They circle the earth 14 times every 24 hours at a height of 570 miles, or 918 kilometres, above the earth.

3. From the photographs sent from the satellites, scientists are learning things about the earth they have never known before.

4. In false colours, water is black, cities are blue-green, rock is brown, healthy plants are red and diseased plants are green. The

222

white areas show barren land.

5. Because photographs from the satellite are taken looking directly down on the land from such a height, they are more accurate than earlier photographs taken from airplanes.

6. The second use of these Landsat photographs is to help find oil and minerals.

7. Although these two Landsats have already produced a lot of very important information about the world, they are just the beginning.

8. Later Landsats may be equipped to photograph even smaller areas or they may be equipped with radar.

Key to Exercises:

Task 1: Learning to Rephrase

Listen to the following sentences. Write the words you think are most important in the space given.

1. (Landsats: 2 butterfly-shaped spacecrafts around the earth 1972 & 1975)

2. (circle the earth 14 times/24 hours, 570 m (918 km) above earth)

3. (photos from satellites, scientists know more about earth)

4. (water black, cities blue-green, rock brown, healthy plants red, diseased plants green, barren land white)

5. (photos from satellites more accurate due to height)

6. (2nd use of Landsat photos: find oil & minerals)

7. (produced a lot of information, but just the beginning)

8. (later Landsats may photograph smaller areas, equipped with radar)

Task 2: Dictation

Body Positions

People often show their feelings by the body positions they adopt. These can contradict what you are saying, especially when you are trying to disguise the way you feel. For example, a very common defensive position, assumed when people feel threatened in some way, is to put your arm or arms across your body. This is a way of shielding yourself from a threatening situation. This shielding action can be disguised as adjusting one's cuff or watchstrap. Leaning back in your chair especially with your arms folded is not only defensive, it's also a way of showing your disapproval, of a need to distance yourself from the rest of the company.

A position which betrays an aggressive attitude is to avoid looking directly at the person you are speaking to. On the other hand, approval and desire to cooperate are shown by copying the position of the person you are speaking to. This shows that you agree or are willing to agree with someone. The position of one's feet also often shows the direction of people's thoughts, for example, feet or a foot pointing towards the door can indicate that a person wishes to leave the room. The direction in which your foot points can also show which of the people in the room you feel most sympathetic towards, even when you are not speaking directly to that person.

Supplementary Reading:

Landsat System Update

Although there have been some problems with the Landsat system, in many ways the satellites have worked even better and longer than scientists had expected.

224

Landsats 1 and 2 were sent into space in 1972 and 1975. They were expected to work for about two years each, but they surprised scientists by sending back information for more than five and a half years. During that unusually long time, there were some changes in their performance.

The first change involved the Landsats' tape-recording capabilities. Originally each Landsat had two tape recorders which enabled them to take pictures of areas where there are no ground stations. The tape recorders held the pictures until the Landsat passed near a ground station. The pictures were then sent down. By the end of 1977, only one tape recorder of the four was working, and it was working only part of the time. During the times it was not working, Landsat pictures could only be sent to earth when the satellite was within range of a ground station.

Second, the orbit of Landsat 1 changed. At the time Landsat 2 was launched in 1975, it was placed so that together the two Landsats would pass over the same spot on earth every nine days. But by the time Landsat 1 had been in orbit four to five years, its orbit had begun to change due to the pull of earth's gravity. Therefore, it was necessary to fire Landsat 1 rockets for a very short time to correct its orbit. With the new orbit, the two satellites no longer followed each other every nine days. Instead, Landsat 1 followed Landsat 2 six days behind it, and Landsat 2 followed Landsat 1 twelve days behind it.

A third change concerned the complex machine that measured colours in order to send pictures back to earth. The machine was intended to measure four colours, but the part of the machine that indicated the colour green in Landsat 1 stopped working, and for a time the spacecraft continued to operate with three colour bands.

Landsat 1 was finally shut down in early 1978 after five and a half years of operation.

Landsat 3 was launched to take the place of Landsat 1. Landsat 3 had the same uses as Landsat 1, and in addition, it was equipped with an infrared system to measure heat. This system failed after about two months. Landsat 4 is scheduled to be launched in 1981. It may also be equipped to measure heat if scientists can solve the problems that they had with Landsat 3. Landsat 5 (Stereosat) will be next. It will provide three-dimensional pictures of geological formations to help gas and oil companies find new sources of oil.

Seasat A was another satellite added to the Landsat system. It was specifically created to gather information about the seas. Microwave instruments on the spacecraft were so accurate that they were supposed to be able to measure the height of the waves in the ocean to within 20 cm. (7.8 in.). Other uses for the Seasat were to watch the weather over the seas, to forecast storms and floods, and to provide information on surface temperatures, currents, and ice. Unfortunately, after operating for only 105 days, Seasat failed in October 1978 because of a loss of power.

The Landsat satellite system has sent back more data than has ever been completely and fully used. The system will continue to change. New ideas will be tried; some will fail and some will succeed. People who are interested in Landsats may read and listen for news about the Landsats in the future. At this point, nobody knows whether the program will be supported and expanded by the government, whether data will be sent to many other countries, and how data will be more fully used.

Lesson 12

Section One:

Tapescript:

Dustbin Day Robbery

Gentleman Jim has worked out a plan to rob a bank. He's telling his gang, Fingers Jones and Ginger Robertson about the plan. Listen to their conversation.

Fingers: Let's see. You're going to walk up to the counter and you're going to start writing a cheque. Then you're going to open the canister of nerve gas, and everyone will go to sleep instantly.

Jim: That's right. This gas will put anyone to sleep for exactly three minutes.

Fingers: And while everyone is asleep, you're going to go round to the manager's desk and steal all the money?

Jim: Exactly. I've worked it out very carefully. There should be about £ 50,000 in used bank notes.

Ginger: Sounds great. There's only one thing. If you open the gas, you'll go to sleep too, won't you?

Jim: I have thought of that. I'll wear a motor-cycle helmet, with an oxygen mask inside. If I wear a helmet, no-one will be able to recognize me afterwards, either.

Ginger: I think it's risky. If the bank clerk sees you take out a gas canister, he won't wait. He'll push the alarm button straight away.

227

Fingers: I've just had an idea. If I came into the bank when you were standing at the counter, no-one would even look at me. Then, if I threw the can of nerve gas, they wouldn't guess that we were connected.

Ginger: Yes, that might be better. Are you going to wear a helmet, too?

Fingers: No. It would look very suspicious if two people were wearing motor-cycle helmets. I'll just open the door, throw in the gas canister, and leave Gentleman Jim to rob the bank.

Jim: I like that idea. Right, we'll do that. Any other problems that you can see?

Ginger: What are you going to do with the money? If you walk out with £50,000 under your arm, somebody will surely notice you.

Jim: You'll be sitting in a get-away car, waiting for me outside the bank.

Ginger: But there is a police station just 50 yards away. If I park the car outside the bank, the police would probably come and ask me to move.

Fingers: Well, what do you suggest? He can't just walk around the town. He'll be carrying £50,000 in bundles of bank notes.

Jim: Just a minute! I've thought of something. What day is this robbery?

Fingers: Monday.

Jim: Monday! You know what happens on Monday, don't you? It's dustbin day!

Ginger: So?

Jim: So, can you think of a better way of moving the money? If you saw a man pick up £50,000 and put it into a car, what would you think?

Fingers: I'd think he was a thief.

Jim: Exactly. But if you saw a man pick up a dustbin and put it into a lorry, what would you think?

228

Fingers: I'd think he was a dustman. Hey! That's clever!

Ginger: And if the £50,000 was in the dustbin, I could pick up the money and nobody would notice. That's brilliant.

Fingers: Er... Is there a dustbin?

Jim: Oh yes, several. They put the dustbins out every Monday. They'll be standing there, outside the bank.

Fingers: But if you put the money in a dustbin, it'll stink. We'll never be able to spend it if it smells like that.

Jim: We don't have to put it in a dustbin. We can put it in a black plastic bag. They often have black plastic bags for rubbish nowadays. If I carry one in my pocket, I can pull it out after you've thrown the gas. OK? Let's run through the plan once more.

Ginger: You go into the bank with a motor-cycle helmet on, and a black rubbish bag in your pocket.

Fingers: I come in a few minutes later. I open the door, throw in the open gas canister, and then go ... where?

Jim: I've hired a room in the building right opposite the bank. Go up in the lift to the top floor and keep a look out. When you get there, radio Ginger, and tell him to come.

Ginger: In the meantime, everyone in the bank has gone to sleep, except you. You take the money, and put it in the plastic bag.

Jim: I come out, and put the bag with the rubbish, and then go back into the bank.

Ginger: Go back?

Jim: Oh yes. If everyone woke up and I wasn't there, they'd know I was one of the thieves. No, I'll go back and pretend to wake up with everyone else.

Fingers: That's a really clever touch.

Ginger: I drive a dustcart and wait in the cul-de-sac behind the bank until Fingers contacts me. Then I come and pick up the rubbish, including the £ 50,000.

Jim: I can't think of any problems, can you?

Key to Exercises:

A. True or False Questions. Write a T in front of a statement if it is true according to the recording and write an F if it is false.

    1. (T) The three men are discussing their plan for a bank robbery.

    2. (F) The three robbers don't think dustbin day is a good day for their robbery.

    3. (F) They plan to take away 15,000 pounds.

    4. (T) If two of them wear motor – cycle helmets, the bank clerks would be suspicious.

    5. (F) If Jim goes back and pretends to wake up with everyone else in the bank, people will think he is the thief.

    6. (F) One of them will wait in a dustcart in front of the bank.

    7. (T) They plan to take away the money together with rubbish.

B. Identification: Identify the items in Column I with those in Column II with regard to their function in the robbery.

Column I	Column II
1. nerve gas	a. to move away the money and robbers
2. motor-cycle-helmet	b. to wrap the money
3. dustbin	c. a parking lot
4. dustcart	d. to put people to sleep instantly
5. plastic bag	e. to keep people from being recognized

230

6. cul – de – sac   f. to put money in

Answer: (1) – (d); (2) – (e); (3) – (f);

(4) – (a); (5) – (b); (6) – (c);

C. Answer the following questions briefly.

1. How will Jim protect himself from going to sleep after he opens the canister of nerve gas?

   Answer: He is going to wear a motorcycle helmet with an oxygen mask inside.

2. What will happen if they park a car in front of the bank?

   Answer: The police will probably come and ask them to move since a police station is just fifty yards away from the bank.

3. Why don't they want to put the money directly into the dustbin?

   Answer: Because it will stink and they'll never be able to use it if it smells like that.

4. Why has Jim hired a room right opposite the bank?

   Answer: Because they can keep a lookout there since the room is on the top floor of the building. And there, Fingers can radio Ginger and tell him to come.

Section Two:

Tapescript:

Task 1: Crime

(Doorbell rings. Door opens.)

Boss: At long last! Why did it take you so long?

1st villain: Er ... I really am sorry about this, boss ...

Boss: Come on! What happened? Where's the money?

231

1st villain: Well, it's a long story. We parked outside the bank OK, on South Street, and I went in and got the money—you know, no problems, they just filled the bag like you said they would. I went outside, jumped into the car, and off we went.

Boss: Yes, yes, yes. And then?

2nd villain: We turned right up Forest Road, and of course the traffic lights at the High Street crossroads were against us. And when they went green the stupid car stalled, didn't it? I mean, it was dead—

1st villain: So I had to get out and push, all the way to the garage opposite the school. I don't know why Jim here couldn't fix it. I mean, the car was your responsibility, wasn't it?

2nd villain: Yeah, but it was you that stole it, wasn't it? Why didn't you get a better one?

1st villain: OK, it was my fault. I'm sorry.

2nd villain: The mechanic said it would take at least two days to fix it—so we just had to leave it there and walk.

1st villain: Well, we crossed over Church Lane, and you'll never believe what happened next, just outside the Police Station, too.

2nd villain: Look, it wasn't my fault. You were responsible for providing the bag—I couldn't help it if the catch broke.

1st villain: It took us five minutes to pick up all the notes again.

Boss: Fine, fine, fine. But where is the money?

2nd villain: We're getting there, boss. Anyway, we ran to where the second car was parked, outside the library in Ox Lane—you know, we were going to switch cars there—and then—you know, this is just unbelievable –

1st villain: —yeah. We drove up Church Lane, but they were dig-

232

ging up the road just by the church, so we had to take the left fork and go all the way round the north side of the park. And then, just before the London Road roundabout—

2nd villain: – some idiot must have driven out from the railway station without looking right into the side of a lorry. The road was completely blocked. There was nothing for it but to abandon the car and walk the rest of the way.

Boss : All right, it's a very fascinating story. But I still want to have a look at the money.

1st villain: Well, that's the thing, boss. I mean, I'm terribly sorry, but this idiot must have left it somewhere.

2nd villain: Who are you calling an idiot? I had nothing to do with it. You were carrying the bag.

1st villain: No. I wasn't. I gave it to you...

Task 2: Shop-lifter

Man: Excuse me, madam.

Woman: Yes?

Man: Would you mind letting me take a look in your bag?

Woman: I beg your pardon?

Man: I'd like to look into your bag, if you don't mind.

Woman: Well I'm afraid I certainly do mind, if it's all the same to you. Now go away. Impertinence!

Man: I'm afraid I shall have to insist, madam.

Woman: And just who are you to insist, may I ask? I advise you to take yourself off, young man, before I call a policeman.

Man: I am a policeman, madam. Here's my identity card.

Woman: What? Oh ... well ... and just what right does that give you to go around looking into people's bags?

Man: None whatsoever, unless I have reason to believe that there's something in the bags belonging to someone else?

Woman: What do you mean belonging to someone else?

Man: Well, perhaps, things that haven't been paid for?

Woman: Are you talking about stolen goods? That's a nice way to talk, I must say. I don't know what things are coming to when perfectly honest citizens get stopped in the street and have their bags examined. A nice state of affairs!

Man: Exactly, but if the citizens are honest, they wouldn't mind, would they? So may I look in your bag, madam? We don't want to make a fuss? do we?

Woman: Fuss? Who's making a fuss? Stopping people in the street and demanding to see what they've got in their bags. Charming! That's what I call it: charming! Now go away; I've got a train to catch.

Man: I'm sorry. I'm trying to do my job as politely as possible, but I'm afraid you're making it rather difficult. However, I must insist on seeing what you have in your bag.

Woman: And what, precisely, do you expect to find in there? The Crown Jewels?

Man: No need to be sarcastic, Madam. I thought I'd made myself plain. If there's nothing in there which doesn't belong to you, you can go straight off and catch your train and I'll apologize for the inconvenience.

Women: Oh, very well. Anything to help the police.

Man: Thank you, madam.

Woman: Not at all; only too happy to co-operate. There you are.

Man: Thank you, Mm. Six lipsticks?

Woman: Yes, nothing unusual in that. I like to change the colour

234

with my mood.

Man: And five powder-compacts?

Woman: I use a lot of powder. I don't want to embarrass you, but I sweat a lot. (Laughs)

Man: And ten men's watches?

Woman: Er, yes. I get very nervous if I don't know the time. Anxiety, you know. We all suffer from it in this day and age.

Man: I see you smoke a lot, too, madam. Fifteen cigarette lighters?

Woman: Yes, I am rather a heavy smoker. And ... and I use them for finding my way in the dark and ... and for finding the keyhole late at night. And ... and I happen to collect lighters. It's my hobby. I have a superb collection at home.

Man: I bet you do, madam. Well, I'm afraid I'm going to have to ask you to come along with me.

Woman: How dare you! I don't go out with strange men. And anyway I told you I have a train to catch.

Man: I'm afraid you won't be catching it today, madam. Now are you going to come along quietly or am I going to have to call for help?

Woman: But this is outrageous! (Start fade) I shall complain to my MP. One has to carry one's valuables around these days; one's house might be broken into while one's out...

Key Exercises:

Task 1: Crime

A. Choose the best answer(a, b or c) to complete each of the following statements.

1. This conversation is about _____.

235

* a. a bank robbery

  b. a burglary into a civilian's house

  c. a theft on a bus

2. They _____ the car they drove.

  a. damaged

* b. stole

  c. bought

3. The money they robbed from the bank _____.

  a. was brought to Boss in safety

* b. was gone on their way to the Boss's

  c. was still in the bank

B. Activities. Write down what happened to the two villains at the following locations.

  (1) South Street: (They parked the car outside the bank.)

  (2) High Street crossroads: (The traffic lights were red.)

  (3) The garage opposite the school: (to repair the car)

  (4) Outside the Police Station: (The catch of the money bag broke and they had to pick up all the notes.)

  (5) Ox Lane: (They switched cars.)

  (6) Church Lane: (Roads were dug up.)

  (7) London Road roundabout: (The road was blocked owing to a traffic accident.)

  (8) The Boss's: (The two arrived empty-handed.)

Task 2: Shop-lifter

A. Choose the best answer (a, b or c) to complete each of the following statements.

  1. This conversation takes place _____.

236

  a. between a shop assistant and a customer

  b. between a shop assistant and a shop-lifter

 * c. between a policeman and a shop-lifter

2. This conversation takes place _____.

  a. in a department store

  b. at a cosmetic shop

 * c. in the street

3. The man stops the woman in order to _____.

 * a. have a look in the woman's bag

  b. start a conversation with her

  c. rob her purse

4. The man has been very _____ while the woman

 _____.

  a. arrogant and rude; polite and co-operative

 * b. polite and insistent; arrogant and dishonest

  c. polite and insistent; friendly and honest

B. Write down what the woman says about the use of the following articles.

1. Six lipsticks: (She likes to change the color with her mood.)

2. Five powder – compacts: (She sweats a lot, so she has to use a lot of powder.)

3. Ten men's watches: (She gets nervous if she doesn't know the time.)

4. Fifteen cigarette lighters: (She is a heavy smoker; she uses lighters for finding her way in the dark and for finding the keyhole late at night. And she is a lighter collector.)

C. Complete the following sentences with what you hear on the tape.

1. Would you mind (letting) me (take a look in) your bag?

2. I advise you (to take yourself off).

3. So may I look in your bag, Madam? We don't want to (make a fuss).

4. I must (insist on seeing) what you have in your bag.

5. No (need) to be (sarcastic), madam. I thought I'd (made myself plain).

6. I'll apologize (for the inconvenience).

7. One has to (carry one's valuables around) these days; one's house might (be broken into) while one's (out) . . .

Section Three:

Tapescript:

Task 1: Learning to Rephrase

1. The American Indians of the Southwest have led an agricultural life since the year 1 A.D., and in some aspects their life is still similar today.

2. At the beginning of this period, the people farmed on the tops of high, flat, mountain plateaus, called mesas. Mesa is the Spanish word for table.

3. They lived on top of the mesas or in the protection of the caves on the sides of the cliffs.

4. In their early history, the Anasazi used baskets for all these purposes. Later they developed pottery. But the change from basketmaking to pottery was so important that it began a series of secondary changes.

5. To cook food in a basket, the women first filled the basket with ground corn mixed with water. They then built a fire.

238

6. But many stones could be heated on the fire and then dropped into the basket of food so it would cook. The stones heated the food quite well, but soon they had to be taken out of the food and heated again.

7. But although the men brought home the idea of pottery, they didn't bring home any instructions on how to make it. Anthropologists have discovered pieces of broken pottery made according to different formulas.

8. Because the Anasazi had solved the problem of cooking and storing food, they could now enjoy a more prosperous, comfortable period of life.

Key to Exercises:

Task 1: Learning to Rephrase

Listen to the following sentences. Write the words you think are most important in the space given.

1. (Am. Indians in Southwest; agricultural life since 1 AD, similar today)

2. (farm on mesas — tops of high, flat mountain plateau — Spanish — table)

3. (live on mesas or in caves on sides of cliffs)

4. (early history: Anasazi used baskets, later pottery, change — important, began a series of secondary changes)

5. (fill basket with ground corn + water, build fire)

6. (many stones heated on fire & dropped into basket of food, but must be heated again soon)

7. (men brought idea but not how to make pottery; shown in anthropological discoveries)

8. (solved problem of cooking & storing food, a more prosperous &

comfortable life)

Acupuncture

There are many forms of alternative medicine which are used in the Western world today. One of the most famous of these is acupuncture, which is a very old form of treatment from China. It is still widely used in China today, where it is said to cure many illnesses, including tonsilitis, arthritis, bronchitis, rheumatism and flu. The Chinese believe that there are special energy lines through the body and that the body's energy runs through these lines. When a person is ill the energy in his or her body does not run as well as normal, perhaps because it's weaker or it's blocked in some way. The Chinese believe that if you put very fine needles into the energy line, this helps the energy to return to normal. In this way the body can help itself to get better.

The acupuncturist puts the needles into special places along the energy line and some of these places can be a long way from the place where the body is ill. For example it's possible to treat a bad headache by putting needles into certain places on the foot. It may surprise you to know that it doesn't hurt when the acupuncturist puts the needles into your body. People who have had acupuncture say that they felt nothing or hardly anything. Western doctors at first did not believe that acupuncture could work. Now they see that it not only can work but that it does work. How and why does it work? No one has been able to explain this. It is one of nature's mysteries.

Section Four:
Enjoy Your English:
Tapescript:

I Just Fall in Love Again

Dreaming, I must be dreaming
Or am I really lying here with you
Baby you take me in your arms
And though I'm wide awake
I know my dream is coming true
And oh I just fall in love again
Just one touch and then it happens every time
There I go
I just fall in love again and when I do
I can't help myself I fall in love with you

Magic, it must be magic
The way I hold you and the night just seems to fly
Easy for you to take me to a star
Heaven is that moment when I look into your eyes
And oh I just fall in love again
Just one touch and then it happens every time
There I go
I just fall in love again and when I do
I can't help myself I fall in love with you
Can't help myself I fall in love with you

Supplementary Reading:

Discovering the Anasazi

Dozens of Anasazi families had already left the mesa by 1299, but the tribe's final departure was sudden. Little food was left, and almost no water. Every winter the people had hoped for snow, and every spring they had prayed for the rain that never came. It had been this way for twenty-four years: a dry period that weakened the strong and killed the weak. Finally the thing happened that people had feared most — the only corn that was left was their seed corn. They did not dare eat that, for then they could never be farmers again. They had to take their seed corn and leave the mesa for a better home.

In their hurry to be gone, they left everything as it was. Perhaps they felt that everything in the pueblos was unlucky; perhaps they were trying to escape the evil spirits of the mesa. Cooking pots and work tools lay there, ready to use, as if the people intended to return soon. But nobody came back.

Soon after they left, the weather changed, and the rain returned. The mesa became green and rich again. People wandered back over the mesa tops; this time they were Navajo Indians. As they discovered the incredible ruins, they stood amazed. Afraid of the spirits in these houses, the Navajos decided not to live there. But from this time, the Indians knew of the cliff dwellings. They spoke about the people who had made them, calling them the "Ancient Ones."

Centuries passed, and the cliff dwellings stood untouched by human beings. The sweeping winds of the mesa blew into the caves and covered the cooking pots and work tools with the dry dust of the Southwest.

Across the oceans, the great nations of Europe were beginning to look to the New World for gold and for land. England, Spain, and France sent their soldiers, priests, and explorers. Slowly they approached the mesa. First to see the large mesa were the Spanish,

242

who gave it its name: Mesa Verde – green table.

Pioneers of the young nation, the United States, were next to command the area. They drove back the Spanish and made a kind of peace with the Indians of the region, the Utes. But none of the newcomers wanted to try farming there, for there was not much rain. Cattle raising became the main occupation around Mesa Verde.

The Wetherill family was friendly with the Ute Indians, and from the Utes they may have heard stories of mysterious houses in the cliffs. To show their friendship, the Utes permitted the Wetherills to keep their cattle on Indian land during the winter. The cowboys gathered their cattle together again in the spring.

This is how, in the spring of 1888, Richard Wetherill and his cousin Charlie Mason came to be on the mesa. Following the tracks of a few lost cattle, they rode to the top of the mesa. They had just come to the edge of a cliff when they paused to rest their horses. Where were the cattle? They looked down into the canyon below – and up again to the top of the neighbouring cliff.

Then suddenly, Wetherill forgot completely about his cattle as he discovered something fantastic! Was it real? How could there be – here in the middle of the lonely mesa – an entire city of perfectly fitted stone blocks, built to hold hundreds of people in its graceful towers and square rooms? And where were the people who had built such a wonder? Wetherill decided that the city was suitable for a king and his family, and he called it Cliff Palace.

Wetherill's discovery changed his whole life. Before the discovery, he had been a cowboy with no advanced education. But because he was a sensitive man, he realized how important his discovery was. Wetherill made two promises to himself: he must discover everything he could about the people who had lived here, and he must protect the ruins for the future. He spent the rest of his life keeping these promises.

Wetherill's situation was not well suited to the job, and he had little support from the general public or the academic world. Still, he invested the small income from his farm in exploratory trips to the ruins. Because his ranch demanded his time during the summer, he had to wait until the cold winters to explore the cliffs. He rose at dawn, dug and searched all day, and then spent the dark evening hours recording his discoveries. He did not want anything to be lost or misplaced. He made careful records of all the pots, tools, and jewellery.

Wetherill's collection of museum pieces would have made the most scholarly archaeologist proud. He found 182 different cliff dwellings in the Mesa Verde area, and he was also the first to discover evidence of the Basketmakers. He realized that there must have been an earlier people who had come before the Pueblo Indians. When he announced his theories and findings to the world, the university anthropologists and archaeologists simply laughed at him. Without even investigating, they refused to believe him!

But the patient Wetherill continued to work and to record his discoveries. Almost ten years after his death, scientists discovered evidence of the Basketmakers for themselves and proved that he had been right. Now a large part of Mesa Verde National Park bears his name: Wetherill Mesa. And so the ruins, which for many years stood quietly unexplored, were finally discovered and preserved. Wetherill was a man very much like the cliff dwellings themselves – quiet, strong, and enduring. He belonged to the area and he brought out one of its greatest secrets.

Lesson 13

Section One:

Tapescript:

Task 1: Guess What People Are Talking About

Lesley: Ah... it's such a lovely day. It reminds me of last week, doesn't it you?

Fiona: Oh don't! I mean that was just so fantastic, that holiday!

Lesley: I love that city, you know.

Fiona: I do too. Really, it's got something about it, a certain sort of charm...

Lesley: Mm, and all that wine and good food...

Fiona: And so cheap. Right, I mean, compared to here...

Lesley: Yes, although the shops are expensive.

Fiona: Mm, yes.

Lesley: I mean, really I bought nothing at all. I just ate and ate and drank and drank.

Fiona: I know. Wasn't that lovely?

Lesley: And I... I... I don't... I like listening to the people talking and sitting outside drinking wine.

Fiona: Yes. Could you understand what they were saying? When they were speaking quickly, I mean.

Lesley: Well, it is difficult, of course. And then I liked that tower, too.

Fiona: You liked that tower? I'm not sure about it, really. (No) It's very unusual, right in the centre of the city.

Lesley: True, but there's a lovely riew from the top.

Fiona: Oh, you went right up, didn't you? (Mm, yes) Oh no, I didn't.

Lesley: Of course you didn't.

Fiona: I remember that day. We weren't together.

Lesley: No, that's right. (Mm) You went down by the river, didn't you?

Fiona: That's it. Oh, walking along the river and all the couples (Yes) and it's so romantic...(Is it true) and the paintings too...

Lesley: They do have artists down by the river, do they? (Yes) Oh, how lovely!

Fiona: Oh, it really is super.

Lesley: Yes. Oh, I think we ought to go back there again next year, don't you?

Fiona: I do, yes. (Mm) If only just to sample some more of the wine.

Lesley: It'd be lovely, wouldn't it?

Fiona: Yes.

Task 2: Nice to See You!

Doorbell rings.

Peter: Hello, John. Nice to see you. Come in. How are you?

John : Fine, thanks. Peter. And how are you? I expect your patients are keeping you busy at this time of year?

Peter: Ah, well. I can't really complain. Let me take your coat. There we are. Well, now, I don't think you've met Ann Patterson, have you? Ann, this is John Middleton. He's the local schoolteacher.

Ann: Oh! How do you do?

246

John: How do you do?

Ann: Well, that's very interesting. Perhaps you'll be looking after my son.

Peter: Yes, that's right. Ann and her family have just moved into the old barn, up by the village hall. They're in the process of doing it up now.

Ann: Yes, there's an awful lot needs doing, of course.

Doorbell rings.

Peter: Er, please excuse me for a moment. I think that was the doorbell.

John : Well, if I can give you a hand with anything ... I'm something of a handyman in my spare time, you know. I live just over the road.

Ann:That's very kind of you. I'm an architect myself, so ... Oh, look! There's someone I know, Eileen!

Eileen: Ann, fancy seeing you here! How's life?

Ann: Oh, mustn't grumble. Moving's never much fun though, is it? Anyway, how are things with you? You're still at the same estate agant's. I suppose?

Eileen: Oh yes. I can't see myself leaving, well, not in the foreseeable future.

Ann: Oh, I quite forgot. Do you two know each other?

John : Yes, actually, we've met on many an occasion. Hello, Eileen. You see, we play in the same orchestra.

Ann: Oh, really? I didn't know anything about that.

Eileen: Yes, actually, just amateur stuff, you know—once a week—I come down from London when I can get a baby-sitter for Joanna.

Paul : Er ... excuse me, I hope you don't mind my butting in. My name's Paul Madison. I couldn't help overhearing what you said about an orchestra.

John : Come and join the party. I'm John Middleton. This is Ann Patterson and Eileen ... or ... I'm terribly sorry. I don't think I know your surname?

Eileen: Hawkes. Pleased to meet you, Paul. You play an instrument, do you?

Paul : Yes, I'm over here on a scholarship to study the bassoon (*loud yawn from Ann*) at the Royal Academy of Music for a couple of years ...

Ann: Oh, I *am* sorry. It must be all that hard work on the barn ...

Paul: Well, anyway ... We've been working very hard ...

Key to Exercises:

Task 1: Guessing What People Are Talking About

A. True or False Questions. Write a T in front of a statement if it is true according to the recording and an F if it is false.

1. (T) Lesley and Fiona are talking about a holiday they had last week.

2. (F) Neither of them likes the city they went to.

3. (F) It was easy for them to understand people no matter how quickly they spoke.

4. (T) Only one of them walked along the river.

5. (F) Neither of them thinks they should go there again next year.

6. (T) They enjoyed themselves very much drinking and eating.

248

B. Write a list of things that Lesley and Fiona liked about the city.
   1. (wine and good food)
   2. (the river)
   3. (walking along the river and all the couples)
   4. (paintings there)

C. Complete the following sentences with what you hear on the tape.
   1. It (reminds) me (of) last week.
   2. Really, it's (got something about it), a certain (sort of charm . . .)
   3. It's very (unusual), right (in the center of) the city.
   4. But there's a lovely view (from the top).
   5. They do have artists (down by the river), don't they?

Task 2: Nice to See You!
A. Choose the best answer (a, b or c) to complete each of the following statements.
   1. The conversation takes place _____.
      a. at John's home
      b. in the village hall
    * c. at Peter's home
   2. Most of the people in the conversation _____.
    * a. meet for the first time
      b. have known each other for a long time
      c. are members of an orchestra

B. Identification. Match the people in Column I with the professions, identity or location in Column II.

249

Column I

Column II

1. Peter   a. architect

2. Ann Patterson   b. estate agent

3. John Middleton   c. London

4. Eileen Hawkes   d. host

5. Paul Madison   e. local schoolteacher

6. Joanna   f. amateur

g. Eileen's daughter

h. Royal Academy of music

i. doctor

Answer: (1) - - (d, i); (2) - - (a); (3) - - (e, f); (4) -
- (b, c, f); (5) - - (h); (6) - - (g);

C. Complete the following sentences with what you hear on the
tape.

1. I expect your patients (are keeping you busy) at this time of
year?

2. They are (in the process) of (doing it up) now.

3. Well, if I can (give you a hand with) anything. . . I'm
(something of) a handyman in my spare time.

4. I can't (see myself leaving), well, not in the (foreseeable)
future.

5. I hope you don't mind (my butting in).

6. I'm (over here on a scholarship) to study the bassoon at (the
Royal Academy of Music) for a couple of years.

Section Two:

Tapescript:

Task 1: What Do You Like About Your Job?

First speaker: I'm a night person. I love the hours, you know? I like going to work at around six at night and then getting home at two or three in the morning. I like being out around people, you know, talking to them, listening to their problems. Some of my regulars are always on the lookout for ways that they can stump me. Like last week, one of them came in and asked for a Ramos gin fizz. He didn't think I knew how to make it. Hah! But I know how to make every drink in the book, and then some. Although some of the nights when I go in I just don't feel like dealing with all the noise. When I get in a big crowd it can be pretty noisy. People talking, the sound system blaring, the pinball machine, the video games. And then at the end of the night you don't always smell so good, either. You smell like cigarettes. But I like the place and I plan on sticking around for a while.

Second speaker: If I had to sit behind a desk all day, I'd go crazy! I'm really glad I have a job where I can keep moving, you know? My favourite part is picking out the music—I use new music for every ten-week session. For my last class I always use the Beatles—it's a great beat to move to, and everybody loves them. I like to sort of educate people about their bodies, and show them, you know, how to do the exercises and movements safely. Like, it just kills me when I see people trying to do situps with straight legs—it' so bad for your back! And...let's see...I—I like to see people make progress—at the end of a session you can really see how people have slimmed down and sort of built up some muscle—it's very gratifying.

The part I don't like is, well, it's hard to keep coming up with new ideas for classes. I mean, you know, there are just so

251

many ways you can move your body, and it's hard to keep coming up with interesting routines and ... and new exercises. And it's hard on my voice—I have to yell all the time so people can hear me above the music, and like after three classes in one day my voice has had it. Then again, having three classes in one day has its compensations—I can eat just about anything I want and not gain any weight!

Third speaker: What do I like about my job? Money. M – O – N – E – Y. No, I like the creativity, and I like my studio. All my tools are like toys to me—you know, my watercolours, pen and inks, coloured pencils, drafting table—I love playing with them. and I have lots of different kinds of clients—I do magazines, book covers, album covers, newspaper articles—so there's lots of variety, which I like. You know, sometimes when I start working on a project I could be doing it for hours and have no conception of how much time has gone by—what some people call a flow experience.

I don't like the pressure, though, and there's plenty of it in this business. You're always working against a tight deadline. And I don't like the business end of it—you know, contacting clients for work, negotiating contracts, which get long and complicated.

Fourth speaker: Well, I'll tell you. At first it was fun, because there was so much to learn, and working with figures and money was interesting. But after about two years the thrill was gone, and now it's very routine. I keep the books, do the payroll, pay the taxes, pay the insurance, pay the bills. I hate paying the bills, because there's never enough money to pay them! I also don't like the pressure of having to remember

252

when all the bills and taxes are due. And my job requires a lot of reading that I don't particularly enjoy—like, I have to keep up to date on all the latest tax forms, and it's pretty dull. I like it when we're making money, though, because I get to see all of my efforts rewarded.

Task 2: What Do You Think of Yourself?

TV Interviewer: In this week's edition of 'Up with People' we went out into the streets and asked a number of people a question they just didn't expect. We asked them to be self-critical ... to ask themselves exactly what they thought they lacked or—the other side of the coin—what virtues they had. Here is what we heard.

Jane Smith: Well ... I ... I don't know really ... it's not the sort of question you ask yourself directly. I know I'm good at my job ... at least my boss calls me hard-working, conscientious, efficient. I'm a secretary by the way. As for when I look at myself in a mirror as it were ... you know ... you sometimes do in the privacy of your own bedroom ... or at your reflection in the ... in the shop windows as you walk up the street ... Well ... then I see someone a bit different. Yes ... I'm different in my private life. And that's probably my main fault I should say ... I'm not exactly—oh how shall I say? —I suppose I'm, not coherent in my behaviour. My office is always in order...but my flat! Well...you'd have to see it to believe it.

Chris Bonner: I think the question is irrelevant. You shouldn't be asking what I think of myself ... but what I think of the state of this country. And this country is in a terrible mess. There's

253

only one hope for it—the National Front. It's law and order that we need. I say get rid of these thugs who call themselves Socialist Workers. . . get rid of them I say. So don't ask about me. I'm the sort of ordinary decent person who wants to bring law and order back to this country. And if we can't do it by peaceful means then . . .

Tommy Finch: Think of myself? Well I'm an easy-going bloke really . . . unless of course you wind me up. Then I'm a bit vicious. You know. I mean you have to live for yourself don't you. And think of your mates. That's what makes a bloke. I ain't got much sympathy like with them what's always thinking of causes . . . civil rights and all that. I mean . . . this is a free country innit? What do we want to fight for civil rights for? We've got them.

Charles Dimmak: Well . . . I'm retired you know. Used to be an army officer. And . . . I think I've kept myself. . . yes I've kept myself respectable—that's the word I'd use—respectable and dignified the whole of my life. I've tried to help those who depended on me. I've done my best. Perhaps you might consider me a bit of a fanatic about organization and discipline— self-discipline comes first—and all that sort of thing. But basically I'm a good chap . . . not too polemic . . . fond of my wife and family . . . That's me.

Arthur Fuller: Well . . . when I was young I was very shy. At times I . . . I was very unhappy . . . especially when I was sent to boarding-school at seven. I didn't make close friends till . . . till quite late in life . . . till I was about . . . what . . . fifteen. Then I became quite good at being by myself. I had no one to rely on . . . and no one to ask for advice. That made me inde-

254

pendent ... and I've always solved my problems myself. My
wife and I have two sons. We ... we didn't want an only child
because I felt ... well I felt I'd missed a lot of things.

Key to Exercises:

Task 1: What Do You Like About You Job?

A. Choose the best answer (a, b or c) to complete each of the following statements.

  1. The first speaker probably works in _____.

  * a. a night club

    b. an evening school

    c. an office

  2. According to the tape, the second speaker _____.

    a. is a pop music singer

    b. produces radio programmes

  * c. is a coach for some body-building courses

  3. The third speaker earns a lot of money by _____.

    a. drawing oil paintings

  * b. art designing

    c. selling magazines, books, etc

  4. The fourth speaker is engaged in _____.

    a. the management of a company

    b. a lot of funny experiences

  * c. bookkeeping

B. True or False Questions. Write a T in front of a statement if it is
true according to the recording and write an F if it is false.

  1. (F) The first speaker does not enjoy working late at night.

  2. (F) The place where the first speaker works is very quiet.

3. (T) The second speaker chooses the music that is new and exciting for the people in her class.
4. (F) During her classes, the second speaker doesn't have to yell because she turns the background music low.
5. (T) The third speaker sometimes is so much obsessed by his work that he forgets about time.
6. (F) The greatest pleasure work has brought to the third speaker is money.
7. (F) The fourth speaker's job does not become routine at all. It's more and more interesting.
8. (T) The fourth speaker certainly takes pleasure in the work, especially when they're making money.

C. Complete the following sentences with what you hear on the tape.
1. I'm (a night person).
2. Some of my regulars are always (on the lookout for) ways that they can (stump me).
3. I like the place and I (plan on sticking around) for a while.
4. For my last class I always used (the Beatles), – – it's (a great beat to move to).
5. It's hard to keep (coming up with) interesting routines.
6. (At the end of) a session you can really see how people (have slimmed down) and sort of (built up) some muscle.
7. You're always working (against a tight deadline).
8. (At first) it was fun, because there was so much to learn, and (working with) figures and money was interesting.

Task 2: What Do You Think of Yourself?

256

A. Choose the best answer (a, b or c) to complete each of the following statements.

1. This interview is shown on a TV programme called
_____.

    * a. Up with People

    b. People Overheard

    c. Life of People

2. The woman interviewed _____.

    a. always has her things in order

    b. looks different in the mirror and shop windows

    * c. is unable to keep her flat tidy

3. The second interviewee Chris Bonner thinks that
_____.

    * a. the whole country is in a terrible mess

    b. his flat is in a mess

    c. he is pretty tidy

4. The third interviewee Tommy Finch thinks _____.

    a. little of himself

    b. much of the civil rights

    * c. much of himself

5. Charles Dimmock, the fourth interviewee, _____.

    a. is an army officer

    * b. used to be an army officer

    c. is going to be retired

6. Arthur Fuller's personality has made him _____.

    * a. shy but independent

    b. shy and dependent

    c. good at making friends

B. Provide as much information as possible about the following people with the help of what you hear on the tape.

1. Jane Smith:
   a. (a secretary)
   b. (good at her job)
   c. (different in her private life)
   d. (pretty tidy in office)
   e. (incoherent in her behaviour)

2. Chris Bonner:
   a. (concerned about state affairs)
   b. (critical of the political system)
   c. (eager to bring law and order to his country)

3. Tommy Finch:
   a. (easy-going)
   b. (a bit vicious when upset)
   c. (not sympathetic)
   d. (not interested in civil rights)

4. Charles Dimmock:
   a. (a retired army officer)
   b. (respectable and dignified)
   c. (helpful to those dependent on him)
   d. (a bit fanatic about organization and descipline)
   e. (not too polemic)
   f. (fond of his wife and family)

5. Arthur Fuller:
   a. (shy and unhappy during childhood)
   b. (unable to make friends till very late)
   c. (good at being by himself)
   d. (self-reliant and independent)

e. (fond of children)

Section Three:
Study Skills: Notetaking 2
Recognizing the Main Idea

Unless, for some reason, you wish to record every word that the lecturer says, you will have to select what to write down. You will naturally want to select the main points, and perhaps some subordinate or subsidiary points which relate to the main points. How does one recognize the main points?

Usually, the speaker will make it clear which ideas he wishes to emphasize by the way in which he presents them. In other words, the main ideas are cued. They are often cued by such semantic markers as:

I would like to emphasize . . .

The general point you must remember is . . .

It is important to note that . . .

I repeat that . . .

The next point is crucial to my argument . . .

Let's move on to another matter . . .

My next point is . . .

Another problem to be discussed is . . .

A related area would be . . .

Very often speakers list their main points.

Other ways in which lecturers may cue their main points while speaking are by emphasis or repetition; or perhaps by visual display (e.g. by putting headings on a blackboard, overhead projector etc).

Sometimes you will find that facial expression and gestures of the lecturer point up his meaning (of course, you will not see these

259

if you are crouched over your notes, scribbling away furiously!).

Often examples and points of lesser importance are also cued. The speaker may use such phrases as:

Let me give you some examples ...

For instance ...

I might add ...

To illustrate this point ...

Examples and points of lesser importance should be related briefly to the main headings.

Sometimes speakers will digress, i. e. mention things which have very little to do with their main topic, or relate to it only in a rather roundabout way. Speakers will sometimes digress deliberately in order to give more spice or variety to their lectures, or because the digression is interesting, amusing or topical. There is, of course, no need to note down digressions.

Digression markers are expressions like:

By the way ...

I might note in passing ...

Tapescript:

Recognizing the Main Idea

1. Bert is a natural listener. He can lose himself in conversation with friends or family. Bert has a few very close friends, and he works hard to keep his friendships strong.

2. One means of contact with friends is the regular exercise that Bert gets. He plays handball and swims with a friend twice a week. Besides that, he tries to stay in shape with morning exercises. Bert enjoys the exercise that he gets for its own sake as well as for the fact that it has kept him healthy all his life.

3. In general, Adam has very few hobbies. He used to enjoy collecting coins and reading, but now can never find enough time. He has practically no release from his job and usually brings some work home with him.

4. Like many modern Americans, neither man is very religious. Both belong to a church, but the religious services are not a sustaining part of their lives. But the difference in their spiritual make-up is nonetheless remarkable.

5. Adam does not enjoy much self-confidence. He has never spent the time to think problems through carefully or to teach himself to think about other things. As a result, he isn't a particularly creative problem solver. He spends quite a lot of time in compulsive, repetitive nervous activity which only frustrates him more.

6. Heart attack victims who have tried to change their behaviour after their first heart attack report that Type B behaviour has given them a new sense of peace, freedom, and happiness. Not for anything in the world would they return to their old lifestyle, which held them trapped like prisoners in an unhappy world of their own making.

Key to Exercises:

Recognizing the Main Idea

Listen to these paragraphs. Then decide what topic heading you would use to describe the main idea of each. Write the topic heading in the space given.

1. (Bert's friendship)
2. (Bert and sports)
3. (Adam's hobbies)
4. (the two men's religious belief)

5. (Adam – – not a creative problem solver)

6. (Heart attack victims enjoy Type B behaviour.)

Lesson 14

Section One:

Tapescript:

News Summary

Here is a summary of the news.

No general election yet says the Prime Minister.

Five people die in an earthquake in central Italy.

And £ 1/4 million is stolen from a security van.

In a speech in the city of London last night, the Prime Minister announced that there will be no general election in the near future. Talk of a quick election was pure speculation, she said. A general election would be held when it was in the best interests of the nation to do so.

In central Italy, several small towns and villages are still cut off by avalanches following the earthquake during the night which killed five people. It was central Italy's strongest earthquake for several years and hundreds of people have been made homeless. In Rome, as well as in Florence, Naples and Perugia, gas pipes were broken, windows shattered and electric cables thrown onto the streets.

Thieves got away with almost £ 1/4 million after a security van was ambushed in central London early this morning. The security van was rammed by a lorry as it was taking a short cut through a narrow street off Piccadilly. Three masked men then threatened the driver and his assistant with shotguns and forced one of them to unlock the van. The thieves made their escape in a car parked nearby. This car was later found abandoned in south London. The driver of the van and his assistant were badly shaken but not seriously hurt.

The flight recorder of the DC 10 airliner which crashed in the Antarctic a fortnight ago has shown that the plane was flying normally just before impact. All two hundred and fifty-seven people on board the aircraft died when it hit the side of a volcano. The investigation into what happened is still going on.

Voting is taking place today in the Euro-Constituency of London South-West. This by-election for the European Parliament is being held because of the death of the previous member, Mr Harold Friend. At the last election Mr Friend had a majority of 17,000 over his nearest opponent.

Talks on a formula for ending the strike at Independent Television get under way in London this afternoon. Looking forward to the meeting, the General Secretary of the Association of Cinematograph, Television and Allied Technicians, Mr Albert Tapper, said it was taking place on the basis of new proposals from the companies. He hoped it would lead to a basis for negotiations but he refused to speculate on the chances of success.

Fifteen people are to appear in court in Manchester today following disturbances on a train bringing football supporters back from matches in London. Eye witnesses report that the trouble began when groups of rival supporters whose teams had both been playing London clubs began to insult each other. After fighting had broken out police boarded the train just outside Manchester and arrests were made. British Rail have announced that they are considering withdrawing all soccer specials operating from Manchester.

Key to Exercises:

A. Summarize each of the following pieces of news in one sentence beginning with the words given.

1. No (general election in Britain in the near future).

2. In central Italy (an earthquake killed five people).

3. Thieves (stole a quarter of a million pounds).

4. Two hundred (and fifty-seven people were killed in an aircraft crash).

5. A by-election (was held in London).

6. Efforts (were made to end the strike at Independent Television).

7. Arrests (were made when a fight between football supporters of rival teams).

B. Choose the best answer (a, b or c) to complete each of the following statements.

1. The Prime Minister announced yesterday that here would be _____ in the near future.

    a. a quick election

  * b. no general election.

    c. a by-election

2. The earthquake in central Italy killed _____ people.

    a. hundreds of

    b. three

  * c. five

3. A quarter of a million pounds was stolen from a security van _____ London.

  * a. in central

    b. in south

c. southwest to

4. The thieves escaped with the money in _____.

   * a. a car parked nearby

     b. a lorry nearby

     c. a van passing by

5. The DC 10 airliner was flying _____ just before it crashed in the Antarctic.

     a. abnormally

     b. downward

   * c. normally

6. An election is being held for the European Parliament because _____.

   * a. the previous member, Mr Harold Friend died

     b. the previous member, Mr Harold Friend resigned

     c. Mr Harold Friend was defeated by his opponent

7. Those on strike at Independent Television have begun talks on a formula for _____ in London.

     a. expanding the strike

   * b. ending the strike

     c. winning the strike

8. Fighting broke out on a train to Manchester _____.

   * a. between football fans supporting rival teams

     b. between football players from rival teams

     c. between football supporters and the police

C. True or False Questions. Write a T in front of a statement if it is true according to the recording and write an F if it is false.

   1. (T) The Prime Minister said the date for general election would be set according to the interests of the nation.

2. (T) Both Naples and Rome were affected by the earthquake.

3. (F) The driver of the security van and his assistant were badly hurt by the masked thieves.

4. (F) The security van was forced to a stop by a car nearby in a narrow street off Piccadilly.

5. (F) At the last election for the European Parliament Mr. Friend had a majority of 70,000 over his nearest opponent.

6. (F) Mr. Albert Tapper was the General Secretary of the Association of Independent Television.

7. (F) Policemen got onto the train after the fight was over just outside Manchester.

8. (T) The fight might lead to the cancellation of all soccer specials operating from Manchester.

D. Complete the following statements with the information you hear on the tape.

1. (The Prime Minister) announced that there will be no general election in the near future.

2. (In central Italy) several small towns and villages are still cut off by (avalanches) following (the earthquake during the night).

3. (Three masked men) then threatened the driver and his assistant (with shotguns) and forced one of them to (unlock the van).

4. All (two hundred and fifty-seven people) on board the aircraft died when it (hit the side of a volcano).

5. He hoped it would lead to (a basis for negotiations) but he refused to speculate on (the chances of success).

6. (Fifteen people) are to appear (in court in Manchester) today

267

following disturbances on a train bringing football supporters
back from (matches in London).

Section Two:
Tapescript:
Task 1: Bearded Lady

Interviewer: Tell me Mrs Clark, how did you come to be a bearded
lady?

Mrs Clark: Well, it all began when I started growing a beard.

Interviewer: Mm ... and when was that exactly?

Mrs Clark: Just after my fourth birthday, I believe.

Interviewer: Really? As early as that? Didn't you see a doctor?

Mrs Clark: Oh, yes, my parents took me to dozens of specialists.

Interviewer: And what did they have to say?

Mrs Clark: They just told me to shave.

Interviewer: That's all the advice they could give? So you started
shaving?

Mrs Clark: Well, I was too young to be allowed to use a razor, and
electric razors weren't even thought of in those days, so my
dad used to shave me once a week before going to church on
Sundays.

Interviewer: And when did you stop shaving?

Mrs Clark: Oh, that would have been when I was around fifteen.
You see it was growing at an enormous rate, something like
five inches a day, I mean you could almost see it growing, and
it was so thick. I mean a razor or scissors were no use.

Interviewer: So you...let it grow?

Mrs Clark: Well, it was taking so much time trying to keep it down
and I was just wasting my time fighting a losing battle. So I

268

thought ... I'll just let it grow ... and that's when I came to work in the circus. I was spotted by a talent scout.

Interviewer: Do you ... ever cut your beard now?

Mrs Clark: Oh, yes every week I chop off a few feet. I have to cut it or I fall over it if I don't remember to wrap it around my waist.

Interviewer: (Laughs) What about the circus? How did you find it at first, being stared at all day?

Mrs Clark: Well, I must admit it was a bit un-nerving at first ... what with people gaping at you as though you were a goldfish in a bowl. I used to feel like saying. 'It's all right, dear, it's not that unusual, you know. It's only a bit of extra hair. It's not another head or something.' But you get used to the pointing and laughing in the end. Don't hardly notice it any more. Even the jokes don't upset me now. It's a bit boring in fact, after thirty years, just sitting here all day being stared at. But still there's always the breaks. and then the Ten Foot Woman and the Midget from next door come in for a cup of tea and a chat, that passes the time nicely.

Interviewer: Would you say there were any advantages to having a fifteen foot long beard?

Mrs Clark: Well, my husband says it keeps his toes warm on cold nights.

Task 2: At a Youth Centre

Paul: Anyone want another Coke or something?

James: I think we're all drinking Paul ... thanks just the same.

Darley: I was thinking ... What would you youngsters do without the youth centre? You'd be pretty lost wouldn't you.

Paul : Huh! It's all right I suppose. But I'm telling you ... we don't need no bloody youth club to find something to do. Me ... well ... I only come when there's a dance on. Them berks what come all the time... well... they need their heads examined. If I want to drink ... well there's the pub, isn't there.

Mrs Brent: But how old are you Paul? Sixteen? You can't drink in pubs − it's illegal.

Paul : No barman's ever turned me out yet. Any, way ... thanks for the drink. What about a dance, Denise?

Denise: I don't mind.

Paul: Come on then.

Finchley: Er ... Would you care to dance Mrs Brent?

Mrs Brent: Thank you ... but no. The music isn't of my generation. You know ... the generation gap. When I was young I'd never have dared speak as Paul just did. Especially with a clergyman present.

James: What sort of world do you think we live in Mrs Brent? It's part of my job to know people ... and especially young people ... as they are.

Mrs Brent: Please don't misunderstand me. I only thought it offensive. If my own son ...

James: Oh, I'm used to it. In a sense I feel it's a kind of compliment that ...

Darley: Compliment?

James: Don't get me wrong. Paul feels free to express himself with me just as he would with his friends. He accepts me as a kind of friend.

Finchley: And really the so-called generation gap is a myth you

270

know. Teenagers aren't really so different. As a teacher I find them quite traditional in their attitudes.

Darley: But look at the way they dress ... and their hair!

James: You haven't got the point I think. Those things are quite superficial. I agree with Mr Finchley ... Basically their attitudes are very similar to those of my generation.

Darley: So you approve of the kind of language we heard from Paul just now ...

James: Now I didn't say that. Anyway the concepts of 'approval' and 'disapproval' tend to over-simplify matters. Every generation creates its ... its own special language ... just as it creates its own styles in clothes and music.

Mrs Brent: It's just that ... er ... the styles and habits of today's teenagers are so ... well basically ... so unacceptable.

Finchley: You mean unacceptable to you.

Mrs Brent: No ... I mean unacceptable to the rest of society.

Darley: When you come to think of it ... I mean I'm always on at my boy about his clothes ...

James: So you find them unacceptable too.

Darley: No ... just let me finish. I was about to say that in fact his clothes are very practical ... very simple.

Finchley: Anyway ... the generation gap is non-existent. I mean ... the idea of teenagers ... of a teenage generation that ... which has rejected the values of its parents for a sort of mixture of violence and lethargy ... well ... it's totally unrealistic.

Mrs Brent: I do wish you had a teenage son or daughter of your own, Mr Finchley.

Finchley: But I have more contact with them ...

Mrs Brent: I'm not implying that you have no understanding of

271

their problems.

Finchley: My contact with them ... as a teacher of English ... is close. You see we have regular discussions ... and they very often carry on after school and here at the youth centre. You'd find them interesting. You could come and sit in sometime if you like.

Darley: That'd be interesting.

Mrs Brent: I'd be too embarrassed to say anything.

Finchley: I don't mean there's any need for you to take part in the discussion. Just listen. And you'd realize I think just how traditional their attitudes are.

James: For example?

Finchley: For example ... you probably wouldn't think so but the majority have ... a firm belief in marriage ... and in the family.

Darley: Those are things I've never talked about with my boy.

Finchley: And one very clear ... very notable thing is that they're always looking for opportunities to help others ...

Mrs Brent: Well, Tony doesn't help much in the house ...

Finchley: ... to help others that is who really need help. Not just helping with the washing-up, Mrs Brent. Anyway ... another point that's come out of the discussions is that nearly all of them — about 90 per cent I should say — get on well with their parents.

Mrs Brent: Oh but I ...

Finchley: Most disagreements seem to be over hair and general appearance.

James: And we've called those superficial.

Finchley: Exactly.

272

Darley: I like the idea of sitting in on a discussion. I'll take you up on that.

Finchley: Fine. And Mrs Brent. As you would find it embarrassing ...

Mrs Brent: Well I ... I didn't really mean embarrassing. It's just that ... you know ...

Finchley: There's a book you ought to read ... published by The National Children's Bureau. It's called Britain's Sixteen-Year-Olds. I'll lend you my copy.

Mrs Brent: That's very kind of you. Look, I'd better be going. From the way my son's dancing he'll be at it all night.

Darley: Have you got a car, Mrs Brent?

Mrs Brent: No. There's a bus.

Darley: Then please let me give you a lift.

Mrs Brent: I wouldn't want to take you out of your way.

Darley: Not at all. Anyway ... we have to take an example from the youngsters don't we. Helping those in need I mean ... Well ... we'll say good night ...

Voices: Good night.

Key to Exercises:

Task 1: Bearded Lady

A. Answer the following question briefly.

    1. What is special of Mrs. Clark?

        Answer: She was a bearded woman.

    2. What advice did all those specialists offer her?

        Answer: They advised her to shave.

    3. When did she decide to let her beard grow?

        Answer: When she realized that she was fighting a losing

battle.

4. What was it like being stared at all day?

   Answer: At first it was a bit unnerving.

5. Is there any advantage of her beard?

   Answer: Her beard keeps her husband's toes warm on cold nights.

B. True or False Questions. Write a T in front of a statement if it is true according to the recording and write an F if it is false.

1. (F) Mrs. Clark started growing beard at age of 5.

2. (F) Her father used electric razor to shave her on Sundays.

3. (T) She stopped shaving when she was around fifteen.

4. (T) Her beard grew too fast for her to shave.

5. (T) Sometimes she has to wrap her beard around her waist in case she should fall over it.

6. (F) She has been in the circus for about thirteen years.

7. (T) The Ten Food Woman and the Midget are members of the circus.

8. (F) Mrs. Clark's beard is fifty foot long.

C. Complete the following sentences with what you hear on the tape.

1. You see it was growing (at an enormous rate), something like (five inches) a day.

2. It was taking so much time (trying to keep it down) and I was just wasting my time (fighting a losing battle).

3. Oh, yes, every week I (chop off a few feet).

4. But you get used to (the pointing and laughing in the end).

Task 2: At a Youth Centre

A. Choose the best answer (a, b or c) to complete each of the following statements.

1. This discussion takes place _____.
   * a. at a youth centre
   b. at a pub
   c. at a night club

2. It is likely that James is _____.
   a. a teacher
   b. a waiter
   * c. a clergyman

3. Most of those involved in the discussion must _____.
   * a. be of the same generation
   b. be of two different generations
   c. be classmates

4. Mr. Finchley _____.
   * a. a teacher of English
   b. a clergyman
   c. a social worker

5. According to Finchley and James, most disagreements between the old and the young seem to _____.
   a. be over hair and general appearance
   b. be superficial
   * c. Both a and b

6. The whole discussion is on _____.
   a. children
   * b. generation gap
   c. hair and dress style

B. Give a list of things that are "unacceptable" to the older people.

a. (drinking under the age of sixteen)

b. (music at the dance ball)

c. (language they use)

d. (their hair and clothes)

C. True and False Questions. Write a T in front of a statement if it is true according to the recording and write an F if it is false.

1. (F) Paul often comes to the Youth Centre to find something to do.

2. (T) It is illegal to sell alcohol to Paul because he is only 16.

3. (T) Mrs. Brent doesn't like the way Paul talks to adults.

4. (F) James thinks that Paul is offensive.

5. (T) Actually the teenager generation has rejected the values of its parents for a mixture of violence and legarthy.

6. (F) Teenagers' helping others means helping those who are doing washing-up.

D. Complete the following statements with what you hear on the tape.

1. No barman's ever (turned me out) yet.

2. Don't get me (wrong).

3. I'm always (on at my boy about) his clothes.

4. But I have more contact (with) them.

5. I don't mean (there's any need) for you to (take part in) the discussion.

6. I like the idea of (sitting in on) a discussion. I'll (take you up on) that.

7. I wouldn't want to (take you out of your way).

276

E. Answer the following questions briefly.

   1. Why does Mrs. Brent refuse to dance?

      Answer: Because she does not think the music played in the
           hall is of her generation.

   2. Why does Finchley say that the so-called generation gap is on-
     ly a myth?

      Answer: Because he believes the young people are quite tradi-
           tional in their attitudes and they are not that differ-
           ent from the old generation.

   3. How does James explain the seemingly different language
     used by the young people?

      Answer: He believes that every generation creates its own
           special language as well as its own styles in clothes
           and music.

   4. Why does Finchley suggest Mrs. Brent to read a book entitled
     Britain's Sixteen-Year-Olds?

      Answer: Because he hopes Mrs Brent to have a better under-
           standing of the young people.

Section Three:

Tapescript:

Recognizing the Main Idea

1. How was trade conducted, then, without money to pay for
goods? The answer is by bartering. Bartering is the process by
which trade takes place through the exchange of goods. Money
is not used as payment. Instead, one good is traded for another
good.

2. As trade became more common as a result of people's interdepen-

dence upon one another, it was necessary to develop or invent a more convenient method of payment. Consequently, a new form of exchange medium, money, was introduced into society.

3. Of course, the evolution from a total barter society to one that was totally monetized didn't occur overnight. In fact, today there are still societies that are not monetized, although they account for an insignificant amount of world trade. In the interim between a barter world and a monetized world, both systems operated together.

4. As I stated earlier, money has a specific value, but due to certain conditions, the money — or currency, as money is referred to — of some countries is more valuable than that of other countries.

5. It is difficult to give examples of barter deals because in most cases the terms of the contract are in disclosed. In some cases, we don't hear about barter transactions simply because they work so well. If one company has arranged a profitable exchange, it will be very quiet about it so that its competitors will not come in and try to make a better deal.

6. It is unlikely that the world will revert to a totally barter-oriented existence, but until the economic disorder that's present in today's world is remedied, bartering will probably become increasingly important as an exchange medium.

Key to Exercises:
Recognizing the Main Idea
Listen to these paragraphs. Then decide what topic heading you would use to describe the main idea of each. Write the topic heading in the space given.

1. (trading without money — barter)

2. (how money came)
3. (shifting from barter society to a monetized world)
4. (different money values in different countries)
5. (why difficult to give examples of barter deals)
6. (prospect of bartering)

Lesson 15

Section One:

Tapescript:

Task 1: Capital Punishment

A: Did you hear on the news today about that ... uh ... murderer who was executed?

B: I can't believe it.

A: Yeah. That's the first time in ten years that they've used capital punishment.

B: I just can't believe in our society today that they would actually kill another human being. Nobody has the right to take another person's life.

A: Oh, I don't agree. Listen, I think capital punishment is – it's about time it came back. I think that's exactly what killers deserve.

B: No, they don't deserve that. Because once you're killing a killer, you're the killer, too. You become a killer as well.

A: No, listen. You take a life, you have to be willing to give up your own. And also, I think that if you have a death penalty it will prevent other people from killing. I think it's a good deterrent.

B: I don't think it's a good deterrent at all. My goodness gracious. I mean, first of all, are you sure the person you've convicted to death is really guilty?

280

A: Well, I think that's a very rare ... very rare incidence.

B: I don't think it's rare, (I don't think it's ...) with all the crackerjack lawyers we have today, (Well, no ... I ...) and the judicial system the way it is.

A: I think it's a rare incidence, and I think it's more important to get rid of the ... the bad seed, you know?

B: But you don't get rid of it. You rehabilitate somebody like that. (Oh ...) You don't eliminate, you rehabilitate.

A: Listen, studies show that criminals are never really rehabilitated. When they're ... when they come out of prison they just go back to a life of crime, and they're hardened by that crime.

B: Because the rehabilitation process has to be more than just what's in jail. I mean, (Oh ... well.) when you're in jail you do have to work, but when you're out of jail there has to be an extensive program. We have to expand on the idea till it works.

A: I don't agree. Listen — and, anyway, the jails and the prisons are already very crowded, and we have to pay, the taxpayers. Our money goes to maintaining murderers' (I ...) lives.

B: I agree with you. That's why it's important to look at the problem on a much larger scale. The real problem is a social problem. (What ... noo ...) There are other problems that cause people to kill. Look at poverty, drugs, discrimination.

A: Some people are just bad. They're just evil and there's nothing you can do.

B: No, there ... it is ... no, it isn't true. There's rehabilitation. (No.) And they ... we're all responsible it ... for ... to humanity. That's one of the reasons ...

A: Well, but in the meantime you have to take care of the people who have already committed ...

B: I agree with you there.

A: Preventative is different, but ...

B: I agree with you there.

Task 2: A New Way of Life

Announcer: On 'TV Magazine' tonight we're looking at people who have given up regular jobs and high salaries to start a new way of life. First of all, we have two interviews with people who decided to leave the 'rat race'. Nicola Burgess spoke to them.

Nicola: This is the Isle of Skye. Behind me you can see the croft belonging to Daniel and Michelle Burns, who gave up their jobs to come to this remote area of Scotland. Daniel was the sales manager of Hi-Vita, the breakfast cereal company, and Michelle was a successful advertising executive. Michelle, can you tell us what made you give up everything to come here?

Michelle: Everything? That's a matter of opinion. A big house and two cars isn't everything! Dan and I both used to work long hours. We had to leave so early in the morning and we came home so late at night, that we hardly ever saw each other. We should have come here years ago, but we were earning such big salaries that we were afraid to leave our jobs. In the end we had so little time together that our marriage was breaking up. So two years ago, we took a week's holiday in the Scottish Highlands. We saw this place and we both fell in love with it. It was for sale, and we liked it so much that we decided to give up our jobs, and here we are!

Nicola: How do you earn a living? If you don't mind me asking.

Michelle: We don't need very much. We keep sheep and goats,

282

grow our own vegetables. We've got a few chickens. It's a very simple life, and we're not in it for profit. We're still so busy that we work from five in the morning until eight at night, but we're together. We're happier than we're ever been and we're leading a natural life.

Nicola: There must be some things you miss, surely.

Michelle: I don't know. We knew such a lot of people in London, but they weren't real friends. We see our neighbours occasionally and there's such a lot to do on the farm that we don't have time to feel lonely. At least we see each other now.

Nicola: The motor-bike I'm sitting on is a very special one. Special because it's been all the way round the world. It belongs to Luke Saunders, who has just returned to England after a three-year motor-cycle journey. Luke, what led you to leave your job and make this trip?

Luke: I worked in a car factory on the assembly line. All I had to do was put four nuts on the bolts that hold the wheels on. It's done by robots now, and a good thing too! The job was so routine that I didn't have to think at all. I bought this Triumph 750 cc bike second-hand, fitted two panniers on the back and just set off for Australia.

Nicola: What did you do for money?

Luke: I had a bit of money to start with, but of course it didn't last long and I had to find work where I could. I've done so many different things – picked fruit, washed up, worked as a mechanic.

Nicola: How did people react to you? In India, for example.

Luke: Everywhere I went, the people were so friendly that problems seemed to solve themselves. There was such a lot of interest in the bike that it was easy to start a conversation. You know, often you can communicate without really knowing the language.

Nicola: Did you ever feel like giving up, turning round and coming home?

Luke : Only once, in Bangladesh. I became so ill with food poisoning that I had to go to hospital. But it didn't last long.

Nicola: You've had such an exciting time that you'll find it difficult to settle down, won't you?

Luke: I'm not going to. Next week I'm off again, but this time I'm going in the opposite direction! See you in about three years' time!

Key to Exercises:

A. Choose the best answer (a, b or c) for each of the following questions.

1. What causes the two women's discussion on capital punishment?

* a. The execution.

  b. The report of a murderer.

  c. The function of judicial system.

2. Why does one of the women thinks that killing a killer is not justified?

  a. Because the killer doesn't have to be killed.

  b. Because the crime is not very serious.

* c. Because once you're killing a killer, you become a killer as well.

3. What, according to one of them, is more important than punishment?

a. Life.

* b. Rehabilitation.

c. Elimination.

4. What are the problems that cause people to kill according to one of the women?

a. Poverty and drugs.

b. Discrimination.

* c. Both a and b.

B. True or False Questions. Write a T in front of a statement if it is true according to the recording and write an F if it is false.

1. (F) The two speakers agree with each other on everything.

2. (T) Capital punishment has not been used for ten years.

3. (T) One of the speakers doubts if the person sentenced to death is really guilty.

4. (F) When criminals come out of prison, they never go back to a life of crime.

5. (T) Prisons are very crowded.

C. Give a list of viewpoints that Speakers A and B hold respectively.

A

a. (Killers deserve death penalty.)

b. (Death penalty will preveut other people from killing.)

c. (It is important to get rid of the bad seed.)

d. (Criminals are never rehabilitated, they are hardened.)

e. (Some people are just bad, evil, and there is nothing one can do.)

B

a. (Nobody has the right to take another person's life.)

b. (Nobody is sure that the person convicted is really guilty.)

c. (Criminals should be rehabilitated instead of being eliminated.)

d. (There should be more extensive programmes.)

e. (It is a social problem. We and society are responsible.

D. Answer the following questions.

1. Why doesn't the second speaker believe that we are sure the person convicted is really guilty?

Answer: Because she has doubts on the lawyers and the judicial system today.

2. Why doesn't the first speaker trust the present rehabilitation program?

Answer: Because studies show that criminals are never rehabilitated.

3. What does the second speaker suggest to improve the rehabilitation program?

Answer: She suggests to expand the programme to an extensive one.

4. What are the two reasons given by the first speaker for not keeping murderers in jail?

Answer: (1) The jails and prisons are already crowded.

(2) The toxpayers have to pay to maintain murderers' lives.

Task 2: A New Way of Life

A. Answer the following questions briefly.

1. Who are being interviewed?

Answer: Michelle Burns and Luke Saunders.

2. What's special about them?

Answer: They have given up regular jobs and high salaries and begun a new way of life.

3. Why did Michelle and her husband decide to come to live in a remote area of Scotland?

Answer: Because they had worked long hours and had hardly seen each other. As a result, their marriage was breaking up.

4. How do they make a living now?

Answer: They raise sheep and goats, grow their own vegetables, and they have some chickens.

5. What is unusual of Mr. Luke Saunders?

Answer: He's been a three-year motor-cycle journey round the world.

6. What did Luke do before his journey?

Answer: He had been a car factory worker on the assembly line.

7. What did he do for money?

Answer: He had a bit of money to start with, then he began to do odd jobs like picking fruit, washing up, etc.

8. What is he going to do how?

Answer: He's going to start a new journey in the opposite direction. And he'll be away for three years again.

B. True or False Questions. Write a T in front of a statement if it is true according to the recording and write an F if it is false.

1. (F) Daniel and Michelle Burns gave up their jobs just because they felt underpaid.

2. (T) Daniel used to be a sales manager and Michelle an ad-

vertising executive.

3. (F) According to Michelle, a big house and two cars mean everything in life.

4. (F) They found this Scottish croft through advertisement.

5. (F) They raise all sorts of animals for money.

6. (T) Living a natural life in the country makes them happy.

7. (T) When he was a factory worker, Luke had to do monotonous work every day.

8. (F) People abroad were uncooperative and Luke had to try hard to solve problems.

9. (T) Luke had friendly relationship with people abroad. He could communicate with them without knowing their language.

10. (F) He had to go to hospital once in India.

C. Complete the following statements with what you hear on the tape.

1. We have two interviews with people who decided to (leave the 'rat race'.

2. We saw this place and we both (fell in love with) it.

3. It's a very simple life, and we're not (in it for profit).

4. There's such a lot to do (on the farm) that we don't have time to (feel lonely).

5. All I had to do was put (four nuts on the bolts) that hold the wheel on.

6. Did you ever feel like (giving up), and (turning round) and (coming hme)?

Section Two:

Tapescript:

Task 1: The Work of Sigmund Freud

Here is an extract from a radio talk on the work of Sigmund Freud by Professor Eric Watkis:

Sigmund Freud developed his system of psychoanalysis while he was studying cases of mental illness. By examining details of the patient's life, he found that the illness could often be traced back to some definite problem or conflict within the person concerned. But he discovered, too, that many of the neuroses observed in mentally ill patients were also present, to a lesser degree, in normal persons. This led him to the realization that the borderline between the normal and the neurotic person is not nearly as clearly marked as was once believed.

In 1914 he published a book called *The Psychopathology of Everyday Life*. This book goes a long way towards explaining some of the strange behaviour of normal, sane people.

A glance at Freud's chapter headings will indicate some of the aspects of behaviour covered by the book:

Forgetting of proper names

Forgetting of foreign words

Childhood and concealing memories

Mistakes in speech

Mistakes in reading and writing

Broadly, Freud demonstrates that there are good reasons for many of the slips and errors that we make. We forget a name because, unconsciously, we do not wish to remember that name. We repress a childhood memory because that memory is painful to us. A slip of the tongue or of the pen betrays a wish or a thought of which we are ashamed.

In these days when every would-be-doctor or writer has access to Freud's accounts of his research, it is worth pausing and remembering the remarkable scope and originality of his ideas.

Task 2: Cheese

Cheese is one of those foods that we tend to take for granted as always having been with us, and it's odd to think that someone somewhere must have discovered the process that takes place when micro-organisms get into milk and bring about changes in its physical and biochemical structure.

Obviously, we don't know who discovered the process, but it's thought that it came from south-west Asia about 8,000 years ago.

Early cheese was probably rather unpalatable stuff, tasteless and bland in the case of the so-called 'fresh cheeses', which are eaten immediately after the milk has coagulated, and rough-tasting and salty in the case of the 'ripened' cheeses, which are made by adding salt to the soft fresh cheese and allowing other biochemical processes to continue so that a stronger taste and a more solid texture result.

The ancient Romans changed all that. They were great pioneers in the art of cheese-making, and the different varieties of cheese they invented and the techniques for producing them spread with them to the countries they invaded. This dissemination of new techniques took place between about 60 BC and 300 AD. You can still trace their influence in the English word 'cheese', which comes ultimately from the Latin word 'caseus', that's C-A-S-E-U-S.

Well, things went on quietly enough after the Roman period with the cheese producers in the different countries getting on with developing their own specialities. It's amazing the variety of flavours you can get from essentially the same process.

At this stage in history, people weren't aware in a scientific way of the role of different micro-organisms and enzymes in producing different types of cheese. But they knew from experience that if you kept your milk or your 'pre-cheese' mixture at a certain temperature or in a certain environment, things would turn out in a certain way. The Roquefort caves in France are an example of a place that was used for centuries for the ripening of a certain sort of cheese, before people knew exactly why they produced the effect they did.

In the nineteenth century, with the increasing knowledge about micro-organisms, there came the next great step forward in cheese-making. Once it was known exactly which micro-organisms were involved in the different stages of producing a cheese, and how the presence of different micro-organisms affected the taste, it was possible to introduce them deliberately, and to industrialize the process.

Cheese started being made on a large scale in factories, although the small producer working from his farm dairy continued to exist and still exist today. Cheese-making moved very much into the world of technology and industrial processes, although, because the aim is still to produce something that people like to eat, there's still an important role for human judgement. People still go round tasting the young cheese at different stages to see how it's getting on, and may add a bit of this or that to improve the final taste. Whatever the scale of production, there is still room for art alongside the technology.

Key to Exercises:

Task 1: The Work of Sigmund Freud

A. Choose the best answer (a, b or c) to complete each of the following statements.

    1. This radio talk is delivered by _____.

        a. a radio announcer

        b. Sigmund Freud

    * c. Eric Watkis

    2. Sigmund Freud developed his system of _____ while he was studying cases of _____.

    * a. psychoanalysis; mental illness

        b. psychoanalysis; memory illness

        c. psychology; mental illness

    3. *The Psychopathology of Everyday Life* was published in _____.

        a. 1940

    * b. 1914

        c. 1904

B. Give a list of the chapter headings of Freud's *The Psychopathology of Everyday Life*. (at least four of them).

    a. (Forgetting of proper names)

    b. (Forgetting of foreign words)

    c. (Childhood and concealing memories)

    d. (Mistakes in speech)

    e. (Mistakes in reading and writing)

C. Complete the following statements according to what you hear on the tape.

292

1. By examining details of the patient's life, he found that the illness could often (be traced back to) some definite (problem or conflict) within the person (concerned).

2. But he discovered, too, that many (of the neuroses) observed in mentally ill patients were (also present), to a lesser degree, (in normal persons).

3. This led him to the realization that (the borderline) between (the normal and the neurotic person) is not (nearly as clearly marked) as was once believed.

4. We repress (a childhood memory) because that memory is (painful to us).

5. Freud demonstrates that there are (good reasons for) many of (the slips and errors) we make.

Task 2: Cheese
A. Choose the best answer (a, b or c) to complete each of the following statements.
  1. The passage is about _____.
  * a. the history of cheese-making
    b. cheese-making
    c. the history of cheese
  2. Cheese _____.
    a. was made originally in Europe between 60 BC and 300 AD
  * b. was introduced from South-West Asia 8,000 years ago
    c. was introduced from France in the nineteenth century
  3. _____ were great pioneers in the art of cheese - making.
  * a. Romans
    b. South - West Asians

c. Frenchmen in the Roquefort canes

4. In cheese – making, _____ play an essential role.
   a. biochemicals
   b. salt and water
 * c. micro – organisms

B. True or False Questions. Write a T in front of a statement if it is true according to the recording and write an F if it is false.

1. (T) Cheese is one of the most popular foods in daily life.
2. (F) Early cheese was rather delicious and tasty like fresh cheese.
3. (T) In order to make cheese stronger in taste and more solid in texture, salt is added to the soft fresh cheese and other biochemical processes are allowed to continue.
4. (T) Romans spread the techniques for producing cheese to the countries they invaded.
5. (T) If you keep your milk or per-cheese mixture at a certain temperature or in a certain environment, things will turn out in a certain way.
6. (F) In the nineteenth century, people still didn't know much about which micro-organisms were involved in the different stages of producing cheese.
7. (T) The presence of different micro-organisms affect the taste of cheese.
8. (T) In terms of final taste, human performance still matters much even though cheese-making processes have become industrialized and developed with technology.

C. Answer the following questions.

1. What was early cheese probably like?

   Answer: Early cheese was probably rather unpalatable and tasteless.

2. What is 'fresh cheese'?

   Answer: 'Fresh cheese' is a kind of cheese to be eaten immediately after the milk has coagulated.

3. What is 'ripened cheese'?

   Answer: 'Ripened cheese' is a kind of cheese with salt added to the soft fresh cheese and other biochemical processes continued in the course of cheese-making.

4. What is the origin of the English word 'cheese'?

   Answer: The Latin word 'caseus'.

5. When did people begin to realize the role of micro-organisms and enzymes in producing different types of cheese?

   Answer: In the nineteenth century.

6. What did people do to make cheeses of different taste before the discovery of micro-organisms?

   Answer: People kept milk at different temperatures and in various environments.

Section Three:

Tapescript:

Recognizing the Main Idea

1. All cultures change, even modern ones. As a matter of fact, change occurs most rapidly in modern cultures, since science brings us so many new discoveries every day. It is rather difficult to follow these changes clearly, since they happened so fast. The civilization that I'll discuss today is easier to observe.

2. No formal history was written for these early Indians, but Navajo

Indians who came along later found evidence of their great civilization. The Navajos called these prehistoric people 'the Anasazi', which means 'the Ancient Ones'.

3. Descendants of the Anasazi still live in the Southwest, and many aspects of their culture are similar to ancient times. Today these people are called Pueblo Indians.

4. There are four different time periods in the development of the Anasazi. Scientists have looked for the one most important theme in this story, a kind of unifying idea to organize all the facts. The most critical and influential improvement in their lives was the way they used containers to cook, store, and carry food and water.

5. The most important job of the man in this society was to learn, teach, and perform the religious ceremonies associated with farming. Women worked in the fields and prepared all the food. women also wove baskets out of yucca fibers.

6. We don't know what the final problem was. It might have been enemy attack, sickness, lack of rain, or over-farmed soil. But in the year 1300 the last of the Anasazi left the cliff dwellings, never to return again. They left behind their beautiful pueblos, which still stand as a monument to them.

Key to Exercises:

Recognizing the Main Idea

Listen to these paragraphs. Then decide what topic heading you would use to describe the main idea of each. Write the topic heading in the space given.

1. (why all cultures change)
2. (the origin of the name 'Anasazi')

296

3. (descendents of the Anasazi)
4. (the theme that unifies the historical development of the Anasazi)
5. (labor distribution of the Anasazi)
6. (the end of the Anasazi)

Supplementary Reading:

1. Capital Punishment

Capital punishment is the infliction of the death penalty on persons convicted of a crime. As ideas about what crimes should be punishable by death have differed, so have the methods of inflicting this penalty. The criminal has been hanged, burned, boiled in oil, thrown to wild beasts, frayed alive, drowned, crushed, crucified, stoned, impaled, strangled, torn apart, beheaded, smothered, disemboweled, shot, gassed, or electrocuted.

Debate on the Value of Capital Punishment.

Arguments about the philosophy of punishment and its methods are largely meaningless unless presented in terms of a particular culture. The following discussion applies principally to the countries of Western civilization, especially the English-speaking countries.

Proponents and opponents of capital punishment argue in terms of its deterrent, retributive, economic, and socially protective effectiveness.

Deterrence. The most frequently advanced and widely accepted argument in favour of capital punishment is that fear of death deters people from committing crimes. Opponents contend that any fear of the death penalty is greatly reduced by the decrease in the number of jurisdictions using it, by the uncertainty of detection, the long delays in court procedures, and the unwillingness of many juries to convict in cases where the death penalty is mandatory, by the decline in the number of executions, and by the nonpublic nature of executions. They argue that statistical studies, although not conclusive, indicate that the use of the death penalty has no significant effect on either the frequency of capital crimes or the safety of law-enforcement officers, and that the humanitarianism of modern society would probably defeat any effort to increase the use of capital punishment.

Proponents of capital punishment not only point to the inconclusiveness of statistical studies but also emphasize that the deterrent influence of the death penalty does not depend merely on the fear it may engender. By attaching this penalty to certain crimes, the law exerts a positive moral influence in the educational process. By strongly stigmatizing these acts, the law helps to develop attitudes of disgust and even horror for them. Further, proponents insist that the deterrent influence of the death penalty reaches across state lines into jurisdictions that have abolished it, and so all are benefited by its continued use in some areas.

Retribution. In favour of capital punishment, it has been insisted that the criminal should die because he has perpetrated a horrible crime, and that only his execution will satisfy the public and prevent it from taking the law into its own hands. Opponents of the death penalty argue that all the evidence points to the opposite conclusion. Many jurisdictions have abolished capital punishment; many others have reduced the number of capital offences; and everywhere authorities have sought to make the method of execution as swift and painless as possible. Opponents also say that studies show no positive correlation between illegal lynchings for revenge and the elimination of the death penalty.

298

The proponents of capital punishment argue that retribution should not be construed as revenge. The almost universal desire for revenge must be kept in check and regulated in modern society by legal retribution if order is to be maintained. Retribution functions interrelatedly with reformation and deterrence, both of which must be expressed in terms of society's moral code. The principal function of retribution is to support this code and thus help unify society against those who violate it. In supporting the moral code, this argument continues, retribution increases the effectiveness of reformation and deterrence.

The law exacts retribution by attaching a penalty to each crime according to its seriousness as measured by the moral code. Thus, explain the proponents, the value of the life of the criminal, as measured by the moral code, may be less than such values as the security of the state, the sanctity of the home, or the life of the innocent victim. The law has always recognized the necessity of such a choice, and justifies killing in self-defence, in he prevention of a felony, in the lawful arrest of a felon, or in war against the enemies of a state. Indeed, proponents contend, not to kill in these cases would jeopardize the welfare of society. Just as the individual has the right and duty to kill to protect himself, so the state has the right and duty to take the life of a criminal to protect greater values, according to this argument.

Proponents further argue that there is no substitute for the death penalty in giving retribution its maximum effectiveness. Life imprisonment, usually advanced as a substitute, can readily be converted into early parole. Thus the malefactor may soon come to see no difference between the breaking of a window and the fracturing of another's skull. What often parades as humanitarianism is merely public indifference to dealing with delinquents and criminals. Such public lethargy endangers the moral code. Opponents, however, say that the limited enforcement of the death penalty has little effect on upholding the moral code.

Economy. Some proponents of capital punishment argue that it is cheaper to execute a prisoner than to keep him in an institution for life or a long term. Opponents insist that it is increasingly expensive to enforce the death penalty. Since a large segment of the public is against capital punishment, juries are more and more reluctant to convict those who may receive this penalty. For those who are convicted, the commonly used process of appealing the decision is costly to the state. Further, a prisoner committed to an institution may be able to support himself and his dependents and make restitution to his victim or to the surviving relatives. Moreover, say the opponents, the economic argument if carried further might be applied to all prisoners who are not self-supporting. If the argument is valid, all prisoners should be executed to save the taxpayer the expense of institutionalizing them. When extended this far, opponents contend, the absurdity of the economic argument becomes obvious.

Protection. A fourth argument in favour of capital punishment is that it protects society from dangerous criminals by ensuring that they will neither repeat their crimes nor pass on undesirable hereditary traits to their offspring. Opponents, however, adduce the following arguments: (1) The improvement of institutional rehabilitation programs and probation and parole procedures could reduce the possibility of sending dangerous persons back into the community. (2) People who commit noncapital offences and are not executed may also have mental and physical defects, and the existence of such defects may not be related in any way to the causation of crime. (3)

300

Mental and physical defects may be caused either by heredity or environment, and in many cases scientists are not able to determine the cause. (4) Many persons who are apparently normal may carry recessive defective genes and have defective children. Therefore, even if all persons who have hereditary defects could be identified and killed, the next generation would still have a new group of defective individuals. (5) Only a very small percentage of all criminals are executed, and, again, the number is declining. (6) The wealth, education, or social position of the accused, rather than his potential threat to society, may determine whether he receives the death penalty, and therefore the penalty can be, and indeed has been, applied arbitrarily. Moreover, society sometimes executes persons who are entirely innocent. Proponents agree that such an occurrence should be guarded against but argue that the possibility of executing innocent persons should not blind people to the important protective and retributive effect of the death penalty on persons of criminal intent.

The opponents of capital punishment have achieved some notable victories in recent decades. The death penalty, however, remains in the laws of most jurisdictions throughout the world. Apparently public opinion still strongly supports its use, at least for those crimes that are considered to offer the most serious threat to society.

2. Sigmund Freud (1856 – 1939)

It was not until modern times that medical men began studying the human mind. The great pioneer in these studies was Sigmund Freud. His theories on the workings of the human mind led to totally new ways of treating mental illness.

Sigmund Freud was born on May 6, 1856, in Freiberg, Moravia (now Pribor, Czechoslovakia). He was the son of a wool merchant. When Sigmund was 4, his father moved to Vienna, Austria, in the hopes of earning a better living. Sigmund missed being able to play outside around Freiberg. But as he grew older he found new pleasures in reading and in studies. He became a brilliant student, first in his class for the last 6 years of school. During these years Sigmund often ate his dinner in his room so that his work would not be interrupted. Throughout his life he continued to work with the same deep interest.

As a young man Freud was unsure what he wanted to be. He entered the University of Vienna to study medicine when he was 17. But he studied and did research in many of the life sciences besides his medical work. Although Freud was extremely poor, he was able to study for 8 years. He earned some money by translating and by teaching. He was also lent money by friends and teachers who liked him and saw his ability. In 1881 Freud received his degree in medicine. but even then he was not sure he wanted to practice. For a while he went back to research he had been doing on nerve cells.

By this time, however, Freud had become engaged to Martha Bernays. He saw that he could not support a family by doing research. Finally he decided to earn his living as a doctor. When he married in 1886, he was still poor. He and his bride had difficulty finding money to furnish their first apartment. But their life together was a happy one. Freud lived and worked in Vienna for the next 52 years. His six children were born and raised there.

Before his marriage Freud had spent time in Paris studying nerve and brain diseases under J. M. Charcot (1825 - 93). Charcot treated many patients who were partially paralysed. Paralysis usually means that a muscle cannot move. This occurs when a nerve fails to carry signals to make the muscle move. The muscle is paralysed because a nerve is damaged or out of order.

Freud began to believe there was a mental cause for some of these illnesses. That is, he thought some paralyses might be caused by a state of mind and not by any bodily illness.

When Freud returned to Vienna, he went to work as a doctor, treating nerve and brain diseases. Some of his patients were like ones he had seen in Paris. Parts of their bodies were paralysed. Sometimes Freud could find no bodily cause for this. He decided these illnesses might very well be mental. Other patients turned out to have little wrong with them. Freud realized that what these patients really wanted was someone to talk to. They had problems in their daily lives that were bothering them.

As Freud worked with these patients he came to believe that mental illness could be traced to childhood fears. A child might see or hear something too frightening to think about. Yet the memory could stay hidden in the mind. It could worry the person later in life − − especially when something similar happened. The result could be mental illness.

Freud got patients to talk about anything that crossed their minds. He noticed things that bothered them and analysed what they said. Then he was able to help patients remember past experiences. Once a person remembered a frightening experience, he could begin to understand it. With understanding, the patient could improve. Freud's method is called psychoanalysis.

Freud got results; many of his patients did improve after psychoanalysis. However, his new method was criticized. Other doctors could not get used to Freud's new ideas. They refused to believe that there might be a mental cause for illness.

Freud expressed his ideas in many books and scientific papers. One of the most famous of his books attempted to explain the meaning of dreams. These writings were often attacked by other doctors. They claimed that psychoanalysis was nonsense and that their older methods were better. But Freud worked on. It was not his way to argue. Instead he kept working and published reports on his work. In time other doctors realized he was right.

Freud was a determined man with great belief in the usefulness of his work. Gradually these qualities gained him followers among doctors.

His followers treated many patients over the years. They developed ideas of their own about mental illness. Many of these doctors, who came from different countries, decided to meet in 1908. Thus they could exchange views on psychoanalysis. This meeting was the first International Congress of Psychoanalysis. Some of Freud's followers later left him and branched out on their own. But all admitted that Freud's idea was right − − there can be a purely mental cause for illness.

By the 1930's Freud's work was widely accepted and honoured. However, in 1938 Nazi Germany took control of Vienna and the rest of Austria. Freud was forced to flee because he was a Jew. Old and suffering from cancer, Freud died in England on September 23, 1939.

Lesson 16

Section One:

Tapescript:

Men and Women

BBC interviewer: It's probably true to say that women have been affected more than men by recent changes in the way we actually live. Over a hundred years ago people began to question whether men were really so much wiser, stronger, altogether more sensible and simply better than women as the laws of the country made out. In the end women got the vote, and very recently – in 1975 – the Sex Discrimination Act was passed.

But it's doubtful whether legislation has changed the way we women actually think. A lot is heard about the dilemma of women's two roles. How could a woman be a wife and mother and have a full-time job as well?

In this new series we are going to try to find out what people are really thinking and feeling about this problem, and how it affects their personal lives. In the studio with me today is Mrs Marina Spiden, who recently experienced the problem of having too much to do at home. With Mrs Spiden are her husband Brian, her mother Mrs Vera Cresswell, and Mr Tom Penman, their local newsagent. Mrs Spiden, tell us what happened will you?

Mrs Spiden: Well... you just said it... the problem of having too much to do at home. I do an afternoon job so I have to get the housework and shopping ... er ... done in the morning. And one morning you see ... er ... I just couldn't stand it no more. The ... the baby was bawling her head off. Jimmy— that's my little boy... he's two – had thrown the radio out of the window...

Interviewer: Really!

Mrs Spiden: Yes really ... The dog ... you know ... made a ... a mess on the carpet. And there was Brian – my husband – there he was snoring away on the settee. Didn't lift a finger he didn't ... not a finger to help me.

Mrs Spiden: Now now love ... Don't get all her up about it again ... I mean that's your side of the story ...

Interviewer: Of course Mr Spiden ... We'd like to hear your side later. So ... what did you do about it?

Mrs Spiden: Well ... What do you do when you've got something you're fed up with or ... or you don't want like... You put them up for sale don't you? And that's exactly what I did do. Put the whole damn lot of'em up for sale.

Interviewer: The family you mean.

Mrs Spiden: Yes ... the family ... including the dog.

Mr Penman: She came into my shop that very day and 'Tom', she says, 'Tom', she says, 'I've just about had enough of it. I'm sick of slaving for a husband what sleeps all day. So here you are,' she says. And she gives me an advert on a card to put up in the window of the paper shop.

Interviewer: What did it say?

Mr Penman: I've got it here.

Interviewer: Read it for us, will you?

Mr Penman: 'For Sale – One house – trained dog, one reasonably trained boy of two years, one baby girl of two weeks and one man that needs training. Any offers considered. Apply within.'

Interviewer: And were there any offers?

Mrs Cresswell: It was me what wrote that advert. You see ... I live with Marina and Brian ...

Mrs Spiden: She and her dog ...

Mr Penman: Oh yes. Caused quite a stir it did. I should say I had inquiries from ... from about a couple of dozen housewives in all.

Interviewer: And what offers did they make?

Mr Penman: Well one woman offered 25p. She said that's all a man was worth.

Interviewer: What about you Mr Spiden? What was your reaction to the advertisement?

Mrs Spiden: Well ... you can imagine ... Me wife told me about it but I thought she was joking. Little did I realize ... I was bloody furious when I saw it there. It wasn't till next morning. We live upstairs of the paper shop and when I come down to go on my milk round ...

Interviewer: Yes of course ... you're a milkman ...

Mrs Spiden: That's right. I often have a dekko at the adverts Tom puts up. And when I saw that one sort of ... staring me in the face ... I nearly blew me top.

Interviewer: What did you do?

Mrs Cresswell: I'll tell you what he did. He came and blamed me for everything.

Mrs Spiden: Well it was you ... wannit ... that egged her on. It was you that wrote the advert.

Mr Penman: It was a big joke really. Just that Brian took it all the wrong way. Know what he did? When he come off his milk round he barges into the shop and he says, 'Take that bloody advert out and put one in for me. Ask some kind taxi-driver or someone to come and take my mother-in-law back to Birmingham.'

Mrs Spiden: But it's all blown over now ... innit. It's done us a world of good in a way. We're the best of friends again. Even the dog started to...

Key to Exercises:

A. True or False Questions. Write a T in front of a statement if it is true according to the recording and write an F if it is false.

1. (F) Women are not affected by recent changes in the way people actually live.

2. (F) A hundred years ago people never questioned whether men were really wiser, stronger, more sensible and better than women.

3. (F) Women get the right to vote in 1875.

4. (T) Women are in a dilemma of two roles: being a wife and mother and having a full-time job.

B. Identification. Match the people in Column I with what they do in Column II.

Column I	Column II
1. Mrs. Spiden	a. being furious at the advert
2. Mr. Spiden	b. living with Brian and Marina
3. Jimmy	c. going on one's milk round

4. the dog   d. getting the housework and shopping

5. Mrs. Cresswell   done in the morning

6. the baby   e. having a dekko at the advert

                     f. making a mess on the carpet

                     g. writing the advert

                     h. throwing a radio out of the window

                     i. putting up an advert to sell the family

                     j. snoring on the settee

                     k. bawling

                     l. never lifting a finger to help with the housework

                     m. having an afternoon job

Answer: (1) – (d, i, m); (2) – (a, c, e, j, l); (3) – (h); (4) – (f); (5) – (b, g); (6) – (k);

C. Complete the following sentences with what you hear on the tape.

1. Don't get (all her up about) it again . . . That's (your side of) the story.

2. Put the whole damn lot of 'em (for sale).

3. For sale – – one (house-trained) dog, one (reasonably trained) boy of (two years), one baby girl of (two weeks) and one man that (needs training). Any offer considered. Apply (within).

4. One woman offered (25p). She said that's (all a man was worth).

5. When I saw that one sort of . . . (staring me in the face) . . . I nearly (blew me top).

6. He came and (blamed me for) everything.

7. It was you . . . that (egged her on).

8. When he (came off) his milk round he (barged into) the shop.

9. It's all (blown over) now . . . It's done us (a world of good).

Section Two:

Tapescript:

Task 1: The Suffragette Movement

Interviewer: I'm going to talk to you now about the suffragette movement. Were you yourself ever a suffragette?

Mrs Bruce: No, I did not approve of suffragettes. I did not want to have the vote. I felt the man of the house should be in charge of that section. And the woman, of course, to look after the home and the children. I think that voting was unnecessary, at that time. But I'm not going to say now, that perhaps it has had its advantages.

Interviewer: How common was your attitude at the time that the suffragettes were being militant?

Mrs Bruce: Oh, I was very much against them. I'd be highly insulted if anybody called me a suffragette. I remember walking with my governess down Downing Street just past Number 10 and they chained themselves to the railings. Of course, I had a good laugh but I thought it wasn't going to be me.

Interviewer: Were they a popular movement in their day?

Mrs Bruce: Well, with a certain number of course. And they tried very hard and eventually they got the vote, er through their efforts, so I suppose their efforts were good in quite a lot of ways. Er, I think women in Parliament—there aren't many,

310

but those that've been there have done a lot of good.

Interviewer: So you think in the long term ...

Mrs Bruce: In the long term, no harm was done. As long as their demonstrations were peaceful.

Interviewer: Do you think it would matter very much if women didn't, hadn't achieved the vote, if they hadn't got the vote at all and still didn't have it?

Mrs Bruce: I don't think it would've made a great deal of difference, no, but there are certain things they've done — those that've been Members of Parliament — that have been very useful in helping women in their jobs, in other vocations. I think it's good that it happened. But I wish it happened a little bit more peacefully, perhaps.

Interviewer: What sort of things can you remember, what other sorts of demonstrations do you remember?

Mrs Bruce: Marching, they were marching. But of course those were much more peaceful days, nobody interfered with their marches. There were a few boos here and there and a lot of clapping. Yes.

Interviewer: Did you, did you actually know any suffragettes yourself?

Mrs Bruce: Well, my friends, my close friends, were not suffragettes but I had one or two friends, not very close friends, that were. And we used to have great arguments and I used to say I didn't want the vote, I don't want to vote.

Interviewer: How did they react to that?

Mrs Bruce: They didn't like that. They said I ought to join the movement but I said, no I don't want to vote.

Interviewer: But, and yet you've done so many exciting things.

You've done so many things that in your day, were probably the exclusive preserve of the man.

Mrs Bruce: Well, yes. But voting didn't make any difference because that's a political thing, voting, I never, I don't care about women entering into politics particularly. Ah, no harm's been done with the few that have entered the House of Commons but, in fact, some have done a great deal of good. But that's quite different to beating men at their own job. Now that's nothing to do with votes. Now, for instance, I always got a great thrill on the race track at Brooklands, if I could beat, well, Sir Henry Seagrave, for instance, in a race, I never did beat him but I did beat Frazer Nash, a famous racing driver in a race, and I was thrilled to death. I thought that was super.

Interviewer: So you don't mind actually joining men in their world of work and sport, but you're happy to leave politics to them.

Mrs Bruce: No. I would rather really leave politics to them.

Task 2: Sex Discrimination

Jan: Changes are very gradual. They're too slow. I mean if you sit under a tree long enough the apple'll fall off and you can eat it but sometimes you've got to stand up and do something. You've got to ... Um I think the law is there to protect people. Because women were being discriminated against, it was necessary for the law to stop that, um at least to some extent. But you can't change the way people think.

Duncan: People's discrimination is based on the fact... a lot of it, that they don't think women are capable of making decisions or have any intelligence at all. I mean a lot of people believe that

312

... and if that ... provided ... once that's proved wrong, that removes the valid grounds for the discrimination and you know you ... the belief is then unjustified. You've got to stamp it out. I mean, it's as simple as that.

Keith: But just in the same way that if I want to become a managing director, I have to look at the company in which I work and prove certain elements of my behaviour or ... or my skills to these people, so must women.

Jan: Yes, but if they're not given the chance, then how can they? I mean it's very sad that the law has to be there at all. I mean that you have to say to somebody who's employing someone you must give ... you must interview men and women ... it it seems a great shame ... you have to tell people to do that. It's also a great shame that you have to tell people not to go around murdering other people. I mean, the law's there because people do stupid things.

Duncan: As I say, the law is ... is not that you have to sort of ... I mean you basically all you have to do is give women the right to apply and the right to be considered in the same way as everybody else and if the law was effective as it should be, there'd be nothing wrong with that. I mean, what's wrong with giving women the chance to apply for a job and giving them the right to be considered on equal terms with men.

Keith: Women could always ... women could always apply.

Duncan: That's not true, though. I mean there are employers who just would not consider them.

David: A woman would not apply if the job was ... if the job advertisement was couched in such terms.

Keith: I mean ... the leading example ...

313

Duncan: I mean the whole point about the ... an advertisement asking for a draughtsman being against the terms of the act, is that it gives the imp ... it's implied that only men will be considered and that's why that would be a legal advertisement if you put at the bottom, um applications from men and women will be considered ... the same with postmen and all the other jobs.

David: Interesting point. How important is the language, Jan, do you think?

Jan: I ... it's symbolic. Um I personally don't find it particularly important. Er if you have a meeting and you call the man or the woman who chairs the meeting the chairman, it just doesn't matter I don't think at all.

Key to Exercises:

Task 1: The Suffragette Movement

A. Choose the best answer (a, b or c) to complete each of the following statements.

  1. Mrs. Bruce, the interviewee, _____.

     a. was a militant suffragette

     b. was a supporter of the suffragette movement

  * c. was not interested in the suffragette movement

  2. Mrs . Bruce doesn't think whether women should vote

    _____.

  * a. made a great deal of difference to her

     b. made things better

     c. was a matter of little importance

  3. According to what Mrs. Bruce says, _____.

  * a. the suffragette movement was not peaceful as she had ex-

314

pected

  b. the suffragette movement died away peacefully

  c. she doesn't care much whether the suffragette movement was peaceful or not.

4. On the whole, Mrs. Bruce _____.

  a. is very much interested in politics

 * b. is not interested in politics at all

  c. is eager to enter the House of Commons

B. Answer the following questions briefly.

1. How would Mrs. Bruce feel she was called a suffragette?

Answer: She would feel highly insulted.

2. What came out of the suffragette movement?

Answer: They got the right to vote and some of them became members of the Parliament.

3. What role does Mrs. Bruce think those women MPs have been playing?

Answer: They have been useful in helping women in their jobs, in other vocations.

4. What did Mrs. Bruce say when her friends asked her to join the suffragette movement?

Answer: She didn't want to vote.

5. What does she think of women joining men their world of work, sport and politics?

Answer: She feels all right joining men in their world of work and sport. But she is happy to leave politics to men.

C. Fill in the blanks with what you hear on the tape.

1. I did not (approve of) suffragette.

2. I had (a good laugh) but It thought it wasn't going to be me.

3. (In the long term), no harm was done.

4. Those were much more peaceful days, nobody (interfered with) their marches. There were (a few boos and there) and a lot of (clapping).

5. But that's quite (different to) beating men (at their own job).

6. I always get (a great thrill on the race track) at Brooklands.

Task 2: Sex Discrimination

A. True or False Questions. Write a T in front of a statement if it is true according to the recording and write an F if it is false.

1. (T) Changes are very gradual, actually too slow to come.

2. (F) People always believe that women are capable of making decision or have intelligence.

3. (T) Applying for a job, women must prove certain elements of her behaviour and skills as men do.

4. (T) The law's there because people do stupid things.

5. (F) Employers consider women on equal terms with men.

6. (F) The first speaker thinks that sex discrimination in language matters much.

B. Fill in the blanks with the information you hear on the tape.

1. If you (sit under) a tree long enough the apple'll (fall off) and you can eat it but sometimes you've (got to stand up) and do something.

2. Because women were (being discriminated against), it was necessary for the law to stop that, (at least to some extent).

3. If . . . that's (proved wrong), that (removes) the (valid grounds for) the discrimination.

4. You've got to (stamp it out).

5. It's also (a great shame) that you have to tell people not to (go round) murdering other people.

Section Three:

Tapescript:

Recognizing the Main Idea

1. When a teacher or lecturer recommends a student to read a book, it's usually for a particular purpose. The book may contain useful information about the topic being studied or it may be invaluable for the ideas or views that it puts forward, and so on. In many cases, the teacher doesn't suggest that the whole book should be read. In fact, he may just refer to a few pages which have a direct bearing on the matter being discussed.

2. On Many occasions, however, the student does not come to the library to borrow a book, or even to consult a book from the shelves. He may well come to the library because it provides a suitable working environment, which is free of charge, spacious, well-lit and adequately heated.

3. Learners of English usually find that writing is the most difficult skill they have to master. The majority of native speakers of English have to make an effort to write accurately and effectively even on those subjects which they know very well. The non-native learner, then, is trying to do something that the average native speaker often finds difficult himself.

4. Students, however, often work out a sentence in their own language and then try to translate it in this way. The result is that

very often the reader simply cannot understand what the student has written. The individual words, or odd phrases, may make sense but the sentence as a whole makes nonsense. The student should, therefore, always try to employ sentence patterns he knows are correct English.

5. Many students seem to think that simplicity is suspect. It is, on the contrary, a quality which is much admired in English. Most readers understand that a difficult subject can only be written up 'simply' if the writer understands it very well. A student should, therefore, organize all his points very carefully before he starts to write.

6. Non-native speakers of English, like their native counterparts, usually find that the opportunity to participate in group discussions is one of the most valuable aspects in their whole academic programme. But in order to obtain full value from this type of activity the student must be proficient in asking questions. If he isn't, then any attempt to resolve his difficulties may lead to further confusion, if not considerable embarrassment.

Key to Exercises:

Recognizing the Main Idea

Listen to these paragraphs. Then decide what topic of each. Write the topic heading in the space given.

1. (Reading for a particular purpose)
2. (Why does a student come to the library)
3. (Writing is the most difficult skill)
4. (How to write a correct sentence)
5. (Simplicity - - a quality much admired)
6. (Participating in group discussions)

318

Supplementary Reading:

Suffrage

Suffrage is the right to vote in an election to choose governmental officers or to decide specific issues of government, such as the vote on a new constitution, a new constitutional provision, or a state or local bond issue.

Ancient societies. In early Western society, as in primitive communities today, suffrage was limited to the heads of a few families or clans. Only the leading chieftains were privileged to discuss and decide vital issues, or to be consulted by the tribal chief. Birth, or heritage, was the qualifying criterion for suffrage, although generally the ownership of property tended to be a factor in the grant of suffrage.

In ancient Greece the territorial unit of the city-state was often so small that the question of the scope of suffrage was not a decisive issue. For a long time, Athens, the most advanced and forward-looking of the Greek city-states, took the lead in developing a more democratic approach to the question of suffrage. Early in the 6th century B.C., distinctions of birth gave way to distinctions of property. This change expressed the transformation of the Athenian social system from a hereditary aristocracy into a commercial civilization based on a rising middle class and the developing intellectual attitudes of rationalism and individualism. The gradual development of critical political analysis, particularly during the great period of Periclean government in 5th century Athens, led to the establishment of suffrage based on citizenship rather than on property. Neither slaves nor women were included in the Greek concept of citizenship, however.

In ancient Rome, at first only the patrician families, endowed with property and social prestige, had the right to vote. But the Roman lower classes resented the denial of suffrage based on lack of property, and after centuries of often bitter social conflict they attained suffrage. As the Roman polity expanded to the Italian peninsula and to the whole Mediterranean basin, Roman citizenship was gradually broadened and, in 212 A.D., all free inhabitants of the Roman Empire were given the status of full-fledged Roman citizens. By that time the government of the Roman Empire had been transformed into an absolute monarchy, so that suffrage was more important in local and vocational, or guild, elections than in matters affecting imperial policy.

Medieval and Modern Evolution. In the Middle Ages, both rights and obligations of a person were determined by his social status. The possession of land, or at least rights of tenure in land, generally determined the kind of suffrage a person possessed. Later on, as the landed economy merged with the commercial and industrial economy, ownership or tenure of land was replaced by other property qualifications, such as the payment of minimum taxes.

England. Even in England, the mother of representative government, the progress from limited to universal suffrage was slow. Until 1832 the suffrage was so designed that a few hundred landowners were heavily represented in Parliament, while large urban areas were either not represented at all, or only very inadequately. The phenomenon of the small "rotten boroughs" led to discontent and political agitation. As a result the Reform Act of 1832 broadened the suffrage by including a larger share of the urban middle classes. Urban workers were added to the electorate in 1867 and farm workers in 1884. In 1918 all male voters 21 years old were

320

given the suffrage. Women were also granted the vote, but the minimum age was 30 years. In 1928 the higher age requirement for women was lifted.

United States. In the United States the growth of the suffrage was slow, though it was more rapid than in any other major democracy. The promises of equality contained in the Declaration of Independence and the Constitution did not materialize at once. Religious qualifications, often required in colonial times, disappeared shortly after the American Revolution, but properly and literacy qualifications continued for a long time. The first breakthrough in American suffrage came in the 1830's, the period of Andrew Jackson's radical democracy based on the equalitarian outlook of the Western frontiersmen, who increasingly asserted themselves in national politics. By 1860 universal suffrage for white males had become an accomplished fact. The 14th and the 15th amendments sought to ensure suffrage for Negroes, but these constitutional provisions were not fully enforced in some states, where poll taxes and literacy tests kept most Negroes from the polls. The 19th Amendment (1920) granted the suffrage to women, though some states had given women the suffrage long before. The 24th Amendment (1964) barred the use of a poll tax in federal elections. The Voting Rights Act of 1965 strengthened the hand of Negroes seeking to register in the South. The 26th Amendment (1971) and subsequent legislation granted suffrage to persons 18 years old or older.

Modern Concepts. Although direct government is impossible in large nation-states in the day-to-day business of state, and use must therefore be made of representative institutions, the suffrage expresses the notion that there can be no free government and no free citizens without some direct participation in the making of political

321

decisions. However, suffrage is only the first step toward such direct participation, and a government can exist only if its citizens supplement the periodic act of voting by continuous political expression on all levels of government - - local, state, and federal. This modern concept of the suffrage as involving responsibilities as well as rights is a return to the classical Greek concept of citizenship as active participation in the government of the community.

Lesson 17

Tapescript:

Task 1: News In Brief

Here is a summary of the news.

Shots are fired in a south London street by escaping bank robbers.

Four rock fans die in a stampede at a concert Chicago.

And how an Air France Concorde was involved in the closest recorded miss in aviation history.

Shots were fired this morning in the course of an 80 m. p. h.
chase along Brixton High Road in London. A police constable was
injured by flying glass when a bullet shattered his windscreen as he
was pursuing a car containing four men who had earlier raided a
branch of Barclays Bank at Stockwell. Police Constable Robert
Cranley had been patrolling near the bank when the alarm was
given. The raiders made their getaway in a stolen Jaguar which was
later found abandoned in Croydon. Officials of the bank later announced that £ 16,000 had been stolen.

Four people were killed and more than fifty injured when fans
rushed to get into a stadium in Chicago yesterday where the British
pop group Fantasy were giving a concert. The incident occurred
when gates were opened to admit a huge crowd of young people
waiting outside the stadium for the sale of unreserved seat tickets.
People were knocked over in the rush and trampled underfoot as the

crowd surged forward. The concert later went ahead as planned with Fantasy unaware of what had happened. A police spokesman said that they had decided to allow the concert to proceed in order to avoid further trouble. There has been criticism of the concert organizers for not ensuring that all the tickets were sold in advance. Roy Thompson, leader of Fantasy, said afterwards that the whole group was 'shattered' when they heard what had happened. They are now considering calling off the rest of their United States tour.

The United States Air Force has admitted that a formation of its fighters and an Air France Concorde recently missed colliding by as little as 10 feet. The Air Force accepts the blame for what was the closest recorded miss in aviation history. According to the Air Force spokesman, when the Concorde was already 70 miles out over the Atlantic, on a scheduled flight to Paris from Dulles International Airport, Washington, four US Air Force F-15s approached at speed from the left. The lead plane missed the underside of Concorde's nose by 10 feet while another passed only 15 feet in front of the cockpit.

Forest fires in the South of France have claimed the life of another fireman as they continue to rage in the hills between Frejus and Cannes. Fanned by strong westerly winds the flames are now threatening several villages and many holiday homes have had to be abandoned. The French army was called in yesterday to assist the fifteen hundred fire fighters that have so far been unable to contain the spread of the blaze.

A demonstration against race prejudice drew thousands of people to central London this morning. It was organized by the Labour Party and the Trades Union Congress under the banner 'United against Racialism'. The march was led by several leading Labour

324

Party and Trades Union officials. It was a column that stretched for over two miles and it took the demonstrators nearly three hours to cover the distance from Speakers' Corner to Trafalgar Square. There were representatives from more than twenty major unions, as well as community workers and various ethnic groups. By the time the march reached Trafalgar Square an estimated fifteen thousand people had joined it.

Heathrow Airport Police are investigating how a mailbag containing nearly £750,000 worth of jewels went missing between Geneva and London. The mailbag was believed to be on its way to a London dealer from a jeweller in Geneva five weeks ago, but it was not realized it was missing until the Post Office reported the fact to Scotland Yard two days ago. The mailbag contained a diamond, an emerald and two rubies valued at £635,200 plus a number of stones of lesser value, according to a police spokesman at Heathrow.

Football. The draw for the semi-final of the F. A. Cup was made earlier today. Liverpool will play Manchester City while Arsenal will meet Nottingham Forest. And that's the end of the news.

Task 2: Old Age and Health

Today I would like to tell you about the effects of old age on health. Actually today a lot of improvements have taken place in the care of old people and old people's health is not nearly so bad as it used to be.

Probably many of the fears that people have of growing old are greatly exaggerated. Most people, for example, dread becoming senile. But in fact very few people become senile. Perhaps only about 15% of those over 65 become senile. Actually a much more common problem is in fact caused by we doctors ourselves. And that is over-medication. Nearly 80% of people over 65 have at least one serious illness, such as high blood pressure, hearing difficulty or heart disease. And very often to combat these they take a number of drugs and of course sometimes there are interaction among those drugs as well as simply being too many. And this can cause a lot of complications from mental confusions, very commonly, to disturbance of the heart rhythm. So this's a problem that doctors have to watch out for.

Probably the most ignored disorder among old people is depression. Maybe about 15% of older people suffer from this condition. A lot of it is caused by this over-medication which we mentioned.

Although it is better now for old people, we have to admit that the body does change as we grow older. The immune system starts to decline and there are changes in metabolism, lungs, the senses, the brain and the skin.

So what should an old person do to counter-act these changes?

He or she should eat a balanced diet — not too much fat — chicken or fish should be eaten rather than eggs or beef. Eat more high fibre and vitamin rich foods, such as vegetables and fruit.

The old person should give up smoking if he hasn't already done so. He should also do regular exercise — at least half an hour, three times a week. No section of the population can benefit more from exercise than the elderly.

Key to Exercises:

Task 1: News in Brief

A. Choose the best answer (a, b or c) to complete each of the following statements.

326

1. Gunshots broke out _____ .

   a. near a branch of Barclays Bank at Stockwell

   b. in Croydon

* c. along Brixton High Road in London

2. People were killed and injured at a Chicago concert when

   _____ .

* a. the waiting crowd rushed to get the unreserved seat tickets

   b. the waiting crowd rushed angrily to the gates

   c. the waiting crowd had a clash with the police

3. An Air France Concorde _____ .

* a. missed colliding with four US Air Force F-15s

   b. collided with a US Air Force F-15

   c. and four US Air Force F-15s collided

4. The French Army was called in to help the fire fighters be - cause _____ .

   a. forest fires are going out

* b. forest fires in the south of France are threatening human property and lives

   c. forest fires are urged between Frejus and Cannes by strong winds from the south

5. _____ organized a demonstration _____ .

   a. The Labour Party, against sex prejudice

* b. The Labour Party and the Trades Union Congress, a-gainst race prejudice

   c. The Trades Union Congress, against race discrimination

6. A mailbag containing nearly _____ worth of jewels was missing _____ .

   a. £ 635,000, at Heathrow Airport

   b. £ 175,000, in Geneva

* c. £ 750,000, between Geneva and London

B. True or False Questions. Write a T in front of a statement if it is true according to the recording and write an F if it is false.

1. (F) A police constable pursuing the bank robber's car was driving at the the speed of 18 miles per hour.

2. (T) The British pop group Fantasy is thinking of cancelling the rest of its US tour because of the bloody incident.

3. (F) The two US Air Force fighters missed colliding the French Concorde by 10 feet and 50 feet respectively.

4. (T) At least two fire fighters were killed in the forest fires in the South of France.

5. (F) Around fifty thousand people turned out in the demonstration against racial discrimination.

6. (F) The case that a mailbag of valuable jewels was missing was first discovered by the Scotland Yard.

C. Identification. Match the incidents in Column I with details in Column II.

Column I	Column II
1. Bank Robbery	a. mailed from Geneva to London
2. Chicago Concert	b. stretched for over two miles
3. Plane Collision	c. the closest recorded miss in aviation history
4. Forest Fires	d. fifty injured, four killed
5. Demonstration in London	e. strong westerly winds fanning the flames
	f. officials from the Labour Party
6. Missing Mailbag	g. window glasses shattered by a bullet

328

7. Football Match   h. people knocked and trampled

                              i. Dulles International Airport

                              j. abandoned villages and holiday homes

                              k. Heathrow Airport Police

                              l. Nottingham Forest and Arsenal

                             m. Trafalgar Square

                              n. Fantasy

                              o. a stolen Jaguar

                              p. 16,000 pounds

                              q. diamond, emerald, ruby, and other stones

Answer: (1) – (g, o, p); (2) – (d, h, n); (3) – (c, i); (4) – (e, j); (5) – (b, f, m); (6) – (a, k, q); (7) – (l);

Task 2: Old Age and Health

A. Choose the best answer (a, b or c) to complete each of the following statements.

1. There are a lot of improvements in the care of old people and the old people's health _____.

  * a. becomes better

    b. is no better than it used to be

    c. is worse

2. A much more common problem with the old people's health

    _____.

    a. is the fears of becoming old

    b. is that they become senile

  * c. is over-medication

3. In order to have good health, one should _____.

* a. follow a balanced died and do regular exercises
  b. eat eggs and beef
  c. never change his way of living

B. Fill in blanks with what you hear on the tape.
   1. Most people . . . dread (becoming senile). But in fact (very few people) become senile.
   2. Perhaps only about (15%) of those (over 65) become senile.
   3. Nearly (80%) of people (over 65) have (at least) one serious disease.
   4. So this's a problem that doctors have to (watch out for).
   5. The (immune system) starts (to decline) and there are changes in metabolism, (lungs), (the senses), (the brain) and the (skin).
   6. No section of the population can (benefit more from) exercise than (the eldly).

Section Two:

Tapescript:

Task 1: At a Small Restaurant

Carl: I hope I'm not interrupting your work, Mr Thornton. You must be very busy at this time of the day.

Paul: Not at all. Come in, come in, Mr Finch. I'm just tasting a few of the dishes we'll be serving this morning.

Carl: That looks interesting. What exactly is it?

Paul: That one is fish − in a special sauce. One of my new creations, actually.

Carl: I'm looking forward to trying it.

Paul: I do hope you've enjoyed your stay with us.

330

Carl: Very much, indeed. We both find it very relaxing here.

Paul: Well, I'm sure there's lots more you'd like to ask, so, please, go ahead.

Carl: Thanks. I notice that you have a sort of team of helpers. How do you organize who does what? Surely it's difficult with so many talented people?

Paul: Everyone contributes ideas, of course, and to a certain extent shares in the decision-making. We all have our different specialities and different ways of doing things, but that's a great advantage in a place like this. If there is any disagreement, I have the final word. After all, I own the business and I'm the boss. But it happens very rarely, I'm glad to say.

Carl: Have you had them with you for long?

Paul: Not all of them, no. Alan's been with me for about five years. I used to have a restaurant on the east coast. Then I got the offer to do a lecture tour of Australia and New Zealand, you know, with practical demonstrations, so I sold the business, and then Alan and I looked around for two young chefs to take with us. Tom and Martin have been working for me ever since (Laughs.) Chefs are not a problem, but I'm having a lot of trouble at the moment finding good, reliable domestic staff.

Carl: How long did the tour last?

Paul: We were away for over two years in the end because more and more organizations wanted to see the show, and one thing led to another.

Carl: Had you been considering this present venture for long?

Paul: For some time, yes. During the tour I began to think it might be interesting to combine the show idea with a permanent es-

331

tablishment. and so here we are.

Carl: And what made you choose this particular spot?

Paul: Quite a few people have been surprised—you're not the first. It does seem a bit out of the way, I know, but I didn't want to start up in London. There's far too much competition. Then I decided to go for a different type of client altogether — the sort of person who wants to get away from it all; who loves peace and quiet, and beautiful scenery but also appreciates good food. When I saw the farmhouse I couldn't resist it. I was brought up not far from here so everything just fell into place.

Carl: To go back to the food, Paul. Do you have a large selection of dishes to choose from or are you always looking for new ideas?

Paul: Both. A lot of the dishes had already been created on the tour, but I encourage my staff to experiment whenever possible. I mean I can't keep serving the same dishes. The people who come here expect something unusual at every course, and some guests, I hope, will want to return.

Carl: I know two who certainly will.

Paul: It's very kind of you to say so. Is there anything else you'd like to know?

Carl: As a matter of fact, there is. Your grapefruit and ginger marmalade tastes delicious. Could you possibly give me the recipe?

Paul: It isn't really my secret to give. It belongs to Alan, but I'm sure if you ask him he'll be glad to oblige you — as long as you promise not to print it in your magazine!

Task 2: The Tree Climbers of Pompeii

Shelagh: Um, it's another one of my adventures as a tourist, um, finding out things you really didn't expect to find out when you went to the place! I went to Pompeii and of course what you go to Pompeii for is, er, the archaeology.

Liz: To see the ruins.

Shelagh: To see the ruins. And I was actually seeing the ruins but, um, suddenly my attention was caught by something else. I was just walking round the corner of a ruin, into a group of trees, pine trees, and I was just looking at them, admiring them and suddenly I saw a man halfway up this tree, and I was looking at him so all I could see was his hands and his feet and he was about 20 or 30 feet up. I thought, 'Goodness, what's going on here. Has he got a ladder or hasn't he?' So I walked round to see if he had a ladder. No, he had just gone straight up the tree.

Liz: He'd shinned up the tree.

Shelagh: He'd shinned up the tree. Like a monkey, more or less, except he was a rather middle-aged monkey ... He was, er, he was all of 50 and (Oh God), what's going on here? Anyway, I walked a bit further and saw other people either up trees or preparing to go up trees, and then I noticed a man standing there directing them, a sort of foreman, and began to wonder what on earth was going on, and then on the ground I saw there were all these polythene buckets and they were full of pine cones and of course what they were doing was collecting pine cones, and I thought, 'Well, how tidy of them to collect pine cones to stop the ruins being, um, made, um, made untidy with all these things.' Then I saw there was a lorry ... full of pine cones ... This was getting ridiculous ... They were really collecting them in a big way. So I, um, asked the, er, foreman what was going on and he said, 'Well you know, um, pine nuts are extremely sought after and valuable in the food industry in Italy.'

Liz: For food (Yeah). Not fuel! I thought you were going to say they were going to put (burn) them on a fire. Yes.

Shelagh: Well, they might burn the, er, cones when they've finished with them but inside these cones are little white things like nuts and, er, I realized that they're used in Italian cooking quite a lot in, er, there's a particular sauce that goes with spaghetti, em, from Genova, I think, called 'pesto' in which these nuts are ground up and of course they come in cakes and sweets and things like that.

Liz: So it's quite a delicacy.

Shelagh: It's quite a delicacy. And of course I'd never thought of how they actually got them 'cos you can't imagine having a pine nut farm. So what he said happens is that private firms like his buy a licence off the Italian State for the right to go round places like Pompeii – archaeological sites and things – and systematically collect all the pine cones that come off the trees and similarly in the, in the forests.

Liz: And of course they have to go up the tree because by the time it's fallen the, the food isn't any good.

Shelagh: That's right. They're pulling them down and he said they were very good at, um, recognizing which ones were ready and which ones were a bit hard and etc. and each of them had a sort of stick with a hook at the end which they were using to pull the pines off, off the trees but clearly it wasn't enough to sit around and wait till they fell down. You, you had to do something about it. There they were. So that was, er, the end of my

334

looking at the ruins for about half an hour. I was too fascinated
by this, er, strange form of er, agriculture.

Liz: Well, what you don't intend to see is always the most interesting.

Shelagh: Much more interesting.

Key to Exercises:

Task 1: At a Small Restaurant

A. Choose the best answer (a, b or c) to complete each of the following statements.

(1) Mr. Paul Thorton is _____.

    a. a chef

    b. a journalist from a magazine

  * c. the owner of the restaurant

(2) Mr. Carl Finch is _____.

    a. a chef of the restaurant

  * b. a journalist from a magazine

    c. the owner of the restaurant

(3) The restaurant is located _____.

  * a. in a quiet and peaceful place away from London

    b. in London

    c. in the country in Australia

(4) The restaurant is attractive because _____.

  * a. everyone contributes new ideas, which has improved the
      dishes greatly

    b. they serve ginger marmalade there

    c. customers are used to those old dishes

B. True or False Questions. Write a T in front of a statement if it is

true according to the recording and write an F if it is false.

(1) (F) The staff members of the restaurant don't share in decision-making.

(2) (T) The owner, Carl, always has the final say when disagreement comes up.

(3) (F) Alan has been with Carl for fifteen years.

(4) (T) Carl once lectured on cooking with practical demonstrations in Australia and New Zealand.

(5) (T) His lecture had been very popular.

(6) (F) Carl once wanted to set up his business in a competitive place.

(7) (T) The restaurant used to be a farmhouse.

(8) (F) Carl feels all right keeping serving the same dishes.

(9) (T) Alan may not want to have his recipe publicized.

C. Answer the following questions.

(1) What kind of trouble does Paul Thorton has with his restaurant?

Answer: He has trouble finding good, reliable domestic staff for his restaurant.

(2) Why did his lecture tour last for two years?

Answer: Because more and more organizations wanted to see his demonstration.

(3) What did he want to open a restaurant for?

Answer: He wanted to combine the demonstration with a permanent establishment.

(4) Why did he choose this place?

Answer: He decided to choose this remote place because he wanted to have a restaurant for those who love

peace and quiet and beautiful scenery and who also
appreciate good food.

Task 2: The Tree Climbers of Pompeii
A. Answer the following questions briefly.
　　1. What attracted Shelagh's attention when he was taking a
　　　　walk in Pompeii?
　　　　Answer: A man was half way up the tree.
　　2. What had Shelagh expected to see in Pompeii?
　　　　Answer: Ruins.
　　3. Why did people in Pompeii climb trees?
　　　　Answer: To collect pine cones.
　　4. What did people in Pompeii do with pine cones?
　　　　Answer: The processed them into some sauce which is used
　　　　　　　　in Italian cooking.
　　5. Could anybody collect pine cones without any permission?
　　　　Answer: No. The foreman bought a licence from the State
　　　　　　　　for the right to go round places collecting pine
　　　　　　　　cones.
　　6. What is more interesting to Shelagh, the ruines in Pompeii or
　　　　the tree climbers there?
　　　　Answer: The tree climbers.

B. Fill in the blanks with what you hear on the tape.
　　1. Suddenly I saw a man (halfway up this tree), and I was
　　　　looking at him so all I could see was (his hands) and (his
　　　　feet) and he was about (20 or 30 feet up).
　　2. Like a monkey, (more or less), except he was (a rather mid-
　　　　dle-aged monkey) . . . He was . . . he was all (of 50).

337

3. 'Well, you know, um, pine nuts are (extremely sought after) and valuable(in the food industry) in Italy.'

4. They were very (good at, um recognizing) which ones were (ready) and which ones were (a bit hard).

5. Clearly it wasn't enough to (sit around) and wait till they (fell down).

Section Three:

Tapescript:

Recognizing the Main Idea

1. In all humility, I accept the nomination ... I am happy to be able to say to you that I come to you unfettered by a single obligation or promise to any living person.

(Thomas Dewey 24/06/48)

2. I'll never tell a lie. I'll never make a misleading statement. I'll never betray the trust of those who have confidence in me. And I will never avoid a controversial issue. Watch me closely, because I won't be any better President than I am a candidate.

(Jimmy Carter 13/11/75)

3. I believe that this nation should commit itself to achieving the goal, before this decade is out, of landing a man on the moon and returning him safely to the earth. No single space project in this period will be more impressive to mankind, or more important for the long-range exploration of space; and none will be so difficult, or expensive to accomplish ... But, in a very real sense, it will not be one man going to the moon. We make this judgement affirmatively, it will be an entire nation ... I believe we should go to the moon.   (John F. Kennedy 25/05/61)

4. Those of us who loved him, and who take him to his rest today,

338

pray that what he was to us, what he wished for others will some day come to pass for all the world. As he said many times, in many parts of this nation, to those he touched and who sought to touch him:"Some men see things as they are and say 'Why?' I dream things that never were and say 'Why not?'".

(Edward M. Kennedy (08/06/68)

5. Because if they don't awake, they're going to find out that this little Negro that they thought was passive has become a roaring, uncontrollable lion right in right at their door — not at their doorstep, inside their house, in their bed, in their kitchen, in their attic, in the basement. (Malcolm X. 28/06/64)

6. I guess I couldn't say that er I wouldn't continue to do that, because I don't want the Carter Administration, and because I don't want Secretary Vance er to have to take the blame for the decisions that I felt that I had to make, decisions which I still feel were very much in the interest of this nation, er I think it best that I remove myself from the formal employ of the government er and pursue er my interests in foreign and domestic policy as a private citizen. (Andrew Young 15/08/79)

Key to Exercises:

Recognizing the Main Idea

Listen to these extracts from some famous speeches. Then decide what main idea each speaker wants to express. Write it out in the space given.

1. (Expressing neutrality after being nominated)
2. (Making a promise of what to do when elected the President)
3. (We should go to the moon.)
4. (Commemorating a person)

5. (The problem of the black people should be considered.)
6. (Why I want to resign)

Supplementary Reading:

Pompeii

Pompeii was an ancient city on the southwestern coast of Italy, on the Bay of Naples. It was founded in the 7th century B.C. by a tribe called the Oscans. Later other peoples − − Etruscans, Samnites, and Greeks − − settled there. In the 1st century B.C. Pompeii was taken over by the Romans.

On August 24 in the year A.D. 79 the volcano Vesuvius, located about 5 miles north of Pompeii, suddenly came alive. Dark clouds, hot cinders and ash, and poisonous gases poured from its cone. The terrifying eruption buried Pompeii beneath 10 to 20 feet of cinders and volcanic ash, killing 2,000 of its more than 20,000 inhabitants and sealing up their homes with the furniture and other belongings inside. The nearby towns of Herculaneum and Stabiac were also destroyed in the eruption. In a matter of 2 days the once flourishing seaside city, where many wealthy Romans had their country homes, disappeared. It lay buried nearly 2,000 years.

In 1748 Charles III, King of Naples and Sicily, ordered the digging out of Pompeii to begin. He hoped that this excavation would uncover treasure to enrich his archaeological collection. Since then, almost all the city has come to light. Most ancient cities either have died of old age or were robbed and destroyed by their conquerors. Pompeii was struck down in one swift blow by a natural disaster.

Today, when you go to Pompeii, you see not a heap of ruins but streets with paving stones worn by chariot wheels, well-pre-

340

served public buildings, wine shops, and restaurants. Some walls are scratched with Latin phrases praising or abusing the wine and food or advertising fights between gladiators in the arena.

Many of the rich country homes and their gardens with ornamental pools can still be seen. The gateways were often guarded by dogs. One unfortunate beast was left tied to a gatepost by a master so anxious to escape that he forgot his pet. In another house an unfinished meal was left on a table when guests fled for their lives. There was little time for citizens to remove their valuables. In the crush near the city gates many inhabitants were choked to death by the poisonous gases. The imprint of their bodies remains in the hardened volcanic ash.

Most of the art treasures, cooking utensils, household furnishings, and implements from Pompeii and Herculaneum are on view in the Naples National Museum. All these articles have been so well preserved that archaeologists are able to piece together in a remarkable way what everyday life was like in Roman times 2,000 years ago.

Lesson 18

Tapescript:

Energy Crisis

'Good evening, and welcome again to the 'Michael Parkhurst Talkabout'. In tonight's programme, we're looking at the problem of energy. The world's energy resources are limited. Nobody knows exactly how much fuel is left, but pessimistic forecasts say that there is only enough coal for 450 years, enough natural gas for 50 years and that oil might run out in 30 years. Obviously we have to do something, and we have to do it soon!

I'd like to welcome our first guest, Professor Marvin Burnham of the New England Institute of Technology. Professor Burnham.'

'Well, we are in an energy crisis and we will have to do something quickly. Fossil fuels (coal, oil and gas) are rapidly running out. The tragedy is that fossil fuels are far too valuable to waste on the production of electricity. Just think of all the things you can make from oil! If we don't start conserving these things now, it will be too late. And nuclear power is the only real alternative. We are getting some electricity from nuclear powerstations already. If we invest in further research now, we'll be ready to face the future. There's been a lot of protest lately against nuclear power—some people will protest at anything—but nuclear power-stations are not as dangerous as some people say. It's far more dangerous to work

342

down a coal-mine or on a North Sea oil-rig. Safety regulations in power-stations are very strict.

If we spent money on research now, we could develop stations which create their own fuel and burn their own waste. In many parts of the world where there are no fossil fuels, nuclear power is the only alternative. If you accept that we need electricity, then we will need nuclear energy. Just imagine what the world would be like if we didn't have electricity—no heating, no lighting, no transport, no radio or TV. Just think about the ways you use electricity every day. Surely we don't want to go back to the Stone Age. That's what will happen if we turn our backs on nuclear research.'

'Thank you, Professor. Our next guest is a member of CANE, the Campaign Against Nuclear Energy, Jennifer Hughes.'

'Right. I must disagree totally with Professor Burnham. Let's look at the facts. First, there is no perfect machine. I mean, why do aeroplanes crash? Machines fail. People make mistakes. What would happen if there were a serious nuclear accident? And an accident must be inevitable—sooner or later. Huge areas would be evacuated. and they could remain contaminated with radioactivity for years. If it happened in your area, you wouldn't get a penny in compensation. No insurance company covers nuclear risks. There are accidents. If the nuclear industry didn't keep them quiet, there would be a public outcry. Radioactivity causes cancer and may affect future generations. Next, nuclear waste. There is no technology for absolutely safe disposal. Some of this waste will remain active for thousands of years. Is that what you want to leave to your children? And their children's children? A reactor only lasts about 25 years. By the year 2000 we'll have 'retired' 26 reactors in the UK.

Next, terrorism. Terrorists could hold the nation to ransom if they captured a reactor. In the USA the Savannah River plant, and Professor Burnham knows this very well, lost (yes, 'lost') enough plutonium between 1955 and 1978 to make 18 (18!) atom bombs. Where is it? Who's got it? I consider that nuclear energy is expensive, dangerous, and evil, and most of all, absolutely unnecessary. But Dr Woodstock will be saying more about that.'

'Thank you Jennifer. Now I'm very pleased to welcome Dr Catherine Woodstock. She is the author of several books on alternative technology.'

'Hello. I'd like to begin by agreeing with Jennifer. We can develop alternative sources of power, and unless we try we'll never succeed. Instead of burning fossil fuels we should be concentrating on more economic uses of electricity, because electricity can be produced from any source of energy. If we didn't waste so much energy, our resources would last longer. You can save more energy by conservation than you can produce for the same money. Unless we do research on solar energy, wind power, wave power, tidal power, hydroelectric schemes etc, our fossil fuels will run out, and we'll all freeze or starve to death. Other countries are spending much more than us on research, and don't forget that energy from the sun, the waves and the wind lasts for ever. We really won't survive unless we start working on cleaner, safer sources of energy.'

'Thank you very much, Dr Woodstock. Our final speaker, before we open the discussion to the studio audience, is Charles Wicks, MP, the Minister for Energy.'

'I've been listening to the other speakers with great interest. By the way, I don't agree with some of the estimates of world energy reserves. More oil and gas is being discovered all the time. If we listened to the pessimists (and there are a lot of them about) none of

344

us would sleep at night. In the short-term, we must continue to rely on the fossil fuels —oil, coal and gas. But we must also look to the future. Our policy must be flexible. Unless we thought new research was necessary, we wouldn't be spending money on it. After all, the Government wouldn't have a Department of Energy unless they thought it was important. The big question is where to spend the money—on conservation of present resources or on research into new forms of power. But I'm fairly optimistic. I wouldn't be in this job unless I were an optimist!'

Key to Exercises:

A. Choose the best answer (a, b or c) to complete the following statements.

1. In order to conserve fossil fuels, _____ strongly suggests that _____.

   a. Dr. Catherine Woodstock; nuclear power stations should be built.

  * b. Prof. Marvin Burnham; nuclear power should be the only alternative.

   c. Prof. Jennifer Hughes; nuclear power should be the safest power to resort to.

2. Prof. Marvin Burnham and Prof. Jennifer Hughes _____.

   a. agree with each other on alternative power resources

  * b. sharply disagree with one another on nuclear power

   c. are trying to reach an agreement on nuclear power

3. According to one of the experts present, nuclear power is _____.

  * a. dangerous in its production and disposal, and is a target for

terrorists

    b. safe, but it is more dangerous to work down a coal-mine

    c. not a source of contamination and radioactivity

4. Dr. Catherine Woodstock thinks _____.

    a. it is more important to save energy by conservation than to produce energy with the game amount of money

    b. there should be research on solar energy, wind power, wave power, tidal power, etc.

  * c. Both a and b.

5. Mr. Charles Wicks _____.

    a. agrees with other speakers on energy crisis

    b. is not interested in his position

  * c. doesn't think the world will run out of energy resources. There will always be some alternatives.

B. Give a list of the pros and cons of nuclear power stations, according to the speakers in the program.

Pros

a. (It is the only alternative when fossil fuel is running out.)

b. (It can produce electricity for our daily use.)

c. (Working at a nuclear power station is far safer than working down a coal-mine or on a North Sea oil-rig.)

d. (It can create its own fuel and burn its waste.)

Cons

a. (Nobody can imagine what will happen if there is a nuclear accident.)

b. (Radioactivity causes cancer and may affect future generations.)

c. (There is no technology for absolutely safe disposal of nuclear

346

waste.)

d. (Therrorists could hold the nation to ransom if they captured a reactor.)

e. (Nuclear energy is expensive, dangerous, evil, and most of all, absolutely unnecessary.)

C. Fill in the blanks with what you hear on the tape.

1. Pessimistic forecasts say that there is only enough coal for (450 years), enough natural gas for (50 years) and that (oil) might run out in (30 years).

2. Surely we don't want to (go back to the Stone Age). That's what will happen if we (turn our backs on) nuclear research.

3. Some of this waste will remain (active for thousands of years).

4. A reactor only last about (25 years). By the year 2000 we'll have (26 'retired' reactors) in the UK.

5. Don't forget that energy from (the sun), (the waves) and (the wind) lasts for ever. We really won't (survive unless) we start (working on) cleaner, safer sources of energy.

6. If we listened to the pessimists (and there are a lot of them about) (none of us) would sleep (at night).

7. (in the short-term), we must continue to (rely on) fossil fuels (oil, coal and gas) ... The big question is where to spend the money—on (conservation of present resources) or on (research into new forms of power).

Section Two:

Task 1: The Years to Come (I)

Mal Carrington: Good morning. Welcome to The Years to Come. I'm Mal Carrington, and every week at this time Channel 5 brings you information on life in the future from an expert in the field.

Today's expert is Dr Reginald Healy from MIT, the famous Massachusetts Institute of Technology. Good morning, Dr Healy. Welcome to The Years to Come.

Dr Healy: Thank you.

Mal Carrington: Well, What are your predictions about the world? What is it going to be like in the year 2000 ?

Dr Healy: Hum, if present trends continue, I'm afraid the world in 2000 will be more crowded and more polluted than the world we live in now.

Mal Carrington: Yes, however, food production is constantly increasing. Don't you think we will be able to cope with the increase in world population?

Dr Healy: I don't think so. Even though production is constantly increasing, the people of the world will be poorer than they are today. For hundreds of millions of the desperately poor, the supply of food and other necessities of life will not be any better. And for many they will be worse, unless the nations of the world do something to change the current trends.

Mal Carrington: What is your estimate of world population in AD 2000?

Dr Healy: Well, already, world population is about 5,000 million.

If present trends continue, that is with the number of births by far exceeding the number of deaths. In 2000 the world population could approach 6,500 million people.

Mal Carrington: How many people are born every day?

Dr Healy: About 250 every minute, but only 100 people die. This means there is an increase of 216,000 people per day, and ninety per cent of this increase is in the poorest countries.

Mal Carrington: That's worrying! And what about energy? Will there be enough oil to satisfy our needs in 2000?

Dr Healy: During the 1990s, world oil production will reach the maximum and the price of oil will begin to increase. At the end of the century, the available supplies will not be sufficient for our needs. So at least part of these needs will have to be met by alternative sources of energy.

Mal Carrington: Yes, water is becoming a problem too.

Dr Healy: Yes, unfortunately. Water shortage will become more severe in the future, and due to the increase of births there will be enough water only for half of the population.

Mal Carrington: Which of the present trends do you think will continue over the next decade?

Dr Healy: Well, significant loss of the world's forests will continue over the next ten years as the demand for wood for fuel and manufacturing purposes increases. Also atmospheric concentration of carbon dioxide and other chemicals is expected to increase at rates that could alter the world's climate due to the 'greenhouse effect'.

Mal Carrington: The 'greenhouse effect'? Could you explain what the 'greenhouse effect' is?

Dr Healy: Sure. Well, the amount of carbon dioxide in the air is progressively increasing and it traps more of the heat of the sun

349

in the lower atmosphere. This has a warming effect which could change the climate and even melt the polar ice caps, which would cause disastrous flooding.

Mal Carrington: I see. Is this the only effect of carbon dioxide?

Dr Healy: No, it isn't. Carbon dioxide and other chemicals which derive from the use of fossil fuels will also increase the quantity of acid rain which is already damaging or even destroying plants, trees and other parts of our environment. Also, there will be a dramatic increase in the number of species becoming extinct. Hundreds of thousands of species will be lost because of the loss of their habitat.

Mal Carrington: That's appalling! What about nuclear plants? Aren't they a constant menace to life on our planet?

Dr Healy: Definitely. And apart from the more obvious danger of accidents, like the one at Chemobyl, there's the problem of the disposal of nuclear waste, that is the waste which is produced by nuclear power stations.

Mal Carrington: Oh, yes. I know that some of the materials keep their radioactivity for hundreds or thousands of years.

Dr Healy: Yeah, for example, strontium 90 needs storing for 500 years, being kept cool all the time. plutonium-239 may need storing for up to half a million years!

Mal Carrington: So, what is going to happen to the Earth in the next few years? Will we be able to reverse this trend towards destruction? What is your prediction?

Dr Healy: Well, I don't want to be pessimistic, but I'm afraid that if this trend doesn't change within five or ten years we won't be able to do very much to save the earth.

Mal Carrington: Well, that's a warning that we all need to take seriously. And with that warning, we end part one of this week's The Years to Come. We'll be back soon after the break.

Task 2: The Years to Come (II)

Mal Carrington: Here we are again with The Years to Come. Now I'd like to tell you about and to show you the pictures of an exciting new project which is the result of the co-operation of scientists, engineers and technicians from virtually all over the world.

Towards the end of the 90s, a bright new celestial body will appear in the night sky like an immense shining star, fully visible from 38 degrees north or south of the equator. It will be a space station, Freedom. The idea for Freedom originated in the USA, but eleven other nations have agreed to contribute a few of the station's many parts.

The space station is not going to be launched into orbit in one piece —the thousands of parts which make up Freedom are going to be assembled directly in space. Twenty trips by the shuttle and two rockets will be needed to deliver Freedom, piece by piece, into a low orbit around the Earth. Then, 250 miles above the Earth, construction crews are going to bolt together the space station's many components. The first batch of parts is going to be launched in 1995. By the end of 1996, the first crew of eight is going to enter the living module to begin what NASA hopes will be a continuous human presence in space. The station has been designed to remain occupied and operational for up to thirty years —a whole generation of living in space. Considering that the first man-made object reached orbit just thirty years ago, that will be quite an accomplishment. The design of a space station must combine the excitement of space with the necessity for safety and comfort. Freedom will be the best solution to date and will also be the most complex computerized house ever built —either on Earth or in space. There will be accommodation for eight people and each crew member will have his or her own room, a shower, a toilet, exercise equipment, a washing machine, a pantry, and a sick bay. Add a television, video, phone and computer to each of the eight private sleeping rooms, then top it off with the best view on Earth. Is this some wild new 'luxury house' of the future? Exactly. Life on board will also be brightened by a plan to fill twenty percent of the larder with fresh refrigerated fruit, vegetable and dairy products.

Behind every space station lies the dream that is at least 120 years old: a colony in space. Freedom is not going to be that colony, for it will always depend on the Earth for supplies. But it is going to be the place where scientists discover how to establish healthy and productive human habitation in space. When new technology is developed to make it less risky, we will see more civilians in space. So an eighteen-year-old can look forward to visiting space by his or her sixty-eighth birthday, in 2050.

And that's the end of this week's programme. Tune in next week for another edition of The Years to Come. The Years to Come is a Channel 5 production and this is Mal Carrington.

Key to Exercises:

Task 1: The Years to Come (I)

A. Choose the best answer (a, b or c) to complete the following

352

statements.

1. This talk is broadcast _____.

   a. on radio

   * b. on TV

   c. neither a or b

2. Dr. Reginald Healy _____.

   * a. is an expert on life in the future from MIT

   b. is an expert on nuclear power

   c. works for The years to come

3. According to what Dr. Healy say, the world in 2000 _____.

   a. will take quite a new look

   b. will be more progressive and the life better

   * c. will be more crowded and polluted

4. Now human beings are faced with _____.

   * a. a shortage of oil, water, forests, etc.

   b. a shortage of labour power

   c. a colder climate

5. Greenhouse effect _____.

   a. is the result of decreasing the amount of carbon dioxide

   b. has reduced the heat of the sun in the lower atmosphere

   * c. could melt the polar ice caps, which would cause disastrous flooding.

6. The most serious problem with nuclear power stations _____.

   a. is the accident at Chemoby 1

   * b. is the disposal of their waste

   c. lies in how much *Strontium* 90 and *Plutonium*-239 are available.

353

B. True or False Questions. Write a T in front of a statement if it is true according to the recording and write an F if it is false.

1. (T) The constantly increasing food production can never catch up with the increasing population.

2. (F) The world population today is 1,500 million and it would reach 6,500 million in 2000.

3. (T) There are 250 births and 100 deaths every minute in the world.

4. (F) Hopefully the world will suffer less from the loss of its forests because very few people use wood fuel now.

5. (F) Carbon dioxide and other chemicals which derive from use of fossil fuels won't increase the quantity of acid rain.

6. (T) Carbon dioxide will cause a number of species to become extinct.

7. (T) Nuclear plants are a constant menace to life on this planet.

8. (F) *Strontium* 90 needs storing for 5,000 years, being kept in any temperature.

C. Complete the following sentences with what you hear on the tape.

1. This means there is an increase of (216,000) people per day, and (ninety percent) of this is (in the poorest countries).

2. So (at least) part of these needs will have to be met by (alternative sources of energy).

3. (Due to) the increase of births there will be enough water only for (half of the population).

4. Hundreds of thousands of (species) will be lost because of

354

(the loss of their habitat).

5. I'm afraid that if this trend doesn't change (within five or
   ten years) we won't be able to do very much to (save the
   earth).

Task 2: The Years to Come (II)

A. Answer the following questions briefly.

1. What is Dr. Healy talking about?

   Answer: A space station to be launched towards the end of
   the 1990s.

2. Is this space station going to be built by the USA?

   Answer: No, eleven other nations have agreed to contribute a
   few of the station's many parts.

3. Where are the thousands of parts going to be assembled?

   Answer: In the space.

4. How many people are going to be involved in the first crew to
   begin their space life?

   Answer: Eight.

5. What lies behind the idea of a space station?

   Answer: A dream that has been cherished for 120 years – – a
   colony in space.

6. Why do scientists set up such a space station?

   Answer: Because they want to use the space station to discover how to establish healthy and productive habitation in space.

B. Give a list of daily necessities that are equipped within the space
   station.

   a. (a room for each crew member)

b. (a shower)

c. (a toilet)

d. (exercise equipment)

e. (a washing machine)

f. (a pantry)

g. (a sick bay)

h. (a television set)

i. (video)

j. (a telephone)

k. (a computer)

C. Fill in the blanks in the following sentences.

1. A bright new (celestial body) will appear in the sky like (a shining star), fully visible from (38 degrees north or south of the equator).

2. (Twenty trips) by the shuttle and (two rockets) will be needed to deliver *Freedom*, (piece by piece), into (a low orbit) around the Earth.

3. (250 miles above the Earth), construction crews are going to (bolt together) the space station's (many components). The first (batch of parts) is going to be launched (in 1995).

Section Three:

Tapescript:

Recognizing the Main Idea

1. Two years ago, ... when I landed on your soil, I said to the people of the Philippines. 'Whence I came I shall return.' Tonight, I repeat those words. I shall return.

(Douglas MacArthur 17/03/44)

2. I have a dream that one day on the red hills of Georgia, sons of former slaves and the sons of former slaveowners will be able to sit down together at the table of brotherhood. I have a dream that one day, even the state of Mississippi, a state sweltering with the heat of injustice, sweltering with the heat of oppression, will be transformed into an oasis of freedom and justice . I have a dream that my four little children will one day live in a nation where they will not be judged by the colour of their skin, but by the content of their character.

(Rev. Martin Luther King. Jr. 28/08/63)

3. One thought him indestructible, so overpowering was he in his energy, warmth and his deep faith in man's inherent goodness. For 25 years he had been my friend, my older brother, my inspiration and my teacher.

(Henry Kissinger 02/02/79)

4. I have said this before, but I shall say it again, and again, and again. Your boys are not going to be sent into any foreign wars.

(Franklin D. Roosevelt 30/10/40)

5. I have never been a quitter. To leave office before my term is completed is abhorrent to every instinct in my body. But, as President, I must put the interests of America first. America needs a full-time President and a full-time Congress. Particularly at this time, with problems we face at home and abroad. To continue to fight through the months ahead for my personal vindication would almost totally absorb the time and attention of both the President and the Congress in a period when our entire focus should be on the great issues of peace abroad and prosperity without inflation at home.

(Richard M. Nixon 08/08/74)

6. In the past several months I have been living in purgatory. I have found myself the recipient of undefined, unclear, unattributed accusations that have surfaced in the largest and the most widely circulated organs of our communications media. I want to say, at this point, clearly and unequivocally: I am innocent of the charges against me.

(Spiro T. Agnew 29/09/73)

Key to Exercises:

Recognizing the Main Idea

Listen to these extracts from famous speeches. Then decide what main idea each speaker wants to express, Write it out in the space given.

1. (I shall return.)
2. (Hoping for a country of equality)
3. (Commemorating a person)
4. (I won't send you to any foreign wars.)
5. (Why I resign)
6. (I'm innocent of the charges against me.)

Section Four:
Enjoy Your English:
Tapescript:

Killing Me Softly With His Song

Strumming my pain with his fingers
Singing my life with his words
Killing me softly with his song
Killing me softly with his song
Telling my whole life with his words
Killing me softly with his song

I heard he sang a good song
I heard he had a style

358

And so I came to see him to listen for a while.
And there he was this young boy
A stranger to my eyes
Strumming my pain with his fingers
Singing my life with his words
Killing me softly with his song
Killing me softly with his song
Telling my whole life with his words
Killing me softly with his song

I felt all flushed with fever
Embarrassed by the crowd
I felt he found my letters and read each one out loud
I prayed that he would finnish
But he just kept right on
Strumming my pain with his fingers
Singing my life with his words
Killing me softly with his song
Killing me softly with his song
Telling my whole life with his words
Killing me softly with his song

He sang as if he knew me in all my dark despair
And then he looked right through me as if I wasn't there
And he just kept on singing
Singing clear and strong
*Strumming my pain with his fingers
Singing my life with his words
Killing me softly with his song
Killing me softly with his song
Telling my whole life with his words

Killing me softly with his song*

Oh, la la
(Repeat *)
Supplementary Reading:

1. Energy Possibilities for the Future

Two imaginative ideas would supply people on earth with energy from space. One idea proposes a solar power station that would orbit the earth and send energy back by microwaves. The other proposes a power-relay satellite. The satellite would transmit power from a solar or nuclear power station located in an isolated place on earth to a receiving station serving a populated area on earth.
The Orbiting Solar Power Station.

This idea calls for a very large solar collector in orbit around the earth. The microwaves would be collected by a very large receiving antenna and converted back to electricity.

An orbiting solar power station has several advantages. There are no clouds to block the sunlight from a solar receiver high in space. The sun is always shining in space; there are no day-and-night cycles. One orbiting station of 15 million kilowatts could supply all the electric needs of a city the size of New York City in the year 2000.

There are several disadvantages to an orbiting solar power system. First, the extremely large solar collector would have to be carried into space piece by piece in rockets and then put together in space by astronauts. This would be very expensive and difficult; some new technological advances will be necessary before this can be done. Second, the solar cells that will be used to collect the solar energy are very expensive at present. Finally, further experiments will be necessary to determine whether it will be possible or even safe to send the electricity back to earth by microwaves. There are still some important problems to be solved, but the designers of outer-space solar power stations think they can be ready for use within twenty years.

This plan calls for a large solar or nuclear power station to operate in an isolated place on earth, perhaps in the desert. A power-relay satellite would be placed in orbit to relay the energy to cities in much the same way that a communications satellite relays TV and telephone calls now. The largest and heaviest parts of the system would stay on the ground; this would reduce the cost and difficulty. Because this idea also calls for relaying the energy by microwave, much more experimentation needs to be done before this idea can become a reality.

2. Air Pollution

Wherever you go, whatever you do ﹣ ﹣ inside, outside, upstairs, downstairs, on top of a mountain, down in the bottom of a coal mine you're always surrounded by a sea of gases that we call air, or the atmosphere. These gases cannot be seen and we are rarely aware of them. But they are of the greatest importance, for without atmosphere neither man, animals, nor plants can live. Of almost equal importance is the quality of the atmosphere ﹣ ﹣ whether it is pure or whether it is impure, or polluted. It is easy to understand why clean air is important to good health, for throughout life, human beings take air into their lungs about 20 times a minute. The air is drawn into the lungs through the nose or mouth. After a few seconds the process is reversed and the air is blown out of the lungs through the nose or mouth. During this process of inhaling and exhaling, the impurities in the air may be absorbed by the body or deposited in the lungs.

The atmosphere is a mixture of about one part oxygen, four

parts nitrogen, very small amounts of carbon dioxide and rare inert gases, and water in the form of water vapour. Oxygen, nitrogen, and water play an essential part in man's survival. The oxygen in the atmosphere is essential for all life processes. The nitrogen is essential for the plant life that provides man with the nutrients he needs for good health. The moisture in the atmosphere is essential for plant growth and agriculture, and for the water or fluid man requires. When air contains more than a small amount of particulate matter (matter containing tiny separate particles) or gases other than the ones mentioned, the air is considered to be polluted.

Even the purest air contains small amounts of pollution. Perhaps really clean air can be found only in experimental laboratories. Even in country areas, far removed from factories and heavy traffic, air may contain pollen from plants, dust from the soil, and occasional bacteria and germs. But these pollutants are generally in such small amounts that they are not important. Throughout the world, air pollution is generally present in all cities, especially those with populations of more than 50,000.

High Cost of air Pollution.

The damage caused by air pollution is enormous. In money alone it represents a loss of billions of dollars each year. Many flower and vegetable crops suffer ill effects from air pollution caused by exhaust gases from automobiles. Trees have been killed by pollution from power plants. Cattle have been poisoned by the fumes from smelters engaged in recovering aluminum from the ore. Air pollution causes rubber tires on automobiles to crack and become porous. Fine buildings become shabby, their walls blackened with soot as a result of the pollution that has settled on building stones and surfaces for years. The average householder is familiar with the increasing

362

amount of washing and dry cleaning needed to maintain the home and the family clothing.

But the high cost of air pollution is strikingly illustrated in its damaging effects on the human body. Besides the unpleasantness of irritated eyes and scratchy throats, it presents a threat to the respiratory tract, contributing to a number of serious diseases. In both the United States and Europe, episodes of high levels of air pollution were implicated in a large number of deaths.

Control of Air Pollution.

Much can be accomplished in the prevention and control of air pollution by proper fuel selection and engineering. The use of only those fuels (oil and coal) that contain little or no sulfur or other harmful substances should be permitted. Improved engineering methods must be developed so that the burning of fuels and refuse will not release pollutants into the air.

It is not easy to bring about the new developments needed to control air pollution. Many people - - doctors, engineers, meteorologists, botanists, and other scientists - - are engaged in research, seeking ways to control air pollution. One project involves the setting up of permanent observatories where the gradual change in atmospheric content can be measured uninterruptedly over long periods of time. The first observatory of this type is located near the top of Mauna Loa mountain in Hawaii. Other stations are being planned for the central United States and for south America.

Some progress has been made in reducing air pollution at the source. Smoke and dust control are being accomplished by redesigning automobile motors and fuel burning apparatus.

Until better methods of control become available, we must make more use of the capacity of the air to accept and carry away air pollutants. For example, chimneys and smokestacks may have to be built much taller in order to discharge smoke high above the ground. Studies of this problem are being made in wind tunnels at New York University and other research institutions.

In the United States, the most important force in the battle against air pollution is the United States Public Health Service. Since 1912, many local communities have had simple smoke abatement programs. In the 1960's and 1970's, several Clean Air Acts were passed. These acts gave impetus to the drive against air pollution. The acts placed all federal authority concerning air pollution in the hands of the Secretary of Health, Education, and Welfare. Substantial funds for research and the training of personnel have been provided. At this time many city and state programs are in operation, with more being created all the time.

Nearly all of the highly industrialized countries throughout the world are moving vigorously to prevent and control air pollution. Among the many countries in which some type of control legislation exists are Belgium, Bulgaria, Canada, France, Germany, Italy, Japan, the Soviet Union, Spain, the United Kingdom, and Yugoslavia.

Vast sums of money will have to be spent in the future to clean the air, but the cost will be justified. Perhaps the day will come when people will be able to breathe pure air in cities in which the sunlight is no longer blacked out by an umbrella of smog.

Lesson 19

Tapescript:

Task 1: Estate Agent

Presenter: This week's financial talk will be given by our property expert, James Milligan, who is here to tell us about some surprising new developments in the London area.

James Milligan: Good afternoon. Not so very long ago it would have been really unusual to pay £1 million for a house. Unfortunately this is no longer so. Decline in the real value of money over the past few years has made property values rocket. The cheap house is a thing of the past. Now, the sale of a £1 million house no longer causes surprise, nor is it likely to be the subject of a newspaper article.

What exactly can we expect to get for £1 million today? Well, first of all, space, of course. Living in large cities has made us all tired of living in those cramped little houses and flats built just after the war. We now want space; space to live and relax in, preferably with a garden. And this, of course, is what puts the price up. Another reason for needing space is the fact that we have larger families growing up under one roof and even quite small children demand their own room these days, while teenagers may demand an extra room where they can entertain their friends privately. Also the trend of going out to eat is dying out due to rising prices of restaurant and transport, so

365

people are once more beginning to entertain and dine at home, which requires a larger dining room. There are numerous new developments in London at the moment which can provide all this and more – – if you have the money!

At the moment the most fashionable places seem to be the Barbican, St John's Wood, Morgan's Walk in Battersea. People wanting quiet in the evening tend to prefer the Barbican situated in the business heart of the city and therefore fairly free of traffic in the evenings, although several theatres have opened there lately. The Barbican is also for those who like living high up, accommodation being situated mostly in tower blocks. St John's Wood, on the other hand, is favoured mostly by upper-middle class families who prefer a detached house surrounded by a walled garden, thus ensuring their privacy. Gardens of course tend to raise the price of a property. Those not interested in gardening can choose from the grand mansions in Battersea where you get a wonderful view of the Thames and are still only a few minutes away from London's theatres and shops.

Look around and take your pick. Oh ... just make sure that you have that million pounds first!

Task 2: Jazz Singer

Interviewer: Now you're the First Lady of Jazz; probably the greatest blues singer the world has ever known. Just what is it that makes you sing as you do?

Singer: I don't know; one night it's a little bit slower, the next night it's a little bit lighter. It's all according to how I feel. I never feel the same way twice. The blues is a mixed up sort of thing. There's two kinds of blues; there's happy blues and there's sad blues. I don't think I ever sing the same way twice.

Interviewer: And how did you become a jazz singer in the first place?

Singer: Well, it was all by accident really. You see, I wanted to be a dancer so I went along to try out, you know, to an audition and I was just a kid, I didn't know how to dance at all. So I kept doing the two steps I did know over and over until they told me to get off the stage. But I guess the pianist felt sort of sorry for me because he called me back and asked me if I could sing. Huh, 'Course I can sing, man,' I told him; 'I've been singing all my life. What the hell use is that?' And then he asked me to sing a blues song, St Louis Blues, I think it was, and I just kept on singing and he just kept on playing, and in the end I had a job. That was on West 42nd Street. Now that was the street for jazz in those days. And slowly I became known; people started coming to see me rather than just to listen to the orchestra, and that's how it started. I mean, it began like that and it's just been going on ever since.

Interviewer: You've never looked back and you've been successful ever since?

Singer: Well, it wasn't quite as easy as it sounds. I mean, when I started out I didn't know anything, I mean like chords and sharps and flats. I just sang. But if you're going to sing jazz you have to know these things. And people were very nice and kind to me and they slowly taught me what key I had to sing each song in. And that's how I really became a professional musician. I mean, the beginning was just luck, but if you want to stay at the top you really have to know your job. You have to

367

know what you're doing and you have to know how to be able to change it to go with the public's taste; with the changing fashions. Otherwise you find yourself out of work and back on the streets where you started from.

Interviewer: But surely, you never needed to go with the fashions? I mean, you've always been popular.

Singer: Well, that's true up to a point. And if you're good enough you can even change the fashions. I've never done that. I've always sung what I wanted and if they didn't like it, they didn't have to buy it. I've never made a fortune from my music because I won't sing just any damn thing. I choose what I want to sing. But anything I do sing is part of my life. So it has to be important to me before I'll sing it. I think this is why people like my music; they know that whatever I say in my songs I really believe and this means something to them and helps them in their lives. I'm not a rich pop singer and never wanted to be. And there's been a lot of scandal attached to my life. Some of it's true, some of it's not. But at least I've always been my true self in my music and I'll always stay that way. I think a guy called Shakespeare once wrote 'Unto thine own self be true and thou canst not then to any man be false'. Well, that's how I feel when I'm singing my songs. You may like them, you may hate them, but nobody can say that I'm not singing from deep down inside myself. I won't ever sing anything I don't believe in although, as I said, it's never the same any two nights running: it may be happy one night and sad the next. It's all according to how I feel. And now I'm feeling the need for a drink of something strong; I've got four hours on stage tonight and that really takes it out of you, believe me.

Interviewer: Go right ahead and thank you for the interview.

Singer: That's OK. Here's a couple of tickets; come and see the show.

Key to Exercises:

Task 1: Estate Agent

A. Choose the best answer (a, b or c) to complete each of the following statements.

1. James Milligan is _____.

  * a. a property expert

    b. a programme expert

    c. a salesman

2. Housing prices rise rapidly in the London area because _____.

    a. more and more people become very rich

    b. buying houses is a fashion

  * c. the real value of money declines

3. James Milligan is talking about _____.

    a. houses that most people can afford

    b. houses at unusual and surprising prices

  * c. houses that cost one million pounds

B. Give a list of reasons that people want to buy houses that cost one million pounds.

1. They want space (to live and relax in) since they are tired of (living in the cramped little houses and flats) built just after (the Second World War).

2. Larger families (are growing up, and very small children demand a room of their own).

3. Teenagers (may demand an extra room to treat their friends privately).

4. Due to rising prices of (restaurant and transport, people are beginning to entertain and dine at home, which requires a larger dining room).

C. Describe the characteristics of the following places mentioned by James Milligan.

1. Barbican:
   a. situated (in the business heart of the city); so quiet and fairly free from (traffic in the evenings);
   b. several theatres (opened recently);
   c. suitable for (those who like living high up since accommodation being situated mostly is tower blocks).

2. St. John's Wood:
   a. favoured mostly by (upper middle class families who prefer a detached house);
   b. a walled garden (surrounding the house and ensuring privacy).

3. Battersea:
   a. suitable for (those who are not interested in gardening);
   b. grand (mansions to be chosen);
   c. a wonderful view (of the Thames);
   d. only a few minutes (away from London's theatres and shops).

Task 2: Jazz Singer

A. Answer the following questions briefly.

1. How successful is the interviewee?

Answer: (She is the First Lady of Jazz, the greatest blues singer the world has ever known.)

2. What did she try to do before she became a singer?

Answer: (To learn dancing. But she failed.)

3. How did she become a singer?

Answer: (All by accident. A pianist discovered her talent.)

4. Has she been successful ever since?

Answer: No, at first she had to learn a lot to become a professional musician; then she has to know a lot about the public and changing fashions in order to keep her top position.)

5. What does she think of the songs she sings?

Answer: (She chooses what she wants to sing. Anything she does sing is a part of her life.)

6. How does she look at the scandal attached to her life?

Answer: (She feels she has always been her true self in her music. And she's singing from deep down inside herself.)

B. True or False Questions. Write a T in front of a statement if it is true according to the recording and write an F if it is false.

1. (T) There are two kinds of blues, the happy blues and the sad blues.

2. (F) West 42nd Street was the street for dance those days.

3. (F) When she started singing, she actually knew quite a lot about singing.

4. (T) She became a successful and professional musician with the help of a lot of other people.

5. (F) She often tries to change the fashions and she has made

it.

6. (T) There is a feeling of understanding between her and her audience.

7. (T) She won't sing anything that she doesn't believe in.

8. (T) She sings according to how she feels and she never sings the same way twice.

C. Complete the following sentences with what you hear on the tape.

1. One night it's a little bit (slower), the next night it's a little bit (lighter). It's all according to (how I feel). I never feel (the same way twice). The blues is (a mixed up sort of thing).

2. If you want to (stay at the top you really have to know your job... Otherwise you find yourself (out of work) and back on the streets) where (you started from).

3. That's true (up to a point).

4. I've never (made a fortune from my music) because I won't sing just (any damn thing).

Section Two:

Tapescript:

Task 1: Setting Up a Home Computer

Now first we must identify the parts of this home computer system. Before we can set up the system, we must all know what the names of the different parts of the computer are and what they do. So first I'm going to tell you the names of the parts and what they are used for in a home computer system.

First, and most important of all, is your instruction manual.

Can you all see that? The instruction manual is the book of instructions —it tells you how to set up your system and then how to use it. OK?

Next, the monitor. The monitor is the part that everyone can recognize immediately because it looks just like a television. The monitor shows you the information you have typed in on the screen. You can change the information, move it around or take it away, while it is on the screen. Right?

Now, when you have finished working with your information and you want a copy of this on paper, then you have to use the printer. The printer prints out on paper what you have on the monitor screen. Then you have a copy of your work on paper.

Now the keyboard. The keyboard contains the actual computer and it looks just like a typewriter. Each piece on the keyboard is called a key. You have keys for letters (a, b, c etc.) and keys for instructions to the computer. You have to be able to type if you want to use a computer properly.

Now what have we got left? Ah yes, the 2 floppy discs and the disc drive. The disc drive is quite simple —it's the part of the system that operates the floppy discs, we say it powers the floppy discs. You put the floppy discs into the disc drive and the disc drive makes them work.

So finally, the two floppy discs. You need two because the first one contains the programme —that is, the instructions —and the second is where you type in your information and where the program works on this information. So you really work on the second floppy disc: then, when you are ready to print, the printer takes everything from the second floppy disc and prints out what you have done.

Now, is that clear? Are there any questions?

Task 2: My Computer Makes Me Sick

There's no doubt that the computer has enlarged man's working capacity as well as his intellectual capacity enormously. Er ... but it brings with it dangers to match the benefits. Now by this, I mean danger to physical and mental well-being of the people who work at computer terminals, not the dangers to personal privacy or national or industrial security.

There's one very alarming set of statistics which come from a survey done in the UK on 800 pregnant women, who happened to use computer terminals for a major part of their working day. In no less than 36% of the subjects there was some severe abnormality during the pregnancy, enough to make a termination necessary. Now these figures compare significantly with a control group of pregnant women of the same age but who did not work with computer terminals. The incidence of severe abnormalities in their case was only 16%. This survey confirms similar investigations carried out in Denmark, Canada, Australia and the USA. Now, no one yet has a clear idea about the exact connection between working with computer terminals and the problems with pregnancy, but the figures at least suggest that there's, well, a cause for alarm.

In more general terms, increased stress and disturbances to vision have been noted in workers exposed for long periods to the video screen, and in many countries trade unions of workers involved with computers have laid down their own guidelines to protect members' health. Erm ... for instance, rest periods, or a change of activity from time to time are recommended, and the terminal should be placed so that there's a source of natural light, and something else to

374

look at, emm, no blank walls behind the terminal, in other words, so that the operator has a chance to rest his eyes from time to time.

Ironically, it seems that it's not only those who work with computers who are at risk. Er ... there's perhaps more danger for people who use computers for interest or pleasure in their own homes. Now, it's obviously not possible to impose in the privacy of people's homes the sort of safeguards that can be applied in the working environment. Most people get so fascinated by what they are doing that they stay in front of the screen for hours on end; some are real fanatics!

But they're also using their computers in environments which are not specially designed. Er they may be dusty or hot, and not particularly well-lit on the whole.

An English magazine for computer enthusiasts recently ran its own survey. The readers were invited to send in an account of any health problems they felt were connected with the use of their computers. Er, interestingly, a long list emerged of complaints both serious and less serious, ranging from constipation because of the long hours spent in sedentary ac ... inactivity, and backache due to crouching over an inconveniently positioned keyboard, er, right through to a general sense of fatigue owing to having puzzled over a problem for longer than was sensible.

The visual disturbances mentioned above were also very common. Some readers who already suffered from short sight found that the condition had worsened, and a rarer complaint, but still one suffered by a significant number, was an itching of the face, which in some cases became a form of dermatitis. It seems that this is due to the electrostatic field of the video sereen attracting dust from the atmosphere, which irritates exposed skin. And ... this is an example of a complaint which is rare in the work situation because there is usually some form of air-conditioning, and quite simply not so much dust and fluff in the air as in a normal home.

Precautions for both types of terminal users remain essentially the same. So, first of all, make sure that there's an alternative source of light from that of the screen itself. Secondly, rest your eyes frequently, if possible looking at something in the distance to give them a change from the close focus used on the screen. Thirdly, make sure the screen is properly tuned; a shaky or fuzzy image can cause nausea or headaches. Fourthly, make sure your seat and working area are designed so that you're sitting in a comfortable position, not er ... screwed up or bent over. And finally, get up regularly and walk about the room. Better still, go out into the fresh air occasionally. Sitting still for hours on end is the best way to encourage a thrombosis in the legs, as well as not being particularly good for the digestion.

These are all common-sense precautions, but how many home-computer owners wrapped up in the intricacies of some programing problem, or fascinated by some game, are going to remember to use their common sense? Does a generation of short-sighted, constipated, hunched, migraine sufferers with skin problems and circulatory troubles await us?

Key to Exercises:

Task 1: Setting Up a Home Computer

A. Choose the best answer (a, b or c) to complete each of the following statements.

1. The speaker is _____.

   a. setting up a home computer

376

* b. telling people the names and the functions of the parts in a home computer system

   c. attending a computer science class

2. The book of instructions is called _____ .

* a. instruction manual

   b. instruction menu

   c. instruction review

3. The monitor _____ .

   a. is a television set

   b. is used to store information

* c. shows on the screen the information that has been typed in

4. _____ are mentioned as other parts of a home com -
puter.

* a. A keyboard, two floppy discs and the disc drive

   b. A keyboard, typewriter and a floppy disc

   c. Two floppy discs, a disc drive and a typewriter

B. True or False Questions. Write a T in front of a statement if it is true according to the recording and write an F if it is false.

1. (T) The book of instructions tells you how to set up your system and then how to use it.

2. (F) Once you type the information on the screen, you can change it no longer.

3. (F) The monitor can print on paper the information on the screen.

4. (T) If you want to use a computer properly, you'll have to be able to type.

5. (F) The disc drive is quite complicated because it is the part of the system that operates the floppy discs.

6. (T) The second floppy disc is where you type in your information and where the programme works on this information.

Task 2: My Computer Makes Me Sick
A. Choose the best answer (a, b or c) to complete each of the following statements.
1. The speaker is delivering a speech on _____.
   a. human capacity enlarged by the computer
   b. benefits the computer brings to human beings
 * c. harm and danger that the computer does to human health
2. Statistics show that _____.
 * a. using computer may cause severe abnormity during women's pregnancy
   b. 36 women using computer had to terminate their pregnancy
   c. 16 women in Denmark didn't get pregnant because they used computer
3. Workers working with computers are protected against _____.
   a. the disturbance of natural light to their vision
   b. watching television for long hours
 * c. increased stress and disturbances to vision for being exposed for long periods to the video screen
4. Without taking the precautions offered by the speaker, we will have a generation of _____.
   a. great intellectual capacity
 * b. deformed sufferers
   c. little common sense

B. Answer the following questions briefly.

1. Is there anyone who has a clear idea about the exact connection between working with computer terminals and the problems with pregnancy?

   Answer: (No, but statistic figures at least suggest that there is a cause of alarm.)

2. What is recommended to those who work with computers?

   Answer: (The terminal should be placed where there is another source of light; no blank wall behind the terminal so that the operator has a chance to rest from time to time, get up regularly and walk about the room.)

3. Who else are at risk besides those who work with computers?

   Answer: (Those who use computers for interest or pleasure in their own homes.)

4. What were the health problems some computer enthusiasts felt connected with the use of computers?

   Answer:

   a. (constipation because of long hours spent in sedentary inactivity;)

   b. (backache due to crouching over an inconveniently positioned key board; and)

   c. (a general sense of fatigue owing to having puzzled over a problem for longer than was sensible.)

5. What happened to those who had already suffered from shortsight?

   Answer: (The condition worsened.)

6. Why did people have an itching face?

Answer: (Because of the electrostatic field of the video screen attracting dust from the atmosphere, which irritates exposed skin.)

7. What sort of image would our next generation have if the speaker's precautions were not taken?

Answer: (A generation of short-sighted, constipated, hunched migraine sufferers with skin problems and circulatory troubles.)

C. Write out a list of the precautions offered by the speaker.

1. Make sure that (there is an alternative source of light from that of the screen);

2. Rest your eyes (frequently, if possible, by looking at something in the distance to give them a change from the close focus used on the screen);

3. Make sure (the screen is properly tuned, for a shaky or fuzzy image can cause nausea or headaches);

4. Make sure your seat (and working area are so designed that you're sitting in a comfortable position, not screwed up or bent over);

5. Get up (regularly and walk about the room. Better go out into the fresh air occasionally).

D. Complete the following sentences with the information you hear on the tape.

1. The computer has enlarged man's (working capacity) as well as his (intellectual capacity) ... but it brings with it (dangers) to match the (benefits).

2. A survey was done in (the UK) on (800 pregnant women),

380

who happened to use (computer termiuals) for (a major part) of their working day. In (no less than 36%) of the subjects there were some (severe abnormality) during the pregnancy.

3. In a (coutrol group) of pregnant women of (the same age) but who did not work with (computer terminals), the incidence of (severe abnormalities) in their case was only (16%).

Section Three:
Study Skills: Note-taking 3
Using Abbreviations

We have said that the student is not concerned with taking down every word that the lecturer says, so have rejected shorthand for normal note taking. Nevertheless, a lot of time and effort can be saved by using abbreviations and symbols. The symbols you use must make sense to you, but it is not necessary for anyone else to be able to understand them. Note-taking is a very individual skill. The main point to remember is to use only abbreviations which you will be able to remember when revising your notes some time later. A student of linguistics, for example, might be ill-advised to use phon. as an abbreviation for phonology: it could equally well stand for phonetics, a related, but different, area of linguistics.

Abbreviations can be of three kinds:

1. Field abbreviations. The student specializing in a certain field will learn certain abbreviations as part of the study of that field. For example, a student of chemistry will know that C stands for Carbon, and Ca for Calcium. Such abbreviations are very useful since they are widely used within each field but not ambiguous, or liable to be misunderstood.

381

2. Commonly understood abbreviations. These are abbreviations in common use, or else easily understood. Some examples are i. e. meaning that is, and = meaning is equal to, or is the same as. For more examples see table below.

Some useful abbreviations and symbols for note taking

From Latin		Symbols			
cf.	compare (with)	$\therefore$	therefore, thus, so	$\geqslant$	much greater than
e. g.	for example	$\because$	because	$\leqslant$	much less than
etc.	et cetera, and so on	=	is equal to, the	$\rightleftharpoons$	equal to, or
et al.	and others		same as		greater than
ibid.	in the same place	$\neq$	is not equal to,	%	per cent
	(in a book or		not the same as	$\div$	divide, divided by
	article)				
i. e.	that is	+	plus, and, more	$\times$	multiply, multi-
					plied by
N. B.	note well (some-	−	miuns, less	$\daleth$	insert (something
	thing important)	>	greater than		which has been
viz.	namely (naming some-	<	less than		omitted)
	one or something you	∞	proportional to	$\rightarrow$	from. . . . to, leads
	have just referred to)		·not proportional to		to, results in

3. Personal abbreviations made up by the student himself. If you find yourself having to frequently note down a certain word it is sensible to find a way of abbreviating it. For example, a student of English literature listening to a lecture on the poet Wordsworth could well use the initial W. instead of writing out the poet's name in full each time he has to refer to it.

Tapescript:

Main Ideas and Supporting Details

1. Of course, scientists have always had their pet theories, and historically all of the following have been linked as companions to heart disease: first, a high level of fat and cholesterol in the diet; second, cigarette smoking; third, physical inactivity; fourth, being overweight; and fifth, high blood pressure.

382

2. There are some similarities between the two men. Both are married, have grown children, are in their mid-fifties, and have been very successful in their business careers. Both are hard workers and have achieved a position of financial security and responsibility in their jobs. Their professional lives are not easy for either of them. But life for Adam has been full of tension, and hostility, whereas for Bert, life has been much more enjoyable.

3. Adam always seems to be fighting time, trying to do more things in a day than he previously has done. If situations beyond his control cause delays in his schedule, he becomes angry and hostile. He resents people who are not on time or who do not move as quickly as he does. It is very important to him that he fill up every minute with some kind of productive activity.

4. However, Bert shows an opposite tendency. Once work is behind him for the day, he devotes himself to three or four interesting hobbies. In addition to his regular physical exercise, he is an enthusiastic reader. He prefers history and historical novels. His special interest is in the second world war, and he prizes all the new information which he can gather about that time period. He also enjoys gardening and likes to fix things around the house. He has a very complete tool collection which he uses to improve his house.

Key to Exercises:

Main Ideas and Supporting Details

A. Suggested Abbreviations:

heart disease: heart dis.	cholesterol: chol.
cigarette: cigat.	exercise: ex.
especially: esp.	similarity: simty.

difference: diffr.   financial: finan.

responsibility: respty.   hostility: hosty.

B. Listen to these paragraphs. Then write in the space given below
   the main idea and supporting details of each paragraph.

   1. (companions to heart dis.) (main idea)

      a. (high level of fat and chol in the diet) (supporting details)

      b. (cigat. smoking)

      c. (physical inactivity)

      d. (over weight)

      e. (high blook pressure)

   2. (Bert's life after work) (main idea)

      a. (physical ex.) (supporting details)

      b. (reading)

         (1) (history)

         (2) (historical novels)

      c. (gardening)

      d. (fixing things around the house —a complete tool collec-
         tion)

   3. (simties. & differs, between Adam & Bert)

      a. (simties.) (supporting details)

         (1) (married)

         (2) (grown children)

         (3) (in mid-5os)

         (4) (successful in business careers)

         (5) (hard workers)

         (6) (in a position of finan, security & respty, in their
            jobs)

         (7) (professional lives not easy)

b. (diffrs.)

    (1) (for Adam: life – full of tension & hosty.)

    (2) (for Bert: life – more enjoyable)

4. (Adam's use of time) (main diea)

a. (fighting time) (supporting details)

b. (If delays in schedule, angry & hostile)

c. (resents people not on time & not moving as quickly)

d. (fill up every minnte with productive activity)

Supplementary Reading:

Jazz

Jazz began in the early 20th century as a music of black Americans. It was intended for singing, for dancing, and for entertainment and atmosphere at parties or social gatherings.

Jazz has continued to develop and has produced some of the United States' leading singers, instrumentalists, and composers. today, it is considered by many to be America's art music. It has also influenced almost every other kind of music in America, Europe, and even the Orient.

The origin of the word "jazz" is not known, but the term came into common use after the first phonograph records of Jazz were made in 1917. Jazz represents a blending of musical elements from Africa and from Europe. Jazz uses some European ideas of harmony and melody, but the rhythms are more African in origin. It is usually said to be "syncopated", that is, it is irregular in rhythm. And jazz is polyrhythmic, which means it uses many rhythms around one basic rhythm.

Another important feature of jazz is improvisation. To improvise means to make something up on the spur of the moment. This is the way jazz is usually played. Jazz musicians have learned to improvise so well that they can make up excellent melodies as they play. A good jazz soloist seldom plays anything the same way twice. Thus, listening to jazz is not like hearing a piece of music that was written long ago. It is like being there when the music is first being made.

A Brief History of Jazz

A great deal is known about jazz after about 1917, when recordings of the music began to be made. Much less is known about how jazz began and where it came from.

In the minstrel shows of about 1890 there was often heard a kind of music called cakewalk. It was named for a high-stepping dance. The dance was originated by black Americans, and the music, too, was influenced by their music. Then, about 1900, a new and highly successful kind of black music appeared, called ragtime. We can get some idea of how music changed in those days by comparing ragtime rhythm with the rhythm of the cakewalk. Cakewalk rhythm has a very heavy beat followed by a light beat, like this: ONE two THREE four. A typical cakewalk song goes "RUfus HI-ram JOHN-son BROWN." Ragtime rhythm is less simple; some of its light beats are divided like this: ONE and a TWO and a THREE and FOUR.

Ragtime was mainly piano music at first. Later it was played on other instruments as well. Since it was basically a type of instrumental music, there were only a few ragtime songs. Most ragtime pieces have three or four different melodies, or sections.

As ragtime became popular, it became simpler. Meanwhile, jazz had arrived on the scene. But to understand jazz, we must look at another form of music, the blues.

The origin of the name "blues" and what the earliest form of this music sounded like are not known. Some people believe that the blues originated in Mississippi. The blues were widely played after 1914.

The blues form is very familiar in American music. Most of us have heard it, even though we may not know it. About a third of jazz music is in the blues form. So are many of the popular rock 'n' roll pieces. Even some of the country and western music of the United States is in the blues form. Because it is often sung, the blues is a form of poetry as well as music. And the blues is the only musical form original to the United States.

In the 1920's it became quite common to hear blues without words played entirely on instruments, and it still is. The blue notes are attempts to imitate on instruments the human voice singing the blues, and blues singers use notes and gliding vocal sounds not usually heard in European music. The blues cover a variety of moods and are not necessarily slow and sad. And blue notes are heard in all styles of jazz.

A major step in the development of jazz was taken by the players in New Orleans. New Orleans jazz, sometimes called Dixieland, was a mixture of different elements. It had the deep emotion of the blues and the Negro spiritual, as well as elements of ragtime and European folk music. The New Orleans style involved improvising that was sometimes complex. Often seven or eight players would improvise at the same time. But the most notable new feature of New Orleans jazz was its more complicated rhythm.

In the 1940's a new approach to jazz began to develop. It had been hinted at in the playing of Lester Young with the Count Basie band. Another important influence on early modern jazz was guitarist Charlie Christian, who was strongly influenced by Lester Young. At first the new jazz was called bebop, and later, modern jazz. Many of the musical ideas of modern jazz were worked out at gatherings in which the players performed for their own amusement and instruction. Jazz musicians called these gatherings jam sessions.

Modern jazz was more complex in harmony and melody than earlier styles of jazz. But a most outstanding feature was its new approach to rhythm. Not only did the players use new rhythms in making their melodies, but the drummers played in a more complex way.

By the late 1950's many concert pieces had been written that included parts for jazz improvisation. These pieces usually took the form of a classical concerto with the jazzmen as soloists. Such works are referred to as parts of a "third stream" of music, the first two "streams" of course being classical music and jazz.

Since the modern jazz of the 1940's and 1950's, jazz has taken another step in its development. This new development is something called "the new thing," or "free jazz."

As in earlier major developments in jazz, "free jazz" is characterized new freshness of rhythm. For example, a whole group of players may change the tempo, or speed, of a piece several times during a performance without planning to do so beforehand. But this does not mean that the music is disorganized.

How Jazzmen Improvise

In early styles of jazz most players improvised on a melody as it was written. They added a few notes here or left out a few notes there or varied it in other ways. But the listener could recognize the original melody. Later, however, players discovered that they could invent entirely new melodies, using only the harmonic structure, or

388

chord progression, of an original piece. For example, on a recording of "Body and Soul" by the Benny Goodman Trio, pianist Teddy Wilson makes up an entirely new melody in his solo. It does not sound at all like the song "Body and Soul," and it is a completely new creation.

In the same way, jazz musicians often make up their own written or memorized melodies to introduce their improvised solos. For these they may also use the harmony, or chord structures, of older popular songs. For example, a jazz piece from 1932 called "Moten Swing" is built on the harmonies of a popular song called "You're Drivin' Me Crazy." One of the most commonly used chord outlines in jazz comes from George Gershwin's song "I Got Rhythm." But the most frequent chord outline used in jazz is still the one that belongs to the blues.

How Jazz Develops

Important changes in the development of jazz usually include new ideas of rhythm. The rhythm of ragtime was new, and so was the rhythm of New Orleans jazz. Louis Armstrong and Charlie Parker also brought new ideas of rhythm to jazz. Each style of jazz also had new ways of making melodies, new uses of harmony, and new ways of expressing emotion. Whenever a great player, such as Armstrong or Parker, appears, other players absorb his ideas. Each man then tries to develop those ideas in his own music, in his own way.

Major events in the history of jazz are often the result of the work of individual players, such as Armstrong and Parker, or of important composers, such as Morton, Ellington, and Monk. A player will give jazz a new style, and a composer finds form for each style. In a good record by a musician like Parker, he is the most important

389

player. But in a record by a composer like Ellington, every player is important.

Lesson 20

Section One:

Tapescript:

Task 1: Fixing an Appointment

Principal: Well it looks to me as if we shall have to fit him in somewhere. What dose Monday morning look like?

Secretary: Well Monday morning is extremely busy. You've got all the short-list interviews.

Principal: Oh goodness. And how long do they go on for?

Secretary: Well the last one is due at ... to come at 10 o'clock and will probably go on through until 10.30.

Principal: And then?

Secretary: Then you've got your Japanese agent and you did tell him you'd probably take him out to lunch.

Principal: Yes, well can't pass that up ... erm ... what's Tuesday morning look like?

Secretary: Tuesday morning is also very full. You've got a committee meeting, starts at 9.30 probably won't finish until 12.30.

Principal: Huh – Huh. And lunch?

Secretary: Lunch is with your publisher.

Principal: Oh yes. And I do remember that I've got something in the afternoon ... erm ... from the examining board, haven't I? I've got ...

Secretary: Yes. At 2.30. You're expecting the chief examiner

(Oh) regarding the review report.

Principal: Oh yes. And I've got ... I've got somebody's parents coming.

Secretary: Yes at 4 o'clock Johan Blun's parents are coming.

Principal: And there ... isn't there a meeting, a principal's meeting after ... anyway he didn't want to be that late ... erm ... well, let's have a look at Monday afternoon. What have we got then?

Secretary: Well the lunch with the Japanese agent is probably likely to last until 2.30. (Mm – Mm) At 2.30 you've got the lawyer regarding the planning permission.

Principal: Oh, I've ... yes ... and?

Secretary: Well at 3.30 there's a tutorial with Maria Rosa ...

Principal: Oh well hang on ... erm ... look what we can do ... you ... if you could give the lawyer a ring and ask him if he can fix it, the appointment, for Wednesday and if he can't make Wednesday, later in the week. It's not absolutely vital that I should do it then. And give Maria Rosa a ring also if you can contact her, otherwise you can tell her when she arrives and ... erm ... I can give I can definitely give her ... I've got Wednesday clear, haven't I? So... erm... (Yes) I can give her a tutorial on Wednesday morning (Yes) and that gives us two hours so you could ring the Cultural Council and fix it for then. His name's Mr Dennis I think, isn't it?

Secretary: Yes. So I'll ring him and tell him you're expecting him at 2.30 on Monday afternoon.

Principal: OK then.

Secretary: Fine. Thank you.

Task 2: Last of the Airships?

At 7.20 pm on May 6th 1937, the world's largest airship, the Hindenburg, floated majestically over Lakehurst airport, New Jersey, after an uneventful crossing from Frankfurt, Germany. There were 97 people on board for the first Atlantic crossing of the season. There were a number of journalists waiting to greet it. Suddenly radio listeners heard the commentator screaming 'Oh, my God! It's broken into flames. It's flashing... flashing. It's flashing terribly.' 32 seconds later the airship had disintegrated and 35 people were dead. The Age of the Airship was over.

The Hindenburg was the last in a series of airships which had been developed over 40 years in both Europe and the United States. They were designed to carry passengers and cargo over long distances. The Hindenburg could carry 50 passengers accommodated in 25 luxury cabins with all the amenities of a first class hotel. All the cabins had hot and cold water and electric heating. There was a diningroom, a bar and a lounge with a dance floor and a baby grand piano. The Hindenburg had been built to compete with the great luxury transatlantic liners. It was 245 metres long with a diameter of 41 metres. It could cruise at a speed of 125 km/h, and was able to cross the Atlantic in less than half the time of a liner. By 1937 it had carried 1000 passengers safely and had even transported circus animals and cars. Its sister ship, the Graf Zeppelin, had flown one and a half million kilometres and it had carried 13,100 passengers without incident.

The Hindenburg was filled with hydrogen, which is a highly flammable gas, and every safety precaution had been taken to prevent accidents. It had a smoking room which was pressurized in order to prevent gas from ever entering it. The cigarette lighters were chained to the tables and both passengers and crew were searched for matches before entering the ship. Special materials, which were used in the construction of the airship, had been chosen to minimize the possibility of accidental sparks, which might cause an explosion.

Nobody knows the exact cause of the Hindenburg disaster. Sabotage has been suggested, but experts at the time believed that it was caused by leaking gas which was ignited by static electricity. It had been waiting to land for three hours because of heavy thunderstorms. The explosion happened just as the first mooring rope, which was wet, touched the ground. Observers saw the first flames appear near the tail, and they began to spread quickly along the hull. There were a number of flashes as the hydrogen-filled compartments exploded. The airship sank to the ground. The most surprising thing is that 62 people managed to escape. The fatalities were highest among the crew, many of whom were working deep inside the airship. After the Hindenburg disaster, all airships were grounded and, until recently, they have never been seriously considered as a commercial proposition.

Key to Exercises:

Task 1: Fixing an Appointment

A. Choose the best answer (a, b or c) to complete each of the following statements.

    1. The conversation is _____.

   * a. between a school principal and her secretary

      b. between Maria Rosa and her secretary

      c. between a tourist and her tour guide

    2. They are making arrangements for _____.

      a. the whole week

b. Wednesday, Thursday and Friday

  * c. Monday, Tuesday and Wednesday

3. From the conversation , it is quite obvious that the woman
   _____.

   a. doesn't have much to do during the week

 * b. has a very busy schedule

   c. is going to be busy next week

B. Fill in the blanks with the information you hear on the tape about
   the woman's schedule.

   1. Monday:

      10.00 a.m.—10.30 a.m.: (the last short-list interview)

      Lunch: (to dine with the Japanese agent)

      2.30 p.m.: (a meeting with the lawyer about planning per-
      mission)

      3.30 p.m.: (a tutorial with Maria Rosa)

   2. Tuesday:

      9.30 a.m.—12.30 p.m.: (a committee meeting)

      2.30 p.m.: (business with the examining board)

      4.00 p.m.: (a meeting with Johan Blun's parents)

C. Fill in the blanks with the information you hear on the tape about
   the changes that have been made to the woman's original schedule.

   1. The meeting with the lawyer (is to be postponed to Wednes-
      day or later in the week).

   2. The tutorial with Maria Rosa (is to be put off till Wednesday
      morning).

   3. Mr. Dennis is expected to come (at 2.30 on monday agter-

noon).

Task 2: Last of the Airships?

A. Choose the best answer (a, b or c) to complete each of the following statements.

1. The story took place _____.
    a. at 7.20 a.m. on May 6th 1937
    b. at 7.20 p.m. on May 16th 1937
    * c. at 7.20 p.m. on May 6th 1937

2. The Hindenburg was _____.
    a. an ocean liner
    * b. an airship with luxurious facilities
    c. a man's name

3. By 1937, it had been _____.
    * a. quite safe to travel by the Hindenburg
    b. very dangerous to cross the Atlantic by the Hindenburg
    c. rare for the Hindenburg to carry passengers

4. After the accident, the exact cause of the disaster

    _____.
    a. was found
    * b. was unknown
    c. was determined to be the leaking gas

5. Since the disaster, _____.
    a. people have been using airships a lot
    b. a lot of improvements have been made to the Hindenburg
    * c. airships have never been seriously considered as a means of commercial transportation

B. True or False Questions. Write a T in front of a statement if it is

396

true according to the recording and write an F if it is false.

1. ·(F) The Hindenburg exploded in the first Atlantic crossing of its voyage.

2. (F) Both Europe and the United States had developed a series of airships over 40 years, among which the Hindenburg was the first one.

3. (T) The Hindenburg had been built to compete with the great luxury transatlantic liners.

4. (T) On the Hindenburg, there were very strict safety regulations.

5. (F) The Hindenburg had to hover in the sky for three more hours because of heavy fog.

6. (T) The first flames appeared near the tail of the Hindenburg.

7. (T) The first explosion happened just as the first mooring rope touched the ground.

8. (T) More crew members died than the passengers.

C. Fill in the blanks will the information you hear on the tape.

1. There were (97) people on the Hindenburg, among whom (35) died and (62) managed to escape.

2. The Hindenburg was designed to carry (50) passengers accommodated in (25) luxury cabins.

3. The Hindenburg was (245) metres long and (41) metres in diameter. It could fly at a speed of (125 km/hr) and was able to cross the Atlantic in (less than half the time) of an ocean liner.

4. The Hindenburg had carried (1, 000 passengers) safely and even (cicrus animals and cars) by (1937).

5. The Hindenburg's sister ship, the Graf Zeppelin, had flown (1½ million) kilometres and it had carried (13,100) passengers without incident.

D. List the safety precautions that had been taken on the Hindenburg.
  1. The smoking room (was pressurized in order to prevent gas from ever entering it).
  2. The cigarette lighters (were chained to the tables).
  3. Both passengers and crew (were searched for matches before entering the ship).
  4. The airship (was made of special materials, which had been chosen to minimize the possibility of accidental sparks, which might cause an explosion).

Section Two:

Tapescript:

Task 1: Looking for a Flat

David: Hello Peggy. What are you doing going through all those newspapers?

Peggy: Oh hallo David. I'm trying to find a flat and I've got to go through all these advertisements. I just can't find anything good.

David: Are you wanting to share or do you want a flat on your own?

Peggy: Well, you know Sara and Mary? I'd really like to share with them.

David: Well, I know of an empty flat. I don't know if you'd like it though. It's on the number ten bus route in Woodside Road. Number 10 I think it is.

Peggy: Oh, I know Woodside Road and the ten bus is the one that brings me to work. Would be a marvellous place. How many rooms has it got?

David: Well, it's got a kitchen and a bathroom. Um, apart from that I think it's got two bedrooms and a sitting-room.

Peggy: Two bedrooms. Mm. Well, I suppose two of us could share, or one of us could sleep in the sitting-room. How much is the rent.

David: I think they want £21 a week for it.

Peggy: Twenty-one. Oh, that's fine, that would be £7 each. I don't really want to spend more than £7.

David: No, but you see the trouble is it might be a bit noisy. Woodside Road is really quite busy. It's on the bus route after all. With all that traffic going past I don't know if you'd really like it.

Peggy: Oh, that doesn't matter, we'd be out all day. It'd be marvellous to be on the ten bus route, we wouldn't have to walk at all and we'd get to work so quickly. Oh thanks so much David. I must go and tell Sara and Mary.

David: Well, I hope it's what you want.

Peggy: Oh yes, thanks a lot.

David: That's all right.

Task 2: Moving In

Rod: Mm, it's not a bad size room, is it?

Liz: Oh, it's great! It's lovely! Oh, and look at that fireplace! Oh, we can have the two chairs right in front of the fireplace there in the middle of the room and toast our feet.

Rod: The first thing we ought to do is just decide where the bed's going.

Liz: Oh, well ... (So) what about right here next to the door
(yes) sort of behind the door as you come in?

Rod: Yes, that's a good idea —just as you come in, just in that
corner there.

Liz: Yes. Well now, let's think. What else?

Rod: What else is there? Erm ... well there's that huge wardrobe
of yours ... (Mm) that's got to go somewhere.

Liz: What about over here—you know—across from the fireplace
there, because then, in that little corner where it ... where
the wall goes back ... look, over there. (Mm) That'd do,
wouldn't it?

Rod: Ok, well we'll put the wardrobe there then. (Yes) OK?

Liz: Er ... (OK) what about your desk? (Er) Where are you going
to put that?

Rod: Er ... I need lots of light, so I think in that far corner in between the two windows, OK?

Liz: Oh, I see in the corner there (Yes) yes. (Erm) Yes, that'd
be good.

Rod: So the desk goes there.

Liz: So you'd have your chair with your back to the fireplace?
(Yes) Yes, that'll be all right.

Rod: Yes. And there's (yes) the chest of drawers.

Liz: Oh, that'd be nice in between the two windows there, right in
the middle. (Yes) It really ... come on, I know you're going
to like it. (OK) Come on, let's shove it over there. (I mean)
I bet ... I er ...

Rod: I knew you'd ask me to move it.

400

Liz: Come on. Let's go.

Rod: OK. Let's go then. All right.

Liz: Nearly there! That's got it.

Rod: God, what on earth have you got in there?

Liz: Well, there's nothing much in there. I emptied it ... most of it out.

Rod: Oh God, my back hurts!

Liz: There! Wait a minute. Let me stand back and have a look.

Rod: Yes, it's not bad ... sticks out a bit.

Liz: No, it's fine. (OK) What about the TV? Where are we going to put that?

Rod: Er ... it's really got to go in the opposite corner, hasn't it? (Mm) Opposite the desk, that is.

Liz: Oh, you mean in the corner between the windows and the fireplace? (Yes) Yes.

Rod: And then the stereo, er ... the amplifier underneath the television and then the two speakers one on either side of the fireplace.

Liz: Yes, that'd be good. (Erm) Well lovely! So it'll all fit in beautifully! (Yes) What else ... what else have we got?

Rod: It's the er ... there's the bookcase, isn't there? Erm ...

Liz: Oh Lord ... where'll we put that?

Rod: Well, as you come in the door, er ... immediately on the er ... left-hand side ...

Liz: Oh along that wall there you mean?

Rod: Because that's ... there's just about enough space there. There's about two feet, so it shouldn't stick out too much, no.

Liz: Yes, it's not very wide is it? So you come in the door (Yes) and then the bookcase is right there on the left. (Yes) There's a long way from your desk, though.

Rod: Well, exercise'll do me good, won't it? Er ... table lamp. Well, we can just put that er ...

Liz: On the chest of drawers. (Yes) When it's ... (Mm) Yes. That'd be nice.

Rod: And no matter who wants to use it, you know.

Liz: Yes. Oh this is going to be lovely. When are we going to get it all in? Now?

Rod: Er ... no, not now. Let's just go to the kitchen and er ... sort that out and have a cup of tea, eh.

Liz: Oh, ha-ha, good. (Right) Yes, I haven't seen the kitchen. Come on.

Rod: Come on then. Let's go.

Key to Exercises:

Task 1: Looking for a Flat

A. Answer the following questions briefly.

  1. What is Peggy reading newspapers for?

     Answer: (She is trying to find a flat in the advertisements in those newspapers.)

  2. Does Peggy want to have a flat on her own?

     Answer: (No, she is going to share it with two other girls.)

  3. Why doesn't Peggy care about the noise in Woodside Road?

     Answer: (Because Peggy and her roommates would be out all day.)

  4. Why does Peggy say it would be marvellous to be on the ten bus route?

     Answer: (Because they wouldn't have to walk at all and

would get to work quickly.)

5. Why must Peggy tell Sara and Mary?

Answer: (Because they are the girls who will share the flat with Peggy.)

B. Give detailed information about the flat according to what you hear on the tape.

1. The number of rooms: (a kitchen and a bethroom, two bedrooms and a stting-room)

2. The rent: (£ 21 a week, £ 7 for each) .

3. The location: (on the No. 10 Bus route in Woodside Road)

Task 2: Moving In

A. Choose the best answer (a, b or c) to complete each of the following statements.

1. Rod and Liz _____.

  * a. are moving into a new house

    b. are looking in the house they are going to rent

    c. are talking about the house they have just bought

2. The first thing they decide to do is _____.

    a. to put two chairs in front of the fireplace

    b. to toast their feet before the fireplace

  * c. to put their bed in the corner behind the door

3. Their desk goes _____.

    a. opposite the fireplace

  * b. in the far corner between the two windows

    c. beside the wardrobe

4. Their TV set is put _____.

    a. opposite the window

* b. in the opposite corner, between the windows and the fireplace
   c. in front of the fireplace
5. Rod doesn't care if the bookcase is far away from his desk
   because _____.
* a. exercise'll do him good
   b. he doesn't write much
   c. he works elsewhere
6. Both Liz and Rod feel it convenient to use the table lamp if it
   is put on _____.
* a. the chest of drawers
   b. the desk
   c. a table
7. Both Rod and Liz want to go to the kitchen because
   _____.
   a. they have to move something into it.
   b. Rod and Liz have never been to it
* c. both of them would like to have a cup of tea there

B. Give a list of the furniture and other household items mentioned
   in the conversation.
   Answer: (two chairs)
           (one bed)
           (a wardrobe)
           (a desk)
           (the chest of drawers)
           (the stereo)
           (the amplifier)
           (the television set)

404

(two speakers)

(the bookcase)

(the table lamp)

C. Fill in the blanks with what you hear on the tape.

1. —Mm, it's not (a bad size room), is it?

　　—Oh, it's great!

2. —God, what (on earth) have you got in there?

　　—Well, there's (nothing much) in there, I emptied it ...
　　　(most of it out).

　　—Oh, God, my back (hurts).

3. —Oh along that wall there (you mean)?

　　—Because that's ... there's just about (enough space)
　　　there. There's about (two feet), so it shouldn't (stick out
　　　too much), no.

4. —Let's just go to the kitchen and er ... (sort that out) and
　　　...

Section Three:

Tapescript:

Main Ideas and Supporting Details

1. Another use for Landsats is to find fresh water. In dry areas such
   as deserts, Landsat photos may show black areas that indicate
   water or they may show red areas that indicate healthy plants.
   People who are trying to find water in these dry areas can save
   time by looking in the places that are black or red on the Landsat
   pictures.

2. The fifth use is to warn us of natural disasters, such as the damage done by large forest fires, melting ice near the North and

South Poles, and lines in the earth where earthquakes might happen.

3. Many experts believe that we must turn to the sun to solve our energy needs. Solar energy is clean and unlimited. It is estimated that the amount of solar energy falling on the continental United States is 700 times our total energy consumption. It is possible to convert, or change, this energy for our use, but the cost is the major problem. The federal government is spending millions of dollars to find ways to convert, or change, sunshine into economical energy. By the year 2000, solar technology could be supplying about 25 percent of the United States' energy needs.

4. The major expense involved in a solar heating system is the purchase cost of all the parts of the system and the cost of their installation. The approximate cost to buy and put a solar heating system into a three-bedroom house at present varies from $7,000 to $12,000. This is a one-time cost that can be financed over many years. This finance charge may be more expensive than heating with oil at present prices.

Key to Exercises:

A. Suggested Abbreviations:

disasters: disas.	North: N.
South: S.	earthquake: ethq.
Consumption: consp.	federal: fed.
government: gov.	millions: mns.
economical: ecol.	year: y.
technology: techgy.	installation: instl.
expensive: exp.	

B. Listen to these paragraphs. Then write in the space given the main idea and supporting details of each.

1. (Landsats used to find fresh water)(main idea)
   a. (in dry areas: black = water, red = healthy plants)(supporting details)
   b. (save time by looking at photos)

2. (5th use: warn us of natural disas)(main idea)
   a. (forest fires)(supporting details)
   b. (melting ice near the N. & S. poles)
   c. (lines where ethqs. might happen)

3. (solar energy)(main idea)
   a. (clean & unlimited)(supporting details)
   b. (solar energy on US: 700 times our consp.)
   c. (fed. gov. spending mns. of dollars to change sunshine into ecol. energy)
   d. (y. 2000: solar techgy. supplying 25%. of us energy needs)

4. (cost of solar heating system)(main idea)
   a. (cost: all parts & their instl.)(supporting details)
   b. (cost for a 3-bedroom house: $7,000 to $12,000)
   c. (one-time cost financed over many years)
   d. (more exp. than heating with oil at present prices)

Supplementary Reading:

Airship

Airship, a powered lighter-than-air craft that gains its lift from gases rather than from aerodynamic forces as airplanes do. Although the airship is derived from the balloon, the axis of a balloon is perpendicular to the direction of forward motion, whereas an airship's axis is parallel to this direction. The airship also differs in having self-contained power, so that it can be steered independently of the wind — — hence the name dirigible (steerable) by which it also is known.

There are three kinds of airship: nonrigid, or blimp; semirigid; and rigid. The nonrigid consists of a large bag, or envelope, filled with lighter-than-air gas and containing separate cells, or ballonets, filled with air. The shape of the nonrigid is maintained by keeping the gases at slightly higher than atmospheric pressure, and the control car is slung from ropes attached to patches glued to the envelope. The semirigid is similar but has a rigid keel suspended beneath the envelope, usually with control surfaces as well as the car and engines attached to this keel. The rigid airship is of different construction, its shape being obtained by stretching a fabric cover over a rigid frame inside which individual gas cells are anchored.

Although some fairly large gas capacities have been achieved with nonrigid constructions — — for example, the United States' ZPG-3W class blimps carried 1.5 million cubic feet (42,400 cubic meters) — — it was the rigid-construction style that served best for large ships with high capacity and long endurance. The largest rigids had gas capacities several times greater than that of the nonrigid craft. They were more than 700 feet (200 meters) long and could carry several tons over transatlantic distances. However, although blimps and semirigids are still in scattered use for various purposes around the world, large rigid airships have not been flown since the late 1930's.

The construction of airships led to important advances in the design and technology of both aircraft and other structures, as in the use of aluminum alloys. The hangars required to house the giant ships were themselves considerable technological achievements, since the wide roofs could have no interior supports.

Periodically there have been proposals to revive the airship industry, but the plans have generally foundered on the rocks of cost, size, docking problems, the slow speed of the airship − − and memories of past disasters. Technology has not been the problem. Research may still be conducted into new hull forms for large airships in which the hull will develop lift as a true airfoil. Rigid airships have been proposed that could carry 500 tons of cargo, with the use of stern propulsion and with loading and unloading being done by helicopter. Suggestions have also been made that airships be used to move large rockets and other bulky items when safe delivery rather than speed is the important factor.

Construction and Operation

Airships owe their lift to lighter-than-air gases, which are contained either in a bag that is an inherent part of the craft's shape, or in cells that are attached inside the hull and transmit their lift to the structure as a whole. The ships are kept as light as possible, and their shape is a compromise between the need for streamlining and the desire to hold gases much as possible relative to total size and weight. All airships, but especially rigids, have to give careful consideration to temperature, humidity, range, fuel, load, and mission as well as to the matters of weight and ballast.

Flight Control. Airships basically used the traditional ballooning method of releasing ballast in order to rise and releasing some of the gas in order to descend. When time was not important, some change of altitude was also possible by using local temperature variations of the atmosphere or simply by the consumption of fuel. The main advantage of airships was that they could stay airborne even if their engines failed, but this was possible only if a ship had sufficient gas left in its cells to provide the necessary lift or if sufficient fuel or ballast could be jettisoned to provide the ship with buoyant equilibrium.

In other respects airships stabilized their height and controlled their changes in direction and altitude as airplanes do, through the movement of control surfaces. These were attached to the rear of the hull and usually took a simple, cross-shaped form of horizontal elevators and vertical rudders, Some ships were equipped with propellers that added to the control power of the elevators.

There was some disagreement among airship designers as to the use of dynamic lift − − that is, whether airships should be driven through the air is a nose-up attitude to create aerodynamic lift over the upper surface of the hull. Barnes Wallis, a British aeronautical engineer who worked on airships in the 1920's, argued against the practice, maintaining that a properly designed airship should always be flown straight and level so as to create minimum drag on the craft. His R-100, following the Zeppelin pattern of World War I, had a fully streamlined hull, whereas most earlier ships had streamlined nose and tail sections but long, parallel sides. The use of the fully streamlined hull prevailed thereafter for rigid airships.

Nonrigids, on the other hand, evolved quickly into a standard, teardrop shape from which a certain amount of lift could be obtained. It was not uncommon for the US. Navy to have its large blimps take off with somewhat excess weight by taking a ground run like an airplane in order to gain sufficient lift to fly. However, such takeoff methods were never developed for rigid airships.

Ground Handling. Small airships were not a serious problem to handle on the ground, since it was possible to fly them right up to a

410

shed door to be taken on in by a ground crew. The big rigids, however, required very large groundhandling parties. In 1917 the British developed the mooring mast as an alternative. The ship was reeled in to the mast and allowed to ride at anchor until the air was motionless enough that it could be walked into its shed. The German solution was to build revolving sheds, so that the ship could be brought in through doors sheltered from the wind, and the ultimate American solution was to use a movable stub mast on rails. By 1930 there was talk of going beyond these methods and building great docks that would use giant arms to hold the hull of the airship, but these were never developed.

Airships – achievements and disasters.

1852   1st airship (43.8m long) flew over Paris.

1910 – 14 Five Zeppelin airships operated commercial flights within Germany, carrying 35,000 people without injury.

1914 – 18 Military Zeppelins took part in 53 bombing raids on London, during first World war.

1919   British 'R34'. First transatlantic crossing. Both directions (10,187km in 183 hours).

1921   British 'R38' broke up over Yorkshire, killing 15 passengers, 29 crew.

1925   US 'Shenandoah' (first helium airship) destroyed in a storm over Ohio. Heavy loss of life.

1926   Italian airship, the 'Norge', flew over North Pole.

1929   German Graf Zeppelin flew round the world. Began commercial transatlantic flights.

1930   British 'R101' (236m long) crashed over Beauvais,

France. Killed 48 out of 54 on board. British airship programme cancelled.

1931   US 'Akron' in service in USA – – could carry 207 passengers.

1933   'Akron' wrecked in a storm.

1935   Sister ship, US 'Macon' wrecked.

1936   Hindenburg built. Carried 117 passengers in one flight.

1937   It crashed.

1938   'Graf Zeppelin II' completed. It never entered service.

1940   Both Graf Zeppelins scrapped.

1958   US Navy built a radar airship, the 'ZPG3-W'. (123m long, 21 crew.)

1960   June. 'ZPG3 – W' crashed in the sea.

1961   US Navy airship programme ended.

1975   US Goodyear company operating small airship fleet. The 'Europa' (58m long) carries a pilot and six passengers.

Lesson 21

Tapescript:

Task 1: Talking About Television

Stuart: What did you do last night then? Did you work all night?

Judy : Yes, I did some work (Yes) but erm ... I watched a bit of TV ... (Uh – huh) got to relax, you know.

Stuart: Did you watch the football?

Judy: No, no I didn't. I can't bear football.

Stuart: Really?

Judy : Yes. (Coo) I really hate it. (Yes) Well, actually, just before the football came on, I switched over (Yes) just to ... just to protest.

Stuart: What did you see then?

Judy : Well, I saw the programme before ... just the end of a film (Uh – huh) that was on before the football. It looked quite good actually. It's a shame I didn't erm ... switch on earlier. It was some kind of love story ... with Dustin Hoffman, you know, the erm ...

Stuart: *The Graduate*?

Judy: That's it. *The Graduate*.

Stuart: Yes. I know. I've seen that. (Yes) Yes, good ... good film.

Judy : Yes, and nice music. (Mm – mm) And then, when the football came on I turned over.

Stuart: Terrible, terrible!

Judy: I hate it! I really can't stand it.

Stuart: It was a great game!

Judy: Yes? (What did) Who was playing?

Stuart: England of course. (Oh) What did you see then that was more important than football?

Judy : Foxes. Yes, a good programme on foxes. (Uh - huh) Yes, they spent ages watching these foxes in a house. (Yes) They were watching them all night and these little baby foxes ... it was tremendous.

Stuart: Yes, sounds all right.

Judy : Yes, it was good; better than football ... and then, then I turned over, back to the other channel (Mm - mm) to see who won the football, but I missed it and I just saw the beginning of the News and packed up and went to bed.

Stuart: Well, I'm sorry you missed it. It was a good game.

Judy: Who did win?

Stuart: England, of course. Who do you think? (Ah) Six nil. (Yes) Yes.

Judy: Must have been quite good then!

Stuart: Yes, it was good, actually. It was very good. (Mm)

Task 2: Games

Commentator: It's Carter to serve—he needs just one more point. He serves. AND SMITH MISSES! WHAT A GREAT SERVE! ... So the championship goes to 19-year-old Harry Carter. Who d've believed it a week ago? Poor old Smith just shakes his head in bewilderment. Well, well! What a way to

414

finish it off! ... And now I'll hand you over to Peter Plumber, who's on court waiting to interview the two finalists.

Plumber: Thank you, David. Well Harry, congratulations on a marvellous victory. You were on tremendous form.

Carter: Thank you, Peter. Nice of you to say so. You know, well, I think I won because, well, I just knew all along I was in with a good chance.

Plumber: Yes, you certainly were pretty convincing today, but what about the earlier rounds? Any nervous moments?

Carter: Well, you know, I was a bit nervous against Jones when he took the lead in the second set, but then ... er ...

Plumber: Yes, that was in the quarterfinals, wasn't it? And of course you met Gardener in the next round, didn't you? Er ... the score was ... er ... 6 – 4, 7 – 5, wasn't it?

Carter: Yes, that was quite a tough match, I suppose, but ... er ...

Plumber: Anything else you'd like to add?

Carter: Well, I would like to say how sorry I am for John Fairlight not making it past the quarter-finals. He's unbeatable, you know, on his day, and ... er ... I'd also like to say what a terrific job the officials here have done you know, the ballboys and linesmen and umpires and so on. You know ... er ... lots of players have been complaining, but ... er ...

Plumber: Well, that's great. Harry, Well done again. And now let's have a quick word with the runner-up to the title, Mark Smith. If you just stand over here, Mark ... that's right ... Well, bad luck, Mark. It wasn't really your day, was it? I mean, what a terrible final set! Anyway, the less said about that the better, as I'm sure you'll agree.

415

Smith: Yeah, but you know, I did pretty well to beat Hutchins in the semis and ... er ... what's his name? ... Brown in the quarter-finals. And, I mean, what a terrible umpire, eh? I mean, half of Carter's points were on ... er ... doubtful decisions, weren't they?

Plumber: Well, that's probably a bit of an exaggeration, but anyway, it's time for us to leave the tournament now at the end of a tremendously exciting week, and I hand you back to the studio in London.

Key to Exercises:

Task 1: Talking About Television

A. Choose the best answer (a, b or c) to complete each of the following statements.

  1. Both the man and the woman spent some time last night

        _____.

        a. playing foottball

        b. watching a film on TV

    * c. watching TV

  2. *The Graduate* _____.

    * a. is a love story

        b. is a sports film

        c. is about Dustin Hoffman

  3. The end of the conversation shows _____.

        a. the woman is not interested in football at all

        b. the woman is only interested in animals

    * c. the woman does have some interest in football

B. True or False Questions. Write a T in front of a statement if it is

416

true according to the recording and write an F if it is false.

1. (F) The woman watched TV all night yesterday.
2. (F) Both the man and the woman like football game very much.
3. (T) The woman regretted that she hadn't switched the TV on earlier.
4. (T) The programme on foxes was great.
5. (F) The woman watched the ending of the football game but missed the beginning of the News.
6. (T) England won the game.
7. (F) The loser, however, scored six goals.
8. (F) Programmes on animals appeared to be more interesting than football matches to both the man and the woman.

C. Fill in the following blanks with what you hear on the tape.
1. I watched (a bit of) TV.
2. Just before the football (came on), I switched (over) just to (protest).
3. It's (a shame) I didn't (switch on) earlier.
4. When the football came on, I (turned over).

Tack 2: Games
A. Choose the best answer (a, b or c) to complete each of the following statements.
1. The interview is _____.
   a. about a basketball match
   b. on a football game
   * c. about a tennis match
2. _____ wins the championship.

417

* a. Harry Carter

   b. Peter Plumber

   c. Mark Smith

3. Harry Carter and Mark Smith _____ .

   a. share the same view about the umpire

   b. feel the final result is convincing

* c. have quite different attitudes towards the umpire

B. True or False Questions. Write a T in front of a statement if it is true according to the recording and write an F if it is false.

1. (T) Harry Carter wins the championship at the age of 19.

2. (F) Harry Carter never felt nervous in the earlier rounds.

3. (T) Gardener was beaten by Harry Carter with the score 4-6, 5-7.

4. (T) According to Carter, John Fairlight is almost unbeatable but he failed in the quarter-finals.

5. (F) Lots of players are satisfied with those umpires.

6. (T) Mark Smith had very bad luck that day.

7. (T) Plumber, the interviewer, does not go along with what Mark Smith says about Carter's points.

C. Identification. Identify who, Harry Carter or Mark Smith, has made the following remarks.

1. "I did pretty well to beat Hutchins in the semis."

2. "I was a bit nervous against Jones when he took the lead in the second set."

3. "What a terrific job the officials here have done, ..."

4. "... half of Carter's points were on doubtful decisions ..."

5. "That was quite a tough match."

6. "... what a terrible umpire ..."

Answer:

Harry Carter: (2, 3, 5)

Mark Smith: (1, 4, 6)

D. Complete the following statements with what you hear on the tape.

1. Poor old Smith (just skakes) his head (in bewilderment). Well, well, what a way to (finish it off)!

2. I just knew all along I was (in with a good chance).

3. I was a bit (nervous against) Jones when he (took the lead) in the second set.

4. And now let's (have a quick work with) the runner-up to the tittle.

Section Two:

Tapescript:

Olympics

Chairman: Good afternoon, ladies and gentlemen, I declare the meeting open, and I take it you all have a copy of the agenda, so we'll take the minutes of our last meeting as read and get straight down to business. Now, the proposal before you is that we should see if we can reduce the size of the Olympic Games in any way and thereby ease the burden placed on the host city. We all know that each time we hold the Games this burden increases because of the vast undertaking it is to host them. Today, however, I only want to sound out your opinion of this proposal, so this is really no more than an exploratory meeting.

Mrs Armstrong: Could I say something straight away, Mr Chairman?

Chairman: Yes, Mrs Armstrong.

Mrs Armstrong: I can't accept your proposal at all on the grounds that I feel that to reduce the size of the Olympic Games would seriously damage their character, detract from their universal appeal and penalize certain countries if we start arbitrarily throwing things out before ...

Herr Müller: Yes, Mrs Armstrong, if I may interrupt you for a moment. I think we all sympathize with your point of view, but we mustn't overlook the main point of this meeting put forward by the Chairman, which is to see if we can cut down the programme a bit, without in any way damaging the overall appeal of the Games, so let's not reject the proposal out of hand before we've had a chance to discuss it.

Mrs Armstrong: Very well, Herr Müller, but I'd like to state here and now that I'm totally opposed to any reduction in the number of events in the Games.

Chairman: Your objections will be noted, Mrs Armstrong, but to get back to the point of the meeting, could I hear from the rest of you what you feel? Sr Cordoba, for example, what's your opinion?

Sr Cordoba: Reluctant as I am to alter the composition of the Olympic Games, I can see the point that in terms of space and financial demands, the host city is subjected to a lot of difficulty. The costs seem to soar phenomenally every time we stage the Olympics, so we might be able to make one or two savings here and there. There is, for instance, quite a strong lobby against boxing because of its apparently violent nature so I did wonder if ...

420

Mrs Armstrong: But that is one of the most popular sports in the world, and one of the oldest.

Sr Cordoba: Agreed, but people get a lot of boxing on their television screens all the year round, so I was just thinking that we might be able to drop that from the programme. Football, too, is another thing which already enjoys a lot of television coverage, and as it takes up a lot of space accommodating all the football pitches, mightn't we also perhaps consider dropping that too?

Mrs Patel: Mr Chairman ...

Chairman: Yes, Mrs Patel.

Mrs Patel: I wholeheartedly endorse what Sr Cordoba said about boxing and football. In my opinion we should concentrate on some of the more unusual sports which are rarely seen on our screens such as fencing and archery, for a change, since it is on TV that the majority of people watch the Games.

Herr Müller: Perhaps we could cut out hockey along with football because, relatively speaking, that too takes up a lot of space, as measured against its universally popular appeal.

Mrs Patel: I can see your point, Herr Müller, and as one of the basic tenets of the Olympic Games is individual excellence, I feel we ought to concentrate on those sports which really are a true test of the individual, I, therefore, suggest we cut out —that is, if we go ahead with this idea − the team games such as basketball, volleyball, football and hockey.

Mrs Armstrong: But then you're sacrificing some of the most interesting items in the programme. People like to watch team games as well as take part in them; it'll be very dull without them.

Chairman: I think Mrs Armstrong has made a very valid point. We ought to keep some of the team games, although I am inclined to agree with what has been said about football.

Sr Cordoba: There's one thing I would like to say about this and that is to suggest that we could remove from the programme sports like sailing and canoeing and possibly the equestrian events, where the test is not so much of the stamina of the competitor but of his skill in handling the boat or whatever.

Mrs Armstrong: What about the pentathlon, then? Riding is one part of that, so we are going to need facilities to cater for that in any case, so why not use them for horse-riding as well—or do you think we should axe that too?

Chairman: Well, let's not get too heated about it, as this is only a preliminary discussion about possibilities and we are not yet in a position to make any final decisions. I will, however, briefly summarize what has been said so far, as I understand it. Mrs Armstrong is totally opposed to reducing the size of the Games in any way at all. There is one body of opinion in favour of removing from the Games those sports which are already well represented in other international contests and in the media. Another strand of thought is that we should concentrate on individual excellence by cutting out the team games featured in the programme, and Mrs Patel suggested we ought to focus attention on the more unusual sports in the programme which do not normally gain so much international attention. Sr Cordoba also brought up the idea that we could drop boxing because of its seemingly violent nature. There was also an opinion voiced that we might exclude events where the skills of a competitor in handling a horse or yacht, for example, were being tested, rather

422

than the stamina of the individual himself, as is the case with, say, athletics. Well, it is quite clear that we shall need to discuss this further, but in the meantime I think we'd better move on to something else ...

Key to Exercises:

A. Choose the best answer (a, b, or c) to complete each of the following statements.

   1. People present at the meeting _____.

      a. may be sportsmen

   * b. are probably members of the Olympic Committee

      c. are probably from the host country of the next Olympic Games

   2. The meeting is held _____.

   * a. to see whether the size of the Olympic Games could be reduced in any way

      b. to decide the size of the Olympic Games

      c. to decide where the next Olympic Games should be held

   3. At the end of the meeting, people persent _____

      a. have reached an agreement

   * b. still hold diversed views

      c. are convinced by the chairman

   4. There are _____ attending the meeting.

      a. four

      b. six

   * c. five

B. Summarize briefly the views presented by the following people.

   1. Mrs. Armstrong: (totally opposed to reducing the size of the

Olympic Games in any way at all)

2. Sr Cordoba: (in favour of removing from the Games those sports which are well presented in other international contests in the media, such as boxing and football)

3. Mrs Patel:

   a. (attention to be focused on the more unusual sports which do not normally gain so much international attention)

   b. (in favour of a true test of individual stamina instead of skills)

4. Chairman: (agreeing to keep some of the team games)

C. True or False Qnestions. Write a T in front of a statement if it is true according to the recording and write an F if it is false.

1. (T) The cost of the Olympics is increasing.

2. (T) According to Mrs Armstrong, reducing the size of the Olympics means damaging the overall appeal of it.

3. (F) Sr Cordoba really thinks that the composition of the Olympic Games should be altered.

4. (F) Nobody present thinks boxing is violent.

5. (T) According to Herr Müller, hockey and football should be cut out because they take a lot of space.

6. (F) The meeting ajourns after the discussion on the Olympics.

D. Write out the names of at least ten kinds of sports mentioned on the tape.

1. (boxing)

2. (football)

3. (fencing)

424

4. (archery)
5. (hochey)
6. (sailing)
7. (pentathlon)
8. (canoeing)
9. (basketball)
10. (volleyball)

E. Fill in the following blanks with what you hear on the tape.
   1. Let's not (reject) the proposal (out of hand) before we've had a chance to (discuss it).
   2. I can see the point that (in terms of) space and (financial demands), the host city is (subjected to) a lot of difficulty.
   3. The costs seem to (soar phenomenally) every time we (stage) the Olympics.
   4. I (am inclined) to agree with what has been said about football.
   5. So why not use them for (horse-riding) – – or do you think we should (axe) that too?
   6. Another (strand of thought) is that we should concentrate on (individual excellence) by (cutting out) the team games (featured) in the programme.

Section Three:

Tapescript:

Main Ideas and Supporting Details

1. The houses they lived in weren't meant to be permanent dwellings; as a matter of fact, we have no remaining evidence of their houses. Probably in the summertime they lived up on the

mesa top near their fields, in temporary structures made of poles and brush. In winter they most likely moved down to the caves in the cliffs for warmth and protection against the snow.

2. People were experimenting and changing their methods of potting; the broken pieces are evidence of the steps in the process.

    The first attempt at pottery came as women mixed clay, a kind of dirt, with water to make pots. When the clay dried, however, it crumbled and fell apart. Clearly this wouldn't work.

    The second idea was to add extra material to bind the clay together: grass, straw, or pieces of bark. This held the pot together very well until it was set on the fire. Then the binding material burned up, leaving a pot full of holes.

    Again the Anasazi women tried to find the secret of success. They added sand or volcanic grit to the clay to make it harder, and they baked the pots before using them. This final step proved to be successful, and it is the basic method which is still used today.

3. The pots which the women made this way were far superior to baskets for carrying, cooking, and storing food and water. Now the people could add beans, a rich source of protein, to their diet. Water could be stored safely over long periods. Life became much easier, and so effort could now be spent on other developments.

4. Their culture developed to its height, and the main improvement was in housing. The earlier pit houses were modified to one-story row houses, made with pieces of stone. Several separate buildings stood near each other like a small village. Some villages were

426

as large as several hundred rooms and could contain as many as a thousand people. The name for this kind of house and for these Indians is "Pueblo", which is the spanish word for "village".

Key to Exercises:
Main Ideas and Supporting Details
A. Suggested Abbreviations:

permanent: perm   protection: protc

development: devlp   hundred: hund

B. Listen to these paragraphs. Then write in the space given the main idea and suppouting details of each.
1. (Houses were not perm.) (main idea)
    a. (summer: mesa top, made of poles & brush) (supporting details)
    b. (winter: caves in cliffs for warmth & protc.)
2. (experimenting with potting) (main idea)
    a. (mixed clay with water: fell apart when dried) (supporting details)
    b. (added grass, straw or pieces of bark to clay: full of holes when burnt)
    c. (added sand or volcanic grit to clay, baked: success)
3. (advantages of pots) (main idea)
    a. (added beans to diet) (supporting details)
    b. (stored food & water over long periods)
    c. (life easier, effort spent on other devlps.)
4. (improvement in housing) (main idea)
    a. (one-story row house) (supporting details)
    b. (made of stone)
    c. (forming a village: several hund. rooms with 1,000 peo-

427

ple)

    d. (these houses & Indians: Pueblo = village in Spanish)

Supplementary Reading:

Tennis

If you are a tennis player or a tennis fan, you are in good company. You are among the millions of people who are enjoying the game in the most exciting period of its history. You are living in the time of the great tennis boom, which began in 1968. As a result of the boom, everyone seems to be playing tennis, not simply sitting back and watching the experts play.

What triggered the tennis explosion? It began with the growth of professionalism (playing for pay). And it happened immediately after the major national championships became "open" events - - that is, after these championships were opened to professionals as well as amateurs. (Amateurs are players whose expenses can be paid but who are not allowed to accept pay directly.)

Soon industrial firms began to sponsor tournaments and offer large cash prizes. Enormous amounts of money poured into what had been strictly a noncommercial sport. Promoters new to the game signed rich contracts with star players and sent the players on tours across the country and around the world. Television coverage carried tennis matches into millions of homes. All these activities helped to change tennis from a minor sport to a major sport within a few short years.

The Changing World of Tennis

During the first 50 years of its history - - from 1873 to the mid-1920's - - tennis was largely a pastime of wealthy people. In the United States it was played chiefly in the northeast and by a

428

scattering of followers in California, the Middle West, and the South. Gradually, though, it took a more democratic turn. Programs for junior players were started, and the number of courts in public parks increased steadily. By the early 1920's a few players had risen to world fame and won wider recognition for tennis. Among them were William ("Big Bill") Tilden of the United States and Suzanne Lenglen of France.

The first big professional promotion was launched in 1926, with prominent players touring under a manager. After that, other well-known players turned professional. But the professional matches lacked the prestige of the main amateur events, and only a few players shared in the big money each year.

Then came the revolution. Britain demanded the right to stage its Wimbledon championships as an open event. And in 1968 the International Lawn Tennis Federation, which governs tennis worldwide, gave in to the demand. The winners of the singles titles in the first Wimbledon Open were Billie Jean King of the United States and Rod Laver of Australia. In the first United States Open, also in 1968, Virginia Wade of Britain and Arthur Ashe of the United States were the winners.

The British went a step further in 1968. They ended all distinctions between amateurs and professionals. All were simply players. In other countries, players who registered with their national associations could represent their countries in international team matches and receive prize money. In a short time amateur tennis declined as a major attraction. And scores of players, both women and men, began to win prize money they had never dreamed of.

With the arrival of open tennis, women took second place to men in sharing the harvest of riches. But they organized themselves and pressed their demand for equal prize money. They achieved equality in the United States Open in 1974, when the singles winners, Billie Jean King and Jimmy Connors, each received $ 22,500. Wimbledon increased the women's share the next year and promised equality in the future.

Spectacular events brought other changes and added to the excitement of tennis. One of these was the "battle of the sexes" between Billie Jean King and Bobby Riggs, a senior player who had won both the Wimbledon and the United States titles in his prime. Riggs lost the match, played in the Houston (Texas) Astrodome in 1973. The World Team Tennis League, an organization new to tennis, made its bow in 1974. A number of top women and men players signed contracts for large amounts to play on the league's teams.

At the same time new equipment came into use, especially metal rackets. And colourful sweaters, shorts, shirts, and dresses appeared on the courts along with the traditional tennis white.

Famous Cups and the Hall of Fame

Changes also came to international competition for the Davis Cup, long the most famous of all trophies in men's tennis. Officially called the International Lawn Tennis Challenge Trophy, it was donated in 1899 by Dwight F. Davis of the United States. During its long history more than 50 nations have taken part in Davis Cup play. But by the early 1970's many of the world's best players were reluctant to compete. The long time required to play through the elimination rounds caused them to miss opportunities for prize money in other competitions.

Many top players dropped out of the Wightman Cup matches, the famous international women's event held each year between the United States and Britain. The cup was donated in 1919 by Hazel

Hotchkiss Wightman, a great United States champion and one of the most honoured players in tennis history. The National Lawn Tennis Hall of Fame and tennis Museum in Newport, Rhode Island, came into being through the efforts of James H. Van Alen of Newport. It was authorized by the United States Lawn Tennis Association in 1953 and was opened in 1954. Each year distinguished tennis players and benefactors are enshrined in the Hall of Fame.

Tennis for Everyone

According to a nationwide survey, there were about 5, 600, 000 tennis players in the United States in 1965. Within 10 years the number had skyrocketed to 34, 000, 000. Hundreds of millions of dollars were being spent to build tennis courts and to buy rackets, balls, clothing, and other equipment. Tennis camps, schools, and commercial clubs were opening in ever-increasing numbers.

There are many reasons for this astonishing rise in the popularity of tennis. Greater publicity in newspapers and magazines and on television has been an important factor. People are interested in physical fitness, and they see tennis as a game that can be played the year round, indoors and out. Equipment for playing need not be expensive. Best of all, tennis is a game that can be enjoyed throughout a lifetime.

Lesson 22

Section One:

Tapescript:

Class in Britain and America

Christine: Harry, as an American, have you noticed any strong class distinctions in English society since you've been here?

Harry: Strong class distinctions? Yes, they haven't changed at all —that's what —that's what amuses me —in fifteen years or fourteen years —that the stratification is exactly the same as it was when I first came. It's extraordinary that it pervades everything.

Anna : What is class distinction? Because I don't know whether it's what job they do or ...

Harry: It's people's accents. In Pygmalion, you know, it goes back to, as soon as you open your mouth in England you're immediately you know placed.

Anna : Do you mean that there aren't different accents in America?

Harry: Not —of course there are different accents —but they're not as —they're not nearly as clearly defined.

Anna : But I mean, don't —doesn't a certain strata of American society use perhaps more slang than another one? More correct?

Harry: Not the way they do in England. In England they seem to really stick together. I mean I went the other week for the first

432

time in my life to a point-to-point and I couldn't believe what I found. There I was in the middle of Lincolnshire and we went through muddy fields and suddenly we came upon this parking lot with nine thousand Range Rovers in it and everyone going 'Oh, hello darling. How are you?' you know and it was hilarious I mean and they were all you know this meeting of the clan and that certainly doesn't happen in America and all those people spoke the same way.

Barrie: But that —yes, I live in the middle of the country in the south and I must say when I moved there I noticed —I mean of course I'd been aware of class before that but I had no idea that the lines between them were so rigid. I lived on an estate of a very big and successful farm until recently, and so the farm of course was run by the landed gentry who all went hunting and to point-to-point and all the rest of it. I lived next door to the groom who was —who despised them because they did all this and he had to just get the horses ready, um but at the same time he was terribly fond of them and they of him and there was all this sort of paternalistic attitude to the country workers that still goes on. I was staggered and nobody knew where to put me because I was living in a tied cottage that was tied to the farm, um but because I didn't work with any of them they were all uneasy with me. Most peculiar.

Christine: But I think you raise a very good point there Barrie because you're in fact talking about yourself not fitting into either of these two extremes and I'd like to ask Harry again how many classes he can see very clearly defined.

Barrie: In England?

Christine: In England, yes.

Harry: Well, I guess, three off the top of my head. I mean not counting immigrants and foreigners. Yes, I mean there's the middle class is the most snobbish of all it seems to me. You know, they're the most aware of the whole system really because they're upwardly mobile usually you know they hope to be, and they're the ones —I mean the upper class are what I find extraordinary —they seem to be totally uninhibited for the most part. I think it's extraordinary. I mean I'm not passing any moral judgements on them but it still exists ...

John: Because they've got the confidence ...

Anna: ... and the money ...

Barrie: ... confidence and the money ...

John: Well no, I don't think money's much to do with it actually.

Anna: How can you change it? I mean how would you change it?

Harry: I'm not saying it should be changed ...

Anna : No, no, no, no. I don't —I mean people do say that it should be changed. Politicians say that we should have total e-quality which I don't believe you can ever have in anything.

Harry: Well there should be equality of opportunity. I mean at least it's a nice ideal to have, isn't it?

Key to Exercises:

A. Choose the best answer (a, b or c) for each of the following questions.

1. What is Harry's nationality?

    a. British.

    b. English.

 * c. American.

2. What can be used to tell people's social status in England?

    a. Their clothes.

* b. Their accent.

    c. Their job.

3. What surprised and amused Harry in Lincolnshire?

    a. The muddy fields.

    b. The large number of people.

* c. People who went there drove the car of the same brand and spoke in the same way.

4. Why was Barrie staggered living in a cottage tied to a farm?

    a. The groom next door did not like him.

    b. He felt uueasy living there.

* c. People in the community did not know how to treat him bccause they did not know which class he belonged to .

5. What does Harry think of the middle class in Britain?

* a. The most snobbish.

    b. Totally uninhibited.

    c. Very extraordinary.

B. True or False Questions. Write a T in front of a statement if it is true according to the recording and write an F if it is false.

1. (F) According to Harry, class distinctions have not changed much in the last forty or fifty years.

2. (T) People's accent is not enough to tell their social position in the U. S.

3. (T) In the country, there was a paternalistic relationship between those farmhands and their masters.

4. (F) The middle-class people in Britain are not aware of the whole system.

5. (T) Equality of opportunity is a nice ideal to have.

C. Fill il the blanks with what you hear on the tape.
   1. In England they seem to (really stick together). There I was (in the middle of) Lincolnshire and we went through (muddy fields) and suddenly we (came upon) this parking lot with (9,000 Range Rovers) in it.
   2. I think you raised (a very good point) there, Barrie, because you're (in fact) talking about yourself not (fitting into either of these two extremes).
   3. I mean (the upper elass) are what I find (extraordinary) — they seem to be (totally uninhibited) for the most part... I'm not (passing moral judgments on them).

Section Two:
Tapescript:

Task 1: Autobiography: Seminole Girl (I)

Public school was hard compared to what I'd had before, day school on the reservation and a year at Sequoyah Government School. I almost flunked eighth grade at the public school, and it was a miracle that I passed. I just didn't know a lot of things, mathematics and stuff. I survived it somehow. I don't know how, but I did. The man who was head of the department of education at the Agency was the only person outside of my family who helped me and encouraged me to get an education. He understood and really helped me with many things I didn't know about. For a long time the white public school for the Big Cypress area would not let Indian children attend. A boy and I were the first Big Cypress Indians to graduate from that school. He is now in the armed forces.

After I graduated from high school, I went to business college, because in high school I didn't take courses that would prepare me for the university. I realized that there was nothing for me to do. I had no training. All I could do was go back to the reservation. I thought maybe I'd go to Haskell Institute, but my mother was in a TB hospital, and I didn't want to go too far away. I did want to go on to school and find some job and work. So the director of education at the Agency said maybe he could work something out for me so I could go to school down here.

I thought bookkeeping would be good because I had had that in high school and loved it. So I enrolled in the business college, but my English was so bad that I had an awful time. I had to take three extra months of English courses. But that helped me.

I never did understand why my English was so bad —whether it was my fault or the English I had in high school. I thought I got by in high school; they never told me that my English was so inferior, but it was not good enough for college. It was terrible having to attend special classes.

At college the hardest thing was not loneliness but schoolwork itself. I had a roommate from Brighton (one of the three reservations), so I had someone to talk to. The landlady was awfully suspicious at first. We were Indians, you know. She would go through our apartment; and if we hadn't done the dishes, she washed them. We didn't like that. But then she learned to trust us.

College was so fast for me. Everyone knew so much more. It was as though I had never been to school before. As soon as I got home, I started studying. I read assignments both before and after the lectures. I read them before so I could understand what the professor was saying, and I read them again afterwards because he

437

talked so fast. I was never sure I understood.

In college they dressed differently from high school, and I didn't know anything about that. I learned how to dress. For the first six weeks, though, I never went anywhere. I stayed home and studied. It was hard —real hard. I can imagine what a real university would be like. And it was so different. If you didn't turn in your work, that was just your tough luck. No one kept at me the way they did in high school. They didn't say, "OK, I'll give you another week."

Gradually I started making friends. I guess some of them thought I was different. One boy asked me what part of India I was from. He didn't even know there were Indians in Florida. I said, "I'm an American." Things like that are kind of hard. I couldn't see my family often, but in a way that was helpful because I had to learn to adjust to my new environment. Nobody could help me but myself.

Task 2: Autobiography: Seminole Girl (II)

Well, I graduated and went down to the bank. The president of the bank had called the agency and said he would like to employ a qualified Indian girl. So I went down there, and they gave me a test, and I was interviewed. And then they told me to come in the following Monday. That's how I went to work. I finished college May 29, and I went to work June 1. I worked there for three years.

In the fall of 1966, my father and the president of the Tribal Board asked me to come back to Big Cypress to manage a new economic enterprise there. It seemed like a dream come true, because I could not go back to live at Big Cypress without a job there.

438

But it was not an easy decision. I liked my bank work. You might say I had fallen in love with banking. But all my life I had wanted to do something to help my people, and I could do that only by leaving my bank job in Miami. Being the person I am, I had to go back. I would have felt guilty if I had a chance to help and I didn't.

But I told my daddy that I couldn't give him an answer right away, and I knew he was upset because he had expected me to jump at the chance to come back. He did understand, though, that I had to think about it. He knew when I went to live off the reservation that I had had a pretty hard time, getting used to a job, getting used to people. He knew I had accomplished a lot, and it wasn't easy for me to give it up. But that's how I felt. I had to think. At one time it seemed to me that I could never go back to reservation life.

But then really, through it all, I always wished there was something, even the smallest thing, that I could do for my people. Maybe I'm helping now. But I can see that I may get tired of it in a year, or even less. But right now I'm glad to help build up the store. If it didn't work out, if the store failed, and I thought I hadn't even tried, I would really feel bad.

The basic thing about my feeling is that my brothers and sisters and nieces and nephews can build later on in the future only through the foundation their parents and I build. Maybe Indian parents don't always show their affection; but they have taught us that, even though we have a problem, we are still supposed to help one another. And that is what I am trying to do. Even when we were kids, if we had something and other kids didn't, we must share what we had . . . .

439

By the age of nine, girls were expected to take complete care of younger children. I too had to take care of my little brother and sister. I grew up fast. That's just what parents expected. Now teenagers don't want to do that, so they get angry and take off. Head Start and nurseries help the working mothers because older children don't tend the little ones anymore. The old ways are changing, and I hope to help some of the people, particularly girls about my age, change to something good.

There are people on the reservation who don't seem to like me. Maybe they are jealous, but I don't know why. I know they resent me somehow. When I used to come from school or from work back to the reservation, I could tell some people felt like this. I don't think that I have ever, ever, even in the smallest way, tried to prove myself better or more knowing than other people. I have two close friends here, so I don't feel too lonely; but other people my age do not make friends with me. I miss my sister, and I miss my roommate from Miami. My two friends here are good friends. I can tell them anything I want. I can talk to them. That's important, that I can talk to them. That's what I look for in a friend, not their education, but for enjoyment of the same things, and understanding. But there are only two of them. I have not been able to find other friends.

The old people think I know everything because I've been to school. But the old people don't have the kind of experience which allows them to understand our problems. They think that it is easy somehow to come back here. They think there is nothing else. They do not understand that there are things I miss on the outside. They do not understand enough to be friends. They are kind, and they are glad that I am educated, but they do not understand my problems. They do not understand loneliness . . . .

Key to Exercises:

Task 1: Autobiography: Seminole Girl (I)

A. Choose the best answer (a, b or c) to complete each of the following statements.

1. The speaker _____.
    * a. is an American Indian
      b. came from India
      c. isn't of American origin
2. _____ prevented her from attending a college far away.
      a. Her tough father
      b. Her brothers and sisters
    * c. Her mother's illness
3. She _____ when college life started.
    * a. realized her English was terrible
      b. realized her knowledge on bookkeeping was too little
      c. had already mastered English
4. During her college days, she _____.
      a. busied herself preparing for the lectures and assignments
      b. managed to adapt herself to the environment and people around her
    * c. Both a and b.

B. State what role the following people and places had played in the speaker's life with the help of the information you hear on the tape.

1. Head of the Department of Education at the Agency:

441

(He was the only person outside her family who helped her and encouraged her to get an education).

2. The white school in the Big Cypress area:
(She graduated from it as one of the first two Indian pupils in that school).

3. The college: (She learned bookkeeping).

4. The landlady of the apartment:
(She was suspicious of the speaker at first but began to trust her gradually).

5. The boy who asked her about her origin:
(She felt hurt and hard being an Indian).

C. True or False Questions. Write a T in front of a statement if it is true according to the recording and write an F if it is false.

1. (F) In high school, she took all the courses that would prepare her for the university.

2. (T) She and her family lived on an Indian reservation in Florida.

3. (T) She spent three extra months on English courses at college.

4. (F) She was always confident that she understood what the professor was saying in class.

Task 2: Autobiography: Seminole Girl (II)

A. Choose the best answer (a, b or c) to complete each of the following statements.

1. _____, the Indian girl found a job in a bank.
   a. A year after she graduated from college
 * b. Two days after she graduated from college

c. Two months after she graduated from college

2. In the fall of 1966 _____ .

* a. her father and the president of the Tribal Board asked her
      to manage an enterprise on the reservation

   b. she just graduated from college

   c. she got a job in a bank at Big Cypress

3. It took her quite some time to decide whether to go back to
   the reservation because _____ .

   a. she didn't like her people on the reservation

* b. she loved her work with the bank and meanwhile she had
      deep affection and a sense of responsibility for her people

   c. the pay offered by the Tribal Board was too low.

4. Some people on the reservation don't seem to like her.
   Maybe it is because _____ .

   a. she tried to prove herself better and more knowledgeable
      than others

   b. of her father

* c. they are jealous of her

5. She is afraid _____ when she comes back to live on the
   reservation again.

* a. she would feel lonely and miss the outside world

   b. she would be resented by her own people

   c. she would lose contact with her friends

B. True or False Questions. Write a T in front of a statement if it is
true according to the recording and write an F if it is false.

1. (T) She went through a lot of difficulty getting used to the
   life outside the reservation.

2. (F) She wouldn't feel guilty if she hadn't helped her people

on the reservation.

3. (T) Being an Indian, she has a strong sense of belonging.

4. (T) Among Indians, there is a tradition that people should help each other and share everything.

5. (F) She doesn't have any close friends to whom she can tell what she wants.

6. (T) Being educated and working off the Indian reservation, she has become different from what her tribal people expected of her.

7. (F) She feels quite at home on the reservation when she is back from Miami.

8. (T) The old people on the reservation, though kind, can hardly understand how she really feels.

C. Fill in the blanks with what you hear on the tape.

1. I knew he was (upset) because he had expected me to (jump at the chance to come back).

2. If it didn't (work out), if the store (failed), and I thought I hadn't even tried, (I would really feel bad).

3. That's (important), that I can talk to them. That's (waht I look for in a friend), not (their education), but (for enjoyment of) the same things, and (understanding).

4. They do not (understand) that there are things I miss (on the outside). They do not understand (enough to be friends).

Section Three:

Tapescript:

Main Ideas and Supporting Details

444

1. One wonders how, then, these students have arrived at such a false conclusion. One reason, of course, may be that they're science students. Scientific terms generally possess only one, precisely defined, meaning. It is, in fact, exactly this quality that makes these words distinctive in English, or indeed in any other language. Another reason could be the way in which these students were taught English. For example, long vocabulary lists are still an important feature in the foreign language learning programmes of many countries. On one side of the page is the word in English; on the other side a single word in the student's native language.

2. Practically all the students think that every word in English had an exact translational equivalent in their own language. Again this is a gross distortion of the truth. Sometimes a word in the student's native language may not have an equivalent in English at all, which may have to employ a phrase as a translation. Sometimes one word in the student's language may be translated by one of two possible words in English. The difficulty that many students have with the two verbs 'do' and 'make' is an example of this. Often the area of meaning covered by one word in the student's language may be wider or narrower than the area of meaning covered by a corresponding word in English. This sometimes happens with the naming of colours, where most students would expect an exact correspondence between their language and English. The borders between the primary colours of the spectrum are, however, drawn at different places in different languages. Translation, in fact, is a particularly difficult thing to do well. It certainly can't be done

by matching single words from one language by single words from another. At first, those computer scientists who attempted to construct an automatic translation machine made this mistake. The machines often produced nonsense.

3. What, then, is the best way to increase one's vocabulary in a foreign language? This can be answered in three words. Firstly, observation: the unknown word should be observed in its context; in other words, the neighbouring words and the grammatical construction should be noted. A good dictionary should be referred to and examples of the usage of the word should be noted. Secondly, imitation: the student should use the new word in appropriate contexts, imitating the examples he has noted. Finally, repetition: he'll need to practise using the word several times before he's confident that he can use it correctly; in other words, repetition is necessary if the new word is to 'stick', and especially if it is to enter the student's active vocabulary.

Key to Exercises:

Main Ideas and Supporting Details

A. Suggested Abbreviations:

false: f	conclusion: concl
scientific: scient	student: st
vocabulary: vocab	English: Eng
translational: transl	equivalent: equiv
appropriate: appro	

B. Listen to these paragraphs. Then write in the space given the main idea and supporting details of each.

446

1. (Causes of the f. concl.) (main idea)
   a. (science students: scient. terms − − one meaning) (supporting details)
   b. (way st's taught Eng. e.g. list of vocab.)
2. (every word with exact transl. equiv. in their own lang.) (main idea)
   a. (no equiv. word need phrase) (supporting details)
   b. (1 word in st's lang.: 2 words in Eng. e.g. do & make)
   c. (meaning covered by 1 word in st's lang.: wider or narrower than Eng. e.g. color)
   d. (trnaslation = diff. to do well; can't be done by match single words e.g. computer scientists)
3. (best way to increase vocab.) (main idea)
   a. (observation: unknown word, observed in context) (supporting details)
   b. (imitation: use word in appro. context)
   c. (repetition: make it enter st's active vocab.)

Supplementary Reading:

Pygmalion

Pygmalion in Greek legend, a king of Cyprus and an accomplished sculptor, distrusted women and vowed that he would never marry. While at work on an ivory statue of a maiden, he became enchanted with its beauty and wished that it could be brought to life. He named the figure Galatea. Aphrodite, the goddess of love, granted his wish, and he and Galatea were married. Their son, Paphos, founded the city named for him, which became sacred to the worship of Aphrodite.

George Bernard Shaw's satirical play Pygmalion is based on the legend. Written in 1912 and first produced in 1914, the play is an adaptation of the myth of Pygmalion and Galatea. Shaw's Pygmalion is Henry Higgins, a speech expert, and his Galatea is Eliza Doolittle, a Cockney flower girl. In the play Higgins transforms Eliza from a tattered, ill-spoken wench, unacceptable in upper-class circles, into a beautiful woman who can pass as a duchess. He accomplishes this by teaching Eliza manners, poise, fashion, and, most importantly, correct and cultivated speech. In Pygmalion, Shaw satirizes British class structure by demonstrating how speech accent helps determine an individual's place in society.

Pygmalion is one of Shaw's most amusing and popular plays. In addition to the well-realized principal characters, Shaw created the unforgettable Alfred Doolittle, Eliza's father, a dustman who is the epitome of vulgarity.

Pygmalion was made into a successful film in 1938 and into the musical My Fair Lady (1956) by Alan Jay Lerner and Frederick Loewe, which was filmed in 1964.

Lesson 23

Section One:

Tapescript:

Task 1: Finding a Job

Interviewer: Hello. My name's Hudson. Disk Hudson.

Applicant: I'm Pamela Gable.

Interviewer: Well take a seat, please. Miss Gable—it is Miss, isn't
it? Thought so. Well, let me just check that I've got these par-
ticulars right. Your surname is Gable, spelt G – A – B – L – E,
and your first names are Pamela Ann ... Fine. You live at 147
Collingdon Road, Croydon ... your telephone number is 246
8008 ... you were born on July the eighth 1965, and ...
that's about it ... OK? Fine ... Now let's see ... what are you
working with at the moment?

Applicant: I'm the personal assistant to the manager of a modelling
agency.

Interviewer: Oh, really? And what does that involve?

Applicant: A bit of everything, really. I have to keep the accounts,
write a few letters, answer the telephone, look after bookings
and engagements and that sort of thing.

Interviewer: You work with people a lot, do you?

Applicant: Oh yes. I have to look after all the models who work for
us, you know, keep them happy, lend an understanding ear to
their heartaches, you know.

449

Interviewer: Have you ever done anything to do with hotels or conferences —hotel management, for instance?

Applicant: No, not really. I did work for a short time as a courier for a tour operator, taking foreigners on guided tours of London. Perhaps that's the sort of thing you mean?

Interviewer: Yes, I think it is. Do you speak any languages?

Applicant: Yes, I do. I speak French and Italian —you see, I spent several years abroad when I was younger.

Interviewer: Oh, did you? That's very interesting. And what about any exams you've taken?

Applicant: Well, I left school at 16. You know, there didn't seem to be any point in staying on somehow; I was sure I could learn much more by getting a job and a bit of experience and independence.

Interviewer: So you have no formal qualifications at all? I see ... Well, I don't suppose it matters.

Applicant: Um ... I was wondering if perhaps you could tell me a bit more about the job? You know, it said in the ad that you wanted a go-ahead girl with car and imagination, but that's not very much to go on.

Interviewer: No, it isn't. Well, we run conferences, and your job as conference co-ordinator would be, well, much the same as the one you have now, I suppose. Meeting people, transporting them from one place to another, making sure they're comfortable, a bit of telephoning, and so on.

Applicant: It sounds like just the sort of thing I want to do.

Interviewer: There is the question of salary, of course.

Applicant: Well, my present salary is £8,000, so I couldn't accept any less than that. Especially if I have to use my car.

450

Interviewer: Ah! We have something like 7,500 in mind, plus of course a generous allowance for the car. But look, if I were you, I'd take some time to think about this. Perhaps you'd care to have a quick look round the office here, see if you like the look of the people who work here.

Applicant: What do you think I should do then ...?

Task 2: Hypnosis

Ann: When did you discover that you had this talent for hypnosis, Dr Parker?

Dr Parker: When I was a final year medical student, actually. I'd been reading a lot about it and decided to try it myself on a few friends, you know —using certain well-tried techniques.

Ann: And you were successful.

Dr Parker: Well, yes. I was amazed at how quickly I was able to do it.

Ann: Could you tell me more about these techniques?

Dr Parker: Certainly. My method has changed very little since I started. To begin with, I get the subject to lie comfortably on a sofa, which helps to relax the body. You see, in order to reach a person's mind, you have to make him forget his body as much as possible. Then I tell him to concentrate on my voice. Some experts claim that the sound of the voice is one of the most powerful tools in hyponsis.

Ann: Do you have an assistant with you?

Dr Parker: Yes, but only as a secretary. He always sits well in the background, taking notes and looking after the recording equipment. Then I tell the subject not to think about what I'm saying but just to accept it.

451

Ann: Don't you use a swinging watch or flashing lights?

Dr Parker: No. At first I used to rely on the ticking of a clock — some say that boring, repetitive sounds help —but now I simply get my patient to stare at some object in the room. At this point I suggest that he's feeling sleepy and that his body's becoming so relaxed that he can hardly feel it.

Ann: Be careful, Dr Parker, I'm beginning to feel very drowsy myself.

Dr Parker: Don't worry. I won't make you do anything silly, I promise.

Ann: What you're saying, then, is that you want to control your patient's mind, and that to do this you have first to take care of the body.

Dr Parker: Yes, You see, the aim of the session is to make the patient remember in great detail an experience which has caused him a lot of pain and suffering, and by doing that to help him to face his problems.

Ann: I've heard a person's memory is far more powerful under hypnosis.

Dr Parker: Indeed it is. Some of the things that patients are able to remember are just incredible.

Ann: Would you mind giving me an example?

Dr Parker: Not at all. During a session, it's standard procedure to take a patient back in time slowly, pausing at certain times in his life and asking a few questions.

Ann: To, sort of, set the scene before you go deeper. Is that what you mean?

Dr Parker: That's it exactly. Well, once, I took a thirty-five-year-old lady back to the age of eight —in fact, I told her it was her

452

eighth birthday and I asked her what day it was. I later checked a calendar for that year and she was right – it was a Tuesday. She even told me who was at her party, their names, what they were wearing and about the presents she received. I mean, can you remember even your last birthday?

Ann: I couldn't even tell you what day my birthday fell on this year.

Dr Parker: Precisely. And when I asked her to write down her address at that time, the handwriting was in a very immature style. I later compared it to a sample from some old school exercise books her mother had kept and it was identical.

Ann: Dr Parker, that's an amazing story.

Dr Parker: I've taken patients back to their first year and a few even further than that ... but that's another story, unless you've got plenty of time ...

Key to Exercises:

Task 1: Finding a Job

A. Complete the information chart for the applicant with what you hear on the tape.

1. Name: (Pamela Gable)
2. Address: (147 Collington Road, Croydon)
3. Telephone number: (2468008)
4. Date of birth: (July 8, 1965)
5. Present job: (personal assistant to the manager of a modelling agency)
6. Languages: (French and Italian)
7. Formal qualifications: (none)
8. Present salary: (8,000 pounds)

B. List Miss Gable's responsibilities with her present job and the would-be responsibilities with the job she is applying for.

1. Responsibilities with the present job
   a. (keeping the accounts)
   b. (writing letters)
   c. (answering the telephone)
   d. (looking after bookings and engagements)
   e. (taking care of all the models who work for the agency)
   f. (keeping those models happy, lending an understanding ear to their heartaches)

2. Responsibilities with the new job
   a. (meeting people)
   b. (transporting them from one place to another)
   c. (making sure they are comfortable)
   d. (a bit of telephoning)

C. True or False Questions. Write a T in front of a statement if it is true according to the recording and write an F if it is false.

1. (T) For some time, Miss Gable worked as a courier for a tour operator.
2. (F) Miss Gable studied business management at college.
3. (F) Miss Gable sounds as if she doesn't like the new job.
4. (T) If Miss Gable takes the new job, She won't earn more than her present salary.
5. (F) Miss Gable's new job is to be a tour guide.
6. (F) If Miss Gable takes the new job, she will use her car a lot without any allowance by the new employer.

454

7. (T) The interviewer asks Miss Gable to think about the new job before she makes the find decision.

Task 2. Hypnosis

A. Choose the best answer (a, b, or c) to complete each of the following statements.

1. Hypnosis _____.
   * a. is a medical treatment dealing with the patient's mind
   b. is a magic way of fortune-telling
   c. deals with people who always feel drowsy

2. _____ , according to Dr. Parker, is one of the most powerful tools in hypnosis.
   a. A swinging watch
   * b. Voice
   c. An assistant

3. When a patient receives the treatment of hypnosis , he'd better _____.
   * a. get completely relaxed
   b. fall asleep
   c. become sensitive

4. The treatment of hypnosis is _____.
   a. to make the patient forget his past
   b. to make the patient lose his memory
   * c. to make the patient remember in great detail what caused him pain and suffering and help him to face his problems

5. _____, Dr Parker has turned out to be _____.
   a. Because his patients were co-operative; very successful
   * b. By using well-tried techniques; very successful
   c. With the help of his secretary; well-established

B. True or False Questions. Write a T in front of a statement if it is true according to the recording and write an F if it is false.

1. (T) Dr. Parker found he had the talent for hypnosis when he was in the last year in a medical school.

2. (F) There have been a lot of changes in Dr Parker's method.

3. (F) Dr Parker asks the patient to sit on a sofa.

4. (F) The secretary usually doesn't take notes or look after the recording equipment.

5. (T) Dr Parker wants to control his patient's mind during the treatment.

6. (F) The standard procedure is to take the patient to the present slowly.

7. (T) The 35-year-old female patient remembered a lot of things in detail far back in time.

C. List the details the thirty-five-year-old lady remembered.

1. (her eighth birthday)

2. (a Tuesday)

3. (those who were present)

4. (the names of those present)

5. (the clothes those present wore)

6. (the presents she received)

7. (her address at that time)

D. Complete the following statements with what you hear on the tape.

1. (In order to reach a person's mind), you have to make him forget his body (as much as possible). Then I'll tell him (to

456

concentrate) on (my voice).

2. Then I tell the subject (not to think about) what I'm saying but (just to accept it).

3. At first I used to (rely on the ticking of a clock) − − some say that (boring, repetitive sounds) help − − but now I simply get my patient to (stare at some object in the room).

4. I've taken patients (back to their first year) and a few even further than that . . . .

Section Two:

Tapescript:

Getting a Job

These days it's hard enough to find a suitable job, let alone get as far as an interview. Dozens of people every day scour the Situations Vacant columns of the press, send off their curriculum vitae or application form, and wait hopefully to be summoned for an interview. Now this, apparently, is where a lot of people fall down, because of their inadequacy at completing their application forms, according to Judith Davidson, author of Getting a Job, a book which has recently come on the market. This book, as the title suggests, is crammed full of useful tips on how to set about finding yourself work in these difficult times. Our reporter, Christopher Shields, decided to look into this apparent inability of the British to sell themselves, and he spoke to Judith Davidson about it.

Judith: Very often a job application or a curriculum vitae will contain basic grammatical or careless spelling mistakes, even from university graduates. Then those that do get as far as an interview become inarticulate or clumsy when they try to talk about themselves. It doesn't matter how highly qualified or brilliant

457

you may be, if you come across as tongue-tied and gauche, your chances of getting a job are pretty small.

Christopher: Judith Davidson lectures at a management training college for young men and women, most of whom have just graduated from university and gone there to take a crash course in management techniques. One of the hardest things is, not passing the course examinations successfully, but actually finding employment afterwards, so Judith now concentrates on helping trainees to set about doing just this.

Judith: Some letters are dirty and untidily written, with fingermarks all over them and ink blots or even coffee stains. Others arrive on lined or flowered or sometimes scented paper —none of which is likely to make a good impression on the average business-like boss.

Christopher: This apparent inability of many people to make that initial impact with an employer by sending him an application which will stand out from the rest and persuade him you're the right one for the job prompted an enterprising young man, called Mark Ashworth, a recruitment consultant himself, to start writing job applications for other people for a fee, as a sideline. He told me he got the idea in America where it's already big business, and in the last few months alone he's written over 250 c.v.s. He feels that 80 per cent of job applications received by personnel managers are inadequate in some way.

Mark: Many people simply can't cope with grammar and spelling and don't know what to put in, or leave out. Sometimes people condense their work experience so much that a future employer doesn't know enough about them. Then, on the other hand, some people go too far the other way. To give you an

458

example, one c. v. I once received in my recruiting role was getting on for thirty pages long.

Christopher: Mark has an initial interview with all his clients in which he tries to make them think about their motivation and why they've done certain things in the past. He can often exploit these experiences in the c. v. he writes for them, and show that they have been valuable preparation for the job now sought. He also believes that well-prepared job history and a good letter of application are absolutely essential.

Mark: Among the most important aspects of applications are spelling, correct grammar, content and layout. A new boss will probably also be impressed with a good reference or a letter of commendation written by a former employer. The type of c. v. I aim to produce depends largely on the kind of job being applied for. They don't always have to be slick or highly sophisticated, but in certain cases this does help.

Christopher: Judith Davidson thought very much along the same lines as Mark. In her opinion, one of the most important aspects of job applications was that they should be easy to read ...

Judith: ... Many applicants send in letters and forms which are virtually unreadable. The essence of handwritten application is that they should be neat, legible and the spelling should be accurate. I stress handwritten because most employers want a sample of their future employee's writing. Many believe this gives some indication of the character of the person who wrote it. Some people forget vital things like putting their own address or the date. Others fail to do what's required of them by a job advertisement.

459

Christopher: Judith believes that job seekers should always send an accompanying letter along with their application form stating clearly why their qualifications make them suitable for the vacancy.

Judith: Personal details have no place in letters of application. I well remember hearing about one such letter which stated, quite bluntly, I need more money to pay for my flat. No boss would be impressed by such directness.

Christopher: She added that the art of applying for jobs successfully was having to be learnt by more and more people these days, with the current unemployment situation. With as many as two or three hundred people applying for one vacancy, a boss would want to see only a small fraction of that number in person for an interview, so your application had to really outshine all the others to get you on the short list.

Key to Exercises:

A. Choose the best answer (a, b or c) to complete each of the following statements.

   1. This discussion is on _____.

     a. how to get a job

     b. how to please the employer

   * c. the problems those job applicants have to sell themselves

   2. Mary applicants fail to get a job _____.

   * a. because of their own inability with application forms and C.V.

     b. because the competition is too fierce

     c. because these employers are too fussy

   3. Writing an application, one should _____.

460

* a. be very careful about spelling, grammar, content and layout
  b. always use a typewriter
  c. feel free to present anything he wants
4. An applicant's handwriting _____.
  a. is a symbol of his educational level
  * b. indicates the applicant's character in a way
  c. doesn't matter at all in a job application
5. With hundreds of people fighting over one vacancy, one has to _____.
  a. write his application longer than others
  b. hire someone to write the application for him
  * c. make his application impressive, well-written and appealing to the employer

B. True or False Questions. Write a T in front of a statement if it is true according to the recording and write an F if it is false.
  1. (F) Those who have been to universities don't make grammatical or careless spelling mistakes.
  2. (T) Some application letters are dirty and untidily written.
  3. (T) Some people are at a loss what to put in an application.
  4. (F) Applying for a job, one doesn't need at all a good reference or a letter of recommendation by a former boss.
  5. (T) The applicant's address and the date he writes the letter are vital things with regard to an application letter.
  6. (T) Highly qualified and brilliant, an applicant will be turned down if he is tongue-tied and gauche during the interview.

C. Identification. Match the people in Column I with the special activities in Column II.

Column I	Column II
1. Christopher Shields	a. lectures at a business training college
2. Mark Ashworth	b. author of *Getting a Job*
3. Judith Davidson	c. recruitment consultant
	d. reporter

Answer: (1) – – (d); (2) – – (c); (3) – – (a, b)

D. Complete the following passages with the information you hear on the tape.

1. In the last (few months alone) he's written over (250 c. v. s.) He feels that (80 percent) of job applications received by personnel managers are (inadequate in a way).

2. Sometimes people (condense) their work experience so much that (a future employer doesn't know enough) about them. Then, on the other hand, some people (go too far the other way) . . . . One c. v. I once received in (my recruiting role) was getting on for (thirty pages long).

3. Many applicants send in letters and forms which are (unreadable). (The essence of) handwritten applications is that they should be (neat, legible) and the spelling should be (accurate).

4. Personal details (have no place in letters of application). I well remember (hearing about) one such letter which (stated, quite bluntly), 'I need (more money to pay) for my flat'. (No boss) would be impressed (by such directness).

Tapescript:

Main Ideas or Supporting Details

1. (Literature)

   We may note in passing that, although Dr Johnson's friend and biographer Boswell was a Scotsman, Johnson despised, or pretended to despise, Scotsmen in general. He once said that the best thing a Scotsman ever saw was the high road to England. In his famous dictionary, Johnson defined oats as 'a grain which in England is generally given to horses, but in Scotland supports the people'. He did not condemn all Scotsmen, however. Once he commented on a distinguished nobleman who had been born in Scotland but educated in England, saying that much could be made of a Scotsman —if he was caught young.

2. (Geography: American Indians)

   The first important point to note about the American Indians is that, in spite of their name, they are in no way related to the peoples of India. This confusion arose, as you probably know, because of a mistake on the part of Christopher Columbus. When he landed in America he thought that he had in fact discovered India. This mistake has been perpetrated, that is kept alive, ever since by the name he gave them. If they are related to any Asian group it is to the Mongols of Northern Asia. Many experts believe that the ancestors of the present American Indians emigrated from Northern Asia across the Bering Strait between 10, 000 and 20, 000 years ago.

3. (Science: methods of scientific discovery)

   A good illustration of how scientific discoveries may be made accidentally is the discovery of penicillin. Alexander Fleming was a bacteriologist who for fifteen years had tried to solve the problem of how to get rid of the disease-carrying germs or microbes in the human body without causing any dangerous side-effects. Fleming was an untidy worker and often had innumerable small dishes containing microbes all around his laboratory. One day, one of the dishes was contaminated with a mould, due to the window having been left open. Fleming noticed that the mould had killed off the microbes, and it was from similar moulds that the miracle drug penicillin was finally developed. Of course, only a brilliant scientist like Fleming would have been able to take advantage of this stroke of luck, but the fact remains that the solution to his problem was given to him, literally, on a plate.

4. (Psychology: memory)

What I want to emphasize to you is this: that people remember things which make sense to them or which they can connect with something they already know. Students who try to memorize what they cannot understand are almost certainly wasting their time.

Key to Exercises:

Comprehensive Exercises: Main Ideas or Supporting Details
You will hear some extracts from four different lectures. For each extract write down whether you think it is a main idea, supporting detail or digression.
Discuss with your classmates why you think the extract falls under the heading You have choose.

1. Answer: (main idea with supporting details)

Reason: ("we may note" for main idea;

"he once said" & "once" for supporting details)

2. Answer: (main idea)

    Reason: ("the first important point to note")

3. Answer: (supporting detail)

    Reason: ("a good illustration of")

4. Answer: (main idea)

    Reason: ("what I want to emphasize to you is this")

Supplementary Reading:

Hypnosis

Hypnosis refers to a complex phenomenon that cannot even be described in a few words and that is still harder to define. Hypnosis is used by medical men to study their patients' problems and to relieve symptoms such as pain. It is also used improperly and with great risk by quacks who allege, for example, that they can enhance the performance of an athlete or cure otherwise hopeless diseases. Still another use or rather abuse of hypnosis is by entertainers. A stage magician, for example, may "put a subject to sleep" by having him watch a light or an object and telling him he is growing sleepy. The hypnotist may then claim that the subject is in his power as long as the trance like state continues.

Calling hypnosis "sleep" is the earliest, simplest and least acceptable attempt at explanation. This article will not give a definition but will instead present facts about the phenomenon, summarizing what scientific investigators know about it.

Some students of the field believe that examples of hypnotism can be found in ancient reports of religious ecstasy and religious trance. However, very little hard information on the subject is older than the work of Franz Anton Mesmer in the late 18th century. Mesmer believed that a "rarefied fluid," which he called animal

465

magnetism, controlled health, he held that he could cure disease by correcting imbalances in this fluid through the use of magnetism. Mesmer's theories about magnetism were discounted by a French investigating commission, although he did cure some patients. Later his cures were ascribed to suggestion. Sometimes a patient who believed he was being helped was in fact improved. Mesmerism for many years was the term for what is now called hypnosis.

Mesmer's results have been explained by the claim that his patients were hypersuggestible. This explanation, however, may amount to nothing more than substituting the term hypersuggestibility for hypnosis. Investigators in the 1950's and 1960's found that some subjects are no more suggestible when hypnotised than when not. Still, hypersuggestibility is probably the most frequently observed phenomenon of the hypnotic state.

Techniques of Hypnosis

Who Can Be Hypnotised?

Most workers in the field believe that one of every three or four persons can, under appropriate conditions, manifest hypnotic phenomena. Hypnotizability doesn't not depend on sex, age, intelligence, personality type, emotional disease, or anything else so far investigated.

As long as a subject's (or patient's) attention can be gained, that person (if hypnotizable at all) can be hypnotised. Good subjects can be hypnotised with or without their knowledge and their conscious consent. All techniques utilize a gradual or rapid narrowing of the focus of conscious awareness. Theoretically, hypnotic induction is possible under the pretext of testing the ability to relax or while discussing interests or symptoms. During experimental closed-circuit telecasts, some members of television audiences have gone into hypnotic trance states while watching or listening to induction procedures. The U. S. television code since 1960 has banned portrayal of trance induction unless this is part of the plot of a play.

Classical Techniques.

All classical induction techniques utilize eyelid closure. The subject (or patient) is instructed to gaze at the hypnotist's eye, his finger, a spot on the wall or ceiling, or a shiny or whirling object, while being told over and over again in a monotonous tone, preferably in cadence with the patient's respiratory rhythm: "Breathe deeply but comfortably, deeply and comfortably, as your eyes grow heavier and heavier, and you grow sleepier, sleepier, sleepier still. Your eyes are so heavy, they feel they must close." The hypnotist may add, "You can close them now", or he may say "They are closing, closing". Some subjects need merely to be told once and matter-of-factly, "Close your eyes so tight that the harder you try to open them, the tighter they close." In either case, if induction is successful and the subject is challenged and tries to open his eyes, he cannot. He moves the wrong muscles. He has, it should be noted, been instructed to grow relaxed or to sleep. With eyes closed, he seems asleep. The stage magician and the medical hypnotist alike use this technique or some variation of it. Any reasonably intelligent adolescent or adult can be taught to hypnotise by this method unless he has an emotional block against doing it.

Contrary to popular belief, no elaborate apparatus is needed. Fixation objects are unnecessary. The blind can be hypnotised; the hypnotist's voice is sufficient. Even this can be dispensed with, for the deaf can be hypnotised through getting them to imitate the hypnotis's actions.

Other Techniques.

Psychiatrists use specialized methods called sensorimotor induction techniques. Certain other techniques, rejected by the medical profession, can be characterized as "trick" methods. One, which is highly dangerous, has been used by an occasional stage magician.

The carotid arteries, one on each side of the neck, carry blood from the aorta, to the head. A sudden blow with the side of the hand on one carotid sinus while the hypnotist commands his subject to "go to sleep," can cause momentary loss of consciousness. On both, it may kill. This technique is extremely dangerous and warrants the harshest condemnation.

Posthypnotic Suggestion.

While under hypnosis, a subject can be given instructions to respond to a signal at a later time. For example, the hypnotist might suggest that, at some time after the hypnotic session, the subject will resume his hypnotic state on signal. These posthypnotic suggestions are not always effective but usually are.

Autohypnosis.

A person can learn to induce a hypnotic state in himself. Usually, he is first hypnotised by someone else. While hypnotised, he is given the posthypnotic suggestion that he will, whenever he wishes, induce the trance state in himself.

Uses And Abuses of Hypnosis

For Entertainment.

To the layman, hypnosis has an aura of mystery and magic. Overpopularization has led to oversimplification, and hypnosis more often than not is regarded as a parlour or theatrical trick, an instrument of the spiritist rather than as a powerful medical and psychological technique. The inherent dangers must be stressed. In one case, two girls in London were hypnotised by a New York stage hypnotist. They posthypnotically developed adverse reactions severe enough to require months of psychiatric treatment. The resulting public furor led Parliament to pass the British Hypnotism Act of 1952, limiting public displays of hypnosis.

The hypnotised subject may be openly susceptible to even veiled suggestion, he may have ready access to his more usually heavily veiled unconscious drives, and he may while hypnotised feel that all social and personal curbs on his behaviour have been removed. For this reason the American Medical Association in 1958 and the American Psychiatric Association in 1961 vigorously condemned all use of hypnosis for entertainment purposes. Unfortunately the dramatic manner in which hypnosis has been presented to the public obscures the fact that it is complex and potentially dangerous.

To Improve Performance.

Some people look to hypnosis to increase physical strength or to improve physical, academic, professional, or artistic performance. For centuries hypnosis has been regarded an occult art bestowing on its practitioners secret Satanic power. Svengali, In George Du Maurier's novel Trilby, is the proto-type of the all-powerful malignant hypnotist. By his "arts" he makes a girl into a famous singer. It is worth noting that Du Maurier has Svengali rehearse Trilby while she is hypnotised, painstakingly teaching voice to her. He does not substitute hypnosis for voice training.

The hypnotised subject's motivation to perform may become pronounced enough for him to expend unusual effort in order to carry out his hypnotist's suggestions. But experimental evidence shows that, if motivation is increased in other ways, the same person when not hypnotised may equal or exceed his performance under hypnosis.

This applies specifically in the field of athletics. In at least two cases, professional athletes did worse after hypnosis than before it. There is an additional danger. In its statement opposing the use of hypnosis in athletics, the AMA explained that hypnotised athletes may go beyond the limits of their physical ability and experience states of serious exhaustion; and because of posthypnotic suggestion they may be so intent on performance as to leave themselves open to injury.

In Research.

Hypnosis has proper uses in psychological and medical (including psychiatric) research. Only a trained psychologist or a trained investigator in medicine or allied health fields can competently conduct research of this type.

As an Aid in Treatment.

Hypnotic techniques have legitimate uses in medical practice. Whenever hypnosis is used, however, it remains a psychiatric technique. There can be no nonpsychiatric clinical use of hypnosis, even though physicians in general practice and in the nonpsychiatric specialities may, and do, hypnotise patients for medical purposes.

Physicians hypnotise (1) to induce analgesia (decreased perception of pain) and anaesthesia (absence of pain or other sensation); (2) to allay apprehension and anxiety; (3) to repress, or suggest away, symptoms; and (4) as an adjunctive technique in the treatment of psychiatric disease.

Until the development of chemical anaesthesia, hypnosis (when applicable and practical) constituted the safest and most effective means for controlling pain. Even during World War II, because of the dearth of chemical anaesthetics in Japanese prison camps, appendectomies were performed with hypnosis as the anaesthetic agent. Women may be delivered of babies under hypnosis, and dentists may

470

use it during oral surgery. Surgeons and anaesthesiologists, with carefully selected patients only, may use hypnosis by itself as the anaesthetic of choice or in conjunction with decreased amounts of other anaesthetic agents. Patients who can be anaesthetized by direct suggestion are merely told under hypnosis either that they will feel no pain or that they will not react to it. Patients with severe burns present fewer nursing problems while hypnotised. They are neither drowsy nor confused (as they would be under drugs) when attending to bowel or bladder functions or while eating.

Symptoms such as the severe itch of a poison ivy or the skull – splitting headache of a brain tumor can be suppressed or suggested away. If symptoms are emotionally based, they may likewise be suppressed or suggested away. This at times may be inadvisable, unless the underlying emotional disease be concurrently treated. To illustrate a schoolteacher with severe back pain was successfully cured of this symptom during a single hypnotic session. His pain, however, was a depressive equivalent – – as long as he focused on his pain, he could evade facing and feeling his underlying depression. His pain, in other words, held his depression in check. But with the hypnotic relief of his pain, his depression was unleashed, and a few days later he plunged to his death from a seventh-story window.

There are particular dangers in using posthypnotic suggestion to relieve symptoms. One patient, for instance, kept ridding himself in this way of headaches caused by a brain tumor, and by the time he was examined, his tumor was inoperable.

Such patients should not have been hypnotised, at least not by a nonpsychiatrist. Selfhypnosis in any case should not posthypnotically have been suggested to them. There is little in the whole field

471

of psychodynamics with so great a potential for harm. If self-, or auto-, hypnotic procedures are suggested even to apparently stable people, as for headache or pain relief, this may be the equivalent of giving them a permanently refillable unlimited prescription for narcotics.

Hypnosis at times may also be used as a diagnostic tool. In most areas of medicine, symptoms can be produced by organic causes, by emotional causes, or by some combination of the two. Emotional imbalances are likely to manifest themselves in a number of ways that would appear to require the specialized attention of a neurologist, dermatologist, or internist. With hypnosis as a diagnostic procedure, physicians can often determine whether a constant headache, for example, is due to tension or brain tumor.

Hypnosis for either physical or psychiatric purposes is neither a therapeutic agent nor a therapeutic technique. Patients with organic diseases, when treated surgically, are operated on not by but under anaesthesia. Similarly, patients with emotional diseases are treated psychotherapeutically under, not by, hypnosis.

In psychiatric practice, hypnotic techniques are used on a highly selective basis during treatment and during or after prior consultation and evaluation. With some patients, through such techniques, the therapist may sometimes more effectively, or more rapidly, study the patient's underlying psychopathology, recognize his defences, assay his personality assets, and be enabled to incorporate them into a therapeutic program. Patients who are readily hypnotizable may, depending upon what is involved, be treated on hypnotic, nonhypnotic, or on mixed levels.

With hypnotic techniques the therapist may utilize a number of extremely specialized manoeuvres, limited only by his own personality, his knowledge of the patient, experience, ingenuity, and understanding of psychodynamics.

One of these techniques is fantasy production. The patient may be asked, after induction into a hypnotic trance, to imagine himself in a movie theatre. The therapist then suggests that a person will appear on the screen exhibiting the same symptoms as the patient. By asking the patient to look behind the screen to discover what is responsible for the disorder in the fantasied screen personality, the therapist can bring significant, and sometimes deeply hidden, material to the fore.

On the surface, one of the most dramatic hypnotic techniques is time manipulation. A patient may be asked to travel backward or forward in time, or his sense of subjective time may be manipulated so that in a few minutes or seconds he seems to live hours, days, months, even years. When a patient is regressed in time, he may be told after being hypnotised that his main emotion, whatever it is, will grow stronger until he feels it fully and completely. This is known as intensification of emotion. The therapist may then suggest that the subject regress to an earlier period in his life when he felt the same way. In this way the patient may seem to return to any point in his life and experience it as he either actually lived it or as he now fantasies he lived it.

When such reliving, or revivification, of past events under hypnosis is accompanied by an appropriate emotional release, the result is the classic example of what Sigmund Freud called abreaction. During abreaction, a soldier, for example may return to a battle situation and experience hallucinations of combat through sight, sound, touch, and smell. When it is developed around a forgotten traumatic experience, abreaction can provide emotional relief – –

473

this is what Freud termed catharsis. Abreaction and catharsis still remain the core of all analytically oriented psychotherapies, including psychoanalysis.

Material enacted, described, or "relived" on hypnotic levels is not necessarily factual. A person may fantasy something has happened and then relive it in vivid detail. For example, reincarnation fantasies have little or nothing to do with fact; their origins can be determined.

Hypnosis and the Law.

Confessions obtained through the use of hypnosis have been declared by the courts to be inadmissible evidence. In the landmark case of Leyra V. Denno, which was fought all the way to the U.S. Supreme Court, a psychiatrist employed by a district attorney's office hypnotised a murder suspect, who then posthypnotically signed three separate confessions. The Supreme Court found that there had been mental coercion with violation of Section One of the 14th Amendment and Article Five of the Constitution. The prisoner was freed, for the only evidence against him was the confessions.

Hypnosis as an investigative tool has severe limitations. Hypnotised subjects, for example, may confess to crimes they have actually committed, to crimes they fantasy having committed, or to crimes their hypnotists think they have committed. They can falsify testimony against themselves and against others or be induced to persuade themselves that they remember committing crimes that in actuality they never committed.

474

Lesson 24

Section One:

Tapescript:

Task 1: I. Q. Tests

Brigid: Mrs Kellerman, why is it that some children perform much better than others at school?

Mrs Kellerman: Obviously, it can't be denied that certain children are brighter than others, but it's not as simple as that. A lot of emphasis is placed on intelligence measured by tests —so-called I. Q. tests, which only measure certain types of intelligence.

Brigid: Such as?

Mrs Kellerman: Basically linguistic and numerical skills —or reading and mathematics, to put it plainly —which is unfortunate because some children are bound to suffer. A good example was a friend of mine's son who was kept out of the top class at school because of his average I. Q. —that's around 100. His father, though he had no idea his son was going to be an architect, always said he was a clever child. Apparently he was able to picture things in his mind and draw accurately at a very early age. The point is that his university life might not have been so difficult if his ability had been recognized sooner.

Brigid: What you're saying, then, is that some children have abilities that are not easy to measure, that aren't appreciated by many schools.

475

Mrs Kellerman: Precisely. And if these skills are not spotted sufficiently early, they cannot be developed. That's why, in my view, there are so many unhappy adults in the world. They are not doing the things they are best at.

Brigid: What are these other kinds of intelligence, and how can we recognize them in our children?

Mrs Kellerman: Well, take musical talent. Many children never get the chance to learn to play an instrument but, while they might not become great artists or composers, they may get a lot of pleasure and satisfaction. Musically gifted children are fascinated by all kinds of sounds —car horns, animal noises and so on. And they can easily recognize tunes and sing them in key.

Brigid: How can a parent encourage them?

Mrs Kellerman: Sing to them and teach them new songs. Buy a piano or even a cheap instrument such as a recorder. If you can afford it, send them to lessons as soon as possible. Play recordings of different instruments to them.

Brigid: What about a child who is good at sport? Could that be described as a form of intelligence?

Mrs Kellerman: Most certainly. We psychologists call it 'motor', or bodily, intelligence. These children move gracefully and handle objects skilfully. A child who finds it easy to take things apart and use various tools may well become an engineer with the right encouragement. We should give them models to make and take them to science museums. However, unless these children are also good with words and numbers, they will probably not do well in school examinations.

Brigid: Is there anything a parent can do to help in this case?

Mrs Kellerman: Yes. It may be worth spending money on private lessons. But, you know, hardly anyone is good at everything. In my opinion a child should be judged on his individual talents. After all, being happy in life is putting your skills to good use, no matter what they are.

Task 2: Why Is It Good For Children to Read

Teacher: I think there are a lot of reasons why it's good for children to read. Er ... Not just reading for pleasure, but all of the subjects, no matter what subject it is, involve some reading, even if it's just art. (Mmm.) They have to read the directions to do an art project, and ... ah. Social Studies they have to read. Science they have to read. And the more they read, ah, the easier, ah, the more their vocabulary will expand, and the better the ... they'll do in their other subjects. Erm ... Also for, for pleasure, erm, es-, er, especially here in Puerto Ordaz where there aren't very many things to do. In ... instead of being out doing something they shouldn't be doing, ah, they can choose reading as a hobby.

Erm ... It also improves their language tremendously. I can read a composition that a student has written that has, that reads a lot and I know, er, that he reads a lot by his use of the language and his vocabulary and a lot of advanced sentence structure that someone of that age normally would not, er, be able to handle.

Erm ... What else? Erm ... Sometimes children who have very limited experiences, whose families don't get out very much, er, maybe not have enough money, er, ah, just stay at home a lot, have real limited experiences and by reading they can expand their experiences about what happens in the

477

world and I've had children who, in a reader, see a picture, an exercise and they see a picture of a lion and they don't know what it is, because either their parents haven't read to them, or they haven't read books, or they haven't been out. And if they haven't been to a zoo to see an actual lion they could have read in a book, or had their parents read to them about, er, lions. And they miss the, the problem, because they may, once you tell them what it is, explain, they they can do the exercise, but because they didn't know, didn't have the experience, they weren't able to do it.

Erm ... er ... For survival later, too. If you can't read, erm, a cook-book or a , a manual to, to repair things, you're lost in that you have to rely on someone else to, always. And you're not, er, independent.

Interviewer: What is it good for children to read?

Teacher: I think children should read everything, that, er, not just limit it to mystery books, or just to science fiction. In fact there are some children who, who say, 'No, no. I just want to read science fiction,' but, er, I think they should read, er, from different areas. Er ... The newspaper, magazines. The school subscribes too, even though it's a small school, we've gotten in the budget approved to have fifteen magazines come in, and during their silent sustained reading time can read magazines.

Erm ... if ... anything that's written down, I think they should read. Whether a sign or newspaper, textbook, everything, and not just limit it to one or two things. Erm ... I think a lot of parents disagree that children, they say if they're reading comic books they're wasting their time, but if I have a

478

child who's a poor student, if he'll read a comic book, er, I'm happy because he's reading something. Or if he's, while he's eating breakfast he's reading the back of the cereal box he's still reading something and I wouldn't take it away from him and say, 'Stop wasting your time,' because that is a step to go on to further reading and if you limit it to certain areas, then that will, it sometimes, it will stifle them and they'll stop reading completely. And they'll say, 'If I can't read the comic book then I don't want to read anything.' But reading the comic book could, erm, they say, 'Well I enjoyed this and I understood this, er, I think I'll try something else,' and that expands their reading. And they can learn something from a comic book.

Erm ... It's also important, erm, if a student, if, a lot of the kids want to play games and they don't, it's a new game they don't know how to play, if they can't read the instructions, then they won't be able to play the game. Or, if they have a new toy, erm, if they can't read the instructions, they could possibly break the toy, and, by not learning how to use it properly.

Key to Exercises:
Task 1: I. Q. Tests
A. Choose the best answer (a, b or c) to complete each of the following statements.
  1. Mrs Kellerman is probably _____.
  * a. a psychologist
    b. a primary school teacher
    c. a doctor

2. I.Q. Test, according Mrs. Kellerman, _____ .

a. can be used to measure all types of intelligence a child has.

* b. can be used to measure certain types of intelligence a child has.

c. can not be used to measures a child's intelligence

3. Musically gifted children _____ .

a. are interested in noises

* b. are fascinated by all kinds of sounds, even animal noises

c. are keen on playing the piano

4. Psychologically speaking, a child who possesses bodily intelligence may _____ .

a. be good at language acquisition

* b. be good at sports

c. become an engineer in the future

5. Parents should _____ if the children find it easy to take things apart and use various tools.

a. show them how to operate a recorder

b. stop them from doing that

* c. give them models to make and take them to science museums

6. According to Mrs Kellerman, _____ since nobody is good at everything.

* a. a child should be judged on his individual talents

b. a child should be judged on his I.Q. scores

c. a child should be judged by his parents who know him better than anybody else

B. True or False Questions. Write a T in front of a statement if it is true according to the recording and write an F if it is false.

480

1. (T) I.Q. tests are most valid in testing a child's ability in linguistic and numerical skill or reading and maths.
2. (T) The earlier a child's talents are recognized, the better.
3. (F) Children who are not good with words and numbers can still do well in school examinations.
4. (F) A child doesn't have to go to private lessons even if he is discovered to have special talents.

C. Fill in the following blanks with what you hear on the tape.
1. Some children have abilities that (are not easy to measure), that aren't (appreciated) by many schools.
2. And if these skills are not (spotted sufficiently early), they cannot be (developed). That's why, (in my view), there are so many (unhappy adults) in the world. They are not doing the things (they are best at).
3. Many children (never get the chance) to learn to play (an instrument) but, while they might not become great (artists) or (composers), they may get a lot of (pleasure and sstisfaction) . . . They can easily recognize (tunes) and sing them (in key).

Task 2: Why Is It Good For Children to Read
A. Write out a list of benefits that reading can bring to a child according to what you hear on the tape.
a. Reading can be (a hobby that a child takes pleasure in);
b. Reading expands (a child's vocabulary);
c. Reading improves (a child's language);
d. Reading enriches (a child's experience);
e. Reading helps (children to become independent in life).

481

B. True or False Questions. Write a T in front of a statement if it is true according to the recording and write an F if it is false.

1. (T) Even doing an art project, a child needs to read.
2. (F) Science fiction is the most important for children.
3. (F) Magazines and newspapers, should be excluded for a child's reading list.
4. (T) Never say it is a waste of time when a child is reading.
5. (T) Even a comic book offers children something to learn.
6. (F) Children don't have to read when they pick up a new game or play a new toy.

C. According to what you hear on the tape, give a list of things that children should be allowed to read.

1. (mystery books)
2. (science fiction)
3. (newspapers and magazines)
4. (signs)
5. (textbooks)
6. (comic books)

D. Fill in the blanks in the following passage based on what you hear on the tape.

If I have a child who is (a poor student), if he'll read (a comic book), I'm happy because (he's reading something). Or if he's, while he's eating breakfast he's reading (the back of the cereal box) he's still reading something and I (wouldn't take it away) from him and say, 'Stop wasting your time', because that is (a step to go on) to further reading and if you (lim-

482

it) it to (certain areas) then, that will, it sometimes, it will (stifle) them and they'll (stop reading completely).

Section Two:

Tapescript:

Task 1: What Is a Koto? (I)

Ever since you started to school, and perhaps before, you have been given tests. One type of test you have probably taken is an intelligence test, a test designed to determine your ability to learn or your ability to change behaviour on the basis of experience.

It is not just test-givers who make judgements about intelligence, however. Most of us make educated guesses or inferences about how smart or intelligent a person is from the way he does certain things. We usually call people intelligent if they learn quickly, know answers to a lot of questions, and can solve difficult problems. When a psychologist studies intelligence, there are many questions that he wants to answer. But the first question he must ask is: What is intelligence?

Most people think of intelligence as one ability. We say, "Ann is smart". But is intelligence really that simple? Is it only one ability? In trying to understand these questions, it might be helpful to look at athletic ability. If Mitch is a good basketball player, do we say that he is a good athlete? What if he is poor in baseball? What if he can't play football? Even if a person is good at sports, is he equally good in all of them?

This is the same kind of problem we have when we ask, "What is intelligence?" What if Estelle is very good in math, but very poor in spelling? Is she intelligent or unintelligent? Maybe there is not just one kind of intelligence, but several different kinds. You probably know people who are very good in some subjects, but not good in others, and it is likely that you are the same way. You find some subjects easier than others and you do better in them. Most people are like that—they are not equally good in everything.

In trying to understand the nature of intelligence, a psychologist tries to find out how various abilities are related to each other. To do this, he devises intelligence tests which have several parts— each part measuring a different ability. The kinds of abilities that these tests measure include:

1. How well words can be defined and understood;
2. How well arithmetic problems can be done;
3. How well facts can be remembered.

Are these abilities related to each other? If a student is good at solving arithmetic problems, will he also be good at remembering facts? If he can define and understand a lot of words, will he also be good in arithmetic? To find the answers to these questions, the psychologist correlates the scores from each part of the test. A correlation is a mathematical way of finding out if these abilities are related to each other. If two abilities are correlated, it means that if you are good at one, you will probably be good at the other—or, if you are poor at one, you will probably be poor at the other. When two abilities are not correlated, it means that they are not related to each other—they do not go together. It means that being good at one has nothing to do with being good at another. For example, success in mathematics is not correlated with success in playing baseball. Some people who are good baseball players are good in math—others are not.

Think of all the mental and athletic abilities shown by your friends and schoolmates. Can you think of some abilities and skills that seem highly correlated? Can you think of some abilities which do not seem to be correlated? Why do you think some abilities are correlated and others are not?

Task 2: What Is a Koto? (II)

There are many factors to keep in mind about intelligence tests. It is especially important to realize that intelligence tests measure how well you do at the time you take the test, but not how well you could do. There are many reasons why a student might not do well on a test in school. A person may do poorly on an intelligence test because he did not have a proper education and not because he is stupid. Also, some of the problems and questions of intelligence tests are not fair to certain groups of people.

For example, suppose that the problems and questions on a test are about ice cream cones, baseball, automobiles and hot dogs. How would a student from another country, where these things do not exist, do on this test? Could he do as well as an average American boy? What if you took an intelligence test which asked questions about the hibachi, tempura and saki? Any Japanese boy could answer these questions, but you probably couldn't. Does this mean that you are not intelligent? No matter how intelligent a person is, he will not be able to answer questions about things he has never seen or heard of. When a test has a lot of "unfair" questions, do the results tell us much about a person's intelligence? Why not?

Some questions would be "unfair" to almost all American test takers. How can you tell if a test question is "unfair"? Here is one to consider: Which of the following four musical instruments is different from the others in an important way: VIOLIN, SITAR, KOTO, TRUMPET.

485

What makes this question unfair to most American boys and girls is that two of the four words are from foreign languages. The test taker has no way of knowing what they mean. Therefore, if you don't know what a word means, how can you decide that it is, or is not, different from the other words?

The same question can be made into a fair intelligence-test question. It can be done very easily by adding pictures next to each word and asking the question again.

To find out if the question without pictures is "unfair", ask people to answer it. Do not let them see the picture next to each word. Ask them why they gave the answer they did. Now show them the question with the pictures. Do the people who are questioned give correct answers more frequently the first time, without pictures, or the second time, with pictures?

In what ways do the pictures help people answer the question? Is it true that the question without pictures is "unfair" and the one with pictures is "fair"? Can you think of a question that would be fair to boys and girls all over the world? Intelligence is partly measured by the ability to put information together and use it to answer questions. How does this apply to the question on musical instruments? Can the most intelligent person you know answer this question: What colour hair does each author of this book have?

Key to Exercises:

Task 1: What Is a Koto (I)

A. Choose the best answer (a, b, or c) to complete each of the following statements.

    1. According to the tape, an intelligence test is designed to
    _____.

* a. determine one's ability to learn and his ability to change behaviour on the basis of experience

b. determine one's ability to work with his hands

c. determine one's potential to become a sportsman or a language learner

2. The question "What is intelligence" _____.

a. is quite easy to answer

b. doesn't require much thinking

* c. is fairly difficult to answer

3. If a person is good at football, we _____.

a. can say he is good at all sports

* b. can't say he is good at other forms of sports as well

c. can say he is very intelligent

4. A psychologist has designed a test based on _____.

a. 2 variables

* b. 3 variables

c. 3 facts

5. This new test aims at finding _____.

* a. correlation among those variables

b. cause-and-effect relationship among the variables

c. finding language and mathematical genius from those tested

B. True or False Questions. Write a T in front of a statement if it is true according to the recording and write an F if it is false.

1. (T) Intelligent people usually learn quickly, know answers to a lot of questions and can solve difficult problems.

2. (F) Intelligent people are equally good in everything.

3. (F) People's abilities are closely related to one another.

487

C. Complete the following passage with what you hear on the tape.

A correlation is (a mathematical way) of finding out if these abilities (are related to each other). If two abilities are correlated, it means that if you are (good at one), you are probably (good at the other)—or, if (you are poor at one), you will probably be (poor at the other). When two abilities are not correlated, it means (they are not related to each other)—They do not (go together). It means that being good at one (has nothing to do with) being good at another.

Task 2: What Is a Koto? (Ⅱ)

A. Choose the best answer (a, b or c) to complete each of the following statements.

1. One has to remember that intelligence test measures

   _____.

   a. how well he could do

   b. all his abilities

   * c. how he does at the time he takes the test

2. Some people do poorly on an intelligence test because .

   _____.

   a. they are not quite interested in doing it

   * b. they did not have a proper education

   c. they are stupid

3. _____ will do better when questions are asked about the hibachi, tempura and saki.

   * a. Japanese

   b. Americans

   c. Indians

4. Some questions would be "unfair" if _____.
* a. the test taker had never seen or heard of what is asked about
   b. they are on musical instruments like koto or sitar
   c. the test taker is a foreigner

B. True or False Questions. Write a T in front of a statement if it is true according to the recording and write an F if it is false.
1. (F) If a person is intelligent, he can answer any questions.
2. (T) Unfair questions will produce unfair results of a test taker's intelligence.
3. (T) One person's experience affects his scores of an intelligence test.
4. (F) American boys and girls have little idea about ice cream cones, base ball, automobiles and hot dogs.
5. (F) Illustrations to a question will certainly help a test taker to work out a better answer.
6. (T) Intelligence is partly measured by the ability to put information together and use it to answer questions.
7. (T) It is very difficult to think of a question that is fair to all boys and girls all over the world.

Section Three:
Tapescript:
Main Ideas and Supporting Details
1. (Politics)

When a party is elected to Parliament in Britain it may not stay in power for more than five years without calling an election. But—now this is an important point—the Prime Minister may 'go to the country', that's to say call an election at any time before the five years are up. This is important because it gives the Prime Minister in Britain a lot of power—he can choose the best time to have an election for his own party. In many other countries the timing of an election is fixed—it must take place on a certain date every four years, or whatever, and this means that in these countries the President or Prime Minister cannot choose the most convenient time for himself, the way a British Prime Minister can.

2. (Medicine)

One of the most dramatic examples of the effect of advances in medical knowledge is the building of the Panama Canal. In 1881 work was started on this canal under the supervision of De Lesseps, the Frenchman who built the Suez Canal. The project had to be abandoned after mosquito-borne diseases of yellow fever and malaria had claimed 16,000 victims among the workers. At the beginning of this century, the area was made healthy by spraying the breeding waters of the mosquitoes with petroleum. Work was able to be started again and the canal was finished in 1914.

3. (Sport)

By the way, since we have mentioned the Olympic Games, you may be interested to know the following curious fact about the ancient Olympic Games as compared to the Modern Olympics. The ancient games were held every four years without interruption for over 1,000 years. The modern games have already been cancelled three times (in 1916, 1940 and 1944) because of world wars.

4. (Zoology)

490

Although it is not strictly speaking relevant to our topic, perhaps I might say something about sharks since they are in the news quite a lot these days. Sharks have got a very bad reputation and probably most people think that all sharks are killers. This is not the case. In fact, the largest sharks of all (I mean the Whale Shark and the Basking Shark) are usually harmless to man.

Key to Exercises:

Comprehensive Exercises: Main Ideas or Supporting Details You will hear some extracts from four different lectures. For each extract write down whether you think it is a main idea, supporting detail or digression. Discuss with your classmates why you think the extract falls under the heading you have chosen.

1. Answer: (main idea)
   Reason: ("this is an important point")
2. Answer: (supporting detail)
   Reason: ("one of the most dramatic example of")
3. Answer: (digression)
   Reason: ("by the way")
4. Answer: (digression)
   Reason: ("although it is not strictly relevant to our topic")

Section Four:
Enjoy Your English:
Tapescript:
Moon River
Moon river wider than a mile
I'm crossing you in style some day
Old dream maker

You heart breaker
Wherever you're going
I'm going your way
Two drifters, off to see the world
There's such a lot of world to see
We're after the same rainbow's end
Waiting round the bend
My Huckleberry friend
Moon river and me

Supplementary Reading:

Intelligence Tests

The IQ. The concept of the IQ, or intelligence quotient, was first suggested in 1912 by the German psychologist Wilhelm Stern, but the credit for popularizing it belongs largely to Terman. The IQ at first represented the ratio of mental age to chronological age, each expressed in months; because each mental age was defined as corresponding to the average performance of individuals of the same chronological age, the average IQ for any large standardization group was very nearly 1.00. For the sake of convenience this figure was multiplied by 100, so that the midpoint of the IQ range is now 100.

A disadvantage of this definition of the IQ is that, as was known very early and repeatedly demonstrated, the ability to learn grows more and more slowly as age increases and, like physical growth, generally ceases in the early teens. Thus it was agreed very early that the maximum chronological age used as a divisor in determining the IQ should not exceed 16 years. The 1937 revision of the Stanford-Binet called for subtracting a gradually increasing number of months from the divisor of the IQ beginning at age 13, and, regardless of the subject's true age, the divisor never exceeded 16 years.

Another method for dealing with this problem was adopted by Otis, whose Self-Administering Test of Mental Ability (1922) was accompanied by a descriptive manual proposing the "Index of Brightness". This index was simply the subject's deviation from the norm of his age, added to or subtracted from 100. If the norm was 42 (as it was for adults on this test) and the subject's score was 35, the index would be 100 + 35 - 42, or 93. The Index of Brightness was later named the Deviation IQ, and the concept was adapted to various other mental tests.

Otis' scheme made no allowance for the growing variability of scores with increasing age. If a single test with a very wide range of difficulty was given to individuals ranging in age from six years to adulthood, the spread of scores on such a test, like the average score, would increase with age and reach a maximum in the early teens. A solution to this problem was suggested by an empirical study of IQ's that extensively surveyed the relevant literature up to about 1940 and concluded that the standard deviation of IQ's was about 16. The computation of Deviation IQ's now takes this fact into account, allowing for changes in the spread of IQ's accompanying increased age.

Test Scores as Predictive.

The most prevalent use of intelligence test scores is to predict degree of academic success. Such scores are used in some communities as bases for admitting able children to schools at ages younger than normal, and they are very generally used to determine admissions to schools beyond public secondary school. Another use com-

493

mon in elementary schools involves comparing such scores with performances in various subjects in order to identify children who are working below capacity.

Intelligence tests provide the best available predictive measures. School grades as determined by teachers not only vary widely from one teacher to another and from one community to another but also are expressed in widely varying ways: sometimes as letter grades, sometimes as percentages. Too rarely are they based on objective tests devised and administered locally.

The greatest problem in using intelligence tests for the purpose of prediction is that no dependable criterion of their accuracy exists. The ideal criteria would be objective and reliable achievement tests following instruction in each subject, but there are few such tests, especially at the college level. Studies have shown that correlations between intelligence tests and achievement tests in various subjects up through secondary school range roughly from 0.5 to 0.8. Such correlations are fairly high, but they do not suggest anywhere near complete agreement.

At the college level there are two major tests used as criteria of admission. By far the more important is the College Entrance Examination, constructed by the Educational Testing Service under contract for the College Entrance Examination Board. These tests are returned to the Educational Testing Service for scoring, and the results are then made available to the various colleges authorized by the student to receive them. The second test of this type is the American College Test, which operates in essentially the same fashion.

Both tests, and certain others of more specialized natures, constitute measures of certain skills, abilities, and knowledges that have been found to be related to success in college. Their correlations

494

with academic success are limited for three outstanding reasons. First, measures of achievement in college are themselves perhaps no more reliable than those in elementary and secondary schools. Second, intellectual factors do not alone determine academic success, especially at the college level. Many students drop out of schools because they are inadequately motivalted or because they dislike the instructional program. Third, corrlations are lowered because the use of such tests for denying admission to some students means that the range of scores for those admitted is restricted, and such restrictions tend to reduce correlation.

Areas of Controversy. Over the years, tests of mental ability have arousd great controversy. One of the most important areas of disagreement concerns the constancy of the IQ. Every test score incorporates a certain degree of chance error, and in the case of IQ's such errors usually amount to 5 points or more, so that an intelligence test score usually can only identify a range of 10 points or more in which a subject's true but unknown IQ lies. In addition to such errors of measurement, there are many factors affecting the performances of subjects, such as variations in the particular contests of tests, in the standardization groups used to determine norms for the tests, in the physical conditions under which the tests are administered, and in the accuracy and adequacy of the administration, the scoring, and the interpretation of the results.

One source of variation in scores is careless or unscrupulous use of tests in the schools. Published tests of mental ability usually have two or more equivalent forms, but some schools, for reasons of economy, use one form again and again. This practice is dangerous and unprofessional in that it magnifies the temptation to coach for the test. This danger includes a hazard for the school, because intelligence test scores are generally accepted as estimates of reasonable achievement; artificial increases in such scores place additional burdens on teachers, who must work harder to produce what seem to be the same results. However, coaching for ability tests is fairly difficult, unless deliberate cheating – giving away answers – is involved. The practice of reusing the same test is more reprehensible in achievement testing, since coaching for such tests is relatively easy; in such cases the practice results in consistent gains in the pupils. scores, which make the community look good while cheating the pupils of instruction of the quality they have a right to expect.

Another area of controversy relates to the use of the same mental test with subjects whose backgrounds differ widely in respect to socioeconomic status, degree of education of parents, and the like. Intelligence test scores in such cases are most useful as measures of present learning potential. As measures of overall potential for learning they are unsafe, but fairness in this respect can be avoided if the tests are applied to more or less homogeneous groups and if the norms for the tests are based on performances by similar groups in schools of the same locality. In this way variations in socioeconomic status and in quality of schooling can be minimized. The greatest danger in using a single test with subjects of widely varying backgrounds is the tendency to think of th test scores as measuring inherited intelligence; it is essential to bear in mind that environmental factors can have considerable effect on intelligence test results.

Another controversy has to do with the extent to which it is legitimate for schools to report the results of mental ability tests to pupils' parents. This is a matter of judgment on which each community must establish its own policy. Such results are often abused by those who are untrained to deal with them. Even so, it seems

496

reasonable to expect a school to do nothing to its pupils that cannot be divulged to their parents. Much can be gained by sharing test scores with parents using local morms, provided that the information is accompanied by an explanation of the limitations of the test and an exposition of the local norms. Knowledge of this sort is essential if the parents are to understand the relationship between their child's ability and his performance in school.

Lesson 25

Section One:

Tapescript:

The Lucky Story of the Holiday Money

Mary: On holiday, one summer, we were camping, of course, (Yes, of course) er, and had been to Italy and, er, back into France (Yeah) and, at the border, we had an awful lot of trouble finding the passport and (Mm) the this and the that, (Mm) to move over from Italy to France, erm, so I was rather disappointed a, at the mess we'd made of it and, as we travelled on into Fance, I spent the rest of that day tidying up the car (Mhm) and I very carefully put into one folder the passports, the tickets, travellers' cheques and all our currency (Yeah) and it was all beautifully packed so that we wouldn't be caught in this position again of not being able to find (Mhm, Mhm) anything. Erm, we eventually decided to stop in a town where we knew there was a camp-site and in the town we stopped at a garage, really to ask the way to the camp-site, (Mm) but while we were there we thought, well, we'll get some petrol, erm, and, er, ask the question at the same time. (Yeah) Erm ... the man put the petrol in the car and, with all efficiency, I took out the folder (Yeah) with the money in it (Mhm) and paid for the petrol and then we went on our way. The camp-site was about two or three miles

498

away. Er, when we got to the camp-site, we went into the office and one of the things one usually carries as a camper is a little sort of card, erm, a camping ticket, if you like, and, er, I ...

Tom: What's that for?

Mary: Well, one gets reduced rates for being a (Oh, I see) member of a camping club, (Mm) or something like that. Erm, and I went to get it from the folder, properly packed folder, (Mm) and I could not find the folder! (Oh, God!) We had everything out of the car, all over the floor on the grass, erm, and each one of us was sure we, er, had seen it somewhere since the garage. And we finally had to say to these people, 'We are very sorry, we have no money, no card, no nothing' And ...

Tom: How much money was involved?

Mary: Well, all our holiday money, you know. Some hundreds of pounds, in travellers' cheques and some in currency, you see, a few pounds ...

Tom: And passports?

Mary: And passports, and tickets for the boat (God!) Erm, so we said we'd go to the police station. So back we went to the town. And we all went into the police station. Erm, and a very friendly policeman said, 'Well, I can do nothing about it. Your best bet is to see the British Consul, er, in the city.' Erm, well this was on a Saturday afternoon and it was five o'clock and he told us that we would be able to get into the, er, Consul on Monday morning when they opened, which didn't encourage us too much. (Quite!) Then it suddenly struck us that somebody must have taken this money, at the garage,

499

(Ah, of course) so back we went the garage (Mhm) and we thought that as we stood talking to the man asking 'Where do you go to the camp-site?', someone else had obviously stolen our folder.

Tom: That was the last time you'd had it ...?

Mary: Yes, indeed, (Mm) you see, erm, that was the last time that we could all agree (Mm) that we must have had it. (Mhm) So, er, John distracted the man's attention and I went into the man's office and went all through his papers on his desk (laughter) looking for it. It was a sort of green - coloured folder (Yeah) which one should have found easily (Yeah) and it wasn't there. And then we saw an old woman across the road, sitting on a window-ledge, and I was sure she was sitting on our folder because something green was sticking out underneath her. And we had to try and work out some way of moving her, to see. And eventually we persuaded her by asking her to give us directions and she stood up to speak to us. But it wasn't our folder at all she was just sitting on a lit- tle green mat (Oh) obviously to keep herself clean. Erm ... and we were feeling pretty desperate by now, (I bet you were. Yeah) so back we went to the camp-site and we were going to beg, 'Please, may we stay tonight and worry (Mm) about it tomorrow?' (Mm) you see. And when we got back they said, 'There's been a phone call. Would you go to this address? Er, someone has found your folder.' So ...

Tom: How would anybody who'd found your folder (have) phoned, the fact, the camp-site?

Mary: Right. Well, this is what we discovered. We were w, wor- ried, because someone might have found it (Mm) and we

500

might get our passports, but what about our money, you know. (Quite, yeah) So we went to the address, (Mhm) and it was a little cycle-repair shop, kept by two brothers. And they told us that they had seen us driving up the road to the camp-site. We had swung round a corner (Mm) and the folder had flown off the top of the car! (Cor) We'd obviously left it (Yes) there, at the garage. And it had fallen at their feet. (Good havens!) They saw the tent and camping stuff (Yeah) on top of the car. (Mm) They saw which way we were going. (Mm) They guessed we were going to the camp-site, because it (Mm) was just a country lane (Mm) and they telephoned! Weren't we lucky? And (Gosh!) when we got there they said, er, 'Would we check that everything (Mm) was there.' (Mm) And certainly everything was there, (mm) nothing gone. And we were so pleased, we'd only got one piece of, erm, French currency — it was on large-value (Mm) note (Mm) — a number of pounds. (Mm) Erm, and we knew that we had to live till Monday, (Yeah) so we asked them if they would change this note for us. Erm, and the man sent a small boy to another shop to get change (Yes) and he came back with two equal value notes, (Oh yes) he'd split it in half (Mm) if you like. So we gave them half (Yeah) and we went back to the camp-site and put up our tent and installed ourselves and then we went out and spent the other half on a celebration. Erm, and er, of course, we had no money all day Sunday (Yes) and had to spend the day eating bread and si . . .

Tom: But you felt rich, because you'd got everything back.

Mary: Indeed, we were so relieved . . .

Tom: How terribly lucky, though! What a lucky story!

Key to Exercises:

A. Answer the following questions briefly.

1. Where had Mary, the female speaker, been travelling?
   Answer: Italy and France.

2. What kind of holiday was Mary going on?
   Answer: A camping holiday.

3. What did Mary put into the folder?
   Answer: The tickets, travellers' cheques, all the currency, passports, tickets for the boat, and a card.

4. When did Mary find the folder had gone?
   Answer: At the campsite.

5. Why did Mary carry a special card with her when camping?
   Answer: With this card, she could get reduced rates for being a member of a camping club.

6. Was the policeman helpful?
   Answer: No, not at all.

7. Were John and Mary suspicious of the people at the garage?
   Answer: Yes.

8. Who recovered the folder?
   Answer: The two brothers at a cycle-repair shop.

B. True or False Questions. Write a T in front of a statement if it is true according to the recording and write an F if it is false.

1. (T) The folder was found missing after they got the petrol.

2. (T) The policeman suggested that Mary should ask for help from the British Consul there.

3. (F) Mary let John go into the garageman's office and go all

502

through the man's papers.

4. (F) They were not suspicious of the old lady with something green sticking out underneath her.

5. (F) They never felt desperate even with all their money and credentials missing.

6. (F) When they heard about the phone call, all their worries were gone.

7. (T) Everything was recovered and nobody had stolen the folder.

8. (F) They did not give the garage men anything as a token of gratitude.

C. Describe, according to the recording, what Mary and John did at the following places.

1. At the border between Italy and France: (Having a lot of trouble finding the passports and this and that.)

2. At a garage in France: (Fueling their car.)

3. At the campsite: (Finding their money, travellers' cheques and passports missing.)

4. At the Police Station: (Asking the officer for help.)

5. At the garage again: (Distracting the man's attention and searching through his papers for the folder.)

6. On the road across: (managing to discover what an old lady was sitting on.)

7. At a cycle-repair shop: (Recovering what they had lost.)

Section Two:

Tapescript:

Task 1: Parking in London

Lesley: Oh Jackie, I've had such a terrible day. You just wouldn't believe ···

Jackie: You look exhausted. What on earth have you been doing?

Lesley: Oh, I've been such a fool! (Oh) You just wouldn't believe what I've done.

Jackie: I would, I would. Come on ··· (You won't) Where've you been?

Lesley: I'm dying to tell someone. I've been down to London (Uh-huh) you see. (Uh-huh) OK, I thought I'd be very sensible, so I'd drive down to the Underground on ··· on the outskirts of London, leave the car and go in by Tube. All right? (Er ··· what you) Very sensible. (Yes) Yes? (OK) OK. So I drove down to London (Uh-huh) and I parked my car by the Tube station and I got the Tube into London. (Uh-huh) Fine! All right? (Well, sounds like it) so far, so good. (Yes) Right. Came back out of London ··· (Uh-huh ··· and you er ··· forgot the car?) Got out of the Tube. No, no, I didn't forget the car. (Oh) I couldn't find the car, Jackie. (You're joking) It'd gone. (You're kidding) No, no, really, it'd gone. I walked out ··· happily out of the Tube, you know, over to where it was (Mm) and I looked and it was a red Mini and mine's green, so (Oh on!) I thought 'Oh no'. So having panicked a bit, I rang the police, you see, and this lovely, new little policeman ··· a young one (Yes, all shiny and bright) came out to help. That's it yes ··· buttons shining ··· (Yes) big, smile ··· came down to help, so I said 'I've lost my car. It's been stolen' and I took him to see it and everything and ···

Jackie: You mean where it wasn't.

Lesley: And sure enough, it wasn't ··· yes, well, right ··· and it wasn't there. And then he coughed a bit and he went very quiet

... (Oh dear) and he took me back into the Tube station (Oh dear) and out the other side into the other car park ... and there was my car, Jackie (Oh Lesley) parked in the other Tube station car park, the other side of the station, because there are two exits, you see, so I walked out of an exit (Yes) not knowing there were two and it was in the other one.

Jackie: Oh Lesley. And was he ever so cross?

Lesley: He was livid, Jackie. (Really) He really ... he went on and on at me and I didn't know what to do. It was (Oh dear) just frightful. I just ... I went red and just shut up and said ' Sorry' all the time.

Jackie: Jumped in your car and (Oh yes) and left.

Lesley: Oh, it was awful. I'm never doing that again ever.

Task 2: Mummy Dust

Today we're going to look at some aspects of life – or perhaps it would be more correct to say 'death' in Ancient Egypt.

Egypt has always fascinated ordinary people as well as scholars engaged in the serious study of the past. To most of us it's a land of mystery and magic. In particular, the custom of preserving the bodies of important people, especially of kings and queens, has quite a hold on the popular imagination. How many thrillers and horror films are based on the idea of finding a mummy in the secret tomb of a lost king, who in the case of horror movies usually comes to life again!

In earlier times the subject exerted a more sinister fascination—so-called 'mummy dust'—the powdered remains of dead Egyptians—was thought to be an essential ingredient in many magical spells and medical remedies—a case of the cure being worse than the disease?

This of course led to a great demand for mummies both inside and outside Egypt, and even to an industry of making 'false mummies' to sell to unsuspecting foreigners. This continued well into the 19th century. Even when, at that time, tighter controls were exerted by the Egyptian authorities, many mummies were still sold on the black market, and even some of the mummies that were acquired for museums for scientific purposes were bought clandestinely.

These days, archaeologists and anthropologists have more moral scruples about the way they treat the dead – even those who have been dead for thousands of years. That's one reason why—even though new techniques of analysis can reveal fascinating information, there is some hesitation about carrying out 'autopsies' on too many mummies in an indiscriminate way. Besides the ethical question, there is the practical one that any analysis must involve at least some degree of destruction.

The studies that have been made in recent years have therefore for the most part been of mummies which were already in poor state of preservation, and the investigators have tried to do the minimum damage possible—taking only tiny samples of tissue for analysis, or using non-destructive means of study such as X rays.

At the end of each study, it is now customary to restore the mummy to a state of 'decent burial'. In this way, the scientists involved have tried to satisfy both their curiosity and their consciences.

In a moment, I'm going to ask Dr. Albert Simons, a noted expert on Egyptian archaeology, to give us an overview of some recent studies and what they have revealed ...

Key to Exercises:

Task 1: Parking in London

A. Choose the best answer (a, b or c) for each of the following questions.

   1. How does Lesley look ?

      a. Excited.

   * b. Exhausted.

      c. Foolish.

   2. What happened to her today?

   * a. She failed to remember where she parked her car.

      b. She could not find where the Tube Station was .

      c. She had a terrible fight with a traffic policeman.

   3. Why didn't she find her car ?

      a. Because she was frightened by the policeman.

      b. Because it was the first time she went to London.

   * c. Because she didn't know at each exit of the Tube Station there was a car park.

   4. Why did Lesley say 'Sorry' all the time ?

   * a. Because the policeman got very angry.

      b. Because she needed the policeman's help.

      c. Because she ran into the policeman.

B. True or False Questions. Write a T in front of a statement if it is true according to the recording and write an F if it is false.

   1. (F) Lesley parked the car in central London.

   2. (T) Lesley went to London by Tube.

   3. (T) Lesley's car was green.

   4. (F) The policeman was old and wore new uniform.

5. (F) There was only one car park at the Tube Station.

6. (F) The policeman was friendly to Lesley all the time.

C. Fill in the blanks in the following sentences with what you hear on the tape.

1. I'm (dying to tell) someone.

2. I thought I'd be very (sensible), so I'd drive down to the Undergrund (on the outskirts of) London.

3. And was he ever so (cross)?

4. He (went on and on at) me.

Task 2: Mummy Dust

A. Choose the bast answer (a, b or c) to complete each of the following statements.

1. The talk is about _____.

   a. Ancient Egypt

 * b. mummies in Ancient Egypt

   c. death in the nineteenth-century Egypt

2. Mummies _____.

 * a. are the well-preserved bodies of important people in ancient Egypt

   b. are the well-preserved bodies of ordinary Egyptians

   c. are the well-preserved bodies of important people in Egypt now

3. The magic story of "mummy dust" led to _____.

   a. a lot of deaths

   b. great improvement in preserving bodies

 * c. a great demand for mummies both inside and outside Egypt.

508

4. With the increasing commercial value of mummies _____.

    a. some people were engaged in making false mummies.

    b. the black market of mummies came into being

* c. Both a and b

5. Nowadays archaeologists and anthropologists are very careful in treating mummies because _____.

    a. they are hesitant to touch such bodies

* b. they don't want to do the least destruction to the mummies

    c. they bought the mummies at high price.

B. True or False Questions. Write a T in front of a statement if it is true according to the recording and write an F if it is fatse.

1. (T) Both ordinary people and scholars are fascinated by Egypt.

2. (F) Nowadays many mummies of ancient kings and queens have come to life again.

3. (T) Mummies were once believed to have medical effect on some diseases.

4. (T) Even in the nineteenth century the Egyptian authorities had to exert tight control over the sale of mummies.

5. (T) Because of the Black Market, scientists had to buy mummies for their research in a secret way.

6. (F) New techniques of analysis won't do any destruction to the mummies.

7. (T) After the analysis, scientists now restore the poorly preserved mummies to a state of "decent burial".

C. Fill in the following blanks with what you hear on the tape.

1. The custom of preserving the bodies of important people...
   (has quite a hold on) the popular imagination.

2. So-called 'mummy dust' —(the powdered remains of dead
   Egyptians) — was thought to be an essential imgredient in
   (Many magical spells)...

3. In this way, the scientists involved have tried to satisfy both
   (their curiosity and their consciences).

Section Three:
Study Skills: Note-taking 4

Outlining — the Standard Topic Outline Form

Outlining is a skill that will be useful to you when you are taking lecture notes, reading, or writing a paper. An outline shows the
organization of a lecture or a written article. It is an organized list of
ideas, grouped together in such a way as to show their relationship
to one another.

We generally use a system of Roman numerals, Arabic
numbers, and letters to show relationships. There is a standard form
for using symbols to show which ideas are most important. The
symbols used, in order of decrasing importance, are Roman numerals, capital letters, Arabic numbers, lower-case letters, and numbers in parentheses. The placement of the topics on the paper is important also, with the most important items farthest to the left.
Lesser items are entered farther and farther to the right.

The blank form looks like this:

I . _____

    A. _____

    B. _____

C. _____

II. _____

   A. _____

      1. _____

         a. _____

         b. _____

            (1) _____

            (2) _____

      2. _____

   B. _____

The letters and numbers are placed about three spaces to the right of the item above. Periods are used after Roman numerals and numbers. Headings of equal importance are indented an equal distance from the left margin (notice II. 1. and II. 2). The purpose of this indentation is to make each idea easy to see and to show just how it is related to the ideas before and after it. Not punctuation is needed at the end of an idea unless it is written as a complete sentence.

Some students may already be familiar with a type of outline that uses the decimal system. This outline form shows the relationship between ideas by giving a decimal rank to each idea.

1. _____

  1.1 _____

  1.2 _____

2. _____

  2.1 _____

    2.11 _____

    2.12 _____

  2.2 _____

If you know how to use the decimal system well already, you can use it throughtout the rest of the notetaking exercises. If not, we suggest you learn the standard topic outline form.

Tapescript :

Burglaries

The figures for burglaries have risen alarmingly over the last few years and are now quite appalling. Let me quote you a few statistics about break-ins.

A house is burgled in Britain now about every two minutes, and over the past three years the number of burglaries reported to the police has risen by approximately 50, 000 to well over 400, 000 this year. The insurance companies report that last year alone household burglary losses rose by 27 per cent over the previous year to £ 138. 2 million, and I believe one or two companies are refusing to provide burglary cover in what we might call high-risk areas.

There are, nevertheless, half a dozen measures which can be taken against burglaries, which I will briefly outline for you. It really only requires some basic common sense and a small outlay, combined with a little knowledge of the way a burglar thinks and operates. You have to put yourself in his position, really. Most burglars are opportunists looking for an easy break-in, so don't make things simple for them. Don't advertise the fact you're out or away, or be careless about security. Even if you're just popping out for a quarter of an hour, don't leave doors and windows open or unlocked. A burglary can take less than ten minutes.

This time element leads me to my second main point, that where a house is hard to get into and will take a long time to do so because you've fitted good locks and bolts on your exterior doors and windows or even burglar alarms, the chances are that the burglar will move on to somewhere easier. There are plenty of these, I can assure you. Milk bottles left on the doorstep, papers by the front door, garage doors wide open, curtains drawn in the daytime or un-drawn at night are all indications. For comparatively little you can buy a programmed time-switch that'll turn on and off a light at appropriate times.

Not all burglaries happen while you are out, of course. You should always be wary of callers at the door who say, for example, that they've come to read the gas meter; always check their credentials, and if in doubt don't let them in. It's also a good idea to keep a record of serial numbers on electrical equipment, radios, TVs and so on, or even to take photographs of valuable jewellery, antiques or pictures.

Any further tips I may not have mentioned can always be got from your local police station, where you should ask to speak to the Crime Prevention Officer.

In the final analysis I think I should say that when it comes to fitting security systems and the like you've really got to strike a balance between the cost of what you spend on installing the system and the value of the property you're trying to protect.

Key to Exercises:

A. Choose the best answer (a, b or c) to complete each of the fol-
    lowing statements.

    1. The text is mainly about _____.

        a. how serious the problem of burglary is

        b. measures against burglary

   * c. a and b

513

2. The number of burglaries reported to the police has risen to
   _____ this year.
   a. 5,000
 * b. 400,000
   c. 50,000
3. The insurance companies lost _____ last year to cover
   household burglary losses.
   a. 148.2 million pounds
   b. 138.2 billion pounds
 * c. 138.2 million pounds
4. Most burglars look for _____.
 * a. easy break-ins
   b. widely open garage doors
   c. unlocked doors
5. People are advised to use a programmed time-switch because
   _____.
   a. it will save electricity
 * b. in this way nobody will know that the owner of the house
      is away for a long time
   c. burglars are often frightened by it
6. The last sentence means that _____.
 * a. your property should be worth the money you spend on se-
      curity systems
   b. a security system is better than none
   c. there's no use fitting security systems

B. Suggested Abbreviations:
   number: no.   credential: cred.
   over: +   equipment: equip.
   514

burglary: burg.   electrical: elect.

previous: prev.   jewellery: jewl.

C. Notetaking: Complete the following outline.

Title: (Burglaries)

I. The figures for burglaries have risen alarmingly.

    A. A house is burgled in Britain (about every 2 minutes).

    B. Over the past 3 years (no. of burg. rise by about 50,000 to 400,000 this y).

    C. Insurance Companies (last y. household burg. losses rose by 27% over the prev. y. to 130.2 mn. pounds).

II. Measures against burglaries

    A. Don't advertise (when you're out or away, or be careless about security).

        1. When out even for a short time, (lock or close doors & windows).

        2. A burglary can take (less than 10 minutes).

    B. Don't leave marks that you're away for a long time.

        1. Marks:

            a. (milk bottles left on the door-step)

            b. (papers by the front door)

            c. (garage doors wide open)

            d. (curtains drawn in the daytime & undrawn at night)

        2. Way to avoid:

        Buy (a programmed time-switch)

    C. Be wary of strangers at the door

        1. Check (their cred.).

        2. If in doubt (don't let them in).

D. Make a note of your properties

   1. Keep a record of (serial nos. on elect. equip., radios, TVs).

   2. Take photographs of (valuable jewl., antique or pictures).

E. Speak to the (Crime Prevention Officer) for any (further tips).

Ⅲ. Strike a balance between (cost of security systems & value of property to be protected).

Supplementary Reading:

Mummy

Mummy is a dead body preserved by embalming. The name arose because the skin and bones of corpses embalmed by the ancient Egyptians are often found to be blackened, an effect mistakenly attributed to the use of bitumen (Arabic, *mumiya*) in the embalming process. The earliest indisputable evidence of attempts to preserve the body by artificial means dates from about 2600 B. C. The remarkable state of preservation of many bodies from earlier times is the result of the natural drying effect of the hot sand in which bodies were interred. Artificial embalming was developed after the use of chambered tombs and wooden coffins had introduced corpse decay, since the Egyptians believed that a complete body was essential for the housing of the spirit in the next life.

For many centuries only the wealthy could afford mummification. Eventually cheaper methods allowed the practice to spread, but for the most part it was confined to the wealthy and to animals sacred to certain gods, such as bulls, cats, and ibises.

No description of the embalming process has been preserved

from Egypt itself. The Greek authors Herodotus and Diodorus Siculus related what they were told about it, and their accounts may now be verified by the results of careful study and chemical analyses.

The essential feature of the process was thorough desiccation, effected by means of dry natron (native sodium carbonate). First the soft internal parts of the body were removed: the brain through the nostrils; the lungs, stomach, and intestines through an incision in the left side. These organs were desiccated, wrapped in linen, and stored in the tomb in special (canopic) jars or chests. The heart and kidneys were not removed from the body. Generally the body cavities were filled with resin, resin-soaked linen, sawdust, or, occasionally, wood pitch. Then the body was dried by completely enclosing it in natron. Following the desiccation came a washing and then on anointing with oil. Finally the body was wrapped, first each digit and each limb, until the entire body was enveloped in strips of fine linen arranged in elaborate patterns. Special care was taken to prevent the nails from falling away. Models in resin-soaked linen of the external genitals were often fitted into place. In some periods a painted cartonnage mask preserved the features.

The entire process took many weeks . According to Egyptian records, 70 days elapsed between death and burial. With changes in the techniques of preparation and wrapping, the practice of embalming continued in Egypt until Christianity became the dominant religion (4th century A.D.). After that it fell into disuse.

Although archaeologists use the word "mummy" for bodies buried in Egypt and elsewhere in the world after that time, these, like the Egyptian predynastic burials, have been preserved by natural means.

Lesson 26

Tapescript:

Sport in Britain

Interest in sport in Britain is widespread, as is indicated by the huge crowds which attend such occasions as the Football Association Cup Final at Wembley Stadium, international rugby matches at Twickenham, Murrayfield or Cardiff Arms Park, the Wimbledon Lawn Tennis Championships and so on. Not only do millions watch these matches on television but there is also growing enthusiasm for active participation in sport and recreation in the country as a whole. People find they have more free time on their hands nowadays, so there is a duty on the part of government to make opportunities and facilities available. Apart from the professional side of it, there is increasing enthusiasm for amateur sport, which has led to a growth in interest in climbing, rambling, boating and other water-based sports, as well as keep fit, and movement and dance activities.

Probably the most popular spectator sport is Association Football, which dates back to the nineteenth century and is controlled by separate football associations in England, Wales, Scotland and Northern Ireland. There are well over 400 clubs affiliated to the English Football Association or FA and some 37,000 clubs to regional or district associations. The main clubs in England and Wales belong to the Football League, 92 in all, and the 38 Scottish clubs

518

belong to the Scottish League. They play in four divisions in England and three in Scotland. During the football season, attendances total some 27 million.

Local authorities provide facilities to cater for a wide range of indoor and outdoor activities; these include such things as golf courses, swimming pools and leisure centres. Total expenditure in the country as a whole on sport and outdoor recreation came to well over £ 500 million last year.

Naturally, publicly maintained schools have to provide by law for the physical education of the pupils, and sometimes these facilities are also extended to the whole community for use out of school hours.

I'd like now to say a word or two about water-based sports. Activities on canals, rivers, lakes and reservoirs are becoming increasingly popular and for this we must thank the British Waterways Board, which as part of its work maintains 1760 kms of cruising waterways for navigation, about 960 kms of other waterways and some 90 reservoirs.

In addition to the facilities which are provided by local authorities, such as the sports centres and golf courses I mentioned earlier, we mustn't forget the local voluntary clubs such as rugby, cricket, tennis, golf and so on. Some clubs are even attached to local businesses and cater for the needs of a firm's employees, and in fact some companies are actively encouraging their staff to take advantage of the facilities provided. I've even heard of employees being given time off in the middle of the working day to do a little sport, a practice which is, I believe, already quite popular in the United States.

'A healthy mind in a healthy body', as the saying goes, so

perhaps this is what is in the minds of these employers. This phrase of course applies very much to the young and, as I said before, all publicly maintained schools must by law provide for the physical education of their pupils. This covers gymnastics, team games, athletics, dancing and swimming. Every school, except those solely for infants, must have a playing field, or the use of one, and most secondary schools have their own gymnasium as well. Some have other amenities such as swimming pools, sports halls and halls designed for dance and movenemt. Sports and recreation facilities are likewise provided at universities, some of which have their own physical education departments, and there are also so-called 'centres of sporting excellence' at universities and other colleges enabling selected young athletes to develop their talents but which also provide for their educational needs.

Key to Exercises:

A. Choose the best answer (a, b or c) to complete each of the following statements.

1. According to the speaker, public enthusiasm for active participation in sports and recreation in Britain _____.
   a. decreases
 * b. grows
   c. remains the same as before

2. As far as the speaker is concerned, _____ to make opportunities and facilities of sports available to the public.
 * a. it is the duty of the government
   b. there is a duty on the part of the individuals
   c. company employers have the duty

3. The most popular spectator sport in Britain is probably

520

_____.

    a. the Wimbledon Lawn Tennis Championship

    b. the international rugby matches at Murrayfield

* c. Association Football

4. Local authorities provide facilities to meet the public demand for indoor and outdoor activities, such as _____.

    a. tennis courts, swimming suits and pubs

* b. golf courses, swimming pools and leisure centres

    c. amusement parks, bars and recreation centres

5. _____ should be legally guaranteed for pupils at _____.

* a. Physical education; publicly maintained schools

    b. Gymnasiums; publicly maintained schools

    c. Physical education; privately maintained schools

B. True or False Questions. Write a T in front of a statement if it is true according to the recording and write an F if it is false.

1. (T) People have become more and more interested in watching sports games and taking an active part in them as well.

2. (F) Association Football has a history of more than 200 years.

3. (F) Britain spent around £ 500 billion on sport and outdoor recreation last year.

4. (T) The British Waterways Board contributes a lot to the popularization of water-based sports.

5. (T) Some companies offer time and facilities to their employees to do a little sport.

6. (T) Sports should be a must in almost all educational institutions.

C. List at least eight of the sport and recreational activities mentioned in what you hear on the tape.
1. (climbing)
2. (rambling)
3. (boating)
4. (daucing)
5. (association football)
6. (golf)
7. (swimming)
8. (rugby)
9. (tennis)

D. Fill in the blanks with what you hear on the tape.
1. There are well over (400 clubs) affiliated to the English Football Association or FA and some (37, 000 clubs to regional or district associations). The main clubs in England and Wales belong to the (Football League), (92 in all), and the (38 Scottish clubs) belong to the Scottish League. They play in (4 seasons) in England and (there) in Scoland. During the football season, attendances total some (27 million).
2. We must thank the British Waterways Board, which as part of its work maintains (1, 760 km of cruising waterways) for navigation, about (960 km) of other waterways and some (90 reservoirs).

Section Two:
Tapescript:
Task 1: A Post-Industrial Society (I)
522

Chairperson: Good evening ladies and gentlemen. It's nice to see so many of you here. Well, I'd like to introduce our two guests this evening: Mr Andrew Frobisher, who's spent many years in Malaysia in the 1950s and 60s and knows the country very well indeed. And, on my right, Dr Harry Benson who's an agricultural economist.

Benson: Good evening.

Frobisher: Good evening.

Chairperson: Well, erm ... the purpose of this evening is to find out more about that fascinating substance. rubber, and the effects that it has on that fascinating country, Malaysia. Erm erm .... I believe erm ... er Mr Frobisher, erm ... that Malaysia is at the same time an extremely rich and rather poor country. Erm ... how is this possible?

Frobisher: Yes, well, that's quite true, Monica. Malaysia's population is by now over 12 million, and er per head o ... on paper the the citizens *are* richer than those of the UK. But...

Benson: But of course that wealth is not so evenly distributed. In fact in 1981, it was estimated that 37% of the population were below the poverty line...

Frobisher: Yeah, well ... whatever that means ... and anyway shouldn't it be, er, *was* below the poverty line.

Benson: Yes, of course. Sorry, Andrew.

Frobisher: Yes, well, erm ... as I was saying, er ... much of Malaysia's wealth is based on rubber. Now, I remember my planting days ...

Benson: Yes, yes, yes yes you're quite right there Andrew. Rubber represents about 20% of the Gross National Product and 30% of export earnings. (Er yes I ...) This puts Malaysia in a very

523

good position internationally since rubber is an example of what we might call a 'post-industrial industry'.

Frobisher: Well, what do you what do you mean by that? I ...

Chairperson: Er ... excuse me ... yes, what does that mean?

Frobisher: What is a post-industrial erm ... society?

Benson: Most manufacturing industries are based on fossil fuels, for example, coal and oil. Now, the problem is that these will not last forever. They are finite. Sooner or later they will run out! Now, rubber is a natural product. The energy source involved in its creation is sunlight. Now sunlight, we hope, will outlast coal and oil, and best of all, sunlight is free. So, it is much cheaper to produce natural rubber which as we all know comes from trees, than to use up all those fossil fuels, both as fuels and as raw materials, in making synthetic rubber in factories. Rubber is one of the world's strategic products, so you can see what a good positin Malaysia is in, and it would help if she could produce more ...

Chairperson: Er ... well, what stands in the way then?

Frobisher: Ah. well, well it's the way they go about cultivating it. You see, I remember in my day just after ...

Benson: Yes, most people have this image of vast estates, centrally run, but that's just not the case, even if almost a quarter of the population is involved, one way and another, with the production of rubber ...

Frobisher: Yeah well, that's if you count the families ...

Nenson: Oh yes, yes, yes almost 3 million people are involved, but the picture is a very fragmented one. Do you realize that there are 2 million hectares of land under cultivation for rubber in Malaysia, but that 70% of this area is divided almongst small-holders – half a million of them – who between them produce 60% of the country's rubber?

Frobisher: Well, there's nothing wrong with that i ... in terms of quality of life, though I remember (yes, quite right ...) just after the war there was...

Benson: Yes, quite right. But being a smallholder does present problems. For example, when it comes to replacing old trees – you'll know about this Andrew – and the average useful life of a rubber tree is about 30 years, (yes, yes,) this can cause financial problems for the small farmer. The problem is being tackled, however, by some very enlightened insurance schemes available to the smallholder which can give him help through the difficult years. After all, the new trees take some years to mature and start producing rubber.

Frobisher: Yes, indeed they do. I... I...

Benson: Look. I've got an overhead projection here, which I think will be useful to make the various problems and their solutions clearer to us all.

Frobisher: Overhead projection. There wasn't anything wrong with the blackboard in my time, you know...

Benson: No, but this is clearer and neater and up-to-date. So, here you see a summary of the position of rubber in Malaysia's economy and here is the first problem, and the solution that has been found through these insurance schemes.

Chairperson: Hm, yes, I see. That's really very clear.

Benson: Now for the second and really major problem.

Frobisher: And may I ask what that is?

Benson: Boredom and fatigue.

Frobisher: Boredom and fatigue? What?

Chairperson: What do you mean by that?

Benson: Well, as with so many societies, the young people are leaving the land for the cities, leaving no one behind to carry on their parents' business. The root cause seems to be simply, boredom. Rubber is just not that entertaining a product to be involved with. It is labour-intensive in the extreme. Each tree on a plantation has to be tapped, by hand, every other day.

Chairperson: Tapped?

Benson: Yes.

Forbisher: Yes, well, we...

Benson: Yes. The trunk is cut and the latex that comes out is collected in a cup. This is collected on the next day. 400 trees per day is the average figure per worker, which means 800 trees under the care of each worker, ten hours a day. Now, as I said previously, the main problem is that of the boredom. The work is not only hard, it is also mind-blowingly tedious.

Task 2: A Post-Industrial Society (II)

Frobosher: So, ha... have you got any suggestions to make things more interesting for them?

Benson: Well, not so much me, but the Malaysians are doing some very good work in this field. One idea is to make the work on the plantations more varied, and and profitable, by introducing other products which are compatible with continuing to grow rubber trees.

Chairperson: Yes for example?

Benson: Well, the most promising line seems to be to encourage small-holders to raise livestock which can live amongst the trees.

526

Frobisher: Yes, yes, I, I hear they've started trying raising chickens and and turkeys.

Benson: Yes, yes, indeed. I have another OHP at this point.

Frobisher: Erm ... OHP?

Benson: Overhead projection...

Frobisher: Ah.

Benson: Anyway, you can see here the different types of animals that have been tried. At first sight, chickens seemed ideal. After all, they did originate as jungle birds. However, hmm hmm excuse me, so far the profits on chickens have proved disappointing. The turkey seemed an excellent choice, since it could live amongst the tress living very well off the seeds of the rubber trees, which lie scattered all over the forest floors and are put to no other use ...

Frobisher: Yes yes... but, but the turkey, it's hardly an established part of the Malaysian diet!

Benson: Exactly! So far the most successful candidate has been the sheep.

Frobisher: Sheep?

Benson: Now ... Sheep. Sheep will eat the weeds, which will save the cultivator money and work, and they are a source of meat which is acceptable both to Hindus and Muslims.

Frobisher: Yes, well, that's most important in multicultural Malaysia.

Benson: Yes, yes, and of course they can also be used for their their milk, their their wool and their skins.

Frobisher: Yes, of course ... Mmm.

Benson: And now, as you can see on my OHP ...

Chairperson: Well, erm ... thank you both very very much to both our guests . . .

Well, what lies ahead for Malaysia? Can her researchers and scientists continue to find ways of increasing the rubber yield? Can the labour-intensive and tedious life of the rubber plantation be made interesting and varied enough to capture the young people's interest and stop the migration to the cities? Well, I'm sure we've all enjoyed and learned a lot from huh what both our guests have had to say. Huh we look forward to the next meeting in the series 'Other lands, other problems' which will be on Monday next. That's at 8.15 and do please come on time.

Frobisher: Hmm hmm. Pushy bastard.

Key to Exercises:

Task 1: A Post-Industrial Society (I)

A. Choose the best answer (a, b or c) to complete each of the following statements.

1. Mr. Andrew Frobisher lived in Malaysia _____.
   a. for ten years
   b. in the 70s
   * c. in the 50s and 60s

2. Dr. Harry Benson is _____.
   * a. an agricultural economist
   b. a post-industrial economist
   c. a rubber specialist

3. Rubber in Malaysia can be said to be _____.
   * a. the lifeblood of its economy
   b. a source of poverty
   c. a problem in the Malaysian

4. Growing rubber trees, a smallholder _____ .

  a. does live an easy life

* b. has to face financial problems and bear boredom and fatigue

  c. compete with others with the help of insurance companies

5. From the talk , it is clear that Mr . Frobisher and Dr . Benson

  _____ .

  a. don't have much interest in the life of people an rubber plantations.

  b. know little about plantation life of those rubber smallholders

* c. are sympathetic with the rubber small-holders in Malaysia.

B. Answer the following questions briefly.

1. Why does Dr. Benson say rubber is an example of post-industrial industry?

  Answer: Rubber production doesn't use fossil fuels. It is based on sunlight. It's cheaper to produce natural rubber than synthetic rubber.

2. How many people in Malaysia are involved in rubber production?

  Answer: Three million.

3. How long does the average useful life of a rubber tree last?

  Answer: Thirty years.

4. What are young people doing on the rubber plantation?

  Answer: They are leaving the land for cities, leaving no-one behind to carry on their parents' business.

5. What is the life like on the rubber plantation?

  Answer: Boring, labour-intensive, and mind-blowingly tedious.

C. Describe in detail what a small-holder of a rubber plantation has to do to his rubber trees with the information on the tape.

1. Each tree (on a plantation has to be tapped).
2. The trunk (is cut and the latex that comes out is collected in a cup).
3. The latex (in the cup is collected the next day).
4. A worker has to (collect 400 trees per day).
5. Each worker has to (take care of 800 trees, which requires 10 hours work per day).

D. With the help of what you hear on the tape, fill in the following blanks with figures about Malaysia.

1. In (1981), it was estimated that (37%) of the population were below the poverty line.
2. Rubber represents about (20%) of the Gross National Product (30%) of export earnings.
3. There are (2) million hectares of land under cultivation for rubber in Malaysia, but that of (70%) of this area is divided amongst small-holders— (half a million) of them—who between them (60%) of the country's rubber.

Task 2: A Post-Industrial Society (II)

A. Choose the best answer (a, b or c) for each of the following questions.

1. What do the Malaysians do to make the work on the planta - tions more varied and profitable?
   a. Making life more interesting.

b. Collecting suggestions about it.

* c. Introducing other products which are compatible with continuing to grow rubber trees.

2. What are small-holders encouraged to do?

* a. To raise livestocks like chickens and turkeys among the trees.

b. To plant more rubber trees.

c. To increase the output of rubber.

3. Why has turkey been replaced by sheep as a by-product in the trees?

a. Raising turkey doesn't bring big profits.

b. Turkey does not go along with chickens among the trees.

* c. The Malaysians don't like eating turkey.

4. Which of the following is NOT the reason for raising sheep among the rubber trees?

a. They supply meat acceptable to Hindus and Muslims in Malaysia.

* b. They feed on the seeds of the rubber trees.

c. Their milk, wool, and skin are of commercial value.

5. What will be the next meeting?

a. At 18:15 next Monday.

* b. At 8:15 next Monday.

c. At 8:50 next Monday.

B. True or False Questions. Write a T in front of a statement if it is true according to the recording and write an F if it is false.

1. (F) Profits on chicken have proved to be encouraging.

2. (T) Turkeys could live well off the seeds of the rubber trees.

3. (T) Raising sheep among the rubber trees is money-saving

and labour-saving, too.

4. (F) With some livestock introduced in rubber production, the rubber plantation small-holders don't have much to worry about.

5. (T) This talk is one of the series "Other lands, Other problems".

Section Three:

Tapescript:

Outlining: Some of the Problems Facing Learners of English

Today I'd like to talk about some of the problems that students face when they follow a course of study through the medium of English - if English is not their mother tongue. The purpose is to show that we're aware of students' problems, and that by analysing them perhaps it'll be possible to suggest how some of them may be overcome.

The problems can be divided into three broad categories: psychological, cultural and linguisitic. The first two categories mainly concern those who come to study in Britain. I'll comment only briefly on these first two and then spend most of the time looking at linguistic difficulties which apply to everyone wherever they are learning English. Some of the common psychological problems really involve fear of the unknown: for example, whether one's academic studies will be too difficult, whether one will fail the examinations, etc. All students share these apprehensions. It's probably best for a student not to look too far ahead but to concentrate day-by-day on increasing his knowledge and developing his ability. The overseas student in Britain may also suffer from separation from his family and possible homesickness; enjoyment of his activities in Britain and the passage of time are the only real help here.

Looking now at the cultural problems, we can see that some of them are of a very practical nature, e. g. arranging satisfactory accommodation, getting used to British money (or the lack of it !), British food and weather (neither is always bad !). Some of the cultural difficulties are less easy to define: they are bound up with the whole range of alien customs, hal.. s and traditions – in other words, the British way of life. Such difficulties include: settling into a strange environment and a new academic routine; learning a new set of social habits, ranging from the times of meals to the meanings of gestures; expressing appropriate greetings; understanding a different kind of humour; and learning how to make friends. Being open-minded and adaptable is the best approach to some of the difficulties listed here.

The largest category is probably linguistic.. Let's look at this in some detail.

Most students will have learnt English at school, but if they've already been to college or university in their own countries they'll have studied mostly in their own language except, perhaps, for reading some textbooks and journals in English. In other words, they'll have had little everyday opportunity to practise using English.

When foreign learners first have the opportunity to speak to an English-speaking person they may have a shock: they often have great difficulty in understanding ! There are a number of reasons for this. I'll just mention three of them.

Firstly, it seems to students that English people speak very quickly. Secondly, they speak with a variety of accents. Thirdly, different styles of speech are used in different situations, e. g. everyday spoken English, which is colloquial and idiomatic, is different from the English used for academic purposes. For all of these reasons students will have difficulty, mainly because they lack practice in listening to English people speaking English. Don't forget, by the way, that if students have difficulty in understanding English-speaking people, these people may also have difficulty in understanding the students!

What can a student do then to oversome these difficulties? Well, obviously, he can benefit from attending English classes and if a language laboratory is available use it as much as possible. He should also listen to programmes in English on the radio and TV. Perhaps most important of all, he should take every available opportunity to meet and speak with native English-speaking people. He should be aware, however, that English people are, by temperament, often reserved and may be unwilling to start a conversation. Nevertheless, if he has the courage to take the initiative, however difficult it may seem to be, most English people will respond. He will need patience and perseverance!

In addition to these problems regarding listening and understanding, the student probably has difficulty in speaking English Fluently. He has the *ideas*, he knows *what* to say (in his own language) but he doesn't know *how* to say it *in English*. The advice here will seem difficult to follow but it's necessary. Firstly, he must simplify his language so that he can express himself reasonably clearly: for example, short sentences will be better than long ones. Secondly, he must try to *think* in English, not translate from his mother tongue. This'll only begin to take place when his use of English becomes automatic: using a language laboratory and listening to as much English as possible will help. In general, he should practise speaking as much as possible. He should also notice the kind of English, and its structure, that educated people use, and try to imitate it.

Key to Exercises:

A. General Comprehension: Write a T in front of a statement if it is true according to the recording and write an F if it is false.

1. (F) There are three types of problems: sociological, cultural and linguistic.

2. (T) The linguistic problems are discussed in the greatest detail.

3. (F) Psychological and cultural problems mainly concern British students and so are discussed briefly.

4. (F) In order to understand English people better the most important thing for a student to do is to listen to the radio and TV.

5. (T) Though English people are often reserved, if the student has the courage to speak to them, they will often respond.

6. (T) The advice given on how to improve spoken English will seem difficult to follow.

7. (T) For student of English short sentences are better than long ones.

8. (F) The only way to make oneself think in English is to practise speaking as much as porsible.

B. Suggested Abbreviations:

problems: probs.   separation: separ.
possible: poss.   accommodation: accom.
British: Brit.   environment: envirt.

very: v.   laboratory: lab.
important: imp.

C. Notetaking: Complete the following outline.

Title: (Some of probs, facing learners of Eng.)

I. Purpose of the speech

    A. aware (sts'. probs.)

    B. suggest (how to overcome)

II. Categories of problems

    A. (Psychological)

        1. fear of fear of. (unknown)

           e.g. (academic studies too diff.)

           solution (not to look too far ahead)

        2. suffer from (separ. from family & poss. homesickness)

        3. solution: a. (enjoy activities)

                b. (passage of time)

    B. Cultural

        1. practical ones

           a. (arranging accom.)

           b. (getting used to Brit. money, food & weather)

        2. Brit. way of life

           a. (settle in strange envirt. & new academic routine)

           b. (learn social habits)

           c. (express appro. greetings)

           d. (understand humour)

           e. (learn to make friends)

        3. Solution: (be open-minded & adaptable)

    C. (Linguistic)

1. Little practice (using Eng.)
   when 1st speak to Eng. person: (shock)
   great diff. (in understanding)
2. Reasons
   a. (Eng. people speak v. quickly)
   b. (Eng. people speak with variety of accents)
   c. Different styles of speech (in diffr. situations)
3. Solution
   a. (attend Eng. classes & use lang. lab)
   b. (listen to radio & TV)
   c. Most impo: (meet Eng. people)
4. How to improve spoken Eng.
   a. (simplify lang. e.g. short sentences)
   b. try to (think in Eng.)
      Not (translate)
   c. practise (speaking as much as poss.)
   d. (Eng. structure – educated use – imitate)

Lesson 27

Tapescript:

Holistic Medicine

Interviewer: I understand you're interested in holistic medicine. Can you explain what holistic medicine is?

Vivienne: OK. Holistic medicine, um, takes into consideration the whole of the person. Now what this means in, in most holistic systems is regarding the person as a physical entity, a mental or emotional person, and also even their spiritual side of them. Um, it also includes looking at the body as a whole rather than looking at individual parts of the body, and as a way of explaining this, we could look at conventional medicine as producing people who are like a cardiologist, who looks at a heart, um, a brain specialist, a person who deals with bones, er, etc. So what we've tended to do in conventional medicine is break things down to a point where we're actually only looking at one part of the person and we're not actually relating terribly well that part to the rest of the body, whereas holistic medicine insists that if there is a problem, er, with your right foot, that is going to somehow, um, affect your entire body.

Interiewer: Um, your speciality is acupuncture. Er, is that a part of holistic medicine?

Vivienne: Acupuncture is very much a holistic system. Um, tradi-

538

tionally the Chinese regarded the person very much as a whole entity and acupuncture itself works on an energy system basically, and in a very simplified way, it's saying that, er, you have an energy system within your body and when that energy becomes blocked or tainted in some way, then you will manifest certain symptoms and the things that we look at in conventional medicine as things like arthritis or rheumatism are, to the Chinese, merely an imbalance of the energy. So, in this way, they may say to you, well, yes, you have rheumatoid arthritis but we're going to actually look at your energy balance and rebalance you, and, as a result, your symptoms should disappear.

Interviewer: Um, is acupuncture essentially a form of preventative medicine?

Vivienne: Traditionally, it was, very much. Um, in fact, traditionally, in China, people only used to pay the doctor while they were well and they used to go to their doctor fairly regularly on, you know, maybe four or five times a year, and they would only pay the doctor when they were kept well. And if they got sick, they didn't pay the doctor. And the doctor had various methods of which acupuncture was one, diet was another, exercise was another, er, of ensuring that the person lived a right life style and their emphasis was on if you're living a right life style, if you're living in tune with the laws of the universe, going to sleep when it's dark, waking up when it's light, working, resting, doing all these things properly, then you won't get sick. Unfortunately, our way of looking at life in the West is very differnt in that we tend to struggle on in spite of our headache and not take terribly much notice of our body when things are not quite right and we tend to struggle on until we

539

fall over and we get carted off to hospital in an ambulance. And so, acupuncture in the West, unfortunately, in a way, has come to be not the preventative medicine that it could be because we're not taking responsibility enough for ourselves in going along and making sure that we stay well.

Key to Exercises:

A. Choose the best answer (a, b or c) to complete each of the following statements.

1. _____ is taken into consideration in holistic medicine.
    a. man's heart
    b. The individual part of the body
  * c. The whole of the person

2. Acupuncture is _____.
  * a. a part of holistic medicine
    b. a part of conventional medicine
    c. a part of modern Chinese medicine

3. According to Chinese medicine, arithritis or rheumatism
    _____.
  * a. is an imbalance of the energy system within the body
    b. are an imbalance of the spiritual side of a patient
    c. are symptoms of a balanced energy system

4. Traditionally in China, people used to pay their doctor
    _____.
    a. when they were ill
  * b. when they were well
    c. when they had to see him

5. In traditional Chinese medicine, the doctor treated the patient with various methods like acupuncture, diet, and exercise so

540

that the patient should _____ .

   a. pay him

   b. get well soon

 * c. live in accordance with the laws of the universe.

B. True or False Questions. Write a T in front of a statement if it is true according to the recording and write an F if it is false.

  1. (T) Holistic medicine looks at the body as a whole rather than the individual parts of the body.

  2. (F) The conventional medicine usually relates a problem one has with his whole body.

  3. (T) Traditional Chinese medicine emphasizes the balance within human body.

  4. (F) The conventional medicine believes in a proper life style with regard to working , resting, eating etc.

  5. (T) People in the West won't pay much attention to their body until they are terribly ill.

  6. (F) Acupuncture is regarded as a form of preventive medicine in the West.

C. Fill in the following blanks with the information you hear on the tape.

  1. What we're tended to do in conventional medicine is to (break things down) to a point where we're actually only looking at (one part of the person).

  2. Holistic medicine insists that if there is a problem (with your right foot), that is going to somehow (affect your entire body).

  3. You have (an energy system) within your body and when

that energy (becomes blocked or tained) in some way, then you will (manifest certain symptoms).

4. Our way of looking at life in (the West) is very (different) in that we tend to struggle on (in spite of our headache) and not take terribly much notice of (our body) when things are (not quite right) and we tend to struggle on until we fall over).

Section Two:

Tapescript:

Task 1: Psychology of Clothes

Janice: So you really believe that clothes carry a kind of message for other people and that what we put on is in some way a reflection of what we feel?

Pauline: Oh yes, very much so. People are beginning now to take seriously the idea of a kind of psychology of clothing, to believe that there is not just individual taste in our clothes but also a thinking behind what we wear which is trying to express something we may not even be aware of ourselves.

Janice: But surely this has always been the case. We all dress up when we want to impress someone, such as for a job interview with a prospective employer; we tend to make an effort and put on something smart.

Pauline: True, but that's a conscious act. What I'm talking about is more of a subconscious thing. Take for example the student who is away from home at college or university: if he tends to wrap himself up more than the others, this is because he is probably feeling homesick. Similarly, a general feeling of insecurity can sometimes take the form of over-dressing in warmer clothes than are necessary.

Janice: Can you give any other examples of this kind?

Pauline: Yes. I think people who are sociable and outgoing tend to dress in an extrovert way, preferring brighter or more dazzling colours – yellows, bright reds, and so on. In the same way, what might be seen as a parallel with the animal kingdom, aggressive clothes might indicate an aggressive personality or attitude to life. Think about the threat displays used by animals when they want to warn off opponents.

Janice: Do you think the care – or lack of it – over the way we actually wear our clothes has anything to tell us?

Pauline: Yes, indeed. The length, for example, of a man's trousers speaks volumes about his awareness of his own image. Or, if his trousers are at half-mast, all sort of hanging down, this probably means he's absorbed by other things.

Janice: Really.

Pauline: Or, to give you other examples, often minority groups, who have perhaps failed to persuade with words, tend to express themselves by wearing unconventional, or what some might consider outrageous clothing, as a way of showing their thoughts and feelings are different from the rest, and so they find an outlet in this way.

Janice: That surely spills over into other things as well.

Pauline: Oh yes, indeed. Haircuts, jewellery, kinds of fabric used – these things can all be a form of rebellion. But to get back to clothes, I would like to add that a whole lot about our personality is conveyed in our clothes and the way we look – aggressiveness, rebelliousness, happiness, sadness, and so on. These can all be interpreted. Think of the aging pop star who may be pushing middle age, he'll keep on dressing up like a rebel to try to prove he's 'with it' still, and in touch with his young fans and current trends.

Janice: Do you think that at work clothes and general appearance have any significance?

Pauline: Definitely. We've already spoken about job interviews a bit, and it's interesting to note that in a recent survey it was suggested that employers prefer young executives to stick to grey, black and dark blue suits if they are men, and classical outfits and dresses in sober colours if they are women, perhaps because they feel this is a reflection of a more responsible and sober attitude to work and will also project this image to customers.

Janice: Do you subscribe to this opinion?

Pauline: I personally think that too much conservatism defeats the object of the clothes industry. They want to create new fashions and colour to sell clothes, so I can't really say that I go along wholeheartedly with it. There shold be room for manoeuvre, leaving people scope to express their individuality in what they are wearing.

Task 2: Fashion Model

We've all seen them on TV commercials, looking out at us from the covers of glossy magazines or showing off the latest creations from Paris, and it must have seemed to us that they have lives which are all glamour. Jeffrey Ingrams has been delving into the world of the fashion model and has come up with some interesting facts.

Denise: The average model can earn roughly the same as a top secretary on the basis, that is, that she's a freelance with an agent who'll send her out for auditions and interviews and get work for her.

Jeffrey: Denise Harper is a model agent. The Central Model Agency, in which she's a partner, is very closely associated with the Metropolitan Academy of Modelling, where dozens of aspiring models have come over the years to pay their money to take a basic course in the techniques of being a model. Just over five years ago, one such aspiring model was eighteen-year-old Margaret Connor, fresh from school.

Margaret: Your mother has told you that you're a pretty girl and you think that you're God's gift. You're not, of course, but the Academy give you the works, how to do make-up, how to walk, how to do your hair, dress sense, the lot.

Jeffrey: Now before we go any further I really ought to give you some idea of what Margaret looks like. She's about 5 feet 8 inches tall, with shoulder-length auburn hair, hazel eyes and a ready smile. Like Margaret, every model has her index card which potential clients can keep in their files to refer to. When not working, Margaret is a rather prettier-than-average girl-next-door, but her photograph alone seemed to show that she can be as versatile and as fashionable as anyone might want. But why did Denise Harper pick her out from the other similar applicants for the modelling course at the Academy?

Denise: I always look for personality, poise, good height and, very important, initiative, all of which Margaret has. You try to find above all a girl who you think will work and is not only in it for the money.

Jeffrey: Naturally, when they've finished the course it doesn't always mean automatically that they are set for stardom. Margaret occasionally gives classes at the Academy and she told me why

545

some girls just pack in the job.

Margaret: Sometimes the work is too hard, sometimes it's too scarce and sometimes you have to push yourself too much. You've got to be a saleswoman to be a model, just sitting back and thinking you're going to be cosseted is no good, you've got to go out there and get work. But once you've got it, OK, fine.

Jeffrey: When work does come along, it could be pretty well anything.

Margaret: Really it's a different job every time — it might be TV advertisements, live advertising promotions, a photo session, anything.

Jeffrey: I asked Margaret to give me some idea of a typical day in her life.

Margaret: This is the fun thing about it, really. You've got no idea what you'll be doing tomorrow, nothing's planned ahead. there's such a variety of ways of spending the day. There's a sort of 'wake-up at 8 o'clock with the phone ringing' day, and next minute you're off abroad somewhere, which is everybody's idea of modelling. Then, other days you have to go round and sell yourself because you've got nothing on at all — seeing photographers, magazines, newspapers, generally getting your face around. On a busy day you've got to dash from job to job, it's all very hectic, but basically you've always got to have everything literally by the phone, be ready to leave at a moment's notice. But there's variety in it. Making TV commercials has in fact now overtaken straightforward fashion as our favourite occupation. It's more fun than photographic work, where one split second decides whether you look nice or not. In a TV commercial there's some acting involved, and you have to keep it up for a while, which is more of a challenge.

Jeffrey: When Margaret said she keept everything by the phone, I wondered what she meant.

Margaret: Definitely your diary, with a pen, waiting for that interview. Then every model has one arm longer than the other (*laughs*) because of all the things she has to cart around in her bag — spare pairs of shoes, make-up, spare tights, and a book — it can get boring waiting around sometimes. I read such a lot of novels! Umm, everything but the kitchen sink — *all* has to be packed in.

Jeffrey: Whatever her motivation, it's quite clear that Margaret enormously enjoys being a model.

Margaret: Yes, I love it! It's fantastic! I just couldn't think of doing anything else. It's always been the glamour that attracted me. To begin with, it's real hard work to get established, but the variety and excitement of not knowing from one day to the next what's going to happen has never ceased to give me a thrill.

Key to Exercises:

Task 1: Psychology of Clothes

A. Choose the best answer (a, b or c) to complete each of the following statements.

   1. The clothes one wears in a way _____

  * a. reflect his personality

    b. show his social position

    c. indicate his economic condition

2. Gnerally speaking , the way people are dressed is
   _____ .
   * a. an unconscious act
     b. a conscious act
     c. determined by different occasions
3. We can tell what a person is like by _____ .
     a. the size of his clothes
   * b. the colour of his clothes, his age, and his social position
     c. the colour and length of his clothes, his haircut, the mate-
        rials he uses, etc.
4. The second speaker feels that many employers ' view on
   clothes are _____ .
     a. quite liberal
   * b. a bit conservative
     c. encouraging to fashion-followers

B. Identification. Based on what you hear on the tape, match the
   person in Column I with the way one is dressed in Column II.

I	II
1. a man absorbed by other things	a. in warmer clothes
2. a person of minority origin	b. in bright reds
3. a homesick student	c. with trousers at
4. a young executive	half-mast
5. a sociable and outgoing	d. unconventionally
person	e. in dark blue suit

   Answer: (1)—(c); (2)—(d); (3)—(a);
           (4)—(e); (5)—(b)

C. True or False Questions. Write a T in front of a statement if it is

true according to the recording and write an F if it is false.

1. (T) People usually wear smart clothes for a job interview in order to impress the employer.
2. (F) Aggressive clothes can never indicate aggressive personality and attitude to life.
3. (T) A middle-aged pop star may be dressed in a rebellious way in order to keep in touch with his young fans and current trends.

D. Fill in the blanks according to what you hear on the tape.
   1. People are beginning now to take seriously the idea of a kind of (psychology of clothing), to believe that there is (not just individual taste) in our clothes (but also a thinking behind what we wear) which is trying to express something we may (not even be aware of ourselves).
   2. They want to (create new fashions and colour) to sell clothes, so I can't really say that I (go along wholeheartedly) with it. There should be (room for manoeuvre), leaving people (scope to express their individuality) in what they are wearing.

Task 2: Fashion Model
A. Choose the best answer (a, b or c) to complete each of the following statements.
   1. Denise Harper is _____.
      a. a model
    * b. a model agent
      c. an announcer
   2. Margaret Connor started her career of a model

549

_____.

   * a. five years ago

     b. nineteen years ago

     c. fifteen years ago

3. As described by Margaret , a model doesn ' t have

_____.

     a. colourful life

   * b. a fixed job with regular working hours

     c. a life with variety.

4. A model has to take with her some spare shoes , make-up, spare tights, etc. in a bag because _____.

     a. she doesn't have any more personal belongings

     b. she is afraid they may be stolen

   * c. she is often called to start working at a moment's notice

5. Margaret likes being a model because _____

     a. of the handsome pay

     b. she is a freelance

   * c. of the variety and excitement of not knowing what's going to happen the next day

B. True or False Questions. Write a T in front of a statement if it is true according to the recording and write an F if it is false.

1. (F) Jeffery Ingrams knows very little about fashion models.

2. (F) The average model doesn't earn as much as a top secretary.

3. (T) Margaret became a model just from school.

4. (T) Clients can refer to index card kept in their files to find the model they need.

5. (T) A model should know how to sell herself.

6. (F) Making TV commercials is not as interesting as photographic work.

C. State the activities of the following people and agencies based on
what you hear on the tape.
1. Denise Harper: (a model agent who sends a model out for auditions and interviews and gets work for her)
2. the Metropolitan Academy of Modelling: (an agency where
aspiring girls take a basic course in the techiniques of being a
model)
3. the girls at the Academy (mentioned above):
(learning how to do make-up, how to work, how to do hair,
dress sense, etc.)

D. Supply the following information about Margaret.
Sex: (female)
Age: (23)
Height: (5 feet 8 inches)
Length of the hair: (shoulder length)
Colour of the hair: (auburn)
Colour of the eyes: (hazel)
General impression of the appearance: (prettier than average
girls)

Section Three:
Tapescript:
Outlining: Solving Problems

Today I am going to talk about some thoughts that psychologists have had on how people go about solving problems.

The first point I want to make is that there is no one way of solving all problems. If you think about it you will realize the obvious fact that there are many different kinds of problems which have to be solved in different ways. Let's take two very different examples.

A student is sitting in his study, trying to solve a problem in Mathematics. After an hour, still unsuccessful, he gives up and goes to bed. The following morning he wakes up and wanders into the study. Suddenly, the solution comes to him.

Now for a very different kind of problem. In the Shakespeare play *Hamlet*, young Hamlet, Prince of Denmark, discovers that his father has been murdered by his uncle. The evidence is based on the appearance of his father's ghost, urging him to revenge his death by killing his uncle. Should he accept the ghost's evidence, and kill his uncle? This is obviously a very different kind of problem. Such moral or emotional problems might have no real solution, or at any rate no solution that everyone might agree on.

There are many other different types of problems apart from these two. In this talk, I'd like to talk about the first kind of problem: the kind that the student of Mathematics was involved with.

The solution to that kind of problem is sometimes called an 'A – ha' solution, because the solution comes suddenly, out of nowhere as it were, and in English people sometimes say 'A – ha' when a good idea comes to them like that. Another, less amusing, name for it is insight. For a long time the student seems to get nowhere, and then there is a sudden flash of insight and the solution appears.

A classic example of insight is the case of the French mathematician POINCARE. For fifteen days Poincare struggled with a mathematical problem and had no success. Then one evening he took black coffee before going to bed (which was not his usal custom). As he lay in bed, he couldn't sleep, and all sorts of ideas came to him. By morning he had solved the problem which had baffled him for over a fornight.

What do psychologists have to say about this process of problem sloving?

A very good and he pful description of the sloving process has been made by Polya, a teacher of Mathematics. I'll spell his name, too. P-o-l-y-a, Polya. Remember that Polya is thinking of insight problems, and in particular, mathematics problems, but his ideas should apply in all sorts of areas.

Polya's description has four stages. They are:
Stage one: *Understanding the problem* : At this stage, the student gathers all the information he needs and asks himself two questions: The first question is:

What is the unknown? What is my *goal*? In other words, what do I want to find out?
The second question is:

What are the data and conditions? What is *given*? In other words, What do I already know?

Stage two: *Devising a plan* : Here the sutdent makes use of his past experience to decide on the method of solution. At this stage he asks himself three questions:
a) Do I know a problem similar to this one?
b) Can I restate the *goal* in a different way that will make it easier

for me to use my past experience? Polya calls restating the golal 'working backwards'.

c) Can I restate what is *given* in a way that relates to my past experience? Polya calls restating what is given as 'working forward'. The student stays at stage two until he has the flash of insight. If necessary he can put the problem to one side for a while and then come back to it. Eventually he will see how the problem can be done.

Stage three: *Carrying out the plan*: The student carries out the plan of solution, checking each step.

Stage four: *Looking back*: The student checks his answer in some way, perhaps by using another method, or whatever. Having done that, he makes it part of his experience by asking himself: 'Can I use this result or method for other problems'?

I will repeat again that not all problems are like the mathematics problems that Polya is thinking about. Not every problem is solvable, and some may even have no satisfactory solution. Nevertheless, it is probably a good idea to do what Polya has done. That is, when you are successful in solving a problem, analyse how you have done it, and remember your method for the next time.

Key to Exercises:

A. General Comprehension: Write a T in front of a statement if it is true according to the recording and write an F if it is false.

1. (T) Not all problems are solvable. The problem of Hamlet belongs to the unsolvable ones.

2. (T) The lecture is largely devoted to how to solve the kind of

problems that the student of Mathematics was involved in.

3. (T) The solution is called an "A-ha" solution because English people sometimes say "A-ha" when they hit upon a good idea.

4. (F) Poincare was a French Psychologist.

5. (F) Polya was a famous mathematician.

6. (T) Although Polya's description of the solving process mainly concerns insight problems, his ideas can be applied in all sorts of areas.

7. (F) Polya's description has four stages, from "understanding the problem" to "looking forward".

8. (T) Finally the lecturer advises people to summarize their successful experience of solving a problem so that they can use the method next time.

B. Suggested abbreviations:

mathematics: maths.　　　　　emotional: emot.

sometimes: s'times.　　　　　mathematician: mathc.

experience: exp.　　　　　　problem: prob.

C. Notetaking: Complete the following outline.

Title: (Solving Problems)

I. Not all problems are solvable

A. The st's (maths) problem can be solved (with insight)

B. Hamlet's (moral or emot.) problem might have (no real solution or no solution that everyone agrees on)

C. Many (other types)

II. Solution to (the 1st kind of probs.)

A. ("A – ha") solution

Also called (insight)

Eng. people s' times say ("A - ha") when (a good idea comes to them suddenly).

e.g. (Poincaré, French mathc.)

B. Polya's description: (4) stages

  1. (Understanding the prob.)

    gathers (information)

    asks a. (What do I want to find out?)

        b. (What do I already know?)

  2. Devising a plan

    makes use of (past exp.) to

    decide on (methods of solution)

    asks: a. (know a prob. similar)

        b. (restate the goal & make it easier)

        Polya calls it (working backwards)

        c. (restate what is given)

        Polya calls it (working forward)

        St. stays here until (flash of insight)

  3. (Carrying out) the plan

    carries out (the plan)

    checks (each stop)

  4. (Looking back)

    asks (use it for other probs.)

III. Conclusion

(Not all probs. solvable, good idea to carry out Polya's method. Summarize exp. & use your method next time.)

Fashion

The first clothes were probably made just to protect people from the cold. But men and women soon wanted their clothes to be more than practical: they wanted them to be beautiful, too. The more advanced a society became, the more attention was paid to the manner of dress. By the time the Egyptians had built the great pyramids, grooming was as important as it is today.

Until recently, beautiful clothes were made by hand. They were usually elaborate and always expensive. Fashion was for the royal, the rich, and the famous. Now mass production has made stylish clothes available to almost everyone. The modern fashion business – from the design room to the store window—is one of the busiest, most imaginative, and most glamourous activities in the world.

In designing a dress the fashion designer works with three things: silhouette, fabric, and colour.

Silhouette

The shape of a dress, suit, or coat—or any article of clothing—is called its silhouette. It is determined by the flare of the skirt and the fit of the bodice (the top of a dress from neck to waistline), the shape of the sleeves, the location of the waistline, and the cut of the neckline. A hat, shoes, and gloves complete and balance a silhouette. Although styles vary from year to year, there are really only a few basic shapes.

The central and most important point of a silhouette is the waistline. It can be high, normal, low, or there can be no waist at all. A high waistline is called Empire, because it was made fashionable by Napoleon's wife Josephine, who set the style for all the ladies of the French Empire. The most common waistline is the normal, or natural, one. It is usually belted. A waistline placed below the natural waist gives a long, slim silhouette that is called a torso look.

The hemline is the second most important part of a silhouette. Hemlines vary in length anywhere from floor length to the short, above-the-knee kilt. In the ever-changing styles of women's clothes, it is the waistline and hemline that change more than any other part of the silhouette.

A shape that closely outlines the figure is the most common silhouette. Another favourite shape is full skirted, or bouffant. Between these two shapes there are a variety of outlines that range from wide triangles and bell shapes to the straight up-and-down look of the chemise, or sack dress.

In the history of European fashion, the natural lines of the body have often been distorted by binding corsets, steel girdles, and wired petticoats. Stiff bodices with tightly bound waists and hoop skirts became fashionable in Spain in the 16th century, and the style spread to England, France, and Italy. When the elegant ladies of the Victorian Age swooned, it was not because they were delicate but because their clothes made breathing difficult.

The body must be free to breathe, to move, and to grow. Clothes must not interfere with health and safety. Today women work, play, and travel; and in today's fashion they are free to move with ease and comfort.

Fabric

The shape of a garment depends on how a fabric falls and how it looks when pinned and belted. Light fabrics such as silk, chiffon, jersey, crepe, and cotton cling to the body or fall around it in soft

558

folds. More definite shapes that stand away from the body can be made of heavier fabrics such as velvet, linen, bulky wools, and flannel. Naturally designers choose fabrics according to the seasons.

Today there is no limit to the kinds of materials designers can use. They can choose fabrics from all over the world. A designer's imagination can be inspired by the prints made in the United states, by the sari silks of the Far East, or the bold designs of the South Pacific.

Fabrics are both natural and man-made. Cotton, linen, and burlap are made from natural fibers that come from plants. Other natural fabrics such as wool, furs, and silk come from animals. Man-made fabrics are called synthetics. They can be made to look like transparent silks or heavy wools. Often in is difficult to tell a synthetic from a pure silk, wool, or cotton. Some materials, like nylon, are completely synthetic; others, like cotton acetates, are a combination of a man-made and a natural fiber. Man-made materials have certain advantages—they frequently wear longer, wash more easily, and do not wrinkle as much as natural fabrics. Often they are less expensive. Since the price of a dress depends partially on the cost of the material out of which it is made, synthetics have made possible a wide choice of inexpensive clothes.

Colour

The colours used in clothes often reflect natural conditions. Prints from Tahiti and Hawaii are as vivid as the flowers and sunsets of the islands. The Pueblo Indians in Arizona weave colours that match the intense shades of the layers of stone in the Grand Ganyon.

Not long ago the color of a dress depended on the season and the time of day when it was worn. Winter wools were always dark, summer cottons always light and pale. Bright colors were worn only by the young or for gala occasions. However, fashion designers have become more daring in their use of color. Vivid combinations are common. We often see bright orange, purple, or red combined with pink, and blue and lavender with bright green. Now wools can be pale and summery, cottons can be dark, and city clothes vivid. Perhaps the only traditional color left is white for the bride.

The Fashion Designer

The fashion designer works in a design room. Here the fabrics are brought together, the shape of the silhouettes developed, and the color schemes decided upon. Some designers create their silhouettes by sketching. From the sketches sample garments are made of muslin (an inexpensive cotton). If the muslin shape is satisfactory, then the garment is made in the desired fabric.

Since the fabric is important to the shape of a dress, some designers work directly with the fabric that will be used. A designer who works with the actual material drapes it on a dressmaker's dummy or a live model. The material is pinned and cut on the model. When the shape of the dress has been decided upon, a rough pattern is made. Then seamstresses, called sample hands, make the first dress, an **original sample**. When the dress is completed, it is given a number and sent to the production department. There the cost of labor, fabric, and general business expenses are figured, and the dress is given a wholesale price.

The group of dresses that a designer creates for one season is called a **collection.** Collections can range anywhere from 25 to over 100 garments or styles. Each season the collection is shown to buyers and newspaper and magazine reporters at a **formal showing.** Usually this takes place in the designer's showroom. In less than an hour, a group of models can show 100 different dresses, coats, or suits.

The Buyer

The store buyer is all-important in the fashion world, and her job is one of the most difficult. She must not only know by experience what sells to her customers, but have an eye for what is new and different.

A large store divides its fashion items into different departments. Very expensive clothes, moderately priced, and budget, or inexpensive, clothes are in separate parts of the store.

Merchandise is divided according to the age of the wearer – such as misses, junior, preteen, and children's clothes – and according to the kind of apparel – evening dresses, daytime dresses, and sportswear. The buyers for these various departments go to New York or Paris to select the new designs. The buyers choose garments according to silhouette and fabric and then pick the colors that they want. Often one silhouette will come in different colors and fabrics.

The Customer

Women learn about new styles from newspapers, television, fashion magazines, and store windows. In the past there were definite fashion cycles; women tended to wear one or two styles and certain colors until a new style was introduced and a new color became popular. Now, because the industry is so large and there are so many different designers, trends and styles change much more rapidly. Also since fashionable clothes are less expensive and women buy more clothes than ever before, it is difficult to determine a fashion cycle. The modern woman selects clothes according to her own taste. She is able to choose what she likes from the many collections. Today the customer, along with the designer, makes

561

trends in fashion.

Elements of Good Fashion

The basic element of good fashion is good grooming. The most stylish clothes will not look good on a woman who does not have good posture and a graceful carriage. Another element of good fashion is individuality. Th clothes of a well-dressed woman always reflect her own personality. To be fashionable, a person must know what is becoming – what silhouettes and fabrics will highlight her figure and what colors are flattering to her. For instance, short women often choose clothes that make them seem taller, while tall women draw attention away from their height.

Centers of Fashion

The French word *couturier* means "dressmaker." In the world of fashion, the word has come to mean "a designer of high fashion" or *haute couture*. It is these designers who begin trends and create new silhouettes. The work of famous couturiers of different countries is copied all over the world. Recently Italian designers have had great influence in setting new styles.

Paris has always been the traditional center of world fashion. There centuries of elegant court life and a delight in beautiful things have inspired some of the loveliest clothes ever made. Today couturier salons such as Dior, Ricci, Balmain, Chanel, Givenchy, and many others carry on the tradition.

French designers guard the secrets of the new designs until their collections are shown to the public. After the showings, pictures of the styles are published in newspapers and magazines all over the world.

People from many countries travel to Paris to buy the clothes and to copy the most recent ideas. In January they come to view spring clothes, in July to see the fall designs.

Because the French couturiers make only a few copies of a dress, each garment is very expensive. Many dress manufacturers from other countries buy the original clothes of the famous French designers. They take them back to their own design rooms, where the clothes are copied line for line to be made in great numbers. Some manufacturers, however, use the Paris styles only as a starting point for their own ideas. Others may adapt only a part of the French design into their own styles.

Copies of Paris designs are still included in some American showings. But since the 1940's American designers have also become fashion trend-setters, and the United States has become a world fashion leader. The American fashion industry, much of it centered in an area around Seventh Avenue in New York City, uses all the techniques of mass-production.

But with the speed of modern communications, especially television, fashion today is almost universal. New styles – from mini, maxi, and midi skirts to all kinds of pants outfits – are worn in Tokyo and Tel Aviv almost as soon as they are in London, Paris, and New York.

And today, too, new fashion trends are as likely to start with young people's fads as they are to come from a "name" designer's sketch pad. Wherever fashion begins, it always keeps pace with a changing world.

Lesson 28

Section One:
Tapescript:

Interviews

Robert: Now, one of the biggest hurdles to cross in getting a good job is the interview. There's no getting away from it, because in nearly every case when you apply for a job you will be called for one, or sometimes even two, interviews. It's quite natural that you might also be dreading it; in fact, some people dread them so much they never turn up at all. What I want to try to do today is to take some of the sting out of the interview and get you over what I call 'job interview jitters' to show you how you can make a good impression and even use the interview to your own advantage. I mentioned two interviews earlier because some companies do a kind of screening interview first, where they try to find out what you're like and if you're suitable for the job before you go on to the main interview. This screening interview would probably be with someone from the personnel department, and I'd like now to show you on the video a couple of examples of these screening interviews, which I hope will help to illustrate how to go about it and how not to. In the first, Walter Edwards of the per sonnnel department of a biscuit factory in Southampton is interviewing Anita Jones for a job as a secretary.

Walter: Come in, I'm Walter Edwards and you're Miss...?

Anita: Anita Jones, er, but my friends call me Nita.

Walter: How do you do, Miss Jones. Do please sit down. Now, your application tells me you were born in these parts. Did you grow up here?

Anita: Er, um, yes. Well, no. I was born here in Southampton, but my dad, that is my father, works in a bank so we, um, moved up north when I was fairly small, which is where I went to school and, um, then we moved back down here, which is why I live round here now, you see.

Walter: Quite. And I see you've just completed a one-year secretarial course. Is this your first job application?

Anita: Yes, er, well, no. I mean, I've had several holiday jobs and part-time jobs but this is, or rather would be my first full-time job. I mean this is the first time I've been looking for one.

Walter: Do you have any special reason for choosing this company?

Anita: Oh, not really. I mean, er, yes, I was attracted by the money but that's not the only reason, of course. (*Laughs.*)

Walter: I see. And could you tell me about your secretarial skills?

Robert: Without going any further, I think we can all see that Anita is a very nervous applicant: hesitant and indecisive. It's quite clear that she is petrified by the whole idea of the interview, and her faltering and stammering delivery is even irritating for Mr Edwards who has, after all, only a few minutes to find out about Anita and to see if she's the right one for the job. Another important point to raise is appearance, which Anita obviously didn't take much care over. Dress is very important and you should never turn up in jeans and an old sweater if you're after a job in an office or a place of work

565

where you will be meeting people, dealing with clients and that sort of thing. Clean, smart clothes are the order of the day, and try to avoid stage fright, like some nervous actor on the opening night of a new play. Job applicants often look upon the interviewer as some kind of ogre who enjoys making interviewees squirm in their seats, a kind of figure to be looked up to and revered. This negative attitude of mind will not help in any way and will only destroy your self-confidence and ensure failure.

Anita also mentioned money straight away, which was bad and made her come across as being mercenary. The one question she did volunteer a lot of information about was her upbringing and that was all highly irrelevant. Before we move on, there's something else I wanted to point out and that was the way Anita moved. As she came into the room she sidled nervously up to the desk and wasn't quite sure whether to shake hands, sit down or what to do and kept looking nervously around her. Throughout the interview she fidgeted about and kept twiddling the strap on her handbag, which she clutched tightly to herself. Furthermore, she sat on the edge of her seat with hunched shoulders and a tense look on her face, all of which indicates to the interviewer she is someone who can't handle pressure and responsibility and who appears indecisive and unsure. You have to remember that you've got about ten or fifteen minutes to show what you're made of, and no matter how good you are normally, it's in these vital minutes that you must project the right image. Now we'll take a look at another interview and see what conclusions can be drawn from that one. In this excerpt, Louise Simpson is being interviewed for a job with a book publishing firm by Audrey Maguire of personnel.

Louise: I'm Louise Simpson.

Audrey: Sit down, please, Miss Simpson. I'm Audrey Maguire.

Louise: How do you do?

Audrey: when you came in, did you happen to notice all the building work going on?

Louise: yes, I did.

Audrey: Well, that's our new office extension and we're moving there within the month, so that's where you'd be working.

Loiuise: Yes, I did read about it in the prospectus you sent me about the firm. I'm sure you're looking forward to the move.

Audrey: Indeed, yes. New I'd like to ask you one or two questions about your previous experience, if that's all right?

Louise: Go right ahead.

Audrey: Have you had any jobs before?

Louise: Yes, I worked as a secretary in a lawyer's office as a summer job, primarily to earn some money to see me through college, but I also gained some useful work experience into the bargain. While I was there I did secretarial work and also took a turn on the reception desk, to help out, and it was very enjoyable meeting people in this way to vary the routine.

Audrey: Did you like working in the lawyer's office?

Louise: From the career point of view it was good to get to know how an office works, but I've always wanted to be in publishing really, which is why I applied for this job.

Audrey: Now, can you tell me ...

Robert: I think we've seen enough to make the distinction between Louise and Anita you saw in the previous slip. Louise gives a

567

totally different image, an image of self-confidence without being too cocky, and she was conducting herself in a relaxed and friendly way. She talked to the interviewer in a normal manner, which was fluent and without the terrible 'ums' and 'ers' of Anita. She also gave the impression that she was there to exchange information with the interviewer rather than be interrogated. She wanted to know if the company was going to suit her as much as they wanted to know if she would suit them. Her clothes were sober and neat, without being too frumpy, and she was relaxed and casual without being too laid-back so that it would appear she didn't care. She had also taken the trouble to read the prospectus she'd been sent, which didn't hurt at all. The basic point about an interview is that it shouldn't be a question-and-answer routine, a boss-and-servant session, but a coming together of two personalities. It's the 'swan technique' which projects the best image in my view, serene on the surface but paddling like mad underneath. And new I'd like to come to the problem of ...

Key to Exercises:

A. Choose the best answer (a, b or c) to complete each of the following statements.

1. The man in the introduction wants to show you
   _____.

    a. there's no getting away from the interview

 * b. how to use the interview to your own advantage

    c. it's natural you might be dreading the interview

2. According to the man in the introduction , some companies
   _____.

a. may ask you to talk with someone from the personnel department first

* b. do a kind of screening interview first

c. may ask you to send them a photo to find out what you look like first

3. According to the man's analysis of the first interview , _____ are very important in job interviews.

* a. appearance, self-confidence and accurate answers to questions.

b. appearance, secretarial experience and self -confidence

c. appearance, self-confidence and family background

4. The man's impression about the second applicant is that she is _____ .

a. full of confidence but too casual

b. full of confidence but too cocky

* c. full of confidence but friendly

B. Complete the following statements concerning the aim of the lecture

1. The man is trying to:

(1) take some of (the sting out of the interview;)

(2) get you over (what he calls 'job interview jitters';)

(3) show you how (you can make a good imgression;)

(4) show you how (you can use the interview to your own advantage;)

(5) illustrate how (to go about it.)

C. Answer the following questions and base your answers on the man's opening remark.

1. What do they try to find out from the screening interview?

   Answer: (They try to find out what you are like and if you

   are suitable for the job.)

2. Who is likely to conduct screening interviews?

   Answer: (Someone from the peroonnel department.)

3. Where does Walter Edwards work?

   Answer: (At the personnel department of a biscuit factory.)

D. True or False Questions. Write a T in front of a statement if it is true according to the first interview and write an F if it is false.

   1. (T) Anita Jones has just completed one-year secretarial course.

   2. (F) Anita Jones has worked at several full-time jobs.

E. Fill in the blanks according to the man's analysis of the first interview.

   1. Anita is a very nervous applicant: (hesitant) and (indecisive).

   2. Anita didn't take much care over (her appearance).

   3. Anita's faltering and stammering (delivery) shows that she is (petrified) by (the whole idea) of (the interview).

   4. The man advises people to avoid (stage fright).

F. Answer the following questions and base your answer or the man's analysis of the first interview.

   1. What do job applicants often think that the interviewer enjoys doing?

      Answer: The interviewer enjoys making interviewees squirm in thir seats.

2. What does the man compare some job applicants to?

Anwer: Nervous actors on the opening night of a new play.

3. How does the man comment on Anita's answer to the question of her upbringing?

Answer: She offers too much information and it is highly irrelevant.

4. What does the man think Anita's nervous movement indicates to the interviewer?

Answer: She can't handle pressure and responsibility and appears indecisive and unsure.

G. Complete the following description given by the man about Anita's movement in the interview.

1. As she came into the room, she

   a. (sidled nervously up) to the desk.

   b. (wasn't quite sure) whether to shake hands, sit down or what to do.

   c. (kept looking nervously around her).

2. Throughout the interview she

   a. (fidgeted about);

   b. (kept twiddling the strap) on her handbag;

   c. (clutched tightly) the handbag to herself.

3. Furthermore , she sat on the edge of her seat with

   a. (hunched shoulders) and

   b. (a tense look) on her face.

H. Choose the best answer (a, b or c) to complete each of the following statements about the second interview.

1. According to the tape Louise is given an interview

_____.

* a. in a publishing firm
  b. in a lawyer's office
  c. in a bookstore

2. Louise got to know the new office extension _____.
   a. by having noticed it when passing by the building site
   b. from the interview
 * c. from the prospectus

3. Louise once worked as a secretary _____.
 * a. as a summer job
   b. as a winter job
   c. as a holiday job

4. When Louise worked in a lawyer's office, she also offered to work occasionally in the office _____.
 * a. as a receptionist
   b. as a typist
   c. as an assistant to the lawyer

I. List the good points that the man finds in Louise's performance at the interview.

1. She gives an image of (self-confidence without being too cocky)..

2. She was conducting herself in a (relaxed and friendly way).

3. She talked to the interviewer in a (normal manner).

4. She also gave the impression that she was there to (exchange inforamtion with the interviewer) rather than (be interrogated).

5. She wanted to know (if the company was going to suit her) as much as (they wanted to know) if she would (suit them).

572

6. Her clothes were (sober) and (neat), without being (too frumpy).

7. She had also taken the trouble to (read the prospectus).

J. Sum up the basic points about an interview according to the man.

1. It shouldn't be a. (a question-and-answer routine),

                b. (a boss-and-servant session).

2. It should be (a coming together of two personalities).

Section Two:

Tapescript:

New Report: Election Review

It is an election day and the Americans of all fifty states are going to the polls. Election observers have predicted a light to moderate turnout, of about forty percent. But some counties' election officials we talked this afternoon were more optimistic.

"I'm in Lamar, Colorado. It's raining. It's a very grey day. I think we are going to have a real good turnout if the weather doesn't getting worse."

"I'm the county auditor in the north – eastern portion of Aberdeen, SouthDakota, Brown, South Dakota. Our turnout in Brown County is absolutely fantastic at this point. The weather is cooperating, is absolutely gorgeous, in South Dakota, sunshining, crisp beautiful day. Couldn't have ordered anything finer."

"We are in Shelby, Montana, the county seat of Toole County. The weather is 59 degrees today, no snow anywhere in our area. It's beautiful. No windy. We expected a very good turnout today."

And it's a small exemplar there. Thirty-six states will elect governors today, in addition there are hundreds of local contests and battle issues to be decided. But the control in the United States senate remains the major item of national interest. A third of the senate, thirty-four seats, will be decided today. Republicans who have held their slim majority in the senate for the past six years are defending twenty-two of those seats. Democrats need a net gain of four seats to win control. According to the latest pre-election polls, the closest senate races were in these nine states, Washington, Idaho, North and South Dakota, North Carolina, Georgia, Alabama, California and Colorado. This would be the most closely watched tonight as county election officials turn their attention from watching the skies to counting the ballots.

Key to Exercises:

A. Complete the following chart according to what you hear on the tape.

1. Time: (Election Day)
2. Place: (the United States)
3. Number of States: (50)
4. Predication of Election Observers: (a light to moderate turnout, of about 40% of voters)

B. Fill in the blanks with the weather information in the following places

1. Lamar, Colorado:
   It's (raining),
   (a very grey day).

2. Aberdeen, Brown County, South Dakota:
   The weather is (cooperating), absolutely (gorgeous, sunshining, crisp beautiful) day.

3. Shelby, Montana:

The weather is (59 degrees) today, (no snow) anywhere (in our area).

It's (beautiful).

No (windy).

C. Fill in the following chart about the election.

1. Governors to be elected in (36 states).

2. Things to be decided locally: (hundreds of local contests and battle issues)

3. Major item of national interest: (the control in the United States senate)

4. Seats to be decided: (34 seats. ⅓ of the senate)

5. Seats possessed by Republicans: (22 seats)

6. Nine states with the closest senate races were:

(Washington, Idaho, North and South Dakota, North Caroline, Georgin, Alabama, California and Colorado)

Section Three:

Tapescript:

Outlining: Listening and Understanding

A student learning English often finds the following problems when he listens to talks or lectures.

Firstly, he doesn't always identify all the words correctly. I refer here to known words. i. e. words which the student would certainly recognize in print. Let's examine some of the reasons for this particular difficulty. In writing, there are clear spaces between each word; in speech, one word runs into the next. It's very difficult to decide, therefore, where one word finishes and the next one begins.

In writing, the words consist of letters of the alphabet. These letters have a fixed shape: they're easy to identify. In speech, however, vowel and consonant sounds are often very difficult to identify. Some of these sounds may not exist in the student's native language. Many of them, particularly the vowel sounds, are given different pronunciations by different English speakers.

Finally, some words in English, words like 'and' or 'there' or 'are' or 'will' are frequently pronounced with their weak or reduced form in speech. This is sometimes so short that non-native speakers, perhaps not accustomed to it, fail to recognize it at all. Many students, for example, don't recognize the normal pronunciation /ðərə/ for the words 'there are' which occur at the beginning of so many English sentences. Furthermore, they encounter a similar problem with unstressed syllables which are part of a longer word. For instance, think of the word 'cotton', which is spelt 'c-o-t-t-o-n'. I'll repeat that: 'c-o-t-t-o-n'. Each letter is the same size; no difference is made between the first syllable 'cot-' and the second syllable '-ton'. In speech, however, the first syllable is stressed, the second is unstressed. The work is not pronounced 'cot-ton' but 'COTn'. The same is true for the word 'carbon', spelt 'c-a-r-b-o-n'; it's not pronounced 'car-bon' but 'CAR bn'

But I want now to come on to the second main problem; the difficulty of remembering what's been said. Again, the problem here is much less difficult in the written rather than the spoken form. Words on a page are permanently fixed in space. They don't disappear like words that are spoken. They remain in front of you. You can choose your own speed to read them whereas in listening you've got to follow the speed of the speaker. A difficult word, or sentence, on the printed page can be read again, whereas a word not clearly heard is rarely repeated. The listener, therefore, finds that he has to concentrate so hard on identifying the words correctly and on understanding them that he has little time left to remember.

In a foreign language his brain simply has too much to do. In his own language, of course, he's able not only to identify and understand the words automatically but also he can often even predict the words which are going to come. His brain, therefore, has much more time to remember.

Thirdly, I want to deal with a problem that worries most students in a lecture. The problem is this – they can't always follow the argument. This is, of course, partly due to the first two difficulties I've discussed. When you have difficulty in identifying or remembering words and sentences, you obviously won't be able to follow the argument. But even those students who can do these two things perfectly well have problems in following a quite straightforward argument. Why is this? I'll suggest three reasons here. Firstly, students don't always recognize the signals which tell the listener that certain points are important. Some of these signals will be quite different from those employed in writing. Secondly, some students try too hard to understand *everything*. When they come to a small but difficutl point, they waste time trying to work it out, and so they may miss a more important point. Thirdly, students must concentrate very hard on taking notes and therefore may miss developments in the argument. But note-taking is a separate subject which will be dealt with in a later talk. ·

There are, however, other problems the student is faced with, which I'd like to mention briefly.

It's always a surprise to students to discover how much the

pronunciation of English changes from one English-speaking country to another, and from region to region. Many lecturers from Britain have a B.B.C.-type accent, the type of English associated mainly with the South of England and most commonly taught to non-native speakers. However, other lecturers will speak differently. To give an example /bʌs/, /lʌv/, /mʌm/ etc., as spoken in the south, are pronounced in Manchester and many other parts as /bɒv/, /lɒv/ and /mɒm/, Southern English /grɑs/, /fɑst/, /pɑθ/ are pronounced in Yorkshire and elsewhere as /græs/, /fæst/ and /pæθ/. It's worth noticing that it's usually the vowels which have variants, though sometimes it may be the consonants. For instance, a Scotsman will roll his 'r's', whereas a Londoner won't. So a lecturer with a particularly strong regional accent will cause non-native speakers considerable difficulty.

Whether a student follows a lecture easily or not depends also on the style of English the lecturer uses. By 'style' I mean the *type* of English chosen to express an idea: at one extreme it may be very formal, at the other colloquial or even slang. Generally speaking, the more formal the style, the easier it is for the student to understand. For example, a lecturer who says, formally, 'This is undoubtedly the writer's central point' will be readily understood. On the other hand if he says, 'That's really what the writer's on about, many students will have difficulty in understanding.

Other factors, which I haven't the time to discuss in detail, may also be involved. These include the speed at which the lecture is delivered, the rather common use of irony, the peculiarly English sense of humour, references which presuppose a knowledge of British culture, etc.

All these factors combine to make it a formidable task for students to follow lectures comfortably. It's clearly helpful to be aware of the problems and to get as much practice as possible in listening to and trying to understand spoken English.

Key to Exercises:

A. General Comprehension: Choose the best answer (a, b or c) to complete each of the following statements.

  1. It is _____ to identify words in speech _____ in print.

    a. easier; than

    * b. more difficult; than

    c. as easy; as

  2. In speech _____ sounds are often difficult to identify.

    a. vowel

    b. consonant

    * c. a and b

  3. The problem of identifying weak forms and unstressed syllables occurs in _____.

    * a. listening

    b. reading

    c. writing

  4. To remember what has been said is _____ to remember what has been written.

    a. as easy as

    * b. more difficult than

    c. easier than

  5. When listening to a foreign language, the student spends most of the time doing the following except _____.

　　　　a. identifying words correctly

　　　　b. understanding words

　　* c. trying to remember

　6. When students understand and remember all the words ,

　　　　_____.

　　　　a. they usually follow the argument

　　* b. they still have problems in following the argument

　　　　c. they often forget the argument

　7. A more colloquial speech is _____ to follow
　　　　_____ a more formal one.

　　　　a. as easy; as

　　* b. less easy; than

　　　　c. easier; than

　8. The text mainly deals with _____.

　　* a. problems in listening

　　　　b. ways to solve the problems in listening

　　　　c. a and b

B. Suggested Abbreviations:

　　consonant: conso　　　　formal: fl.

　　foreign: for.　　　　　　note: N.B.

　　development: dev.　　　　informal: infl.

　　pronunciation: pron.

C. Notetaking: Complete the following outline.

　Title: (Listening and Understanding)

　I. Probs. in listening

　　A. Doesn't identify (all the words correctly)

　　　　Reasons: 1. in speech 1 word (runs into next)

580

2. (in specch vowels & conso. sounds) diff. to identify
3. Some words pronounced (with weak or reduced form)

   e. g. (there are)

   Also (unstressed syllables)

   e. g. *cot*ton, *car*bon

B. Remembering (what's been said)

    1. In listening got to (follow the speed of the speaker)

    2. Concentrate on (understanding words correctly & understanding them)

    3. In for. lang. brain (too much to do).

    4. In own lang. (more time to remember)

C. Can't follow (the argument)

  Reasons: 1. (don't recognize signals of important points)

      2. (try too hard to understand everything)

      3. (take notes, miss dev. of argument)

II. Other prob.

A. Pron. of Eng. changes (country to country) and from (region to region)

e. g. (Southern Eng. /gras/ /fast/ Yorkshire /græs/ /fæst/)

N. B. usually vowels (have variants)

B. Style of Eng.

    1. v. formal vs. (colloquial or slang)

    2. more formal: (easier) to understand

      e. g. (This is undoubtedly the writer's ceutral point. – fl.

That's really what the writer's on
about. – infl.)

C. Also: 1. (speed)

    2. (common use of irony)

    3. (Eng. sense of humour)

    4. (Brit. culture)

Lesson 29

Section One:

Tapescript:

The Sad Life of an Old Man

Linda: Oh, yes, I remember. We were conducting a survey into the, the needs of disabled people in the borough (Yes) in which I work in London. And we got a request from an old man to go along and, and see him in connection with this survey. Well, some of the people that I'd seen on the survey before were really quite poor and lived in very bad housing conditions. (Yes) They were also ... tended to be elderly and to really have some quite bad disabilities, so I was quite prepared for, for anything I thought that I might meet. Anyway, I went along to, to this house and it was not at all what I'd expected. It was a, a large house and really had an air of fa, faded gentility about it. It was in a part of the borough which had (Really?) once been quite fashionable. Er, I knocked at the door and th, the old man, Mr Sinclair, came to, to let me in and showed me into a back room, which he lived in. The rest of the house, I think, must have been shut up and he was just living in one or two rooms. (How extraordinary!) Anyway, we started the interview which I had to, to conduct with him and he was very, very willing to talk but he never stopped grumbling. He grumbled about ... young people, about the rising cost of living,

583

about the government, about how the area had gone down, and so on and so forth. He didn't seem to have a good word to say for anybody at all. (S . . .)

Janet: Got a real chip on his shoulder?

Linda: Well, he was. He was a really grumpy old man and not very likeable with it. But he was . . . rather frail and in his eighties and . . . I just accepted that perhaps, you know, he'd had a hard life in, in some way an, and hadn't really resolved it. Anyway, I left the er, the house and went back to the office, wrote up the interview and didn't think any more about it. And then about a week later, I got a phone call from him saying that he thought he'd left out some important things about himself (Really?) that I should know, and would I go and see him again. So I explained that it was a survey that we were doing and that it wasn't really very usual to go back and see somebody a second time, but if he felt it was really important then, of course, I would go. (Yeah) So I went along and exactly the same thing happened as had happened before. He showed me into the back room and he started grumbling again and this went on for about half an hour and I began to wonder why on earth he'd asked me to go back a second time.

Janet: He didn't tell you anything new about himself?

Linda: Well, he . . . after about half an hour he started. He said, ' I, I expect you wonder why I've asked you to come back, ' (Quite) and I said, 'Well, as a matter of fact, yes I do.' So he said, 'Well, I think I should tell you a bit about myself and perhaps explain why I, I seem to have a chip on my shoulder, ' which took me aback, back a bit, you know. Anyway, apparently, he had come from a, a family which was . . . really quite

584

well-to-do but not spectacularly rich and his father had a, a small grocery business and had supported his mother and, and his two sisters. Well, his mother and father both died quite early on in his life and he took over the business (Yes) and it fell to him, of course, to support his two sisters. (Yes) Well, gradually the, the business began to, to flourish. He opened up new lines in the shops, he bought in some foreign foods and he (He ...) acquired new premises.

Janet: He really built the whole thing up.

Linda: Well yes. He didn't become a multi-millionaire or anything like that, but he was certainly very comfortably off. Anyway, he ... one of his sisters got married and the other sister emigrated to Australia but he himself never, never married.

Janet: He just stayed on in the house by himself?

Linda: He stayed on in, in this house which had been the family house for a number of years.

Janet: Completely alone?

Linda: Completely alone, yes. And he ... really cut himself off from his friends, or friends of the family, because he was giving all day, every day, to the growth of his business. So he kept going for a number of years but eventually, of course, he began to, to grow older and with age came arthritis (Oh dear) and ... gradually the, the condition worsened and he became more and more in pain, more and more frail but he still battled on, I think, for a number of years (Yes) but eventually he was forced to give up. And it left him completely alone. He was still, of course, well off, (Yes) but that wasn't in itself enough, and while he was telling me this he was, he was so upset because he'd remembered when telling me the excitement

585

and the thrill he'd felt (Yes) when he was completing these. transactions, of what it m, meant to be both powerful, respected and really somebody of note (Yes) in the area, whereas now he was old, (H...) frail, in pain.

Janet: He'd lost everything.

Linda: Yes, he had. His, his neighbours were very good to him, but it wasn't that that he wanted. (No) And I felt so ... helpless because it wasn't that he needed more money, it wasn't that he really needed visitors – he didn't particularly want visitor. (No) What he wanted was to be, to be young again and to be in a position of, of building something up and seeing the results (Yes) from it.

Janet: Oh, what a sad story!

Key to Exercises:

A. Choose the best answer (a, b or c) to complete each of the following statements.

  1. Linda , the main speaker , got to know the old man when

    _____ .

    a. she was working in the borough in London

    b. she was taking care of the disabled people

   * c. she was making a survey of the needs of disabled people

  2. To Linda's surprise, the old man _____ .

    a. lived in a very bad housing condition

    b. was locked up in a small, dark room

   * c. lived in a large house

  3. The old man was very _____ .

    a. garrulous

    b. introversive

* c. discontent

4. Linda was asked to visit the old man again by _____.

    a. a message left in her house

* b. a phone call from him

    c. a letter from him

5. The old man's father was _____.

    a. very rich

    b. very poor

* c. quite well-to-do

6. Linda felt helpless with the old man because he _____.

    a. needed more care

    b. wanted to become richer

* c. wanted to be young again

B. Fill in the blanks according to the tape.

    1. Linda had prepared herself for

        a. any very bad (housing conditions) that disabled people might be in, and

        b. some quite bad (disabilities) that they might have.

    2. The old man grumbled about

        a. (young people),

        b. (the rising cost of living),

        c. (the governemnt), and

        d. (how the area had gone down).

C. Choose the best answer (a, b or c) to complete each of the following statements.

1. The other woman thought the old man was extraordinary because _____.
   a. all the rooms in the large house were used by only himself
   * b. he had shut up all the rooms except one or two
   c. he lived in a back room
2. Linda told the old man _____ that they go back and
   see somebody a second time.
   a. it wasn't unusual
   * b. it was very rare
   c. it was very often
3. The house in which the old men now lived _____.
   a. had been bought by him
   * b. had been the family house
   c. had been inherited from his grandfather

D. Answer the following questions.
   1. Why did the old man cut himself off from his friends?
      Answer: Because he was giving all day to the growth of his
              business.
   2. Why did he become more and more in pain?
      Answer: Because he was getting older and more frail. He was
              left completely alone and had lost everything.

Section Two:

Tapescript:

New Report: A New Victim in LA

Los Angeles police yesterday added a new name to the list of
victims of what they believe is a new serial killer. Like the first four
victims Joseph Griffin was a homeless man shot on the head while

sleeping alone. NPR's Salas Wason reports from Los Angeles.

Early this month the police department sent notices to every homeless shelter about the transient killer. Staff member Marcotte Tears reads from the Xerox post near the check-in window at the Union Rescue Mission downtown.

"Four men have been shot in the head in the last three weeks. The men were all transients and sleeping alone at the time of the killings. Please tell everyone in this chapel and those along the streets to come indoors at night to any of the missions or shelters. When they are full please tell the men to group together, not to be alone at night, but huddle for safety. The lives of the men may depend upon their following these instructions."

Since that notice was distributed, police have searched their records and added five more victims to the list. Except for the victim added yesterday they are not transients, but they were all shot while out on the streets in the early morning hours. Commander William Booth, a spokesman for the police department, won't confirm it, but reportedly all the men were shot with a small caliber gun. So far Booth says the task force working on the case doesn't have many clues and only a little bit of information about the murderer.

"Frankly not nearly enough. We have a brief description: a male black, who is tall, slim, a hundred fifty to a hundred and seventy pounds, twenty-five to thirty years old. With a medium to large Afro haircut."

The first victim was shot on September 4th, the most recent October 7th. The crime took place in several Los Angeles neighborhoods. All five homeless men killed were sleeping outside downtown. Not in the skid road area, but nearby. Although the city's transients have been urged to sleep in shelters, there are thousands more men than beds are available. And not all the homeless choose to stay in the shelters. Still most of the men at the Union Rescue Mission know about the transient killer and admit to some concern.

Los Angeles police are still looking for another serial murderer. This outside slayer is suspected of killing seventeen women, mostly prostitutes during the past three years. I'm Salas Wason in Los Angeles.

Key to Exercises:

A. Fill in the information according to what you hear on the tape.
   1. Event: (A man was shot in the head.)
   2. Name of the victim: (Joseph Griffin)
   3. Place: (Los Angeles)
   4. The victim is a (homeless man).
   5. He is (the fifth one) shot by the killer.
   6. The killer is believed to be (a new serial killer).

B. Complete the notice at the Union Rescue Mission.
   (Four) men have been (shot) in the (head) in (the last three weeks). The men were all (transients) and (sleeping alone) at the time of the (killing). Please (tell everyone) in this (chapel) and those along the streets to (come indoors) at night to any of the (missions) or (shelters). When they are (full) please tell the men to (group together), not to be (alone) at night, but (huddle for safety). The lives of the men may (depend upon their following these instructions).

C. Fill in the description of the murderer.

590

Complexion: (black)

Height: (tall)

Build: (slim)

Weight: (150 – 170 pounds)

Age: (25 – 30 years)

Sex: (male)

Haircut: (medium – large Afro)

D. Answer the following questions.

1. When was the first victim shot?

   Answer: On September 4.

2. When did the most recent killing occur?

   Answer: On October 7.

3. What were the five homeless men doing when they were killed?

   Answer: They were sleeping.

4. Why do many transients still sleep outside?

   Answer: Because there are thousands more men than beds available. And on the other hand, not all the homeless choose to stay in shelters.

5. What are Los Angeles police still looking for?

   Anwer: Another serial murderer.

6. How many people is this murderer suspected of killing?

   Answer: 17.

7. What were most of the victims?

   Anwer: Most of them were women, chiefly prostitutes.

8. When were they killed?

   Answer: In the past three years.

Section Three:

Tapescript:

Outlining: How to Present a Seminar Paper

In this talk, I am going to give some advice on how to present a seminar paper.

At one time, most university teaching took the form of giving formal lectures. Nowadays, many university teachers try to involve their students more actively in the learning process. One of the ways in which this is done is by conducting seminars. In a seminar, what usually happens is this. One student is chosen to give his ideas on a certain topic. These ideas are then discussed by the other students (the participants) in the seminar.

What I'd like to discuss with you today is the techniques of presenting a paper at a seminar. As you know, there are two main stages involved in this. One is the preparation stage which involves researching and writing up a topic. The other stage is the presentation stage when you actually present the paper to your audience. It is this second stage that I am concerned with now. Let us therefore imagine that you have been asked to lead off a seminar discussion and that you've done all the necessary preparation. In other words you've done your research and you've written it up. How are you going to present it?

There are two ways in which this can be done.

The first method is to circulate copies of the paper in advance to all the participants. This gives them time to read it before the seminar, so that they can come already prepared with their own ideas about what you have written. The second method is where there is no time for previous circulation, or there is some other reason why the paper cannot be circulated. In that case, of course, the paper will

592

have to read aloud to the group, who will probably make their own notes on it while they are listening.

In this talk, I am going to concentrate on the first method, where the paper is circulated in advance, as this is the most efficient way of conducting a seminar; but most of what I am going to say also applies to the second method; and indeed may be useful to remember any time you have to speak in public.

You will probably be expected to introduce your paper even if it has been circulated beforehand. There are two good reasons for this. One is that the participants may have read the paper but forgotten some of the main points. The second reason is that some of the participants may not in fact have had time to read your paper, although they may have glanced through it quickly. They will therefore not be in a position to comment on it, unless they get some idea of what it's all about.

When you are introducing your paper, what you must not do is simply read the whole paper aloud. This is because:

Firstly, if the paper is a fairly long one, there may not be enough time for discussion. From your point of view, the discussion is the most important thing. It is very helpful for you if other people criticize your work: in that way you can improve it.

Secondly, a lot of information can be understood when one is reading. It is not so easy to pick up detailed information when one is listening. In other words, there may be lack of comprehension or understanding.

Thirdly, it can be very boring listening to something being read aloud. Anyway some of your audience may have read your paper carefully and will not thank you for having to go through all of it again.

Therefore, what you must do is follow the following nine points:

1. Decide on a time limit for your talk. Tell your audience what it is. Stick to your time limit. This is very important.

2. Write out your spoken presentation in the way that you intend to say it. This means that you must do some of the work of writing the paper again, in a sense. You may think that this is a waste of time, but it isn't. If a speaker tries to make a summary of his paper while he is standing in front of his audience, the results are usually disastrous.

3. Concentrate only on the main points. Ignore details. Hammer home the essence of your argument. If necessary, find ways of making your basic points so that your audience will be clear about what they are.

4. Try to make your spoken presentation lively and interesting. This does not necessarily mean telling jokes and anecdotes. But if you can think of interesting or amusing examples to illustrate your argument, use them.

5. If you are not used to speaking in public, write out everything you have to say, including examples, etc. Rehearse what you are going to say until you are word perfect.

6. When you know exactly what you are going to say, reduce it to outline notes. Rehearse your talk again, this time from the outline notes. Make sure you can find your way easily from the outline notes to the full notes, in case you forget something.

7. At the seminar, speak from the outline notes. But bring both sets of notes and your original paper to the meeting. Knowing that you have a full set of notes available will be good for your self-confidence.

8. Look at your audience while your are speaking. The technique to use is this. First read the appropriate parts of your notes silently (if you are using outline notes, this won't take you long). Then look up at your audience and say what you have to say. Never speak while you are still reading. While you are looking at your audience, try to judge what they are thinking. Are they following you? You will never make contact with your audience if your eyes are fixed on the paper in front of you.

9. Make a strong ending. One good way of doing this is to repeat your main points briefly and invite questions or comments.

Perhaps I can sum up by saying this. Remember that listening is very different from reading. Something that is going to be listened to has therefore got to be prepared in a different way from something that is intended to be read.

Key to Exercises:
A. General Comprehension. Write a T in front of a statement if it is true according to the recording and write an F if it is false.
  1. (T) Seminar is one of the ways in which students can be actively involved in the learning process.
  2. (F) The preparation stage refers to the time the students write the seminar papers.
  3. (F) There is no use circulating one's copies of the paper in advance to all participants because often they don't read it at all.
  4. (T) No matter whether you have circulated copies of your paper in advance, you'd better give a brief presentation in class.
  5. (T) Writing out your presentation doesn't mean making a

summary of your paper.

6. (F) In order to make your presentation interesting, you should always remember to tell jokes or anecdotes.

7. (T) Try to look at your audience when you are speaking, otherwise you will never make contact with your audience.

8. (T) Your presentation must be prepared in a different way from your paper because it is intended to be listened to.

B. Suggested Abbreviations:

participants: parts.   comprehension: compr.

presentation: pres.   something: sth.

C. Notetaking: Complete the following outline.

Title: (How to Present a Seminar Paper)

I. What is a seminar?

(1 st. gives ideas which are discussed by other sts.)

II. Stages of presenting a seminar

A. (Preparation)

1. (researching)

2. (writing up a topic)

B. (Presentation)

1. Two ways

a.. (circulate copies in advance)

b. (read aloud the paper in class)

2. First method

can be applied to (2nd method or any time you have to speak in public)

a. Introduce (your paper)

Reasons: (1)(parts, forget main ideas)

（2）(parts, only glanced at paper)

    b. Do not (read the whole paper aloud)

    Reasons: (1)(not enough time for discussion)

              (2) (lack of compr. or understanding)

              (3)(boring)

C. Procedure

  1. (Decide on a time limit)

  2. (Write out spoken pres.)

  3. (concentrate on the main points)

  4. (Make spoken pres. lively & interesting)

  5. (Write out everything, rehearse)

  6. (Reduce to outline notes)

    Make sure you can find your way easily (from out-
line notes to full notes), in case you forget something.

  7. (Speak from outline notes)

  8. (Look at the andience while speaking)

  9. (Make a strong ending)

III. Conclusion

  (The oral pres. should be prepared in a different way from
sth. intended to be read.)

Lesson 30

Section One:

Tapescript:

An Alarming Experience on the Road

Jane : Now look, er, what's all this, er, story about you and this car l've been hearing so much about? Everybody else has been hearing it, but you haven't told me. (Mhm)

John : Well, I was driving to Norwich with a friend, erm, we teach there and, erm, I was driving behind a Lotus Elan sports-car (Yes) on dual-carriageway and, erm, after about, er, three or four miles, er, behind this car, er, we, we left(the) dual-carriageway and, erm, entered a two-way road. And, er, this Lotus suddenly slowed down for no reason whatsoever. (There ...)

Jane: Not a side road or anything?

John : No, no, no turning off, no lay-bys, and it just slowed down, and, er, I thought, that's, that's odd and, er, I overtook the Lotus, er, slowly and, erm, looked over at the driver, ... and as I did, I saw him slump over the wheel.

Jane: oh, how awful!

John: Yes.

Jane: So what did you do next?

John : So, erm, I pulled into the kerb about thirty yards or so, er, in front of the Lotus (Yes) and, erm...my, er, passenger and

598

myself got out and we, we walked back towards his car. My
friend was on the grass verge and, er, I was in the middle of
the road. we never even, erm, reached the car. I was about
five yards from the car when, er, suddenly, erm, there was a
noise of full acceleration and the car just shot forward – nearly
ran me down. So I had to leap for my life. I was absolutely
shaken because the car must have missed me by about half an
inch or so, (I mean,), (How dread...) it just shot past me
and I saw my car smashed in front of my eyes. (How
dreadful!) Yea, just, just smashed to smithereens, pieces of
car flying all over the road and, erm, both cars locked together
went down the road and there was a bend at the bottom of the
road and I thought well, th ... , the next thing is going to be
a head-on collision. (Yes, of course.) Erm. But, fortunately,
nothing came in the opposite direction and, erm, and then
both cars went across the road and, erm, up a grass bank,
which ... it was quite a tall bank and, erm, and, er, at the
top of the bank there was a large hedge. Well, my car left the
Lotus a, and literally took off and shot through the hedge
(Oh, goodness!) and landed in a ploughed field. (Yes) But
the Lotus veered to the left and got stuck in the hedge, in the
thick part of the hedge. And, erm, the acceleration was still
on full and the back wheels were tearing up the grass verge,
throwing mud and soil, earth and grass all over the road, er, it
was just, you know, absolutely terrif ... (How terrify ...)
Yes, (Yes) because the Lotus, erm, radiator burst and, and
there was steam everywhere; it was like a, like a cloud of
steam and smoke, and, er, the first thing, erm, of course, we
thought of doing was to get the driver out (Well, of course.)

Yes. (Quite) So, erm, we tried to get the passenger door open, (Yes) but it was locked, so we had to climb through the hedge and, er, get round to the driving-door. Well, by that time, there was so much steam we couldn't see, so it was a matter of fumbling in the, in the steam and smoke and thinking any moment the car was going to explode.

Jane : Yes, it wasn't on fire, in fact, that, at that point, was it?

John : No, no, it wasn't on fire, but, erm, with the noise of the engine an, and all the steam it was just you know, very, frightening. (Oh, how dreadful!) Erm, well we managed to get the driver out, turn the ignition off. We laid him in the mud actually because it was a ploughed field and, (Yes) er, I ran out in the road and shouted for help and, erm ... er, a car driver told me help, er, was already on its way and, erm, I, er, managed to get blankets from people that had stopped and, er, we tried to make the man comfortable, and erm ... a man appeared shortly afterwards and he was from a nearby American airbase and, er, er, he was a medical man, so he was able to, erm, (Examine him) e, examine him and, er, I helped him, tried to, you know, er, make the man, er, well, you know, do all we could for the man. Erm ...

Jane: He was unconscious, was he?

John : Yes, yes; ... and then the police, a ..., police arrived and (the) fire brigade (Yes) and, er, ... er, we were told to, er, leave the scene by the police and go to the police station and, erm, there we had to make a statement, (Yes, of course.) and, er, I had to have a breathalyser test, and ...

Jane : But they thought you'd been in the car ... of course they did. Yes

600

John : Because, because they thought I'd, th, they automatically thought I'd been driving the car (Of course. Yes) and, er, when I told them the story they had to apologize for giving me a breathalyser and they said, 'Gosh,' you know, 'how, how incredible'.

Jane: So, what happened to the man?

John : And, erm, we were in the middle of making the statements and, erm, the telephone rang and the, the policeman, erm, was told that, that the man was dead, (Oh!) and, erm, and then two days later we had to attend a Coroner's inquest where we were told that the man had died of a heart attack and, in fact, he was dead, erm, before he crashed into my car.

Jane: Oh－h－h! What an alarming story! How dreadful!

John: Yes.

Key to Exercises:

A. Choose the best answer (a, b or c) to complete each of the following statements.

1. The narrator _____ when the accident happened.

    a. was driving in his car

  * b. was walking along the road

    c. was standing by the side road

2. The narrator's car _____.

  * a. was smashed to pieces

    b. exploded in the collision

    c. was left intact

3. The driver was pulled out _____.

  * a. through the driving-door

    b. through the passenger door

c. through the front window

4. The narrator first managed to get help from _____.

   a. residents nearby

   b. people in a nearby American airbase

* c. people that had stopped

5. The driver died _____.

   a. when he crashed into the other car

   b. when he was on the way to the hospital

* c. before the car crash

B. True or False Questions. Write a T in front of a statement if it is true according to the recording and write an F if it is false.

1. (T) The narrator is probably a teacher.

2. (F) A man was driving a Lotus Elan Sports-car behind the narrator.

3. (F) The narrator noticed the Lotus suddenly slowed down when he left it and took another road.

C. Answer the following questions.

1. Why did the narrator and his passenger get off their car?

   Answer: Because they saw the driver of the Lotus slump over the wheel. They wanted to help him.

2. What happened when the narrator got near the Lotus?

   Answer: It suddenly shot forward and nearly ran him down.

3. How did the narrator manage to save his life when the Lotus suddenly changed into full acceleration?

   Answer: He leapt for his life and the car missed him by about half an inch.

4. What would be the next thing, according to the narrator?

602

Answer: A head-on collision.

5. Why did the narrator think so?

Answer: Because there was a bend at the bottom of the road.
If there was a car coming in the opposite direction,
the two locked cars would crash into it.

D. Give a description about things happened to the two cars . Complete the following statements according to what you hear on the tape.

1. The narrator's car:

(1) It left (the Lotus), took off and shot (through the hedge).

(2) It landed (in a ploughed field).

2. The Lotus:

(1) It veered (to the left) and got stuck (in the thick part of the hedge).

(2) The acceleration was still (on full).

(3) The back wheels (were tearing up the grass verge) throwing (mud and soil, earth and grass) all over (the road).

(4) The radiator (burst) and there was (steam) everywhere.

E. Complete the following list of things that the narrator managed to do after the crash.

1. We tried to get (the passenger door open).

2. We had to (climb through the hedge) and get round (to the driving door).

3. We managed to get (the driver out), turn (the ignition off).

4. We laid (him in the mud).

5. I ran (out in the road) and shouted (for help).

6. I managed to get (blankets) from people that had stopped.

7. We tried to make (the man comfortable).

F. Answer the following questions.

1. Who arrived at the scene later?

Answer: The police and the fire brigade.

2. What did the police ask the narrator and his friend to do?

Answer: The police asked them to go to the police station, make a statemeat and have a breathalyser test.

3. How did the man die ?

Answer: he died of a heart attack.

Section Two:

Tapescript:

New Report: Air Controllers Removed from Job for Drug Use

Today the Federal Aviation Administration reviewed that five air traffic controllers based in Kansas City have been taken off the job because of drug use. Earlier this month thirteen controllers at the southern California centre were removed from their jobs for off-duty drug use. Also today the FAA continued to investigate alleged drug use at the nation's sixth largest airlines, US Air. NPR's Wendy Kaufman reports.

"Drug use, even off – duty, is banned for controllers under Federal Aviation Administration rules. So far the FAA has conducted investigations into alleged drug use by controllers at two facilities – Palmdale in southern California and now Kansas City.

In southern California thirty-four controllers were taken off their radar scopes. Pending the outcome of investigation, thirteen tested positive for drugs, and we were told they could quit or enter a treatment program, or opt for treatment. In Kansas City thirty-six controllers were investigated. The five who tested positive for drugs have all agreed to undergo treatment. Three controllers are still under investigation. The proportion of drug users is small. Of the roughly five hundred controllers at the two facilities only seventy were suspect, and of those only eighteen tested positive for drugs. Air traffic control supervisors say they don't see drug use as a serious problem in their work force. Still as one FAA official put it, one drug user is one too many.

Right now there is no routine drug testing for controllers though that will change around the first of the year. There will be pre-employment urine test and test along with the annual physical exam. According to the FAA, there has never been a fatal accident involving a major US airline in which alcohol or drug abuse was a factor for the controllers or for the pilots. But there have been a sizeable number of fatal accidents in which commuter pilots, air taxi pilots and private pilots had been drinking, and a much smaller number of cases in which drugs were a factor.

On another matter, drug use, or, more precisely, alleged drug use by flight crews at US Air has been front-page news in Pittsburgh, the airline's operating base. A grand jury is conducting an investigation into alleged drug use, sales and distribution. Over the weekend, a Pittsburgh press newspaper quoted area hospital officials, who said they had treated about twenty US Air flight crew members for cocaine overdoses. US Air acknowledges that one pilot nearly died of an overdose. He had last flown on September 7th, and was taken to the hospital on September 10th. The airline has removed him from flight duty, and the FAA is considering revoking

605

his medical certificate that would mean he could not fly any aircraft. Meanwhile the FAA is conducting an investigation of the airline and is working with the grand jury and the FBI. I'm Wendy Kaufman in Washington.

Key to Exercises:

A. Fill in the following chart according to what you hear on the tape.

Place	No. of controllers investigated	No. of controllers removed from jobs	Reason
Kansas City	36	5	drug use
Palmdale	34	13	off-duty drug use

B. Complete the following information according to what you hear.

1. Today the FAA continued to (investigate alleged drug use) at (the nation's sixth largest airlines, US Air).

2. So far the FAA has conducted (investigations into alleged drug use by controllers) at (two facilities) Palmdale in (southern California) and now (Kansas City).

C. Choose the best answer (a, b or c) which is opposite to the fact discussed in the recording.

1. Controllers _____.
   a. will be given pre-employment urine test
   b. will be given the annual physical exam
   * c. have been given routine drug testing

2. Alcohol or drug abuse was a major factor for fatal accidents for _____.
   a. commuter pilots

606

        b. taxi pilots

    *   c. controllers

D. Complete the following information according to what you hear
   on the tape.

    1. A grand jury is conducting an investigation into

        a. (alleged drug use),

        b. (sales), and

        c. (distribution).

    2. Pittsburg area hospital had treated about (20 US Air flight
       crew members) for (cocaine overdoses).

E. Answer the following questions.

    1. What does US Air acknowledge ?

       Answer: US Air acknowledges that a pilot nearly died of an
               overdose.

    2. When was the pilot's last flight ?

       Answer: September 7.

    3. What has the airline done to the pilot ?

       Answer: It has removed him from flight duty.

    4. What is the FAA planning to do with the pilot ?

       Answer: To revoke his medical certificate.

Section Three:

Tapescript:

Outlining: Lectures and Notetaking

   Notetaking is a complex activity which requires a high level of
ability in many separate skills. Today I'm going to analyse the four
most important of these skills.

Firstly, the student has to understand what the lecturer says as he says it. The student cannot stop the lecture in order to look up a new word or check an unfamiliar sentence pattern. This puts the non-native speaker of English under a particularly severe strain. Often – as we've already seen in a previous lecture – he may not be able to recognize words in speech which he understands straight away in print. He'll also meet words in a lecture which are completely new to him. While he should, of course, try to develop the ability to infer their meaning from the context, he won't always be able to do this successfully. He must not allow failure of this kind to discourage him however. It's often possible to understand much of a lecture by concentrating solely on those points which are most important. But how does the student decide what's important? This is in itself another skill he must try to develop. It is, in fact, the second of the four skills I want to talk about today.

Probably the most important piece of information in a lecture is the title itself. If this is printed (or referred to) beforehand the student should study it carefully and make sure he's in no doubt about its meaning. Whatever happens he should make sure that he writes it down accurately and completely. A title often implies many of the major points that will later be covered in the lecture itself. It should help the student therefore to decide what the main point of the lecture will be.

A good lecturer, of course, often signals what's important or unimportant. He may give direct signals or indirect signals. Many lecturers, for example, explicitly tell their audience that a point is important and that the student should write it down. Unfortunately, the lecturer who's trying to establish a friendly relationship with his audience is likely on these occasions to employ a colloquial style. He might say such things as 'This is, of course, the crunch' or 'Perhaps you'd like to get it down'. Although this will help the student who's a native English-speaker, it may very well cause difficulty for the non-native English speaker. He'll therefore have to make a big effort to get used to the various styles of his lecturers.

It's worth remembering that most lecturers also give indirect signals to indicate what's important. They either pause or speak slowly or speak loudly or use a greater range of intonation, or they employ a combination of these devices, when they say something important. Conversely, their sentences are delivered quickly, softly, within a narrow range of intonation and with short or infrequent pauses when they are saying something which is incidental. It is, of course, helpful for the student to be aware of this and for him to focus his attention accordingly.

Having sorted out the main points, however, the student still has to write them down. And he has to do this quickly and clearly. This is, in fact, the third basic skill he must learn to develop. In order to write at speed most students find it helps to abbreviate. They also try to select only those words which give maximum information. These are usually nouns, but sometimes verbs or adjectives. Writing only one point on each line also helps the student to understand his notes when he comes to read them later. An important difficulty is, of course, finding time to write the notes. If the student chooses the wrong moment to write he may miss a point of greater importance. Connecting words or connectives may guide him to a correct choice here. Those connectives which indicate that the argument is proceeding in the same direction also tell the listener that it's a safe time to write. 'Moreover', 'furthermore', 'also', etc., are examples of this. Connectives such as 'however', 'on the other hand' or 'nevertheless' usually mean that new and perhaps unexpected information is going to follow. Therefore, it may, on these occasions, be more appropriate to listen.

The fourth skill that the student must develop is one that is frequently neglected. He must learn to show the connections between the various points he's noted. This can often be done more effectively by a visual presentation than by a lengthy statement in words. Thus the use of spacing, of underlining, and of conventional symbols plays an important part in efficient note-taking. Points should be numbered, too, wherever possible. In this way the student can see at a glance the framework of the lecture.

Key to Exercises:

A. General Comprehension: Write a T in front of a statement if it is true according to the recording and write an F if it is false.

1. (T) A student normally has only one chance to understand the lecturer.

2. (F) Students should not be discouraged by the new words in lectures, because they can always look them up in the dictionary later.

3. (T) Students should always write down the title correctly and completely, for it will help the students catch the main points of the lecture.

4. (F) You can always be sure that a lecturer will always indicate if an important point is to follow.

5. (T) Students should also pay attention to the indirect signals a lecturer uses to indicate an important point.

6. (F) A student needs to make a note of every point that the

lecturer makes.

7. (F) A student should write his notes when the lecturer is giving important information.

8. (T) Spacing and underlining help to show the structure of
the lecture. .

B. Suggested Abbreviations:

unfamiliar: unfam.	concentrate: concen.
important: imp.	information: info.
intonation: into.	maximum: max.
usually: usu.	verb: v.
adjective: adj.	argument: argu.

C. Notetaking: Complete the following outline.

  Title: (Lectures and Notetaking)

Skills of notetaking:

  I. Understand what the lecturer says (as he says it).

  A. It's diff. to understand a lecture.

    1. Cannot stop (the lecturer to look up a new word
    or unfam. pattern).

    2. May not recog. (words he understands in print)

    3. Meet (completely new words).

  B. Solutions:

    1. Infer (meaning of a word from context)

    2. Don't be discouraged if (can't guess the
    meaning).

    3. Often poss. to understand much by (concen. sole-
    ly on imp. points.

  II. What's imp.?

611

A. Most imp. info: (title)

.Make sure to write it down. (accurately & completely).

Implies (many major points).

B. Direct signals & indirect signals.

1. Direct signals:

a. Explicit: (write it down)

b. Colloquial: (get used to)

2. Indirect signals:

a. Sth. imp.: (pause, speak slowly or loudly, use a greater range of into. combination of these)

b. Sth. incidental: (sentences delivered quickly & softly, narrow range of into., short or infrequent pauses)

III. Writing down (main points)

A. Use (abbreviations)

B. Select (words that give max. info.)

usu. (nouns) s'times (v. or adj.)

C. Write (1 point on each line)

D. Time to write:

1. Connectives that indicate (the argu. is proceeding in the same direction): write

e.g. (moreover, furthermore, also).

2. Connectives that indicate (new or unexpected info).: Listen

e.g. (however, on the other hand, nevertheless).

IV. Show (connections between points noted down) by

(visual) presentation.

A. (spacing)

B. (underlining)

C. (conversational symbols)

D. (points numbered)

Section Four:

Enjoy Your English:

Tapescript:

The Way We Were

Memories, light the corners of my mind,

Misty watercolour memories,

Of the way we were,

Scattered pictures of the smiles we left behind,

Smiles we gave to one another,

For the way we were,

Can it be that it was all so simple then,

Or has time rewritten every line,

If we had the chance to do it all again,

Tell me, would we, could we.

Memories may be beautiful and yet,

What's too painful to remember,

We simply choose to forget,

So it's the laughter we will remember,

Whenever we remember the way we were,

The way we were.

Lesson 31

Tapescript:

Graphology

Denise: On the contrary, I don't agree at all with people who say graphology is all nonsense. I think that at last it is beginning to be taken seriously as a proper science and not as some kind of fairground entertainment.

Leo: How did you start to become interested in graphology?

Denise: I've always been fascinated by people and what they are like, and then one day I was just looking at a book about different styles of handwriting and I got to thinking that it must all mean something, because we all have a different and individual style of our own. So that's how I began.

Leo: What exactly is the connection between the way we write and the way we are?

Denise: If you think about it, our handwriting, and our doodling too, are all products of our brain – a kind of extension of ourselves on paper, so, consciously or unconsciously, we are giving a kind of 'computer printout' of what we think or feel when we write. As the brain is where our thoughts and feelings lie, there is every reason to assume that our character is transmitted into our handwriting.

Leo: Now I know that a number of European firms have used

614

graphology to evaluate potential employees for some time now, but I believe it's catching on in America too.

Denise: I'm now running my own San Francisco-based consultancy firm, which I started a decade ago, and now over two hundred firms come to me for advice on would-be employees.

Leo: How does it work out, then? Do they show you samples of an applicant's handwriting?

Denise: Yes, most companies nowadays require their new job applicants to provide at least a one-page writing sample which is then passed over to me for interpretation.

Leo: How long does it take you to analyse a sample?

Denise: Oh, anything from three to eight hours, depending on the amount of detail required by the client.

Leo: And what can you tell from the sample you get?

Denise: A whole range of personality traits can be assessed, such as enthusiasm, ambition, imagination, diligence, sincerity, secretiveness – just about everything, in fact.

Leo: Can you give us some tell-tale clues about the way we write? I'm sure our listeners will all be dying to hear something.

Denise: OK, you just write the letter 't', not a capital but an ordinary 't', please, Leo.

Leo: All right. There you are. Now what can you tell me from that?

Denise: Mmm ... well, the 't' you've written, which is more or less straight up and crossed with a diagonal stroke from south-west to north-east, as it were, indicates an optimistic kind of character to me. Would you describe yourself in that way?

Leo: Mmm, yes, I think so. Can you describe any other kinds of 't' for the benefit of our listeners?

Denise: Yes, of course. If, for example, you had written a 't' but crossed it only with a stroke on the left of the vertical stem, which didn't even reach it in fact, that would indicate a procrastinating character, someone who puts things off until tomorrow. Inefficiency can be identified by a 't' where there are two vertical strokes in the stem, reaching up to a rounded point, and then crossed right through. Mmm, what else can I say? A thick cross on the left of the stem, tapering to a point on the right of the stem, tells me that the writer is a sarcastic kind of person. Another thing is that a very practical sort of person always crosses his 't' halfway down the letter, whereas a 't' crossed high up the stem shows a dreamer. The letters 'm' and 'n' are also indicative of personality, depending on whether they are rounded or wedge-shaped.

Leo: I see. That's most interesting.

Denise: One little success story of mine, which I must tell you about, concerns Royal Office Products of New York. They once took a big chance on my analysis of an applicant's writing. His name was Harry Benson, in fact, and he was after an executive job, and he was a person they would never have taken on otherwise ... because he came across very badly orally and in his appearance. However, on the strength of my interpretation of his writing they took him on, and now, only a few years later, he's already President of the company.

Leo: I'd like now to turn to doodling because most of us doodle away merrily, quite absentmindedly, and hear what you have to say about that.

Denise: Oh, you can tell a great deal about people from their doodles as well as their handwriting. The doodle, to my mind, is a

616

message straight from the subconscious. The reason you are feeling the way you are is always written in your doodles.

Leo: Can you give us some indication of what you mean?

Denise: Take, for example, very angular or tangled horizontal lines ... Now, if a person when doodling does a lot of them, it is very indicative of hidden anger and frustration. Arrows, when drawn, stand for ambition, and when they are aimed in a lot of different directions, this will mean confusion in reaching goals.

Leo: Before we started the programme, I happened to be doodling on this pad here. What does that tell you about me? – that's if you can repeat it! (Laughs).

Denise: Well, let me see. You've drawn a very detailed and symmetrical design which tells me, superficially at any rate, that you are a very orderly and rather precise person – a conformist, if you like – who doesn't like chaos and has to have everything planned.

Leo: Yes, well, you're right to some extent. I've got one or two others here done by people in the studio. What can you say about them?

Denise: This one here, which has lots of little stars on it – now, they generally represent hope. And here, on this one, somebody has drawn a human eye, which is indicative of a suspicious or distrustful nature.

Leo: I'd better not tell you who is the artist, then!

Denise: Now, in this one, somebody has drawn a little human figure, which probably means they make friends very easily – and enemies too, incidentally.

Leo: Does everybody doodle?

Denise: Most people do it because they are bored, but some do it

617

more than others. Creative people like architects or fashion designers do a great deal of aimless doodling, whereas writers, on the other hand, do very little because they have a way of expressing themselves in words. I think probably people with disabilities are the best doodlers, because their normal outlets are blocked.

Leo: What about actual writing implements, does it make any difference what you choose to write with?

Denise: Indeed, yes. If you give people a choice of writing implements — say a pencil, a felt tip or an ordinary pen — the middle-of-the-roaders will go for the ordinary pen, those who want to leave the biggest impression with the least amount of work will take the felt tip. As for pencils, I won't say it's true in every case, some pencil users aren't very honest; pencils can be erased, you see, so it's a way of leaving no traces. Criminals will almost always choose a pencil, although of course I'm not suggesting that all pencil users are criminals, of course.

Leo: Well, thank you very much, Denise. That was very interesting, and I'm sure from now on we'll all be careful not to leave our doodles lying around.

Key to Exercises:

A. Answer the following questions.

1. Has graphology been widely accepted by people?

   Answer: No. But it is beginning to be taken seriously as a proper science.

2. What is the connection between the way we write and the way we are?

   Answer: Handwriting and doodling are a kind of extension of

618

ourselves on paper. We are giving a kind of 'computer printout' of what we think or feel when we write. Therefore our character is transmitted into our handwriting.

3. How did the interviewee become interested in graphology?

Answer: He has always been fascinated by people and what they are like. And by looking at a book about different styles of handwriting one day, he realized that it must all mean something, and then he started his study.

4. According to the interviewer, where is graphology being used now?

Answer: A number of European firms and American ones.

5. How many firms come to the interviewee's consultancy firm?

Answer: Over two hundred.

6. What do these firms come for?

Answer: They come for advice on would-be employees.

7. What do the clients have to provide to the interviewee for interpretation?

Answer: At least a one-page writing sample.

8. How long does it take for the interviewee to analyse a sample?

Answer: It takes him anything from three to eight hours, depending on the amount of detail required by the client.

9. What can the interviewee tell from the sample?

Answer: A whole range of personality traits can be assessed, such as enthusiasm, ambition, imagination, diligence, sincerity, and secretiveness.

B. Fill in the following chart about the interviewee's interpretation of the different handwritings of the letter "t".

Sample	Shape	Interpretation
1	It's more or less (straight up) and (crossed) with a (diagonal stroke) from (south – west) to (north – east).	An optimistic kind of person
2	It's (crossed) only with (a stroke) on the (left) of the (vertical stem), which doesn't even (reach) the stem.	A procrastinating character
3	There are (2 vertical strokes) in the (stem), reaching up to (a rounded point), and then (crossed) right through.	Inefficiency
4	A (thick cross) on the (left) of the (stem), tapering to (a point) on the (right) of the (stem).	A sarcastic kind of person
5	It's (crossed halfway) down the (letter).	A very practical sort of person
6	It's (crossed high) up the (stem).	A dreamer

C. Complete the following information based on the "success story".

Company: (Royal Office Products of New York)

Job Applicant: (Harry Benson)

Job Applied: (an executive officer)

Reason for not being hired: (He came across very badly orally and in his appearance.)

Present Position: (President of the company)

D. Answer the following questions.

1. How do most people doodle?

Answer: They doodle away merrily and absentmindedly.

2. What does doodling mean to the interviewee?

Answer: It is a message straight from the subconscious.

3. What do a lot of angular or tangled horizontal lines mean in the doodle?

Answer: They indicate hidden anger and frustration.

4. What do arrows stand for?

Answer: They stand for ambition.

5. What does it mean when arrows are aimed in a lot of different directions?

Answer: It means confusion in reaching goals.

E. Identification. Match each item in Column I with one item in Column II by recognizing the description of the doodle and its indication.

Column I	Column II
1. a human eye	a. hope
2. lots of little stars	b. a conformist
3. a little human figure	c. a suspicious or distrustful nature
4. a very detailed and symmetrical design	d. make friends very easily and enemies indicentally

Answer: (1) – (c); (2) – (a); (3) – (d); (4) – (b)

F. Fill up the following information chart according to the tape.

1. Best doodles: (people with disabilities)

Reason: (Their normal outlets are blocked.)

2. People who do a great deal of aimless doodling:

(creative people like architects or fashion designers)

3. People who do very little doodling:

   (writers)

   Reason: (They have a way of expressing themselves in words.)

4. Reason for most people who do doodling:

   (They are bored.)

G. Complete the chart about writing implements.

Writing implements	User
ordinary pen	(the middle-of-the-roaders)
felt tip	(those who want to leave the biggest impression with the least amount of work)
pencil	(people who want to leave no traces, who are not honest; criminals)

Section Two:

Tapescript:

New Report: Smoking Harms Baby During Pregnancy

The number of adult smokers in the United States keeps going down, down, down, almost twenty percent in the past decade, according to a new survey by the American Cancer Society. Their report based on the government's statistics shows that, while more and more women are taking up the smoking habit, more than enough men are quitting to make up for it. But that news about the women troubles Dr. Ervin Mann, an obstetrician at Paxtang, Pennsylvania and he's decided to do something about it. If you are a pregnant woman and if you smoke cigarettes, then Dr. Mann will make you an offer that he hopes you can't refuse.

"What we will do is, if you will not smoke throughout your pregnancy, then we'll offer you one hundred dollars off the obstetric bill."

"And how much is the typical bill, so how big is this discount going to be?"

"Basically the obstetric bill is one thousand two hundred dollars. So it's a little less than ten percent."

"What inspired you to try this hundred-dollar rebate?"

"We know that smoking during pregnancy results in lower birthrate insense. In other words because of smoking babies are small at birth. And that's the one thing we really know. There have been other things that've been implicated that there is increasing birth defects in smoking women."

"You should explain to me, explain to our listeners why that is of a concern to a doctor, or to a mother and her baby?"

"We know that smaller weight babies have more difficulty in thriving in an early life, so that it takes both babies who are light in weight at the time of birth, will take at least a year of good care before they will come up to the standards."

"So what are the results, does money talk in this case, or are women in your practice buying the idea?"

"Well, money partially talks. We have had seventy-five women who have completed their pregnancy who have previously smoked. And of those seventy-five women, thirty-five of them have gone without smoking during the pregnancy."

"Ah, so they're getting the hundred dollars."

"They are getting the hundred dollars back. Certainly we

haven't had any low birth weight children in that group of patients."

"How do you know for sure that those thirty-five women have indeed not smoked at all? Maybe they're misleading you."

"It's all an honor system. Each time they come for an examination they reaffirm their refusal to smoke. And certainly we trust those patients and feel that they are following it. Other patients, of course, have stated they have started smoking again. So I think it's a pretty good cross section."

"And just one more thing. And when, if we come back to you in a year from now, how much do you think ..."

"I can improve those figures."

"Let me ask you this though, How much do you think you will be paying women to stop smoking?"

"Well, we'll probably be raising it up to two-hundred- or two-hundred-fifty-dollar range, I would think."

Ervin Mann is an obstetrician at paxtang, Pennsylvania.

Key to Exercises:

A. Complete the following information according to what you hear on the tape.

1. The US. government's statistics show:

    a. the number of adult smokers keeps (going down, down, down);

    b. more and more women are (taking up the smoking habit);

    c. more than enough men are (quitting to make up for it).

B. True or False Questions. Write a T in front of a statement if it is

true according to the recording and write an F if it is false.

1. (F) Dr. Ervin Mann's is working in the American Cancer society.

2. (F) Dr. Ervin Mann's offer equals one thousand two hundred dollars.

3. (T) One result of smoking during pregnancy is that babies are small at birth.

4. (F) Seventy-five women have completed their pregnancy without smoking during the pregnancy.

C. Choose the best answer (a, b or c) to complete each of the following statements.

1. The ' figures ' the interviewee mentioned at the end refers to _____.

   * a. the number of pregnant women who would quit smoking
   b. the weight of babies at birth
   c. the money he will give away in a year from now

2. The offer will be raised up to _____.

   * a. 200 or 250 dollars
   b. 300 or 350 dollars
   c. 500 or 550 dollars

D. Fill in the blanks.

1. We know that (smaller weight babies) have more difficulty in (thriving in an early life), so that it takes both babies who are (light in weight) at the time of birth, will take at least (a year of good care) before they will come up (to the standards).

2. It's all (an honor system). Each time they come (for an ex-

amination) they reaffirm (their refusal to smoke). And certainly we (trust)those patients and feel that (they are following it). Other patients, of course, have stated they (have started smoking again). So I think it's (a pretty good cross section).

Section Three:
Tapescript:
Outlining: Marriage Customs

Today we are going to look at the social custom of marriage from a sociological point of view. All societies make provisions for who may mate with whom. The benefits of the social recognition of marriage for children are obvious. It gives them an identity, membership of a socially recognized group and some indication of who must support them and their mother.

Now then all societies have marriage, but there are wide variations in marriage systems. I will give three of the important areas of variation, and some details of each area. The three areas I shall deal with are: firstly, the number of mates each marriage partner may have; secondly, the locality of the marriage (that is, where do the newly married partners set up home?); and thirdly, what arrangements there are for the transfer of wealth after the marriage. Let me deal with each of these in turn.

First, how many mates? In existing human societies there are three possibilities. Most societies recognize POLYGYNY or the right of a man to take more than one wife. In a few societies (not in Africa) there is POLYANDRY, in which a woman is married to two or more men at the same time. Finally, especially in Europe and societies of European origin, there is MONOGAMY. Monogamy limits one man to one wife and vice-versa.

The second area of variation is, as we have said, the locality of the marriage. Here there seem to be three possibilities: at the husband's home, at the wife's home, or in some new place. The old term for the arrangement when a wife moves to her husband's family's household is a PATRILOCAL marriage; a more modern term is VIRILOCAL. The opposite, when the man moves, is termed MATRILOCAL or UXORILOCAL marriage. The third possibility when they set up a new household somewhere else is called NEOLOCAL marriage.

The last area of variation is transfer of wealth on marriage. Here, once more, we seem to have three possibilities. Firstly we have BRIDEWEALTH. In this system wealth is transferred by the husband or his relatives to the bride's family.

This, of course, is the system familiar in Africa. We should remember that the bridewealth may take the form of the husband's labour services to his father-in-law rather than giving cattle or money. In some other societies the opposite system prevails and the wife brings with her a portion or DOWRY in the form of money or other wealth such as land. This was the system of, for example, traditional European societies, and is still practised in the Irish countryside. The third possibility is for the transfer of wealth to take the form of gifts to help the young couple set up the new household. This system is associated with the neolocal type of marriage. In England, these gifts are called wedding-presents. The near kin (that is, the near relatives) of both bride and groom contribute and so do friends, neighbours and workmates. The presents customarily take the form of useful household goods, such as saucepans, tea sets or blankets.

627

Key to Exercises:

A. General Comprehension: Give brief answers to the following questions.

    1. What are the benefits of the social recognition of marriage for children?

        Answer: It gives them an identity, membership of a socially recognised group and some indication of who must support them and their mother.

    2. What are the three areas the speaker will deal with in this lecture?

        Answer: (a) Number of mates;

                (b) locality of marriage;

                (c) transfer of wealth.

    3. What are the three possibilities for the number of mates?

        Answer: (a) Polygyny;

                (b) polyandry;

                (c) monogamy.

    4. What are the possibilities for the locality of the marriage?

        Answer: (a) Patrilocal;

                (b) matrilocal;

                (c) neolocal.

    5. What are the possibilities for the transfer of wealth?

        Answer: (a) Bridewealth;

                (b) dowry;

                (c) gifts.

B. Suggested Abbreviations.

marriage: ma.

628

C. Notetaking: Complete the following outline.

Title: (Marriage customs)

I. Benefits of ma. for children

    A. (identity)

    B. (membership of a social group)

    C. (who must support them)

II. No. of mates

    A. (polygyny: 1 man ＋ more than 1 wife － － most societies)

    B. (polyandry: 1 woman ＋ more than 1 husband － － few societies, not in Africa)

    C. (monogamy: 1 man ＋ 1 wife － － Europe)

III. Locality of the marriage

    A. (patrilocal: at husband's home)

    B. (matrilocal: at wife's home)

    C. (neolocal: in some new place)

IV. Transfer of wealth

    A. (bridewealth: wealth from husband or his relatives to bride's family － － Africa)

    form: (labor service)

    B. (dowry: brought by wife － － Europe, still in Irish countryside) form: (money, land)

    C. (gifts: England － － wedding presents from near kin, friends, neighbors & workmates)

    form: (useful household goods, e. g. saucepans, tea sets, blankets)

Supplementary Reading:

Graphology

Graphology is the study of handwriting. Often the term refers to analysis of handwriting to discover the personality traits of the writer. Much handwriting analysis is pseudoscience, closer to fortune-telling than to serious research. On the other hand, some psychologists believe that the relation of personality to style of writing is worth further study.

Doubts about the validity of graphology do not apply to forensic graphology, the technical study of handwriting for such purposes as demonstrating in court that a signature or document is genuine or forged.

Pseudoscientific Graphology. For centuries, self-appointed experts have tried to discern people's traits and to predict their behaviour by studying samples of their writing. Hundreds of books present "do-it-yourself" guides to graphology. Intuitive analysts believe that they can make interpretations on the basis of their total impression of a person's handwriting. Other interpretations stress isolated signs as clues. For example, it may be claimed that the way a man dots his i's or slants his letters shows whether he is careful or rash, forceful or vacillating.

Scientific Studies. Scientific investigations of handwriting in relation to personality have continued along with popularized analysis. For example, a 19th century German investigator, Ludwig Klages, discredited the isolated signs approach. He stated that meaningful interpretations were possible only if signs were integrated into patterns. The French psychologist Alfred Binet tried to make an experimental test of the validity of graphology. Using writing samples from 37 highly successful men and 37 less outstanding men, he asked seven graphologists to distinguish the groups. One graphologist was correct in 92% of his diagnoses, and in general the results suggested that the analysts were able to draw correct inferences from handwriting.

Different results were obtained from a more recent experiment carried out at the University of Chicago. A graphologist attempted to rate 22 subjects on five personality traits, using samples of handwriting as his only evidence. His ratings were compared with clinical observations of the same subjects by two counseling psychologists. There was a moderate degree of agreement between the two counselors in describing the personalities of the subjects, but there was little agreement between the graphologist and either of the counselors. Attempts have also been made to analyse handwriting by means of electronic devices and computers, but no technique has produced proof that graphology is a valid measure of personal characteristics.

The available evidence seems to leave open the question of whether graphology can be used as a tool of scientific psychology. It is true that personality traits are reflected in behaviour. And it has been found, of course, that handwriting changes as a result of age, illness, and emotional stress. Yet no clear relationships have so far been found between the bits of behaviour demonstrated in handwriting and basic personality patterns.

Lesson 32

Section One:

Tapescript:

How to Keep Fit?

Interviewer: Could you tell me how we should keep fit?

Dr Davis: Well really what we should do is to try to erm keep fit all round. Now what do I mean by that? I mean er such things as keeping up our strength and our suppleness and our stamina. Now er you may say why do we need all three of those things? Well, erm strength is useful really just so that we erm don't strain muscles or pull ligaments and tendons when we suddenly have to do something er a bit energetic like lift a heavy suitcase or er perhaps er shift a wardrobe or even get out of a chair or a bath. Erm. Suppleness is important er obviously so that you can can bend and and move freely and reach things, again without injuring yourself. And stamina is particularly important so that you can sort of keep going without without losing breath so you have you have endurance. One other great plus about developing stamina is that if you er maintain your stamina over a period of years, it actually has an effect of protecting the heart against heart disease.

Interviewer: So out of those three, which is the most important?

Dr Davis: Well, it depends who you are and what you want to do. I mean, the the reason for keeping fit is to keep fit for your way of life, the life you choose. Now, you may say 'Well, if I choose to sort of flop about in an armchair all day watching telly, I don't need to keep very fit, do I?' Well, that's unfortunately not true because there are always times when you have to make a little bit of extra demand on your body. Erm by force of circumstance. You may have to suddenly lift something heavy or move something or may have to er run for a bus or whatever. In which case you could do yourself an injury and you may even actually erm harm something important, like your heart. So it is important to actually to try to keep your fitness a little bit ahead of the sort of erm way of life that you have. Just to give you ... to push yourself just that little bit harder and get yourself just that little bit fitter.

Interviewer: So how do you do it?

Dr Davis: Well it doesn't have to be all grim and irksome. I mean, people have this view of fitness er freaks you know, who sort of are jogging grim-faced round the park you know, or who are er working weights, doing all sorts of horrible exercises you know. PT ... Very grim indeed. It doesn't have to be like that. To keep yourself fit, or get yourself fitter, which is really what it's about, you just have to do a little bit more each day, erm or even every other day for that matter. By a little bit more I mean erm for instance just er walking a bit more often, a bit further, perhaps getting off the bus a stop or two sooner. Erm perhaps er doing a bit of a bit of cycling instead of travelling by public transport. Using the stairs instead of going up in the lift. It's surprising the number of people that erm I see on the London tube who are actually standing on the escalators going down you know, just standing there slowly going down.

633

And the same with lifts. People who take the lift down I mean, that's ridiculous. You should at least walk down, but preferably walk up, because by walking upstairs you actually perform really quite a useful aerobic exercise, that's an exercise that develops stamina, and that's having a beneficial effect on your whole body, toning you up and helping to protect against heart disease.

Interviewer: So it isn't necessary to play squash three times a week or go swimming three times a week?

Dr Davis: It isn't necessary. Er actually swimming is a rather good way of keeping fit because it's particularly excellent for erm all three of the S-Factors if you like, the strength, the suppleness and the stamina. It helps to develop all three of those rather well, and er it's also a very pleasant and relaxing way to keep yourself in shape. Three times a week would be just about right actually, or even twice a week, or even once a week. Em. Squash though is not a good way to get fit. You have to actually get fit to play squash. Squash is a very demanding game. A very very er energetic game, and in fact you could do yourself a lot of damage by playing squash if you're not in good physical shape to start with.

Interviewer: I have a lot of friends who play sport, and they always seem to have bad backs and pulled tendons, so what would you say to them?

Dr Davis: I'd say to them they're they're going about it the wrong way. Erm. They're forcing themselves into into sports, perhaps before they're ready, before they've got themselves in shape first. You have to get in shape to play these sports. Erm. And also for people who force themselves into these

634

things generally. That's bad. Mustn't do that. Whenever you're exercising, or or just carrying out some physical activity, never push yourself beyond comfort. Anything that's uncomfortable, don't do it. Stop. Slow down. It's basically got to be fun. I mean, to keep yourself in shape you've got to carry on exercising week in week out, month in month out, year in year out, Now that sounds awful, but if you choose something which you enjoy doing, er, it's fun, then you will keep it up. You see you can't put fitness in the bank as it were. If you don't carry on exercising, all the benefits that you get from exercising will all disappear within about 6 to 8 weeks. All go and you'll be back where you started so you have to keep it up, and to keep it up, it has to be something you enjoy, it has to be fun. So choose something which you get a lot of pleasure out of, and that way it won't seem irksome at all.

Interviewer: What do you do to keep fit?

Dr Davis: Ah well, I'm glad you asked me that question. Actually, what I... I live in London and I work in London, er so what I what I do to keep fit is to certainly do quite a lot of walking. I certainly walk upstairs er a lot, but also I do a fair amount of cycling, er and as I'm dashing round London I I use the bike. I find it the fastest way to get around town and it's er it's really good for keeping in shape. I'm a little worried about the traffic fumes, I have to admit, but actually er it makes me feel very good to cycle around there and I get there on time!

Key to Exercises:

A. Fill in the blanks according to what you hear on the tape.

    1. The three S-Factors are (strength, suppleness and stamina).

2. Strength is useful so that we don't (strain muscles) or (pull ligaments) and (tendons) when we suddenly (have to do something) a bit energetic like (lift a heavy suitcase) or perhaps (shift a wardrobe) or even get out of a (chair) or a (bath).

3. Suppleness is important so that you can (bend) and (move freely) and reach things without (injuring) yourself.

4. Stamina is particularly important so that you can (keep going) without (losing breath). You have (endurance).

5. If you maintain your stamina over a period of years it has (an effect) of (protecting the heart) against (heart disease).

B. Choose the best answer (a, b or c) for each of the following questions.

1. Which of the three S-Factors is the most important?
   a. Stamina.
   b. Suppleness or strength.
 * c. It depends.

2. Which of the three choices helps to develop all the three S-Factors rather well?
 * a. Swimming.
   b. Playing squash.
   c. Cycling.

3. Which kind of physical activity should you choose to keep fit?
   a. Something comfort.
   b. Something demanding.
 * c. Something enjoyable.

C. Complete the following advice given by the speaker.

1. To keep fit you may:
    a. (walk) a bit (more often), a bit (further);
    b. (get off) the bus (a stop) or (two) sooner;
    c. (do) a bit of (cycling) instead of (travelling) by public (transport);
    d. (use the stairs) instead of (going up) in the (lift).

Section Two:

Tapescript:

New Report: Neo-Nazi

In September bombs went off in Coeur d'Alene, Idaho. They were the work allegedly of a group of Neo-Nazis, three of whom now sit in an Idaho jail awaiting trial. While they wait, commentator Clay Morgan has been thinking about the bombings, the bombers and what it all means for his part of the country.

I lived in a promised land. We got trouble here right now. Some Neo-Nazis declared the north-west to be the homeland for the white races. In the past several weeks we've had four bombs blow up. The situation here is serious. I had a hope that they just go away. I was embarrassed by the news coverage. Every time I saw a story, I cringed and thought my God this will make four more of them move here. Then the bombs exploded in Coeur d'Alene. Let me describe these people to you. They are men mostly. They like to live in forts, and dress up like Hitler. They wear jackboots, brown shirts and military caps. They march around and act tough. What they are is evil. These are the cowardly little boys who never grow up. It is our misfortune that they came here. The north-west attracts these people with all the attributes of a promised land. A promised land you see is a place that's far away, isolated and sparsely populated by people who try to mind their own business. The north-west fits that bill. Ninety percent of some of our states are public lands, owned by everybody. That's everybody. This is a place to breath in. The pioneers came here on the Oregon trail. The Mormons came here to practice their religion. The Basques came here to escape poverty and persecution in Spain. Wyoming was the first state to give women the vote, the first to elect a woman governor. Idaho was the first to have a Jewish governor. Now we are attracting fascists like we were Paraguay. Bad things are happening in a good place.

We would like to have the sheriff go to them and say, "Pack up! Clear up! Get out of the state by sundown!" But we cannot. It is not against the law to believe in evil. The white supremacists protected by laws are meant to protect everybody. That's everybody. And we are to keep those laws. We can only watch these creeps and be ready when they make their move. The people who set off those bombs in Coeur d'Alene meant to rob the bank and ransack the armory. But when the bombs went off, the law came down so fast and hard the perpetrators lost their nerve. They got caught. There were several others who were not in jail yet. But we know about them. We can stand up to them. Those bombs did not scare Coeur d' Alene. So get ready for a good ending to a bad story. After all this embarrassment, Coeur d'Alene would be the town that stands up to evil and wins. And this promised land, maybe, would drop out the news and we can mind our own business again.

Writer Clay Morgan lives in McCall, Idaho. He comes to us by way of member station KBSU in Voizy, Idaho.

Key to Exercises:

638

A. Fill in the chart according to what you hear on the tape.

1. Event: (bombs went off).
2. Place: (Coeur d'Alene, Idaho)
3. Time: (September)
4. Perpetrator: (a group of Neo-Nazis)
5. Number in jail: (three)
6. Declaration: (the north-west is the homeland for the white races).

B. Complete the following description of those Neo-Nazis.

1. Most of them are (men).
2. They like to live (in forts).
3. They dress up like (Hitler).
4. They wear (jack boots), (brown shirts) and (military caps).

C. Complete the following definition based on what you hear on the tape.

1. A promised land is a place that's
   a. (far away),
   b. (isolated),
   c. (sparsely populated).
2. The pioneers mentioned are
   a. (Mormons) who came here to (practise their religion).
   b. (Basques) who came here to (escape poverty and persecution) in (Spain).

D. True or False Questions. Write a T in front of a statement if it is true according to the recording and write an F if it is false.

1. (F) Those Neo-Nazis had been warned by the sheriff before

639

they made their move.

2. (T) We can do nothing to those creeps because it is not a-
gainst law to believe in evil.

3. (F) Those Neo-Nazis had tried to rob the bank and ransack
the armory before they set off those bombs in Coeur d'Alene.

Section Three:

Tapescript:

Outlining: What Your Sense of Time Tells about You (I)

Imagine you are a high school principal. A teacher bursts
breathless into your office. "There's a fist fight in the lunchroom,"
she gasps. The responsibility is yours to stop the fight. How do you
meet it?

(1) Perhaps you, as a youngster, took part in fights and your
present-day ties with students are warm and strong. You can stop
the fight because your prestige is high among them.

(2) You have a plan prepared. Other schools have been disrupted so you have already planned a way to stop any fight.

(3) You are totally confident of your abilities in a crisis. You
are ready to stride into the lunchroom and take charge without a single qualm. Stopping the fight will be easy.

(4) You fervently wish that you could delegate the job since
you know that you're not a talented peacemaker. You wish you
could return to the job of planning for the school's needs ten years
hence.

One of these four reactions would be the first you'd feel, but
only one – not two or three of them, say three psychologists. These
psychologists – Dr. Harriet Mann, Dr. Humphrey Osmond and
Miriam Siegler – have come up with a scheme for sorting people re-

gardless of their education, age or situation.

The concept is based on the premise that all people have a basic way of seeing time. Each of us is predisposed to seeing all events from one time vantage point. Either it reminds you of the past (past-oriented), how the event fits in to today, yesterday and tomorrow (time line), what it is today (present), or how it will develop (future).

The three began working in 1968 when Dr. Mann and Mrs. Siegler were assistants to Dr. Osmond, director, at the Bureau of Research, New Jersey Neuro-Psychiatric Institute in Princeton. Dr. Osmond is currently devising ways to make empirical studies of the theory and Dr. Mann is in Cambridge, Massachusetts, writing a book on the Worlds of Time. Their take-off point was an interest in observations made by Swiss psychologist Carl Gustav Jung, who described in the 1920s the temperamental differences of four psychological types. Jung is known as the founder of analytic psychology. Since Jung's work in 1921, however, no one had conceived of a theoretical framework that would account for the four types. Without such a framework, there was no possibility of substantiating that people of different types experience the world very differently.

Time and space are the touchstones in the system. Each person, after all, uses his time somehow and exists within and acts upon the space around him. Dr. Mann and company propose that certain traits are shared by persons falling in each of the four categories.

The first type, the past type, sees time as being circular. For him, the past crops up in the present and then returns to the past as a memory. He enjoys collecting souvenirs and keeping diaries. He tells stories about Great Aunt Hattie and always remembers your

641

birthday.

Past types are pegged by this system as emotional people who see the world in a highly subjective way. For instance, School Principal I (past type) could identify with the fight and know how to handle it because of some past experience – whether it be similar fights as a child himself or ones previously dealt with as the school principal. In addition, past types usually follow strict moral codes and often are valued more for what they are than for what they do. This quality itself – because it lends authoritarian strength to one who possesses it – might cause the students to quit fighting. Past types often have been found to be skillful at assessing the exact emotional tenor of an event and are adept at influencing others' emotions, according to the Mann group.

Research reveals that many past-oriented people are flexible in early years when they do not have much of a personal past to draw upon. However, the dash of youth is often replaced by a need for stability and usually is rooted by age thirty-five or so. From this age onward, they are conservatives.

"They need to see things in the ways which were popular, fashionable and appropriate in their younger days," explains Dr. Mann. This applies, with exceptions of course, to personal taste in clothing fashions, music appreciation, and other social and environmental factors. In short, the past type often clings to the well-established way with nostalgic verve. Also, the past type finds it difficult to be punctual since the on-going feeling is more important than his next task.

The goal of these people is "to develop a language of the heart, rather than of the mind. To develop those techniques which make memories live, and to dignify any act of remembrance; those are the

642

essential concerns of past-oriented types, " explain the authors in the Journal of Analytical Psychology.

Key to Exercises:

A. General Comprehension: Write a T in front of a statement if it is true according to the recording and write an F if it is false.

1. (F) As a school principal you can have four kinds of reactions towards the teacher's report.

2. (T) The three psychologists presuppose that everyone of us sees all events from one time vantage.

3. (F) The three psychologists started in 1968 based on the observations they had made in the 1920s.

4. (T) Time and space are the criteria used to differentiate person from person in this system.

5. (T) There are four types of people according to this system, but only the first type, the past type, has been discussed in this section of the lecture.

6. (F) The past type people are conservatives from their early years.

B. Suggested Abbreviations.

research: re.   New Jersey: N.J.

institute: ins.   psychologist: psyt.

subjective: subj.   develop: dev.

C. Notetaking: Complete the following outline.

Title: (What your sense of time tells about you)

I. Background

    A. The scheme

1. Premise: (all have basic way of seeing time)
2. Sort people according to (time vantage point).
3. Types of people: (a. past-oriented; b. time line; c. present; d. future)

B. The experiment
1. Began in (1968) at (Bureau of Re. NJ Neuro-Psychiatric Ins. in Princeton)
2. Done by (Dr. Osmond, Dr. Mann & Mrs. Siegler)
3. Take-off point: (interest in observations by Swiss psyt. Jung in the 1920s)
4. The theory: (Time & space) are the touchstones. Each person (uses time somehow & exists within & acts upon space) around him. Certain traits are (shared by people of the same kind).

II. Categories of people
A. (past type)
1. sees time (as being circular)
   enjoys (collecting souvenirs & keeping diaries)
   tells stories about (Great Aunt Hattie)
   remembers (your birthday).
2. emotional people who (see the world in highly subj. way)
3. in early years (flexible, no past to draw upon)
   from 35 (conservatives from personal tast to social factors)
   diff. to be (punctual)
4. goal (dev. lang. of heart not mind)

Lesson 33

Tapescript:

A Coincidence in New York

Angela: Would you like ...

Angela: to tell me about it?

Denise: Yes, I think ...

Denise: ... it's rather a unique experience, actually. I was in New York, er, er, a few years ago and I wanted to read a particular poem, so I went along to the public library. (I see) Now, the public library is different from any, er, library that I'd ever seen, because you never see a book on a shelf, and, er, I went into the building and I was directed to Room 101, where I had to fill in a form with the author and the title of the book that I wanted. I was handed a disc and directed to another room which looked like a cinema. I sat down in this room and waited for the number on my disc to flash on the screen. I waited and waited and waited and noticed that people who came in after me, er, were leaving (Mhm) and so I went back to the original room to find out what had happened and I was told that, erm, they couldn't read the writing on my form, (oh dear) so I filled in another form and was on my way to, er, th, the cinema — like room when, erm, I saw, er, a woman standing in the, in the corridor. Now she was obviously trying to attract some-

645

body's attention. She was dressed very poorly and she had what looked like, er, a sor . . ., some kind of fur hat, a rather mangy fur hat, and on this hat was fixed a ra, a crook-like feather, a very, very long crook-like feather. And, er, this, this attracted, er, my attention I think more than anything, so I stopped and asked her if I could help her and she told me what I thought then was a rather a, an appalling story. She'd come in from the outskirts of New York, erm, to see a sick friend, and just as, as she had been coming out of the underground train, the doors had closed and her handbag had been snatched and her umbrella, er, was caught in the closing door. She managed to wrench the umbrella out and a little bit was chipped off. She showed me where it had been chipped off. (M) she said that she had no money to return home and also she'd had nothing to eat all day. So I forgot about the poetry and we went over the road to a little tea-shop. And I must say it was when we got to the tea-shop and I was getting the tea and had left my bag on the chair that I began just to be a tiny little bit suspicious and I looked back at her but she was sitting quite innocently at the table. (M) Anyway, we had a little conversation — she was quite an interesting woman — and then I sa . . ., I realized that it was about time I was making my way home. So I said to her, 'Well, erm, I've got two dollars and ten dollars. Er, how much will you need?' And she said, 'Well, the ten dollars will do me fine'. I thought that was little bit much at the time so I said, 'No, I'll give you the two dollars', which I did. (M) And then we, we, we bade each other good-bye and I was just . . . going off when she called me back and said, 'May I, er, take your address, so that I can return the two dollars?'

646

which, er, I gave her and then I went off. I had sundry other things to do. I think I went to a book-shop, and I went to buy a scarf or pair of gloves and, er, er, all these things on my way home and when I got home I was still thinking about the two dollars and I opened my purse to, to count my money and I found that I had about fourteen or fifteen dollars when I'd, when I had only had the twelve when I set off originally. (Mm) (Nasty) So somebody along the way had given me the wrong change. I did think about retracing my steps, but it seemed too much trouble, so I didn't. I waited about a week, half expecting my two dollars back but, of course, it didn't come back, so I realized that, er, I'd been conned, I think the word is. (Yes) Well, a month later, I was walking around – it was the end of January — I was walking around, er, in New York and it really was freezing. I couldn't feel my hands or my feet. So I went into the Barbazon Plaza Hotel to warm myself, because all the buildings in New York ate centrally heated, and as soon as I'd got into the hotel, I noticed that the foyer was covered with mirrors and, in one corner of the foyer, I saw this old woman. Now the reason why I recognized her was that she was dressed in a Persian lamb coat this time — very, very expensive Persian lamb coat — and she had a Persian lamb hat on her head. But affixed to this Persian lamb hat was the same long crook-like feather!

Angela: How funny!

Denise: So I thought to myself, 'Well, it's amazing. I, I, I wonder if I will get the same story if I go over there.' So I went over to the mirror and took out my comb and compact and pretended to set about, er, righting my face, when the lady came

647

up to me and without any ado at all poured out the same story.
So I turned to her and looked her straight in the face and I said,
'You and I met a month ago in the public library'. And then I
walked off.

Key to Exercises:

A. Answer the following questions:

1. What did the narrator want in the public library?

   Answer: A particular poem.

2. Why did the narrator leave the cinema-like room?

   Answer: Because she had waited too long and she wanted to
   find out what had happened.

3. Why did they keep her so long?

   Answer: Because they couldn't read her writing on her
   form.

4. How was the woman dressed in the corridor?

   Answer: Poorly.

5. What was the story told by the woman?

   Answer: She said that she had come to see a sick friend, but
   her handbag had been snatched away and she had
   no money left to return home.

6. How much did the narrator give that woman?

   Answer: Two dollars.

7. What was the coincidence the narrator had when she was in a
   hotel?

   Answer: She saw the woman once again and the woman told
   her the same story.

8. How was the woman dressed this time?

   Answer: She was well dressed this time.

B. True or False Questions. Write a T in front of a statement if it is true according to the recording and write an F if it is false.

1. (T) The public library is different from any other libraries because you cannot find a book on a shelf.

2. (F) The narrator's attention was attracted by a woman wearing a new fur hat with a long crook-like feather in the library.

3. (F) The woman said her handbag and umbrella had been caught in the closing door of the underground train.

4. (F) The woman appeared quite innocent after she had opened the bag when the narrator went to get the tea and left her bag on the chair.

5. (T) The narrator was surprised to find that there were about fourteen dollars in her bag while she had taken only twelve with her when she set off.

C. Fill in the detailed information according to what you hear on the tape.

So I thought to myself "well, it's (amazing). I wonder if I will (get the same story) if I go over there. So I went over to the (mirror) and took out my (comb) and (compact) and pretended to (set about righting) my face, when the lady (came up) to me and without (any ado) at all (poured out) the same story. So I turned to her and looked her (straight in the face) and I said, "You and I (met a month ago) in the (public library." And then I (walked off).

Section Two:

Tapescript:

New Report: Election in Mexico

In this country, today was a day of waiting by voters to learn if their candidate won or lost. That provides more suspense than is typical in elections in Mexico. In that country, the ruling Institutional Revolutionary Party has not lost a single state or national election since its founding in 1929. Critics of the system in Mexico say it is not truly democratic because the opposition parties had virtually no chance of taking power. But those parties have grown stronger in recent years and there is increasing pressure to change the procedures for elections. Today the Mexican Congress began work on a package of reforms that eventually could give opposition parties a greater voice in politics in Mexico. NPR's Tom Julton reports in Mexico City.

A week ago Sunday, voters in the Mexican state of Sinaloa elected a new governor. But in a few days, spokesmen for the National Action Party, the opposition, were claiming victory. But yesterday the government announced a different result. The winner, the government said, was the candidate of the ruling party, the PRI, by its initials in Spanish, and by a three-to-one margin. The National Action Party immediately charged that the PRI with the government's help has stolen the election. The accusation has become routine. Opposition parties in Mexico from the left to the right claimed the government here manipulates elections to guarantee that the PRI always wins. Government funds, the opposition says, pay for PRI campaigns, and government employees are forced to support PRI candidates as the price of keeping their jobs. When that is not enough to ensure a PRI victory, opposition leaders say, the govern-

650

ment will stuff the ballot boxes, falsify voter registrations or even change the final tally.

Government officials say the charges are unfair, but they admit to having a credibility problem both at home and abroad. So Mexican President Miguel de la Madrid announced last summer that he would propose sweeping changes in election system. This morning his suggestions were presented to the Mexican Congress. Some of the proposals satisfy long standing demands of the opposition. The most important may be the introduction of the translucent ballot boxes so that official poll watchers can verify that no one has stuffed the boxes beforehand. A new federal elections commission will be established with the power to judge the fairness of the elections and a permanent list of voters would be prepared with the assistance of all political parties.

The reforms would also give opposition parties more representation in the national Congress. Two hundred out of five hundred congressional seats will be awarded to opposition parties in proportion to the number of votes they receive. It's the most ambitious political reform in recent Mexican history but opposition leaders here are still not satisfied. Sisirial Romaro, a Congress woman from the National Action Party, says no real reform is possible in Mexico until the bond between the government and its official party the PRI is broken.

Opposition leaders today responded to the President's reform package by offering one of their own. They propose that all the seats in the national Congress be distributed in proportion to party votes. And they want the elections to be overseen by a separate tribunal completely independent of the government. But the opposition's proposals have no chance of being approved since the PRI totally

651

controls the national Congress and enacts virtually everything the government proposes. In Mexico City, I'm Tom Julton.

Key to Exercises:

A. Choose the best answer (a, b or c) to complete each of the following statements.

1. Today was a day _____ in Mexico.
   a. waiting for voters to be present at the poll.
   * b. of waiting by voters to learn the result of the election.
   c. waiting for the government to announce the result

2. Since its founding in 1 9 2 9 , the ruling Institutional Revolu-tionary Party _____.
   * a. has never failed in the elections
   b. has once failed in the elections
   c. has only lost votes in one city in the elections

3. Critics of the system in Mexico say it is not democratic because _____.
   a. other parties are not allowed to take turns in ruling the country
   b. not all the political parties are given a chance to take part in the general election
   * c. the opposition parties were not given a chance to take power

4. Today the Mexican Congress began work on a package of reforms _____.
   a. that would increase pressure upon the government
   b. that would allow the opposition parties to grow stronger
   * c. that could give opposition parties a greater voice in politics in Mexico

B. True or False Questions. Write a T in front of a statement if it is true according to the recording and write an F if it is false.

1. (F) A week ago Saturday, a new governor was elected in the Mexican state of Sinaloa.

2. (F) The National Action Party was said to win the election according to the government.

3. (T) The election was won by a three-to-one margin.

4. (F) Government officials admit they have done something to the election in order to guarantee the victory.

5. (T) Mexico President Miguel de la Madrid promised to propose sweeping changes in election system last summer.

6. (T) Some of the President's proposals had also long been demanded by the opposition parties.

C. Fill in the blanks with detailed information about the government.

1. The government was said to have
   a. (manipulated elections) to guarantee that the PRI always win;
   b. (paid for) PRI campaigns;
   c. (forced their employees to support) PRI candidates as the price of keeping their jobs.

2. The opposition leaders say that, to ensure a PRI victory, the government will
   a. (stuff the ballot) boxes;
   b. (falsify voter) registrations;
   c. (change the final) tally.

653

D. Identification. Match the proposal in Column I with its result in Column II.

Column I

1. the establishment of a new federal elections commission
2. the preparation of a permanent list of voters
3. the introduction of the translucent ballot boxes

Column II

a. official poll watchers can verify that no one has stuffed the boxes beforehand
b. judge the fairness of the elections
c. with the assistance of all political parties

Answer: (1)—(b); (2)—(c); (3)—(a).

E. Fill in the blanks with the information you hear on the tape.

The reforms would also give (opposition parties) more (representation) in the national Congress. (Two) hundred out of (five hundred) congressional seats will be awarded to opposition parties (in proportion to) the number of votes they receive. It's the most (ambitous) political reform in recent Mexican (history) but opposition leaders here are still not (satisfied). Sisirial Romaro, a (Congress) woman from the National Action Party, says (no real reform) is possible in Mexico until the (bond) between the government and its (official party) the PRI is (broken).

F. Answer the following questions.

1. What have the opposition leaders proposed in answer to the president's reform package?

   Answer: All the seats in the national congress should be distributed in proportion to party votes.

2. What do the opposition parties demand about the elections?

654

Answer: They want the election to be overseen by a separate tribunal completely independent of the government.

3. Have the opposition's proposals got any chance of being approved? Why or why not?

Answer: No. Because the PRI totally controls the national Congress and enacts virtually everything the government proposes.

Section Three:

Tapescript:

Outlining: What Your Sense of Time Tells about You (II)

Time line people see time as flowing, too. For them, however, no one situation is important. Rather, life is a carpet, rolling from the past into the present and onward to the future. Any instance is but a footfall on the carpet.

For the time line people, for whom yesterday, today and tomorrow are an integrated whole, the past is not a past of personal feeling. It is the detached, historical past. Any given event must fit into a larger picture, even if pushed and tugged into place. The desire to put events in historical order enables the time line type to frame hypotheses, to draw conclusions and to make predictions; in short, to be scientific. Naturally, only a few are likely to have true scientific insights but all share the mental process, initial research indicates.

Before starting any project the time line person examines the whole situation and tries to see it in ideal terms. He wants to make up his mind and arrive at a logical conclusion before he acts. School Principal 2 — a time line type — is probably prepared to deal with a fight before it even occurs, since fights among students are a potential hazard in most schools.

The desire to envision the whole picture is often seen as a lack of enthusiasm in the time line people. They are often reputed to be cold, detached and uncaring. They are really none of these things. However, they are happiest when they can project their view far forward and far backward in time.

You say to your time line father, "Let's buy a boat. Joe saw one that's going to be auctioned this afternoon. It looks great."

An inquisition will follow: "Whose boat was it? Has it ever been in a wreck? Is it fiberglass or wood? How do you know it is seaworthy? Where would you use it? How do you know it won't be bid up to a huge price? Does it have a trailer? Have you shopped enough for boats to know if it is a good one? Where would you store it in the winter?" When the questions are through, you probably wish you had never mentioned the boat in the first place, but you know from past experience that a time line person will always ask lots of questions.

On the other hand, if you do buy the boat, a time line person is a comfort at the helm. He will have checked all of the safety factors, will know the weather forecast, will have a good liferaft stowed, will have purchased charts of the area, will have seen that extra supplies are available and will know where the best fishing is reported. He will be a competent captain and will know not only his own duties, but the jobs of the crew.

The third type of person is the present type. He is totally concerned with the immediate and the present, reports the Mann research team. He has the greatest ability to understand the present moment with all of its shadings and ramifications. This total reliance on the present creates most of his strongest traits. For him, life is a

656

happening. Where it is going, where it comes from, is of little interest. He does not integrate past experiences into present activities.

School Principal 3, the one who knew he could take charge, was a present type person. Dr. Mann and her colleagues theorize that this time type responds without hesitation to the stimulus presented by the object or person before him. No prearranged plan or commitment gets in this type's way, according to Mann's research.

A present type is superbly equipped to deal with crises and emergencies. He responds to slight cues and acts immediately. He doesn't have to decide between various courses of action. The event itself tells him what to do.

Your brother, for example, might be a present type. He is happy as a policeman, making quick decisions and acting promptly. Or he is a volunteer Red Cross organizer, quick with answers in a flood disaster area.

Because he does not feel any future, even a slight delay will annoy a present type. Waiting is the same as denial. He will not wait. He may try to manoeuvre others into his wishes and, if unable to get his own way, is quite likely to dissolve the relationship.

The fourth type is the person who places faith in the future. He first perceives the future and then works backwards from that vision into, for him, the lesser reality of the present.

Future types are more concerned with trying to ascertain what is possible rather than what exists now. "For one of this type, the present is a pale shadow, the past a mist, warmth and sunshine, bright lights and excitement are to be found beyond the next bend in the road, on the other side of the mountain. But rounding a bend only leads temporarily to a straight path; there is always another curve," explain the psychologists. All of the life of a future type is spent dashing around the next bend.

Principal 4 is a future type, happier with his plans for breaking up future fights than the one that has materialized.

If you are a future type, you might have looked at a course catalogue in college and found you lacked a listed prerequisite for just the course you wanted to take. Chances are you were always a little lost because you didn't have the prescribed background. "Why does it have to be typed letter-perfect?" you've always exclaimed when you handed in a paper.

You also inspire others with your ideas. If you are active in the local Citizens for Environment, you were the one that dreamed up the biggest fund-raising scheme in years. However, most likely someone else worked out the details because you are terribly impatient with them.

If the three psychologists are correct, we have a new tool for understanding one another. It will make it easier to get along with those who basically differ from us. Dr. Osmond envisions a time when we could use the theory to aid in selecting the kind of politician best suited for the current problems. "If we are right," he explains, "there is no such thing as a philosopher-king. You either get a philosopher with an interest in ruling or a king who enjoys philosophy, but you will never get a philosopher-king; it doesn't happen."

Key to Exercises:

A. General Comprehension: Write a T in front of a statement if it is true according to the recording and write an F if it is false.

  1. (F) The time line people pay more attention to the present and the future.

  2. (F) The time line people are not enthusiastic because they

658

tend to envision the whole picture.

3. (T) The present type people can understand the present very well and make quick responses.

4. (T) The present type people are the best in dealing with crises and emergencies.

5. (F) The future types are satisfied with the present, but believe the future is the best.

6. (T) The future types are often better prepared for the future than the present.

B. Suggested abbreviations:

prediction: pred.   enthusiasm: enth.

ramification: ramif.   emergency: emerg.

environment: envir.

C. Notetaking: Complete the following outline.

B. (Time line people).

1. Life: (like a carpet rolling from past to present to future).

2. Way of thinking: (frame hypotheses, draw conclusions & make pred).

3. Impressions given to others: (lack enth, cold, detached & uncaring).

e.g. (buying a boat).

C. (Present type).

1. Life: (a happening, past & future are of little interest).

2. Characteristics:

a. Has the greatest ability to (understand the present with its shadings and ramif).

b. Superbly equipped to (deal with crises & emergs).

c. Responds to (slight cues & acts) immediately.

d. e.g.(policeman, Red Cross Organizer).

D. (Future type).

1. Life:

a. present: (pale shadow).

b. past: (mist).

c. future: (warmth, sunshine, bright lights, excitement).

2. Characteristics:

a. Perceives (the future) and then (works backward into
present).

b. e.g. (at college or Citizens for Envir).

III. Conclusion:

(If the 3 psychologists are correct, a new tool for understanding one another).

Supplementary Reading:

New York City

Visitors approach New York City in many ways. A great ocean
liner steams proudly into New York Harbour. On deck, people
crane to marvel at the graceful curve of the Verrazano-Narrows
Bridge. Beyond the bridge all eyes focus on the Statue of Liberty.
The panorama of New York's skyline looms steadily larger as tugs
push and pull the great ship into its Hudson River berth.

Overhead, huge jets seem to hover in the sky. Airplane passengers en route to John F. Kennedy International and La Guardia airports peer through the windows at the city spread out below.
Skyscrapers reach upward like huge, stone fingers. Rivers twist

around and through the city like silver necklaces. Thousands of windows twinkle in the sun's reflection.

Millions of people arrive in buses and cars, which stream over highways, through tunnels, and across bridges to be swallowed up in the narrow canyons that lie between rows of tall buildings.

Railroad trains streak across the country to plunge under rivers and emerge at last to disgorge passengers into the domed vastness of the city's railroad terminals.

Regardless of how a visitor reaches New York or what he has heard about the city, the newcomer is overwhelmed by the city's size, the crush of its people, the endless streams of traffic and the steel and glass towers that crowd in on every side. There are subways, buses, taxis, trucks, private cars, and even boats. And there are millions upon millions of peole.

This giant of a city has many faces. New York is the cultural capital of the country. It has more museums, theaters, concert halls, libraries, and publishing houses than any other city in the United States. But New York is a city of astonishing contrasts. There are wealth and poverty, beauty and ugliness, towering skyscrapers and little neighborhood shops, multistoried apartment houses and one-family homes. There are miles and miles of concrete pavement and hundres of acres of park land. There are huge baseball stadiums and little neighborhood playgrounds.

Geography

New York City is located on the eastern coast of the United States where the Hudson River meets the Atlantic Ocean. The city's fine harbor and strategic location in the center of the great northeastern metropolitan region have helped to make New York the largest city in the United States.

661

Islands. New York is a city of islands. The city is made up of five sections called boroughs: the Bronx, Queens, Brooklyn, Manhattan, and Staten Island. Only the Bronx is on the mainland, Brooklyn and Queens are part of Long Island. Manhattan and Staten Island are also island boroughts. Liberty Island (formerly Bedloe's Island) is the site of the Statue of Liberty. Ellis Island was the immigration station through which millions of immigrants entered the United States. Governors Island served as an army base for many years. Today it is a Untied States Coast Guard training center. Some city hospitals are located on Roosevelt Island. Randalls Island has recreation areas and a stadium for sports events, concerts, and other forms of entertainment. Some of the city's prison facilities are on Rikers Island.

Climate. New York City, like the rest of the northeastern United States, has a varied climate. It is temperate enough for the city's harbor to be navigable all year. Spring and fall are generally mild and pleasant. Summers are often hot and humid. Rain Falls irregularly throughout the year, and snowfalls are sometimes heavy. Winter temperatures often range a few degrees on either side of the freezing point.

The Five Boroughs and Counties

Each of New York City's five boroughs is also a county of New York State. In the rest of the state each county contains many villages, towns, and cities. But New York City is so heavily populated that the city has been divided into five different counties. The county and the borough names are the same except for Manhattan (New York County), Brooklyn (Kings County), and Staten Island (Richmond Cunty). Bridges connect Manhattan, the core of the city, with all the boroughs except Staten Island. Ferryboats link Staten

662

Island and Manhattan.

Manhattan was founded in 1624 as New Netherland. Although it is the smallest in area (about 57 square kilometers, or 22 square miles), it is by far the most important of the boroughs. It has the greatest concentraion of business, finance, and entertainment.

Brooklyn was founded in 1646 as the little Dutch village of Breuckelen. Today Brooklyn is the second largest borough in area (about 207 km², or 80 sq mi) and the most heavily populated. Brooklyn sometimes is called the borough of homes and churches. But it is also an important port. Nearly half of New York City's foreign trade is handled at Brooklyn's busy waterfront. Much of the city's heavy industry is located in Brooklyn. The borough is one of the largest manufacturing centers in the United States.

Queens was founded in 1645 at Vlissingen (today called Flushing). It is the largest borough in area, covering about 297 km², or 115 sq mi. Queens is one of the city's most popular residential areas. The borough is important for its concentration of railroads and heavy industry in the Long Island City area. New York City's main airports – John F. Kennedy International and La Guardia – are in Queens. Two world's fairs (1939 – 40 and 1964 – 65) were held in Queens.

The Bronx began as Jonas Bronck's farm in 1641. The Bronx, the second smallest borough in area (about 111 km², or 43 sq mi), is largely residential, although many industries have grown up near the East and Harlem rivers.

Staten Island was first called Staaten Eylandt. It began in 1661 with a village called Oude Dorp. This island borough, in New York Bay, was formerly called Richmond. Its area is about 157 square kilometers, or 61 square miles. Its population is the smallest of those of the five boroughs. Staten Island is growing rapidly; but many small homes and even some farms still are found there. Although the island is mainly residential, many industries are located in its northern section.

Education, Recreation, and Culture

A large part of the city's budget is spent on education. Over 1,000,000 students attend New York's public schools. The city University of New York has an enrollment of about 200,000. the university includes 10 senior colleges, a graduate division, an affiliated medical school, and eight 2-year community colleges. Medgar Evers College in Brooklyn is the newest school to join the university, which also includes City College, Hunter College, Brooklyn College, and Queens College.

Twenty-six private colleges, universities, and technical institutes also are located in the city. New York University is one of the largest in the United States. Columbia University, the oldest in the city, was founded in 1754 as King's College. Fordham University, St. John's University, Long Island University, Yeshiva University, the New School for Social Research, the Polytechnic Institute of Brooklyn, Pratt Institute, and Cooper Union are also in the city.

Libraries. Public libraries are maintained in all the boroughs. Among libraries in the United States, the New York Public Library at 5th Avenue and 42nd Street is second in size only to the Library of Congress in Washington, D. C. Special libraries and Collections include the Library for the Blind, the Schomburg Collection of Negro Literature and History, the Educational Library, an the Municipal Reference Library.

Museums. There are about 35 museums in the city. There are

664

museums of art, science, and history as well as many specialized museums. Fine arts collections can be seen in the Metropolitan Museum of Art and its Cloisters, the Museum of Modern Art, the Frick Collection, and the Whitney Museum of American Art. Also world famous are the American Museum of Natural History (and the nearby Hayden Planetarium), the Brooklyn Museum, and the Solomon R. Guggenheim Museum. Local history is featured at the Museum of the City of New York and at the New-York Historical Society.

Theater, Music, and Dance. New York is known for its many theaters in the Broadway area of Manhattan, many small off-Broadway theaters are scattered around the city. New York is also the center of music and dance for the United States. The Metropolitan Opera, the New York Philharmonic Orchestra, and the New York City Ballet are world famous. Linclon Center for the Performing Arts has modern auditoriums for opera, concerts, theater, and dance programs. Carnegie Hall is also used for concerts and recitals.

Parks. The city's park system includes Central Park, which covers 840 acres in the center of Manhattan. It was begun in 1857 as the first formally planned park in the United States. Here it is possible to ride a merry-go-round, visit a children's zoo, listen to a concert, or watch a play by Shakespeare. The New York Zoological Park in the Bronx is a world-famous zoo. Every borough except Manhattan contains one or more golf courses. Hundreds of small neighborhood parks are found throughout the city.

The Future

Like all large cities, New York has old problems to solve and new ones to face, Slums must be cleared, and new housing built. Traffic congestion continues to plague the city's overcrowded streets. Not only must new highways be constructed, but old ones must be repaired. Protecting the health and safety of New Yorkers requires an army of police, firemen, and sanitation workers. Finding an adequate water supply is a constant problem, as is the attraction of new business and industry to boost the city's economy. Caring for the sick, educating the young, providing for the needy, and helping newcomers to adjust to big city life are additional tasks that the city must perform.

Im spite of New York's problems, millions of visitors continue to flock to the city each year. Thousands stay to work and live in the city, adding to New York's human resources. new Yorkers are working hard to meet their city's needs and to keep it a world center of culture, industry, and commerce. New York buzzes with the sounds of machines tearing down and building up the city, changing its face for tomorrow's world.

Lesson 34

Tapescript:

Interpreting Hands

Like most of us, I was pretty sceptical about palmistry, and I still am to some extent, but I have found one or two interesting things which I'd like to mention. There are, in fact, three kinds of hand interpretation which have to be considered. Most people tend to think immediately of chiromancy when they hear about palmistry — the study of the lines on the hand. This suffers from a bad press, really, because of the gypsy fortune-teller associations it has, but I will explain more fully about that later. The second type of hand interpretation is called chirognomy. This is concerned with the shape of the hand, the thickness and form of the palm, length of fingers and thumb, flexibility and so on. Then dermatoglyphics is the name given to the study of the ridges and furrows which make a pattern on our hands. It is this, incidentally, which is the basis for police identification of fingerprints and so on.

I want to speak briefly today about the first two of these, which is where the bulk of my research was done, and I'll start by saying something about chirognomy. The hand is divided into four areas which I will briefly describe by using this diagram here on the screen. There is, by the way, a connection with astrology. The signs of the Zodiac are, for instance, divided into four distinct groups of three, linked to the four elements, as are modern hand shapes. Now, looking at the diagram, this area here, which includes the little finger, ring finger, half the middle finger and the area below all three, is the inner active area, and this area, area A, relates to close relationships, your love life and your relationship to your partner. Now the second area, B, is called the outer active area around the base of the index finger and the other half of the middle finger, and that relates to our social attitudes, what we might call our relationships to the outside world. Area C is the inner passive area, which lies below the inner active area, and relates to the subconscious part of the mind, and then last of all is the part relating to our energy and our creative potential, area D, which is the outer passive area ... right here, and the area all around the base of the thumb.

Now I can already hear you asking yourselves why should there be any connection between us—our character, that is—and our hands. Well, the only possible explanation I can give is that there is a large part of the brain concerned with the hand, and there are more nerve endings in the hand than elsewhere in the body, proportional to size, so it just may be—and I stressed may be—that the traffic is two-way; that not only does the brain gain information from the hand, but also passes it back again. So, in this way the hand reflects the way the brain operates.

Now I'd like to say a word about the fingers, and this is where the connection with astrology can also be seen, in the names given to the individual fingers. These are taken from the names of the old Roman gods, just like the planets' names. The index finger is the finger of Jupiter, and in this can be seen the worldly tendencies of a person—ambition, life energy, prospects for success. The finger of

668

Saturn is the name given to the middle finger, which reveals the presence of saturnine qualities, as the name would suggest—brooding, melancholy, that type of thing. The third finger or ring finger is the one with which we move towards inner concerns, and this is the finger of Apollo or the Sun. And finally, the little finger or finger of Mercury reveals a lot about human relationships. Palmists look, too, at the shape of the fingers and their flexibility and general position in relation to the hand.

Look now, if you will, at my second diagram where I've illustrated five types of fingers and I'll try to explain the characteristics people with these types of fingers are supposed to have. Now, the square shape illustrated here, where the nails and finger ends are squared off, this type reflects a cautious, thoughtful kind of person. Secondly, the spatulate type of finger, which you can see here, shaped like a spoon, narrow before the tip and then getting wider and flatter, these are the fingers of energetic and active people. Then the pointed type of finger with the tapering end; this belongs to the sensitive and artistic kind of person. Finger number three with the smooth joints indicates a quick-thinking and impulsive kind of character, and then finally the rather crooked type of finger with the knotty joints means a deep-thinking, dignified and methodical nature.

Now I've got another diagram to show you about chirognomy, and that concerns the little bumps we all have on the palm of our hand, which are said to reveal a whole lot about ourselves. Look first, if you will, at the mount of Venus, which is situated at the base of the thumb. This, you may remember, is the area of the hand relating to energy and creativity. Notice, too, the signs used to indicate these bumps: Venus, for example, as in astrology, is

669

shown by the female sign of a circle and a cross underneath it. In the hand where this mount is very flat and under-developed it implies a person with a detached and self-contained nature. Where it is large it implies a person with lots of vitality, and where normal-sized it implies a person who is healthy, warm-hearted and sincere, with plenty of compassion. Moving across to the other side of the hand opposite the mount of Venus but, like it, just above the wrist, is the mount of the Moon. A normal-sized mount of this kind will sup-. posedly be indicative of a sensitive, romantic and imaginative type. If flat, the contrary is indicated, that is, an unimaginative, possibly unstable and even bigoted character. Where it is large, then we can interpret that as being a person who is over-imaginative and intro-spective. Directly above the mount of the Moon is the upper mount of Mars. It would seem that it's best to have a normal-sized one of these, because if this is the case you are meant to be morally coura-geous. If it's flat, then you're cowardly, and if it's large you're bad-tempered and cruel. We'll contrast this with the lower mount of Mars on the far side of the hand, above the mount of Venus I spoke about first of all. With this mount, if it's normal size you're meant to be physically brave and not a panicky sort of person; you' re violent and argumentative if it's large. and cowardly if it's flat. The other four mounts are at the base of the fingers, The mount of Jupiter lies below the index finger, and next to that the mount of Saturn. Below the ring finger, here, is the mount of Apollo, and then next to that is the mount of Mercury. In the first of these four, the mount of Jupiter, if your mount is flat then that means you are a selfish, lazy individual, and if it's normal that is supposed to indicate enthusiasm, self-confidence and friendliness, whereas if large it would indicate an overbearing and very ambitious nature.

The next one right beside it, Saturn, if normal would mean a serious and studious type of personality, and if flat would seem to indicate dullness, and if large a gloomy, reclusive and withdrawn nature, none of which is very promising. The mount of Apollo, when normal, corresponds to a lucky, sunny and pleasant nature, but if flat would indicate a lack of purpose and a philistine nature. Where this mount is large, an extravagant, hedonistic and pleasure-seeking nature would seem to be implied. Finally I'll come to the mount of Mercury, and where this is of normal size it would seem to indicate a lively, persuasive and hard-working character; where flat a gullible and humourless one, and where large a person with a good sense of humour.

I'd like now to ...

Key to Exercises:

A. Answer the following questions briefly.

1. What is chiromancy concerned with?

   Answer: Lines of the hand.

2. What is chirognomy concerned with?

   Answer: The shape of the hand (thickness, form), length of fingers and thumb and flexibility and so on.

3. What is dermatoglyphics concerned with?

   Answer: The ridges and furrows which make a pattern on the hand.

4. In which area has the man focused his research?

   Answer: Chiromancy and chirognomy.

5. How many parts are there in one hand according to chirognomy?

   Answer: Four.

6. Why is there connection between our character and our hands?

   Answer: Because a large part of the brain is connected with the hand, and there are many nerve endings in the hand. Not only does the brain gain information from the hand, but the hand also reflects the way the brain operates.

7. Where are the names of the four fingers taken from?

   Answer: They are taken from the names of the old Roman gods.

B. Fill in the chart according to what you hear on the tape.

CHIROGNOMY

Area	Parts of hand included	Relation
A	Little finger, ring finger, half of the middle finger and the area below all three	close relation, love life and the relation to one's partner (Inner active area)
B	around the base of the index finger and the other half of the middle finger	one's social attitudes, one's relation to the outside world (Outer active area)
C	below the inner active area	the subconscious part of the mind (Inner passive area)
D	around the base of the thumb	one's energy and creative potential (Outer passive area)

C. Identification. Match each item in Column I with one in Column II and Column III

Column I   Column II

1. the finger of Apollo   a. inner concerns
2. the finger of Mercury   b. ambition, life energy,
                               prospects for success
3. the finger of Jupiter   c. human relationship
4. the finger of Saturn   d. presence of saturnine
                               qualities

Column III

i. the index finger
ii. the middle finger
iii. the ring finger
iv. the little finger

Answer: (1)—(a)—(iii); (2)—(c)—(iv); (3)—(b)—(i);
        (4)—(d)—(ii)

D. Complete the following information according to what you hear
on the tape.

1. The square shape finger reflects (a cautious, thoughtful kind
   of person).
2. The spatulate type of finger is the finger of (energetic and active people).
3. The pointed type of finger belongs to (the sensitive and artistic kind of people).
4. Finger with the smooth joints indicates (a quick-thinking and
   impulsive kind of character).
5. The crooked type of finger means (a deep-thinking, dignified
   and methodical nature).

673

Section Two:
Tapescript:
Outlining: Negotiations in the Philippines

In the Philippines today, Cardinal Haimi Sung, the influential Archbishop of Manila, endorsed President Corazon Aquino's efforts to negotiate with Communist insurgence of the New People's Army. Leaders of the Philippine military, however, and members of her own cabinet have criticized Aquino's attempts at negotiation. The NPA rebels had proposed a one-hundred-day cease-fire to begin in December.

A group of civilian negotiators and military advisers will meet tomorrow with rebel leaders to discuss the possible truce. Garis Porter, an assistant professor at the American University's School of International Service, says the rebel proposal is a response to President Aquino's earlier offer for a thirty-day cease-fire.

"I think they're proposing a hundred-day cease-fire primarily because they want to regain initiative, because they do have to have the appearance of being open to a cease-fire, in fact, being at least as open to cease-fire as the government is. The real question, of course, is what terms the cease-fire will be implemented on. And there is where you are going to find a lot of worms which neither side, I think, is really quite clear on exactly what they're yet ready to settle for."

"They suggested five talking points. And some of those talking points I would think could meet with some pretty stiff opposition from the Philippine military."

"Well, there's no question that the military is going to oppose, at least a couple of them very strongly."

"Such as which one?"

674

"The first one, the most important one, I think for both sides at this point is the disposition of the Philippine military, the New Armed Forces of the Philippines, NAFP, during a cease-fire. The Communists have, from the beginning, made it clear that they would insist on the pull back of NAFP units from areas which they claim to control. And the military, on the other hand, has also made equally clear that they reject any terms which would not allow them to claim clear control of all of the countryside.

"Is President Corazon Aquino being naive, as some of her military officials suggest, and thinking that she can negotiate some kind of cease-fire agreement with the Communists that will not ultimately work to their advantage?"

"I don't think 'naive' is the term to describe Aquino's policy towards the insurgency. There are two points here. One is that she understands that the intentions of the Communist side are at best unclear in terms of the cease-fire. She understands that they have their own interests and cease-fire will fit into those interests in a way that may or may not be an interest to the government. The other point, however, I think this is more important to her and perhaps objectively more important in looking at the situation. She understands that the military on her side is simply not capable of controlling the NPA through military means. And by threatening to unleash the military she may actually be making a threat which does not have much credibility. But I think she would almost do anything possible to put off having to go to primarily military strategy for dealing with the insurgency. So in a sense she is playing for time."

"If they manage to agree on a cease-fire, then what happens after that? What happens when the hundred days is up?"

"Nobody wants to be the first one to break the cease-fire once it's put into effect. So I think the agreement to a hundred-day cease-fire is, . . . has much longer term and much broader implication, if in fact they could come to that agreement, which at this point I think it is still very much up in the air."

"If it fails, if it fails, does that mean an escalation in the military complex?"

"Well, I think the pressures on Aquino for letting the military go back to its preferred strategy, attempting to go on the offensive, to carry out major military operations, particularly in Central Luzon and in the Southern Tagalog, that is south of Manila, is very strong. And that she will probably make concessions to the military which would allow it to resume the offenses to, at least, try that out."

Garis Porter is assistant professor at the American University's School of International Service in Washington, D.C.

Key to Exercises:

A. Identification. Identify the following characters' title and function as mentioned in the news report.

1. Corazon Aquino: (President, who made efforts to negotiate with the Communist NPA).

2. Haimi Sung: (Archbishop of Manila, who endorsed the President's efforts).

3. Garis Porter: (assistant prof. at the Am Univ.'s School of International Service).

B. Match each item in Column I with one in Column II by recognizing the person's action or comment.

<table>
<tr><td>Column I</td><td>Column II</td></tr>
<tr><td>1. Corazon Aquino</td><td>a. have criticized Aquino's</td></tr>
</table>

676

		attempts at negotiation
2. military leaders	b.	will meet with rebel leaders tomorrow
3. the NPA rebels	c.	proposed a one-hundred-day cease-fire
4. Garis Porter	d.	offered a thirty-day cease-fire
5. civilian negotiators	e.	says that the rebel proposal is a response to Aquino's earlier offer

Answer: (1)—(d); (2)—(a); (3)—(c); (4)—(e); (5)—(b)

C. Answer the following questions briefly.

1. Who suggested the five talking points?

Answer: The rebel leaders.

2. How would these talking points be received by the Philippine military?

Answer: It is likely that some of the talking points would meet stiff opposition from the philippine military.

D. True or False Questions. Write a T in front of a statement if it is true according to the recording and write an F if it is false.

1. (F) The most important talking point is the disposition of the New People's Army.

2. (T) Some of Corazon Aquino's military officials think that Aquino is naive to negotiate some kind of cease-fire agreement with the Communists.

3. (T) According to the speaker, the military on Aquino's side is simply not capable of controlling the NPA through mili-

677

tary means.

E. Fill in the detailed information according to what you hear on the tape.

　　Nobody (wants) to be the first one to (break) the cease-fire once it's (put into effect). So I think the (agreement) to a hundred-day cease-fire is, ... has much (longer term) and much (broader implication), if in fact they could (come to) that (agreement), which at this point I think it is still very much (up in the air).

Section Three:

Tapescript:

Outlining: Technology and the Future (I)

　　The title of my talk is 'Technology and the Future', and it's only fair to start with a couple of warnings. I have never been interested in the near future—only the more distant one. So if you take my predictions too seriously, you'll go broke; but if your children don't take them seriously enough, they'll go broke. I'll deal first with transportation and communication, because they are inextricably linked together and do more than anything else to shape society. For near-earth applications, both communication and transportation may now be approaching their practical limits and may reach them by the turn of the century.

　　For terrestrial transportation, I don't see any real need for much advance beyond the currently planned supersonic transports, operating at almost two thousand miles per hour.

　　True, one could build pure rocket vehicles to go from pole to pole in about one hour, but I don't think the public will enjoy fifteen minutes of high acceleration and fifteen minutes of high deceleration, separated by half an hour of complete weightlessness.

Rather more practical, and of much more immediate importance, will be ground-effect vehicles, or hovercraft. I think we'll have them in the thousand-ton and ten-thousand ton class by the end of the century.

The political effect of such vehicles may be enormous, as they can go over land and sea and can cross most reasonable obstacles as if they aren't there. You could have the great 'ports' of the world at the centre of the continents, if you wanted to.

That private hovercraft will ever be popular, I rather doubt. They are noisy and have poor efficiency and poor control. You can't t put on the brakes in a hurry if you're riding on a bubble of air. However, they are splendid for opening up terrain where conventional vehicles cannot travel — such as shallow rivers, swamps, ice fields, coral reefs at low tide, and similar types of fascinating and now inaccessible wilderness.

I hope to see the automatic car before I die. Personally, I refuse to drive a car — I won't have anything to do with any kind of transport in which I can't read. I can see a time when it's illegal for a human being to drive a car on a main highway.

More seriously, we'll certainly have to get rid of the petrol engine, and everybody is now waking up to the urgent necessity of this. Apart from the facts of air pollution, we have much more important uses for petroleum than burning it.

To make non-petrol cars and other vehicles practical, we need some new power source. Fuel cells are already here, but they are only a marginal improvement. I don't know how we're going to do it, but we want something at least a hundred times lighter and more compact than present batteries.

Key to Exercises:

A. General Comprehension: Give brief answers to the following
   questions.

   1. What future is the speaker more interested in?

     Answer: Distant future.

   2. Why does the speaker want to deal with transportation and
     communication first?

     Answer: They are closely linked and do more than anything
           else to shape society.

   3. What will happen to communication and transportation by
     the turn of the century?

     Answer: They will reach their practical limits.

   4. Which vehicle will be more practical to develop for terrestrial
     transportation? Why?

     Answer: Hovercraft. They can go over land and sea and can
           cross most reasonable obstacles.

   5. Why will private hovercraft not be popular?

     Answer: They are noisy and have poor efficiency and control

   6. Why should we get rid of the petrol engine?

     Answer: a. Air pollution;

            b. Other uses for petroleum.

B. Suggested abbreviations:

   transportation: transp.   communication: comu.

   century: c.   continent: cont.

   hovercraft: ho   petroleum: p.

   because: ∴

680

C. Notetaking: Make an outline for the first part of the lecture you have heard on the tape.

Suggested outline:

Title: Technology and the Future

I. Warning: distant future, predicting for your children's generation.

II. Transp. & comu.

   A. Transp.

      1. supersonic transports: no need to go beyond; 2, 000m/hour

      2. rocket vehicles: pole to pole in 1 hour; 15 minutes up, 15 minutes down, 30 minutes weightless; not enjoyable

      3. hovercraft: more practical; 1,000 ton and 10,000 ton end of c.

      political effect: go over land & sea;

      have ports at centre of cont.

      private ho.: not popular – noisy,

      poor efficiency & control.

      4. automatic car: get rid of petrol engine

        ∴a. air pollution

         b. other important uses for p.

      5. new power source:

        a. fuel cells – marginal improvement

        b. 100 times lighter & more compact than present batteries.

Supplementary Reading:

Palmistry

Palmistry is the attempt to analyse a person's character or predict his destiny by studying the features of his hand, particularly his palm. Palm reading, also called chiromancy, is considered by scientific students of human behaviour to be a form of pseudoscience. It is often used in fortune-telling.

A palmist gives particular attention to seven mounts and four lines in the hand. Each mount is named for a heavenly body — Jupiter, Saturn, Apollo (or the Sun), Mercury, Mars, the Moon, and Venus — and in this respect palmistry relies on beliefs connected with astrology. The development of each mount is supposed to reveal features of character. Jupiter is supposedly associated with such traits as ambition, concern for honour, and interest in religion. Thus overdevelopment of this mount is said to reveal pride and superstition. A highly developed mount of Mars would indicate bravery and a martial character, and lesser development would suggest cowardice. The mount of Saturn is related to luck and to wisdom; of Apollo, to intelligence; and of Venus, to amorousness.

The four principal lines in the palm are those of the head, the heart, life and fortune. Palmists study the relative length and depth of these lines. They would say, for example, that a short or broken life line forecasts early death or serious illness.

The nature of the head line is taken to indicate a person's intelligence, the heart line relates to affection, and the line of fortune is used as a predictor of success or failure in life.

Palmistry has a long history. It was practised in ancient Egypt, Greece, and Rome, and extensively in China. Modern practices in palmistry may have been imported into Europe from Asia by gypsies during the Renaissance. This period was marked by a flourishing of beliefs in divining personality by studying parts of the body. Twentieth century Palmists — who operate, for example, as carnival entertainers — are more concerned with foretelling a person's future than with analyzing his character.

Lesson 35

Tapescript:

The Unfortunate Story of the Lost Money

Tom: ... when I was living ... in North Africa, and I had a cook, and I'd been there for several years, you see. And I was just coming on leave to England, you see, and obviously it was quite a long leave, you know. I was coming for ... three months, I think it was. So I had to, I had a house and I had to sort of close the house up, obviously, and, erm, this chap who worked for me, who was a sort of ... cook, erm, he was ... obviously going to go off, you know, for three months—there wasn't any point in him staying there—so it was, I was getting everything ready, anyway. And I had a lot of things to fix up, so I'd got rather a lot of cash out of the bank. You know, I had a lot of bills to pay (Yes) and things to do, and, erm, I had about sixty-five pounds, I think it was. And one particular evening, I was just sort of, you know, clearing up the sitting-room and going to go to bed, I put the sixty-five quid under the papers in the top left-hand drawer of my desk and then I went out of the door on to the veranda and locked the door. And the point was, all the rooms of the house sort of opened on to a veranda, on to a courtyard, if you see what I mean. There weren't passages inside the house. And, erm, then I went to bed. So, the next morning I got up, and, erm ... after I'd had my breakfast, I was going out into the town to do various things for which I needed the money, you see (Yes) and, erm, I went to the drawer to get it ... and it wasn't there! I immediately thought, well maybe my cook, Idris, has taken this, because, the thing was, that the rooms were all locked and you couldn't have got in to the, erm, to the room, or any of the rooms of the house, without showing some sort of sign of entry, if you see what I mean. (Yes) And, er, he had access to all the keys in the house, you know. (Oh, I see.) So, erm, I went to his room. And, erm, he'd gone off already. 'He'd gone shopping, in fact. In fact, his room was locked. Erm, I got the keys, unlocked it, went in, sort of searched the room, ... felt rather sort of ... guilty, you know, at sort of going through his personal possessions in this way. But there was nothing there. So, you know, I thought, 'Well, hell, what do I do next? I'd better go to the police'. And, erm, my mind was still very much on him, that ... it must be him. Erm, so I went down to the police station and, erm, said that the money'd been stolen and would the police please come to the house, and investigate. And would they also ... investigate my cook, whom I suspected. And they said, erm, well, they wouldn't come and search the cook or look round the house unless I made a definite accusation a-gainst him. And if I made a definite accusation against him, they'd come along and, er, take him back to the police sta-tion and really sort it out. Well, I wasn't very happy about that, because I felt, erm, I didn't really have any evidence, you know, I was just extremely suspicious of him because of the circumstances. So, erm, I said, ' No, ' and, but felt pretty desperate about it then. So I went back to the house ... Anyway, later in the day, I said to him, 'You know, I had sixty-five pounds, which I put in the desk, and it's disappeared.' And he sort of said, 'Oh, yeah'. You know, he didn, didn't register anything at all. Er, so I said, ' Yes, sixty-five pounds has disappeared and nobody seems to have come into the house'. And he sort of said, 'Oh yeah, well', (you know). So I said, 'Yes, I'm going to get the police'. And he still didn't sort of register anything, you know. He just sort of shrugged his shoulders. So then I thought, ' Well, the only thing to do is that I'll have to tell him that, erm, that's it, you know, I don't want him to work for me any more'. But, erm, being a coward over these sort of things, I let it drift for about a couple of days, and then, the day I was actually going, erm, I said to him, er, you know, 'Idris, I'm afraid that, er, I don't want you to come back after the holidays. I think it's better if you don't work for me any more.' And, er, he immediately made a tremendous speech, he said what the hell did I think I was doing, etcetera, etcetera, why, what were my reasons, etcetera, etcetera. So I said, probably very stupidly, but I said to him, ' Well, you know about that sixty-five pounds that disappeared, well, I'm not saying you took it, but I just think you might have taken it, and therefore I don't feel I can trust you any more and, er, so I just don't think you can go on working for me.' So, of course, that was it! He absolutely went through the roof at this! And, erm, you know, gave me a sort of tremendous ... tirade. Anyway, I'd quite made up my mind, although I'd taken so long to tell him ... And I said, 'Well, sorry', you know, 'that's it.' Then, in fact, erm, a friend dropped in, erm, who, who, who was a great friend. He, he, he lived there, he was a local person. And, erm, Osman came in and he sort of ... started getting involved in the conversation, ... anyway, I wasn't going to change my attitude over it. Then Idris got terribly upset and was all sort of sad about it and upset about it and started to cry, said I was ruining his life, etcetera. But, anyway, I was completely sort of hard-hearted about it and didn't do anything about it and that was it. And he went. I, er, I mean I ... paid him, ... you know, quite a bit of money in lieu of notice and everything but, I mean, he still felt extremely upset, and it was one of those, erm, very kind of unpleasant things, which left one ... feeling ... rather ... upset about it and not knowing... I never knew whether I'd done quite the right thing or not. Well, I worked there for a couple of years more and when I was finally leaving after two years I was throwing out lots and lots of things like magazines, books and so on, and this chap, Osman, who'd actually been there the afternoon Idris had finally left amidst all these rows, I gave him some old magazines, including actually, er, an old *Encounter* and, erm, he came back a few days later and he said, 'You know, I didn't know whether to actually come and tell you or not, but I was looking through that copy of *Encounter* you gave me and I found sixty-five pounds (laughter) in the back of the magazine.' Terribly difficult because I was leaving the country, never to come back, you know, in

687

about twenty-four hours after that ... feeling that one had
done something wrong which one couldn't put right! And I
didn't have any idea what had happened to Idris, in fact.
Pretty unfortunate!

Key to Exercises:

A. Choose the best answer (a, b or c) to complete each of the following statements.

1. The narrator had been in _____ for several years.

    a. North America

  * b. North Africa

    c. England

2. The narrator would have a three - month holiday back
_____.

    a. in North America

    b. in North Africa

  * c. in England

3. He would _____ when he left.

  * a. close his house up

    b. ask his cook to manage the house

    c. ask the police to keep a careful watch on the house

4. All the rooms of the house opened on to _____.

    a. a corridor

    b. a balcony

  * c. a veranda

5. The police refused to come and search the cook or look round
the house unless _____.

    a. the narrator had got some evidence against him

  * b. the narrator made a definite accusation against him

c. the narrator had got a witness of what had happened

B. True or False Questions. Write a T in front of a statement if it is true according to the recording and write an F if it is false.

1. (F) The narrator remembered putting his sixty-five pounds into the papers in the top left-hand drawer of his desk.

2. (T) Idris knew where to get the keys to all the rooms in the house.

3. (F) Thinking Idris was a coward at admitting stealing the money, the narrator waited for a couple of days.

4. (T) The narrator continued to work there for another couple of years after he sent away Idris.

5. (F) The narrator finally found his lost money when he was reading a magazine.

C. Fill in the blanks.

1. He absolutely (went through the roof) at this and gave me a (tremendous tirade). Anyway, I had quite made up my mind although I (had taken) so long to tell him.

2. Terrible difficult because I (was leaving the country), never to come back in about (24 hours) after that ... feeling that one had done something wrong which one (couldn't put right). And I didn't (have any idea) what had happened to Idris, in fact. (Pretty unfortunate).

Section Two:
Tapescript:
New Report: Drive-in Theatres in Trouble

In the summer of 1933, the world's first drive-in movie theatre opened in Camden, New Jersey. Drive-ins became popular after World War II and in the '50s there were nearly five thousand theatres across the country. But today, less than three thousand remained. Drive-ins are in trouble. Land values near cities are increasing and drive-ins are being torn down to make way for malls. And families are more likely to stay home for an evening of cheap entertainment with their VCRs and cable TV. When one more drive-in closed recently outside Jeffersonville, Indiana, reporter Bob Hanson was there, the last night at the Lakewood Drive-in.

The sun set as the last cars entered the Lakewood Drive-in. At the ticket booth Laura Boyle filled in for her daughter who's away at college. No money changed hands. The show was on the house.

Thirty years ago John Walley opened the Lakewood Drive-in on his father's farmland in southern Indiana. Corn fields still surround the theatre. Since 1956 people have driven for miles to get to the drive-in. They came in Studebakers, and Fords, Ramblars, and Corvats. But the '80s haven't been so kind to the drive-in. And on this night John Walley is closing up.

Before the show started, parents took their children to a playground in the front of the theatre. Framed by an orange sky and in the humid Mid-western air, they played on swings and slides. Inside the snack bar, the menu was timeless.

"Forty cents is your change, thank you."

Thelma Wilson stuffed hotdogs in buns and wrapped them in aluminum foil bags. For twenty-three years Thelma has cooked hotdogs, popped popcorn and filled drinks in the Lakewood Drive-in.

In the mid-sixties, five hundred cars would fill the ashfall and dirt theatre. But in the eighties, seventy-five cars was considered a good night. And sometimes the movie's played to just twenty.

Carlo Crown switched on the thirty-five millimeter projector for the last time. About a hundred seventy-five cars pointed at the crumbling while screen. As word got out that the Lakewood Drive-in was closing up, people came from throughout the area. As the black and white images flickered on the screen, some people found themselves back in time. Like Linda King, who spent her wedding night here twenty-two years ago.

"There's a lot of memories here. I've brought all my kids here, my grandkids, and they are not going to be here any more. So they aren't going to bring their children here when they're grown."

Johnny Buckman and his wife Merilyn watched the movie from their tinted glass window. The two went out on dates here twenty-seven years ago.

"I have been thinking about, you know, when we were young, and when he put his arms around me and . . . and just a lot of old memories, you know." John Walley stood outside the snack bar and talked to old friends and customers. He talked about how hard it was to compete with air-conditioned theatres and couldn't get first-run movies any more. And most of all he just reminisced.

"This is nice to go out to the country and watch a movie on a big screen. The young people just don't know what they are missing because there won't be any drive-ins around in another ten years.

Some people watched the movie from the hood of their car. Others sat on lawn chairs. Many just walked around. John Walley plastered auction off the equipment from the drive-in. But in the dark people tried not to think about that. By the way, tonight's final film – The Last Picture Show. For National Public Radio, I'm Bob Henson in southern Indiana.

691

Key to Exercises:

A. Fill in the following chart with information about drive-in movie theatres.

Time	summer of 1933	
Place	(Camden, New Jersey)	
Event	(the world's 1st drive-in opened)	
Days of Popularity		(after WWII)
Number of drive-ins in the '50s		(nearly 5,000)
Number of drive-ins remained		(less than 3,000)
End for drive-ins		(torn down for malls)

B. Choose the best answer (a, b or c) to complete each of the following statements.

1. _____ when the last cars entered the Lakewood Drive-in.

   a. It was in the morning

* b. It was at dusk

   c. it was in the late evening

2. " Laura Boyle filled in for her daughter " means _____.

   a. she signed the name for her daughter

* b. she replaced her daughter as a ticket-collector

   c. she handed in the ticket for her daughter

3. "The show was on the house" means _____.

* a. the show was freee of charge

   b. the film was shown on the wall of the house

c. the projector was placed on the roof of the house

C. Fill in the detailed information according to what you hear on the tape.

Thirty Years ago, John walley opened the Lakewood drive-in on (his father's farmland) in southern Indiana. (Corn field) still surround the theatre. Since (1956) people (have driven) for miles to get to the drive-in. But the '80s (haven't been so kind) to the drive-in. And on this night John Walley (is closing up).

D. True or False Questions. Write a T in front of a statement if it is true according to the recording and write an F if it is false.
   1. (F) Before the show started, parents took their children to a playground in front of the theatre.
   2. (F) Inside the snack bar, the menu was brought to the customers in no time.
   3. (T) Hotdogs, popped popcorn and drinks were served in the snack bar for twenty-three years.
   4. (T) People heard that the Lakewood Drive-in was closing up, so they came from all over that area.
   5. (T) It was hard for the Lakewood Drive-in to compete with air-conditioned theatres and to get new movies.
   6. (F) People paid no attention to what was going on in the Lakewood drive-in while watching the film.

E. Fill in the blanks with the numbers according to what you hear.
   1. In the (mid-'60s), (500) cars would fill the Lakewood Drive-in.
   2. In the ('805), (75) cars was considered a good night.

3. Sometimes the movie's played to just (20).

F. Identification. Match each item in Column I with one in Column II by recognizing the person's identity.

Column I	Column II
1. Johnny Buckman	a. cook in the snack bar
2. Johnny Walley	b. ticket collector at the Lakewood drive-in
3. Bob Hanson	c. projectionist at the Lakewood drive-in
4. Laura Boyle	d. frequent customer who went out on dates at the Lakewood drive-in twenty-seven years ago
5. Carlo Crown	e. reporter from National Public Radio
6. Linda King	f. owner of the Lakewood drive-in
7. Thelma Wilson	g. customer who spent her wedding night at the Lakewood drive-in twenty-two years ago
8. Merilyn	

Answer: (1)—(d);(2)—(f);(3)—(e);(4)—(b);
　　　　(5)—(c);(6)—(g);(7)—(a);(8)—(d)

Section Three:
Tapescript:
Outlining: Technology and the Future (II)

Now I would like to say a word about communications. The revolution in communications that has already taken place is still not fully understood. One way of appreciating it is to do a kind of communications strip tease. I would like you to abolish in your minds TV, then radio, then telephones, then the postal service, then the

694

newspapers. In other words, to revert to the Middle Ages. In such a situation, we should feel deaf and blind, like prisoners in solitary confinement. Well, we'll appear this way to our grandchildren. Don't forget that a generation has already grown up that never knew a world without TV. One communications revolution has taken place in our lifetime. The next revolution, perhaps the final one, will be the result of satellites and microelectronics, which will enable us to do literally anything we want to in the field of communications and information transfer—including, ultimately, not only sound and vision but all sense impressions.

I am particularly interested in TV broadcasting from satellites directly into the home, bypassing today's ground stations—a proposal I first described twenty-two years ago. This will mean the abolition of all present geographical restrictions to TV; via satellites, any country can broadcast to any other. Direct-broadcast TV will be possible within five years and may be most important to undeveloped countries that have no ground stations, and now may never require any. Africa, China, and South America could be opened up by direct TV broadcast, and whole populations brought into the modern world. I believe that communications satellites may bring about the long-overdue end of the Stone Age.

They will certainly lead to a global telephone system and end long-distance calls — for all calls will be 'local'! There will be the same flat rate everywhere.

Newspapers will, I think, receive their final body blow from these new communications techniques. How I look forward to the day when I can press a button and get any type of news, editorials, book and theatre reviews, etc., merely by dialling the right channel. Moreover, not only today's but any newspaper ever published will be available. Some sort of TV-like console connected to a central electronic library, could make available any information ever printed in any form.

Electronic 'mail' delivery is another exciting prospect of the very near future. Letters, will be automatically read and flashed from continent to continent and reproduced at receiving stations within a few minutes of transmission.

All these things are associated with information processing, and one-third of the Gross National Product is now spent on this in one form of another—data storage, TV, radio, books, and so forth. This radio is increasing; our society is changing from a goods-producing society to an information-processing one. I have devoted much of one book *Voices from the Sky* to the social consequences of this, and can mention only a few here.

One could be the establishment of English as the world language, through the direct telecast satellites mentioned above. Within the next ten years the future language of mankind will be decided, in a bloodless battle twenty-two thousand miles above the equator.

Another very important consequence will be a change in the patterns of transport, for a man and his work need no longer be in the same place. When these new information-and-communications consoles are available, almost anybody who does any kind of mental work can live wherever he pleases. Beyond this, any kind of manipulative skill can also be transferred from one point to another. I can imagine a time when even a brain surgeon can live in one place and operate on patients all over the world, through remote-controlled artificial hands, like those used in atomic energy plants.

Yet these developments will not necessarily mean an overall reduction of transport. I see a great reduction of transport for work, but increased transport for pleasure.

A result of this will be that vast uninhabited areas of the Earth could be opened up, because people will have far greater freedom to choose where they will live.

These trends will inevitably accelerate the disintegration of the cities, whose historical function is now passing. Cities will go on growing, of course, like dinosaurs — for the same reasons, and with the same results.

Key to Exercises:

A. General Comprehension: Write a T in front of a statement if it is true according to the recording and write an F if it is false.

1. (T) We would feel deaf and blind if we were to live in the Middle Ages, because of the lack of communication.

2. (F) Satellites and microelectronics have enabled us to do anything we want to in the field of communication.

3. (F) In the future there will be no local calls because there will be no cities or countries.

4. (T) *Voices from the Sky* is a book written by the speaker.

5. (F) The speaker is very sure that English will be the world language in the future.

6. (T) According to the speaker, people will transport more for pleasure than for work.

B. Suggested abbreviations:

general: gen.   microelectronics: microel.

C. Notetaking: Make an outline for the second part of the lecture you have heard on the tape.

Suggested outline

B. Comu.

  1. Gen. vision:

    1 revolution in our time; next or final – result of satellites & microel. ; transfer: sound, vision, all sense impressions.

  2. Specific:

    a. TV: broadcast via satellites; direct broadcast poss. within 5 ys. ; good for underdeveloped countries.

    b. Telephone: global system, no local call

    c. Newspapers: press a button, get any info. by dialling the right channel; get any published paper from a TV-like console connected to a library.

    d. Mail: electronic delivery.

  3. Info. processing:

    a. ⅓ GNP spent on it; increasing

    b. Consequences:

      (1) a world lang.

      (2) Pattern of transport: not for work but for pleasure

        Result: (a) live where people want to live

             (b) cities disintegrated

Lesson 36

Section One:

Tapescript:

Home Computers

Just before I give a few details about the—er—fun aspect of computers, that is, for use at home and for entertainment—I'd like to mention a couple of facts about the outlook for ISDN – that's the integrated services digital network—and it foresees a world-wide telecommunications network which could transmit telex and voice signals and, indeed, full-colour video images and high-speed computer data. Now, can you just imagine having a meeting with your colleagues around the world without even leaving your office? Well, that's what world-wide video teleconferencing can do, and it's on the cards that internal toll-free telephones may be available and also faster computer transmission with a digital network. And how are all these marvellous things achieved? Well, there are satellite relays, and digital packet switching, and laser devices which transmit over fibre-optic cables. But more about that another time.

And after that slight diversion I'll get back to a totally different aspect of modern technology—home computers, or PCs—that stands for personal computers. First, a bit of background. Some people attribute this growth industry to the recession which led to redundancies and a shorter working week, and this in turn led to more leisure time. So what are people doing with this extra free time that's on their hands? They're indulging in home entertainment, that's what! Hundreds of companies have sprung up to fill this gap, and the sports, DIY and home entertainment industries are achieving phenomenal success. In 1983 in the US, there were four million PCs, and game-playing was the principal use, with educational use a close second; and in third place was the financial function for things like budgeting, balancing cheque books, accounting and forecasting and so on.

To illustrate this with a few concrete figures, from the States again, in 1983, 52 per cent of the software was for entertainment programs, whereas only 16 percent was educational. Possibly this could be explained by the short life span of computer games, and having teenagers in the home was a decisive factor in the purchase of a personal computer, as households with children in this age-range were 50 per cent more likely to buy them. As far as the interest versus disapproval statistics go, in the 18-19 age-group, 25 per cent expressed interest in PCs and 18 per cent disapproval; and at the other end of the scale, the over-60s showed only 3 per cent interest and a resounding 87 per cent disapproval!

And this trend towards PCs is likely to continue as users become more knowledgeable and want more expensive machines with all kinds of new things. And there's a wide range in sizes, too, as the portable market expands, and now you can buy a featherweight lap-size model that's less than 2 kgs, or something larger at around 12 kgs but still portable.

Just to digress slightly, I'd like to point out that microtechnology has hit other aspects of the home and leisure industry as well. With more time on our hands it seems we're spending more time keeping fit, and fitness has become a real growth industry, and it seems prone to gadgetry as well! There are all sorts of new things on the market these days. Take, for example, the watches that monitor your pulse rate as you jog or do aerobics, or exercise bicycles with sensors in the handgrips to check your pulse rate and then display it on a screen. And for those of you who remember that famous toy of the early 80s—Rubik's cube, the one with six sides, each composed of nine rotating faces, with 43 quintillion combinations—well, anyway, in a lab in the US they're working on a Cubot—that's a self-contained robot using microprocessors and mechanics—to solve it. But I'm getting off the track again, so back to our home computers with a final warning.

The technical innovations of the last couple of decades have led to a host of new words in our vocabulary, and one of these is hacker—that's H-A-C-K-E-R and it simply means an enthusiast who breaks into computers. And, not so long ago in the States, teenagers who were hackers used their home computers to break into supposedly secure government and business computers, for example in banks, labs and research centres. They just tried out different passwords until they found the right one. And as one seventeen-year-old said, 'It was like child's play.' And all that's needed is a home computer and a modem—that's M-O-D-E-M—which is a device that allows computers to transmit data over the phone lines—and, of course, a basic knowledge of how to operate a computer! And this has led to tangled legal and ethical problems—but we won't go into that here. But, as you can see, home computers are indeed a handy thing to have around, not only for entertainment but also for educational value. And no doubt in future . . .

Key to Exercises:

701

A. Answer the following questions.
1. What do they stand for?
   a. ISDN:
      (the integrated services digital network)
   b. PCs:
      (personal computers)
   c. DIY:
      (do it yourself)
2. What do they mean?
   a. hacker:
      (an enthusiast who breaks into computers)
   b. modem:
      (a device that allows computers to transmit data over the phone lines)
3. What could the future world-wide telecommunications network do?
   Answer: It could transmit telex and voice signals and full-colour video images and high speed computer data.
4. What could world-wide video teleconferencing do?
   Answer: It could enable you to stay in your office and have a meeting with your colleagues around the world.
5. What has caused the growth in computer industry according to some people?
   Answer: More leisure time.

B. Identification. Divide the following phrases into two groups by recognizing the group each item belongs to.
1. digital packet switching
2. faster computer transmission with a digital network

702

3. world-wide video teleconferencing
4. satellite relays
5. internal toll-free telephones
6. laser devices

  Group 1: the marvellous things to be achieved

   1. (world-wide video teleconferencing)

   2. (internal toll-free telephones)

   3. (faster computer transmission with a digital network)

  Group 2: the means that help to achieve those marvellous things

   1. (satellite relays)

   2. (digital packet switching)

   3. (laser devices)

C. Write out the different uses of PCs according to the sequence listed below.

1. Principal use: (game-playing)

2. Close second: (education)

3. Third place: (financial function)

D. Fill in the chart about the reception of PCs in the US.

Age Group	Interest	Disapproval
18—19	(25%)	(18%)
over 60s	(3%)	(87%)

New Report: Miami Has Become a Dangerous Place

Dade County, Florida, which includes the city of Miami, is a dangerous place to be these days, that according to a Miami *Herald* poll released this week. The survey reports that forty-two percent of people interviewed or their family members have been victims of burglary, robbery or assault in the past five years. Almost one half say they need guns to feel safe in Dade County, although most people won't say whether they do own weapons. The *Herald* conducted the survey in the wake of a widely publicized booby trap killing, in which a store owner killed a would-be burglar. And now the poll suggests a lot more people want to take law into their own hands. *Herald* reporter Andre Vicluchee has been covering the story.

"The one part I think that that was a little surprising was the number of people who feel that it is okay to shoot, to kill an intruder that comes into your house. We found sixty-three percent feel that they should have the right to kill an intruder in their house."

"Whether or not the person is armed or not only if . . ."

"Whether they know or not if the person is armed. It surprised us; we figured there would be something of a hard-line attitude out there. But this was probably above what we expected."

"Well, it seems, though, that people are perceiving at least in Dade County that crimes are really in bad situation that they are willing to do something about it with violence."

"Yes. I went back and questioned more at length another fifteen or twenty responded from the poll. And they all seem to feel that, if they find themselves in a situation in which they have to take some action, even if it means killing somebody, they'll do it."

"I'll take it that Miami *Herald* poll and perhaps that a lot of people's feelings about crimes stem in part from this case of the booby trap victim, a store owner booby trapped his variety store raider in a black neighborhood. Tell us about that case."

"The man's name is Prentice Raschid. He is a black business man who has a small store in a black high-crime area of town. He has been burglarized, I think, seven or eight times over the past few weeks, had asked for help from the police and had not gotten any answer to his satisfaction. So he went ahead and set up an electrical booby trap in the store. About a week and a half ago one morning, they found a young man dead in the booby trap who had been electrocuted while trying to carry out some stuff from the store."

"In what has the public reaction been then?"

"The public reaction has been an overwhelming support for Mr. Raschid. He has been charged with man slaughter, and with setting up an illegal man trap. But our poll found that seventy-nine percent of the population here feel he should not be prosecuted."

"Has this case, this booby trap case, led to inspire any other similar instances of citizen store-owners fighting back against burglars?"

"I don't know if it directly inspired them, but it may have been a coincidence. But in the following week there were another five incidents in which citizens, if you will, turn the tables on assailants. In fact these all six incidents left four people dead, four alleged criminals dead and two others wounded in the hospital."

"Is there anything about Dade County that is making it a particularly blood thirsty place at the moment, as crime's really on the increase in Dade County . . ."

"I believe the situation is, we have a city here that's grown a lot in the last few years."

"In what way? What's been the source of the growth?"

"Immigration for the most part, and a lot of people coming in from Cuba, Cuban refugees, a lot of Haitian refugees, and from all over Latin America. What is interesting about the Raschid case in this context is that, as Mr. Raschid has pointed out himself, that although he is a black business man operating in a black area, his support has come from all groups, Hispanic, white and black."

"Andre, do you carry around a gun when you are doing your reporting?"

"I don't. But I know some reporters that do."

Andre Vigluche is a reporter for the Miami *Herald*.

Key to Exercises:

A. Choose the best answer (a, b or c) to complete each of the following statements.

1. In a poll conducted by Miami's *Herald*, _____ interviewed have been victims of some violent crimes in the past five years.

   a. forty-two out of thos

   b. the forty-two people

 * c. forty-two percent of people

2. _____ admit they need weapons to feel safe in Dade County.

 * a. Almost half of the people interviewed

   b. Forty-two percent of the people interviewed

   c. Half of the people in the area

3. To the reporter who has been covering the story, the surprising part of the story is _____.

706

a. that a large number of people have been victims of violent crimes

b. that a lot of people intend to take law into their own hands

* c. that many people think it acceptable to shoot an intruder

4. Prentice Raschid , a black business man was charged with man slaughter because _____ .

a. he had used an illegal gun to kill an intruder into his store

* b. he had electrocuted a burglar with a man trap

c. he had not reported the intrusion to the police

5. All the six incidents mentioned left _____ dead and _____ wounded.

* a. four; two

b. six; four

c. two; six

B. Answer the following questions.

1. Why did Prentice Raschid, the black business man, set up a booby trap?

Answer: He had been burglarized seven or eight times in the course of a few weeks. He had asked for help from the police but he had not got a satisfactory response.

2. What is the chief cause for the increase of crime in Dade County, according to the reporter?

Answer: It is the rapid growth of the city Miami in the last few years.

3. What is the public reaction to the Raschid case?

Answer: There has been an overwhelming support for Mr. Raschid, the black businessman.

Section Three:

Tapescript:

Outlining: Technology and the Future (III)

Now I would like to discuss environment, which is very much a function of transportation and communication. But it is also a function of population. As everybody knows, we are now in a population explosion—but probably around the turn of the century this particular explosion will be controlled and the world population may be shrinking again.

Nevertheless, even with a six billion population there may be more room than is generally imagined today. By the twenty-first century, agriculture will be on the way out. It's a ridiculous process: a whole acre is needed to feed one person, because growing plants are extremely inefficient devices for trapping sunlight. If we could develop a biological system working at a mere five per cent efficiency—today's solar cells can double that—it would require twenty square feet, not one acre, to feed one person.

Food production is the last major industry to yield to technology. Only now are we doing something about it, probably too little and too late.

One promising field of research is the production of proteins from petroleum by microbiological conversion, which sounds most unappetizing—but we do use microbes to make wine. This process gives high-quality proteins, some of them better balanced for human consumption than natural vegetable proteins. It would take only three per cent of today's petroleum output to provide the total protein needs of the entire human race.

With the exception of luxury items—and the Russians, I've

heard, have already started to export synthetic caviare! —most foods will be factory-made in the next century. This will free vast areas of agricultural land for other purposes—living, parks, recreation, hunting—above all, for wilderness.

As a source of raw materials, the sea seems inexhaustible. Any element you care to mention is there, in solution or lying on the sea bed. We will also be forced to use it for more and more of our water supply, through desalination techniques.

I'm sorry to leave the sea so hastily, but space is a lot bigger and I must spend more time on that.

Our current ideas of space and its potentialities are badly distorted by the primitive nature of our techniques. To prove this, here is a statistic that will surprise you.

The amount of energy needed to lift a man to the Moon is about 1000 kilowatt-hours and that costs only ten to twenty dollars! The difference of nine zeros between this and the Apollo budget is a measure of our present incompetence. Ultimately, there's no reason why space travel should be, in terms of future incomes, much more expensive than jet flight today.

Space communities will be established first on the Moon, then on Mars, and later on other worlds. But much closer to the Earth, orbital space stations of many kinds will be in wide use by the year 2000. In May 1967, I was in Dallas to attend the first conference on the commercial uses of space—including tourism. Barron Hilton gave a talk on the Hilton Orbiter Hotel, which he hopes to see in his lifetime. Space tourism is going to be a major industry in the twenty-first century.

Another tremendously important use of space stations will be for medical research. One paper given at Dallas discussed the engineering problem of a hospital in orbit.

Which brings a poignant memory to mind. The last letter I ever received from that great scientist professor J. B. S. Haldane was written when he was dying of cancer and in considerable pain from his operations. In it, he said what a boon the weightless environment of a space hospital would be to patients like himself not to mention burn victims, sufferers from heart complaints, and those afflicted with muscle diseases. I am convinced that research in space will open up unguessed regions of medical knowledge and give us a vast range of new therapies. So I get pretty mad when I hear ignorant but well-intentioned people ask, 'Why not spend the space budget on something useful—like cancer research?' When we do find a cancer cure, part of the basic knowledge will have come from space. And ultimately we will find even more important secrets there: perhaps, some day, a cure for death itself ...

Key to Exercises:

A. General Comprehension: Give brief answers to the following questions.

1. What will happen to our population around the turn of the century?

   Answer: It will be controlled and may be shrinking again.

2. What will happen to agriculture by the twenty-first century?

   Answer: It will be on the way out.

3. How can protein be produced from petroleum?

   Answer: By microbiological conversion.

4. What will be a major industry in the twenty-first century?

   Answer: Space tourism.

5. Apart from tourism, what else can space stations be used

710

for?

Answer: Medical research.

B. Suggested abbreviations:

population: popu.   agriculture: agr.

kilowatt: kw.

C. Notetaking: Make an outline for the third part of the lecture you
have heard on the tape.

(Suggested outline:

III. Envir.

   function of transp. & comu. & popu.

   A. Agr.:

      1. by 21st c. on the way out

      2. now: 1 acre—1 person

      3. future: 20 sq. feet—1 person by a biological system

   B. Food production:

      1. protein:

         from petroleum by microbi. conversion;

         better than natural protein;

         3% of today's p. output for protein of all

      2. food:

         factory-made;

         land for living, parks, recreation, hunting & wilder-
         ness

   C. Raw materials:

      1. sea: inexhaustible; water supply

      2. space:

         a. cheaper - - 1 man to the moon: 1,000 kw-hrs for

711

techniques now primitive

   b. space communities: Moon, Mars, etc.

   c. space stations:

      (1) space tourism: Hilton Orbiter Hotel

      (2) medical research: a cure for cancer, even death

Section Four:

Enjoy Your English:

Tapescript:

Scarborough Fair

* Are you going to Scarborough Fair

Parsley, sage, rosemary and thyme

Remember me to one who lives there

She once was a true love of mine *

Tell her to make me a cambric shirt

(On the side of a hill in the deep forest green)

Parsley, sage, rosemary and thyme

(Tracing of sparrow on the snow-crested brown)

Without no seams nor needle work

(Blankets and bedclothes the child of the mountain)

Then she'll be a true love of mine

(Sleeps unaware of the clarion call)

Tell her to find me an acre of land

(On the side of a hill a sprinkling of leaves)

Parsley, sage, rosemary and thyme

(Washes the grave with silvery tears)

Between the salt water and the sea strands

(A soldier cleans and polishes a gun)

Then she'll be a true love of mine

Tell her to reap it with a sickle of leather

(War bellows blazing in scarlet battalions)

Parsley, sage, rosemary and thyme

(Generals order their soldiers to kill)

And gather it all in a bunch of heather

(and to fight for a cause they've long ago forgotten)

Then she'll be a true love of mine

(Repeat *)